Fiction and Society in the Age of Pushkin

Fiction and Society in the Age of Pushkin

Ideology, Institutions, and Narrative

William Mills Todd III

Harvard University Press
Cambridge, Massachusetts
and London, England
1986

This book is printed on acid-free paper, and its binding
materials have been chosen for strength and durability.

Library of Congress Cataloging in Publication Data

Todd, William Mills, 1944–
Fiction and society in the age of Pushkin.

Includes index.
1. Russian fiction—19th century—History and criticism.
2. Russian fiction—19th century—Social aspects.
3. Pushkin, Aleksandr Sergeevich, 1799–1837—
Criticism and interpretation.
4. Lermontov, Mikhail IUr´evich, 1814–1841—
Criticism and interpretation.
5. Gogol´, Nikolaĭ Vasil´evich, 1809–1852—
Criticism and interpretation.
I. Title.
PG3098.3.T6   1986   891.73'3'09   85–21987
ISBN 0–674–29945–0 (alk. paper)

For
D. S. von Mohrenschildt
J. L. I. Fennell
R. A. Maguire

Acknowledgments

WITH THIS BOOK my aim is to contribute to understanding and further study in several areas: literary theory, the social history of literature, cultural history, and literary interpretation. Such a goal, which disciplinary shifts within academic life are beginning to encourage, would not have been conceivable without extensive library resources, time for research and writing, and the advice of experienced colleagues. Many institutions and individuals have generously provided them.

A Fulbright-Hays Fellowship and a grant from the International Research and Exchanges Board (Autumn 1976) permitted me to begin research and to consult with Soviet colleagues. A summer stipend from the National Endowment for the Humanities (1978) allowed me to read intensively in social theory and social history. A Guggenheim Fellowship (1979–80) enabled me to begin writing; a grant from the Pew Foundation (Summer 1983) and sabbatical leave from Stanford University (1984–85) enabled me to finish. The Mellon Faculty Seminar on Interpretation has provided a continuous and indispensable forum since 1979.

I am very grateful to the Academy of Sciences' Institute of Russian Literature (Pushkinskii Dom), to the Green Library at Stanford, and to the Institut d'Études Slaves for the generosity of their resources and for the scholarly hospitality, knowledge, and efficiency of their librarians.

Among the happiest moments in the project have been those spent in consultation and debate with friends and colleagues. Some, such as Edward J. Brown, Gregory Freidin, Herbert Lindenberger, and Victor Ripp, have read nearly all of the drafts as they came out of the printer. Other colleagues have provided initial guidance, suggestions for research, saving advice, or extensive critiques of the nearly completed manuscript. Among these are L. Ia. Ginzburg, I. Z. Serman, G. P. Makogonenko, Robin Feuer Miller, Donald Fanger, Robert Louis Jackson, John Bender, Russell Berman, Caroline Wellbery, David

Wellbery, Gary Saul Morson, Nicholas Riasanovsky, Dana Polan, Nancy Ruttenburg, Joan Nabseth Stevenson, Irina Paperno, Jeffrey Brooks, Monika Dudli Frenkel, Terence Emmons, Stephen L. Baehr, and Irina Reyfman. All flaws that have survived their advice and scrutiny are products of my obstinacy.

Maud Wilcox of Harvard University Press provided support and encouragement at critical stages. Ann Waters wrestled ably and considerately with the convolutions of my word-processor syntax. Anisa Kurbanali provided expert help with a variety of technical problems.

I have taken the liberty of dedicating the book to three remarkable teachers, whose commitment to Russian literature and culture has always inspired me.

An earlier version of Chapter 1 appeared as "A Russian Ideology," in *Stanford Literature Review*, 1 (1):85–118, and of Chapter 3 as *"Eugene Onegin:* 'Life's Novel,' " in William Mills Todd III, ed., *Literature and Society in Imperial Russia: 1800–1914* (Stanford: Stanford University Press, 1978), 203–235. I thank the journal and publisher for permission to make use of this material. I am also grateful to the following publishers for permission to quote from their editions of *Eugene Onegin:* E. P. Dutton, for A. S. Pushkin, *Eugene Onegin,* 2nd rev. ed., trans. Walter Arndt (1981); and Princeton University Press, for A. S. Pushkin, *Eugene Onegin,* rev. ed., trans. Vladimir Nabokov (1975).

Contents

Fiction and Society in the Age of Pushkin

Note on Transliteration

Russian names, places, titles, and texts appear in the Roman alphabet according to the Library of Congress system of transliteration with these exceptions: (1) names of familiar authors and literary characters appear in their usual spelling (Gogol, Tolstoy, Tatiana); (2) surnames (except Polish ones that end in *-ski*) appear with the ending *-sky* (as in Viazemsky); (3) names of foreign origin in most cases appear according to the spelling of the original ethnic group (as in Benckendorff).

Introduction

> More events take place in Russia in ten years than
> occur in other states in half a century.
>
> Nikolai Gogol, *Selected Passages from Correspondence
> with Friends*

FEW PERIODS in the history of literature so demand—and con-
found—social criticism as the early decades of the nineteenth
century in Imperial Russia. A sequence of catastrophic events (the
assassination of Paul I, the Napoleonic invasion, the Decembrist rebellion, the cholera epidemic, the Polish uprising) punctuate the important historical processes of the age: the impoverishment of the
gentry, the secularization of Russian culture, the growth of educational institutions and media of mass communication, the expansion
of the imperial bureaucracy into all aspects of life, and the growing
opposition of the educated public to that bureaucracy. Simultaneously
and in subtle and elusive relationship to these events and processes,
Russian literature grew with unusual vigor, beginning to produce the
masterpieces that have become canonical in both Russian and world
literature. With all the sentimentality, nostalgia, and mythic rever-
berations that the term evokes, posterity has called this the "golden
age" of Russian letters.

Plenitude, often chaotic, marked nearly every facet of this literary
situation. The beginnings of a secular literature in eighteenth-century
Russia had been nourished by patronage, both academic and imperial,
and it continued into the new century, but the first four decades of
the nineteenth century witnessed a proliferation of salons and literary
circles, which sheltered gentleman amateurs, then the rapid emer-
gence of a nascent literary profession, protected by copyright laws,
financed by journals and booksellers, consumed by an increasing (if
yet indefinable) readership, and practiced by writers of both gentle
and not-so-gentle birth.

This rapid succession—to a large extent coexistence—of disparate modes of literary life accompanied a no less varied array of international styles and orientations: Classicism, the Enlightenment, Sentimentalism, Romanticism, and Realism, to list the more common labels that literary historians of the last hundred and fifty years have attached to the literary tendencies of the period. Continuing scholarly battles concerning the boundaries and populations of these sovereign domains—one recent foray claims the entire period for the Renaissance—demonstrate the lively cultural syncretism of these decades.[1]

The variety of institutional forms and literary styles, not to mention the wealth of genres associated with these styles, points in turn to a more fundamental aspect of early nineteenth-century Russian culture: its attempt to confront in mere decades and almost simultaneously an interrelated *complex* of problems that Western cultures had been addressing more sequentially over the course of several centuries: the secularization of culture; the nature and place of literature in a secular culture; the role of the national language in literature; the codification of that national language and exploration of its wealth; the orientation of a culture toward its own traditions (folk, religious) and toward cosmopolitan models, past and present (Athens, Rome, Paris); the place of an individual in society. Russians confronted these problems in a proliferation of discourses and texts that was unprecedented in their culture. But Russian writers of the early nineteenth century, unlike their French or English confrères, worked with a literary language that had but recently coalesced, a relatively minuscule reading public, and a native literary tradition scarcely a century old.

To discuss each of these problems in appropriate detail would require many volumes. Fortunately some of these volumes have already been written: V. V. Vinogradov, V. D. Levin, Iu. M. Lotman, and B. A. Uspensky have analyzed problems of language and literature in remarkable depth; Donald Fanger has illuminated Gogol's oeuvre with a nuanced reading of that writer's relationship with his audience, real and imagined; André Meynieux has studied Pushkin in the context of literary professionalism, as has Boris Eikhenbaum; a number of scholars have catalogued the styles and groupings of early nineteenth-century Russian writers, and others have described literary genres; historians have examined the political movements (particularly the Decembrists), educational institutions, economic situation, and intellectual trends of the period. My debts to them will be duly acknowledged.

Here, however, I propose a project that is essentially different in focus and approach. It is at once more limited—to examine three of the first Russian novels, produced during these decades—and less so, to examine them in their social context, as that context was generated by the educated Russian public, "society" (*obshchestvo*), as it nebulously called itself. By strikingly different means Alexander Pushkin's *Eugene Onegin: A Novel in Verse* (first edition, 1833), Mikhail Lermontov's *A Hero of Our Time* (1840), and Nikolai Gogol's *Dead Souls: A Narrative Poem* (1842) provide narrative models of their culture's "polite society," offering in their own irrepressibly complicated ways a multiplicity of perspectives upon the possibilities and limitations of this cultural formation, which was not yet an intelligentsia or Bohemia and even less a Western-style bourgeoisie. At the same time, critical attention to the ideals of practices of the regnant cultural group, the educated, Westernized gentry, can illuminate not merely the overt social referent of early nineteenth-century literature, including these three novels, but also its very structures, social functions, and implied author-reader relationships.

Participants in the salon phase of the Russian Enlightenment, which dominated Russian culture in Pushkin's youth and which retained, in part, its productive vitality into the early 1840s, regarded the polite society of seventeenth- and eighteenth-century Paris as a cosmopolitan norm. As Ernst Cassirer notes with respect to this period of European culture, aesthetic ideals became social ones;[2] the reverse, however, must be equally underscored. Critics awarded the prized aesthetic quality of verisimilitude to literary works which modeled the idealized relationships of polite society. This norm, then, functioned as "la belle nature" that was so dear to Classical aesthetics; it had little to do with the subsequent historical, social, and economic commitments of literary Realism.[3] Local aberrations from the universal norms of polite society could appear in literary works, but only as the stuff of comedy or satire, just as deviation from these norms in social behavior was labeled (depending on the circumstances) ridiculous, eccentric, or insane. Moreover, the Russian poet was instructed by such critics as M. N. Murav'ev, N. M. Karamzin, and K. N. Batiushkov to participate in polite society, to entertain it according to its interests, and to speak its refined language.[4] Polite society elevated its forms of communication—letters, conversations, social gatherings—to the aesthetic, and it cultivated literary forms that catered to its interests and limited attention span ("album" verse, bouts-rimés, epigrams). Polite society became an arbiter not only of aesthetic and social form, but of personal existence (the harmonious individual, the honnête homme, later the dandy) and of morality (civility, friendship, social harmony). As such it provided, physically and ideologically, the meeting ground where the period's wealth of literary forms and orientations could be communicated and debated. This vital harmonizing function emerges from a notebook entry by Prince Viazemsky, as he wonders at the ability of Aleksandr Turgenev, a talented cultural reporter and international salon figure, and Petr Chaadaev, who has fair claim to the title of Russia's first systematic secular philosopher, to get along with each other:

> The only points of contact between them were intellect, education, nobility, honorable independence, civility (not only in the sense of politeness, but more in the sense of good upbringing—in a word, civilization of concepts and manners, civilization which, let it be said in passing, takes root and develops only in a milieu that is propitious and prepared by time). These conventions, these similar properties, were sufficient for respectable people to come together on the neutral ground of mutual sympathies, despite certain differences of opinion and character. These are the unmistakable marks of people raised in the school of truly high and elite society. Chaadaev and Turgenev adhered to these conventions.[5]

Nevertheless, even the most casual glance at Russian history shows that this ideal of a civilized, secular society—introduced to Russia by Peter the Great (superficially, with balls and etiquette manuals) and developed through the eighteenth and early nineteenth centuries, yet inaccessible to the vast illiterate majority of the population—was a fragile one. The autocracy found harsher ways to marshal its subjects; those in opposition found ever more radical means of resistance. As hopes for the gradual amelioration of Russian society through the spread of civility faded, and as the advent of new literary movements and writers (Byron, Rousseau, Scott, later Balzac and Sand) helped foster the conflicting views on polite society that were arising within Russian culture, its fragility, exclusiveness, and potential for hypocrisy and self-delusion became increasingly apparent to many Russian thinkers: to the Decembrists, to the playwright Griboedov, to the authors of "society tales" (svetskie povesti), but especially to Pushkin, Lermontov, and Gogol.

The first and final chapters of Eugene Onegin are set in the grande monde, and the rest of the novel stands in relation to it through the concepts of fashion, tradition, and conventionality. Much of the novel revolves around regional variants of the social-aesthetic forms of the Russian gentry—balls, letters, a salon. It probes their harmonizing power from the perspectives of the varied literary-ideological posi-

tions available to a cultured member of that gentry: Romantic alienation, a Sentimentalist cult of friendship and love, the familiar worldliness of a gentleman-author. The most comprehending characters are
those (such as the heroine and the author-narrator) who can play the
greatest number of literary and social conventions off against each
other. But *Eugene Onegin*, with its wealth of parodies, imitations, and
metaliterary comments, becomes the first Russian literary work to
come adequately to grips with the cultural plenitude and contradictions of post-Petrine Russia by allowing none of its characters (including the author-narrator) any refuge from the interplay of its many
discourses (folk, aristocratic, "Russian," Westernized). Finding no
retreat into nature, dream, or art that is not charted by these discourses, no channel of communication that is not regulated in some
way by them, all of the characters become subject to the tragedies of
mistiming and misinterpretation that attend a syncretic culture.

Lermontov set the longest part of *A Hero of Our Time* ("Princess
Mary") in a fashionable resort in the Caucasus. The other parts of
the novel open ethnographic, metaphysical, and literary perspectives—refracted through a variety of Romantic prose genres—upon
this polite society's vicious competitions, which have replaced the
polite, harmonizing rituals of *Eugene Onegin*. Ideology's blend of the
aesthetic, the social, and the moral separates; the social forms remain
(balls, parties, excursions), but now a naked and self-serving theatricality of behavior allows these forms to fulfill no ameliorating function. Differently from Pushkin's novel, Lermontov's questions the
apparent plenitude and freedom of culture, reducing them in this
case nearly to a vanishing point, as it focuses instead on the socializing, leveling power of polite society.

No writer could seem further from an interest in polite society than
the author of *Taras Bul'ba* or the "Diary of a Madman," yet in *Dead
Souls* Gogol's protagonist leads many of the other characters astray
through his manipulation of good manners and the discursive conventions of polite society. The later chapters of the novel take place
in a travesty of high society, as that society holds balls, exchanges
visiting cards with hyperbolic solemnity, and talks politely periphrastic nonsense. The first ball scene in *Dead Souls* brings the society of
that novel properly together, but the final one witnesses an explosion
that tears apart all ties—friendship, infatuation, acquaintance, indeed
the very ties between the characters' linguistic signs and their refer-
ents. The light fictionality of sociable talk yields to Nozdrev's outrageous lies and to Chichikov's macabre scheme. Manners here con-

stitute but a fragile barrier against—and simultaneously a mask for—the chaos and power of the passions, which brook no amelioration.

In each of these three novels, the ideology of polite society becomes problematic not only for the characters, but also for a self-conscious author-narrator, who must contend with the prejudices, tastes, conventions, and stylistic expectations of the readership he projects. The aesthetic and social problems that the author-narrator and the characters confront on their respective ontological levels illuminate each other and illuminate the two levels in a variety of ways that call for both social and literary awareness on the part of the reader.

This process of reading the novels in terms of the cultural situation in which they were written would seem to embroil the project in a venerable interpretive dilemma. It makes sense of the individual parts (the texts) in terms of a whole, yet it knows this whole only from constituent texts. This problem, easily forgotten when the "whole" is a familiar one (such as Romanticism, the European novel, bourgeois society), cannot be so easily dismissed when the whole in question has not yet become an established scholarly category, as is the case with "polite society," both as a historical example of social organization and as an ideology, a systematic understanding of which was articulated by no single contemporary.

The solution that I propose to bring to this problem is to make the hermeneutic circle a sphere, so to speak. My hypotheses about polite society and the novel will be tested and conclusions reached by reconstituting polite society from many perspectives. Polite society, although it cherished a self-image of harmony and homogeneity, did weave itself from many strands (individuals, groups, institutions, cultures), and different viewpoints addressed different strands of this intricate fabric. They did so not merely because writers differed from each other in talent, outlook, and life experience, but because the texts stood in generically, functionally different relationships to polite society. Some genres (familiar letters, conversation, album verse, for example) were central to its working. Comedies, which made persistent sport of Russian Gallomania, provided a favorite form of entertainment.[6] "Society tales" would come, in the 1830s, to view society from the fictional viewpoint of talented protagonists either excluded from it or emotionally maimed by it.[7] Novels and journals, which became increasingly popular during the early decades of the century, were marginal to the life of polite society, in some ways inside, in others not. Consequently they developed complicated relationships to polite society and a variety of perspectives upon it, in ways that I shall discuss. But of all these forms, the novel—marked in Bakhtin's terms by its clashing plurality of discourses, generic fragments, and ideologies—remains the most generous source of insights, less in any direct sense than indirectly, by presenting the inconsistencies, silences, and allure of "society" to critical examination.[8]

Meanwhile, I shall supplement the comparison of these contemporary perspectives on polite society with further dimensions of intertextual confrontation: subsequent memoir accounts by members of polite society, critical interpretations by later readers, and modern works of literary and social theory that touch upon problems which the novels of Pushkin, Lermontov, and Gogol themselves addressed, such as conventionality, self-presentation, oral performance, ritual, and conflict.

This proposed solution to the interpretive problem raises, in turn, a major problem in aesthetics. In comparing these novels with nonliterary texts (including behavioral ones) and in applying the categories of nonliterary disciplines (such as the sociology of knowledge or social history) to them, am I failing to distinguish between the social and the aesthetic, and thereby losing a sense of the specificity of verbal art? Such reservations about the sociology of literature have been raised by both Western and Soviet critics, who have sought to protect imaginative literature from vulgar social analysis and from the crude instrumental uses to which it has frequently been put.[9]

The answers to this are several. First of all, I have intertwined the social and the aesthetic in keeping with the cultural practices of the early nineteenth century, which aestheticized the everyday life of the Westernized gentry and, concomitantly, brought the matter and manner of this everyday life into literature. Social gatherings became aesthetic forms, and literary patterns served as models for behavior and its interpretation. Consequently, differences between the interpretive conventions that governed fiction and nonfiction tended to be less sharp than they have become in our subsequent institutionalizations of literature, and modern readers who would understand the texts of the early nineteenth century cannot afford to ignore these social conventions.

Second, criticism which has limited itself to the traditional aesthetic categories (such as plot, character, diction) has fallen silent before entire sections of the early nineteenth-century novels: Tatiana's salon, the social gatherings of *A Hero of Our Time*, the town settings of *Dead Souls* (which constitute nearly half of the novel). Awareness of the cultural context would aid in specifying and accounting for the ways in which the novels have adapted traditional categories to produce their oft-mentioned plotlessness, their shifting narrative voices, and their curious ways of relating character to setting. What seems "plot-less" to a modern reader may be charged with a coherent sequence of significant events for a different time and place; shifts in narrative voice that represent a striking technique to a twentieth-century analyst may seem natural to a culture that constitutes the human subject differently from ours; abrupt changes in character may likewise be culturally determinate.

Finally, just as early nineteenth-century Russia neglected the "purity" of the aesthetic in putting the social and the aesthetic at each other's service for purposes of cultural transformation, so the concepts that I have adopted for the study of this earlier period are themselves hybrids, adapted from literature or linguistics by modern social theory for its analytic ends: Erving Goffman's account of the presentation of self in everyday life, which employs a theatrical metaphor; Goffman's work on frame analysis, which draws on literary studies of point of view; Clifford Geertz's work on the interpretation of cultures, which depends on a notion of culture as text; or Iurii Lotman's "culturological" project, which treats culture as a system of variably formalized semiotic systems. When literary criticism employs such theories for the interpretation of texts, it reclaims its own, enriched in the passage through other disciplines by broader perspectives and (frequently) greater theoretical coherence.[10]

The chapters that follow—on the ideology of polite society, on the institutionalization of literature, and on the three novels—will stress plenitude, tensions, and discontinuities. The case has already been made that these are the first in a line of great Russian social-psychological novels and that their authors (Pushkin and Gogol, anyway) did much to found the modern institution of literature in Russia.[11] When the Russian classics came to be constituted as such in the early twentieth century, these novels were among the first to be canonized, but this canonization has smoothed away much of their abrasiveness, that is, their self-consciousness and critical intentionality; it has, in large part, neglected their strained relationships with the culture in which they were produced.[12] Yet, paradoxically, it was precisely such self-consciousness, critical intentionality, and strain which at this historical moment helped lay the foundations for the great and unique institution that Russian literature would shortly become. This study, written at a time when literature is again questioning its possibilities in fundamental ways, aims to reexamine these novels' attempts to confront uncertainties of literary institutionalization, to challenge an ideology, and to practice a form in which confrontation and challenge could be most effectively essayed. Because the concepts "institution" and "ideology" are relatively underdeveloped in Russian studies and certainly controversial in any context, I shall define my use of them at the beginning of the first two chapters. I shall discuss generic problems in connection with each of the three novels separately, since in very different ways *Eugene Onegin*, *A Hero of Our Time*, and *Dead Souls* stretch most familiar conceptions of the novel nearly to the breaking point, not only our conceptions, but those of their initial readers, a century and a half ago.

I

A Russian Ideology

It would be difficult to name a period in Russian life
in which oral speech—conversations, friendly talk,
sermons, angry philippics—played such a role.
Iu. M. Lotman, "The Decembrist in Everyday Life"

D URING the first four decades of the nineteenth century, the elegant Laval mansion on the English Embankment in St. Petersburg served as the stage for a full gamut of activities: brilliant balls attended by Petersburg high society, the imperial family, and the diplomatic corps; a lively literary salon that numbered Mme. de Staël, Mickiewicz, Karamzin, Griboedov, Pushkin, and Lermontov among its visitors; and, until December 1825, meetings of the Northern Society of the Decembrist conspirators, headed by the family's son-in-law, Prince S. P. Trubetskoi, and involving the less aristocratic writers Kornilovich, Ryleev, and Bestuzhev together with many other members of polite society.[1]

The ideology that did much to determine and legitimate the structure, social function, and author-reader relationships of early nineteenth-century Russian letters escapes rigid delineation, as does the composition of the social formation to which these authors and readers belonged. But this image of the Laval mansion—with its whirl of activities and interests, its cosmopolitanism, its commitments to talk and social transformation, and its visitors from various social groups and callings—provides a convenient reference point during a discussion of this group and ideology. The term "society" (*obshchestvo*) could for the moment label both group and ideology, if it could be used not in the broad sense ("all the members of a community") but in the exclusive one that was favored by such writers as Karamzin, Zhukovsky, Pushkin, and Lermontov ("the polite or fashionable world").[2] "World" in this English definition is, in turn, a calque from the French *monde*, as is the Russian equivalent, *svet*, which Russian used as a synonym for *obshchestvo* in the exclusive sense.[3] This parallel semantic alteration of the Russian and English languages bears witness to the extraordinary impact of French culture and of its enlightenment, which Nicholas Riasanovsky has called "the last true unifying ideology in the Western world."[4]

Before outlining this particular ideology and following its refraction in the Russian novel, I am compelled by the many different conceptions of the term "ideology" and by its explosive implications to locate my conception among its past and possible understandings. After defining ideology and emphasizing its manifestations in everyday life and language use, and after elaborating upon "society's" definition of itself, I will examine some particulars of the ideology of polite society: its policy of linguistic *exclusion* (the banishment of the discourses of church and bureaucracy) and *expansion* (into the spheres governed by these excluded discourses). From these topics, I shall move to a discussion of the period's privileged mode of language use, "talk," and its decisive impact upon the aesthetic activities, psychological self-awareness, social rituals, and political movements of the period.

Ideology

> Ideology, then, is not to be reduced to misrecognition,
> but is to be seen as signifying a set of practical relations
> with the "real."
> Terry Eagleton, "Ideology, Fiction, Narrative"

Two axes will help the cartographer of ideology with the process of orientation and mapping.[5] The first of them would locate ideology between philosophy and social tactics. One of the finest modern dictionaries of Russian, Ushakov's (1939–40) tends toward the former extreme—"a world view, a system of views and ideas"—a definition shared by other Russian dictionaries and by such Russian literary scholars as Bakhtin and Uspensky.[6] This enabled Ushakov to offer such phrases as "an ideologue of Marxism" or "the proletarian ideology," uses that had already been questioned by Marx himself. Marx believed that ideology would disappear when the rule of the proletariat put an end to alienation and the division of labor, and he presented his "scientific" view of reality in opposition to ideology's distorted vision.[7] Thus Marx drove the definition of ideology toward one of conscious or unconscious social tactics, a position it occupies today in the work of such disparate thinkers as Solzhenitsyn or Roland

Barthes. Marx treats ideology as interested mystification or false consciousness that rationalizes regnant production relations, perfects a dominant class's illusions about itself, transforms the contingent and historical into the enduring and natural, affirms false answers, and prevents new questions from even being asked.[8] From such a perspective, any "philosophical" approach to ideology would itself seem an attempt to depoliticize and depragmatize thought.

It is, in fact, an extreme version of Marx's tactical, pejorative definition of ideology that Solzhenitsyn has turned against the very followers of Marx. The *Gulag Archipelago* indicts ideological thinking as the villain of our time—a license for the evil that would crush all love, morality, and basic human decency. Here ideology simply becomes the social theory (*obshchestvennaia teoriia*) that whitewashes an evildoer's acts, and Solzhenitsyn provides a list of examples that spans post-medieval Western history: "Christianity" for the Inquisition; "civilization" for the colonial powers; "race" for the Nazis; and (an echo of Dostoevsky) "equality, fraternity, and the happiness of future generations" for early and latter-day Jacobins.[9] While justified in its context, such an approach will not lead very far into the labyrinth of social practices and understandings that constituted "polite society" in early nineteenth-century Russia, and I shall avoid it here as much as possible, although the exclusions that this particular ideology occasioned cannot, of course, be ignored.

The second axis of definition spans the problem of consciousness: to what extent is the ideologue a knowing system builder or manipulator, and to what extent an "innocent" or crazed victim of illusion, or its beneficiary. No less than the first opposition, philosophy–social tactics, this second one is frequently overladen with satirical connotations, as it is not uncommon for the analyst of ideas—the "ideologist" in the word's now-unused etymological sense—to present the bearers of an ideology as myopic dupes or lifeless schemers; Marx's scorn for the adepts of Hegelian idealism, Roland Barthes's sarcasm toward the ever-battered yet resilient bourgeoisie, or the McCarthy era's caricature ("master of deceit") spring immediately to mind. Developing on a more serious analytic level the "unconscious" theory, one study of Dostoevsky presents his writing in the "ideological mode" as a product of his occasionally uncontrollable psychic drives.[10] Whatever the merits of this piece of psychoanalysis for Dostoevsky himself, it captures a turn in the development of his ideological heroes, whom ideas drive to frenzies of contradiction, brain fever, and suicide. Solzhenitsyn, by contrast, exploits the prototypical Enlightenment conception of ideology (compare Condorcet) as conscious deceit, *le trahison des clercs*, in order to fix moral responsibility upon his ideological evildoers.

Novelists have commonly treated ideology in terms of a narrative movement between the poles of unconsciousness and consciousness, but the device is not limited to them alone. Hegel, whose term "spirit of the people" bears some resemblance to what I have called a "philosophical" definition of ideology, offers in his *General Introduction to the Philosophy of History* a narrative scheme that moves a particular form along this axis from unconsciousness of itself to consciousness to ultimate fragmentation.[11] Marx himself, turning the Hegelian dialectic "on its feet," presented consciousness as a process of development, and this made a narrative form inevitable.[12]

These definitions of ideology in terms of philosophy versus social tactics or of consciousness versus unconsciousness help to orient the analysis of a particular ideology within a culture or within a literary work, particularly if the analyst is sensitive to gradations and movement along each axis. Nevertheless, studies that depend solely upon these axes—especially when they appropriate such techniques as invective or satire—risk loss of critical perspective. While any discourse about ideology is bound to be itself ideological, a discourse that opens itself to expanding its range and categories of investigation and to reflecting upon its own categories will inevitably present a more subtle understanding of its object than one that does not.

In particular, such loss of critical perspective limits the ability of ideological studies to examine certain fundamental linguistic links between the literary work and the world. Language itself, to quote Voloshinov's formulation, is "filled with ideological or life content and significance."[13] Consequently, discourse fulfills a multiplicity of functions as the theater, weapon, and objective of ideological conflict. To the extent that literature is a mode of discourse among other modes of discourse, a basic critical approach to the problem of literature and ideology would commence with verbal signification, the dynamics of discourse, and the institutionalization of linguistic and generic codes. The crucial question now for literary study in this area of inquiry involves literature's relationship to these discursive practices.

Major contributions to the discovery and description of such links have appeared in a number of recent works. In his essay "Discourse in the Novel," Bakhtin treats that genre as a battleground of "languages," including the author's, that are each replete with ideology. Roland Barthes's *Mythologies* examines the rhetoric of ideology and its surreptitious, now-you-see-it-now-you-don't appropriation of signs. Iurii Lotman in his study of the Decembrists in everyday life refuses to reduce them to their overt political programs, providing instead a poetics of the behavior they bequeathed to Russian culture; in another article he and Boris Uspensky analyze the language controversies in early nineteenth-century Russia, illuminating such concepts as a "noble language" from the perspectives of linguistics, literary history, and sociology.[14]

Perhaps the most thorough studies of literature and ideology, however, have been produced by the post-Althusserian Marxists, such as Pierre Macherey, Terry Eagleton, or Fredric Jameson, who explore the problem with critical concepts and awareness culled from a variety of sources—Lacanian psychoanalysis (with its decentering of the ego), a Marxist view of society (revised to stress its structural, not positivist or historicist aspects), and a post-structuralist sense of the fissured literary text as a playground of codes for the signifier.[15] In these studies ideology appears not as a readily detachable filter between the individual and the "real" or between the text and the "real." On the contrary, it is embedded in "experience," in "common sense," in taste, in discourse, in all acts of signification.[16] Imaginative literature works upon the ideology that presents itself to the text in language and, according to Macherey, wrests ideology into a new, nonideological (yet non-"scientific" in the Marxist sense) form through techniques of isolation, caricature, and figuration, thereby demystifying ideology and revealing its unacknowledged absences and contradictions.[17] Eagleton challenges this apparent privileging of literary form, however, because it slights the persistent coherence of ideology and because, to Eagleton, ideology does not merely mystify or screen history. In his own formulation, literary form becomes not an escape from the "shame of the merely ideological," but a production of the ideological to the second power; it does to ideology what ideology does to history (makes it seem "natural"):

> But the work simultaneously reveals (to criticism, if not to the casually inspecting glance) how that naturalness is the effect of a particular production. If the text displays itself as "natural," it manifests itself equally as constructed artifice; and it is in this duality that its relation to ideology can be discerned.[18]

This last point has particular relevance to our three highly self-conscious novels. In them the "talk" that formed the linguistic basis of polite society becomes fixed on the printed page, and situated with respect to characters, actions, and consequences in fictional worlds that readers can relate to their own. Modern readers may no longer hear a distant culture's "hum and buzz of implication," to quote Lionel Trilling's deft phrase, but they can certainly witness that culture being produced through the conventionality (*Onegin*), theatricality (*Hero of Our Time*), and performance (*Dead Souls*) that impose themselves upon the readers' awareness. Such operations break the spell of the spontaneous, lived experience that these novels also produce and make the readers aware of the tactics and value systems at work in the texts.[19]

Meanwhile, Eagleton theorizes that subformations of a general ideology, subformations which he calls the "authorial ideology" and the "aesthetic ideology"—the latter includes literary conventions, theory of literature, and literary tradition—complicate by their multiplicity, interplay, and potential contradictions the text's production of the general ideology. Moreover, the interplay of subformations renders methodologically invalid traditional scholarly attempts to posit a simple homological relationship between a general mode of production, a dominant ideology, and a literary work, attempts which have justly laid literary sociology open to charges of equivocation.[20] By the time that the logic of this argument leads Eagleton to acknowledge—without recourse to shaky notions of authorial consciousness or unconsciousness—that every author and every work of every author produce what is, to some extent, a unique ideology, he has provided an important set of critical concepts for making the discriminations, comparisons, and intertextual confrontations that permit ideological formations to be named and analyzed.

Society

In the best society they learned to fathom the secret play of the passions, to observe manners, to maintain all conventions and social relations, and to speak clearly, lightly, and pleasantly.

K. N. Batiushkov, "Discourse on the Influence of Light Poetry on the Language"

Equipped with this conception of an ideology as a subjectively coherent, at least implicitly tactical set of values and understandings, manifested through language in the cultural productions and daily life of a group or individual, it should be possible to study the ideology of polite society more closely. From the outset, however, such an investigation is hindered not only by the lack of a thorough social history of the time, but even more by the lack of a clear definition of the social body that produced the period's dominant ideology and outstanding cultural works.[21] Among contemporary definitions of the group—ideologically significant in their vagueness—one finds *ob-shchestvo* and *svet* with several variations: "the best homes" (Karamzin, 1802),[22] "the great world" (Pushkin, *Eugene Onegin*, 1:42; Zhukovsky, 1808; Gogol, 1832),[23] "the best society" (Gogol, 1847, VIII, 409), or "good society" (P. I. Makarov, 1803).[24] Pushkin's comment on "good society"—"it can also exist outside the highest circle, and anywhere that there are honorable, intelligent, and educated people" (XI, 98)—illustrates the elusiveness of this terminology and the seeming universality of the ideal it represents, "seeming" because honor, intelligence (as wit), and education as Pushkin understood them were generally the property of a narrow range of Russian society.

Provoked by debates over the literary "aristocracy" that I shall discuss in the next chapter, Pushkin soon arrived at a more specific definition, "the enlightened gentry" (XI, 172). Shortly thereafter, in 1836, Gogol would distinguish the highly competent, "enlightened," segment of the reading public from the "ingenuous" remainder (VIII, 166). Yet this, too, beclouds the issue, for "enlightenment" in early nineteenth-century Russia bore a wide range of associations, some of which should more properly be linked to the European reaction against the French Revolution, the anti-Enlightenment. The poet Zhukovsky's definition of enlightenment—"the art of living, the art of perfecting oneself in that circle in which the Hand of Providence has enclosed you"—captures the Pietist, Masonic connotations that the word could carry.[25] S. S. Uvarov's list of "all" that people moved by a love of enlightenment would discuss—"literary events; new poems; news of theaters, books, and paintings"—stresses the importance of aesthetic concerns to this Russian "Enlightenment."[26] When, in his *Selected Passages from Correspondence with Friends* (1847), Gogol reminded his readers that the Russian word for enlightenment, *prosveshchenie*, had been used by the Church for a thousand years (VIII, 285), he was, in his accustomed manner, exaggerating a cultural tendency almost beyond recognition. Among modern attempts, Andrzej Walicki's term, "the educated, Westernized gentry," more precisely focuses upon the cultural attributes that separated members of this social formation from nonmembers.[27]

Among the contemporaries of Pushkin, Lermontov, and Gogol, Zhukovsky provides perhaps the most concerted effort to come to grips with the values, characteristics, and relationships that distinguished "society":

A circle of select people—I will not say the best—preeminent in wealth, education, dignity, descent; it is a republic with its own laws, obedient to its own ideal ruler, who arbitrarily changes every minute—fashion— where common sense [*obshchee mnenie*] exists, where selective taste reigns, where all rewards are given, where the evaluation of virtue and talent takes place. Imagine a multitude of people of both sexes, gifted by fortune with either wealth or nobility, joined together by a natural inclination toward polite sociability, ordaining pleasure alone as the aim of its association, pleasure consisting solely in appealing to one another—imagine this, and you will obtain a rather clear understanding of the "great world" . . . a vast theater, where each is at once both actor and spectator.[28]

Zhukovsky goes on to write of the leveling and educational function of "society" in the exclusive sense. For the most part this is compatible with the idea of an "educated, Westernized gentry," although richer in suggesting the ideal dynamics of the group and poorer in that it fails to acknowledge the element of Westernization, which is evident in the very style and theme of this passage, and its source, a German essay that Zhukovsky adapted for the *Messenger of Europe*.[29] Nor does Zhukovsky specifically refer to the group by its historical title (*dvorianstvo*, gentry) and mention its historical function (state service). This exemption of "society" from historical delimitation, reiterated in Zhukovsky's phrase "natural inclination" (*estestvennaia sklonnost'*) represents again one of the salient features of this ideology, the elevation of its practices to universal validity.

Zhukovsky's presentation of this exclusive society and the writer's place in it is far from pessimistic, although he notes that some separation is inevitable: the writer will need time and privacy apart from polite society in order to write, as well as a smaller circle of friends to provide amicable criticism. Here the writer will be a success, even if not in the "great world" proper, from which he may be alienated by a passion for writing, authorial vanity, and reduced circumstances. As the essay makes this distinction, several social fragments join together that voice both the ideology of polite society and the aspirations of Russia's nascent profession of letters. Thus tribute to the overwhelmingly attractive socializing power of the "great world" with its pleasures and entertainments and a Sentimentalist vision of the writer surrounded by his friends and family stand uncomfortably beside both an awareness of the writer as someone who must be concerned with his finances and a suspicion of aristocracy inherent in this type of journalism, consciously derived from Addison and Steele's *Spectator*.[30] These subtle confrontations, together with

Zhukovsky's awareness that wealth and position *do* count after all and that the ideology of society is ultimately one of exclusion, predict the problems that, as we shall see in the next chapter, came to vex and ultimately to devastate the literature of familiar association, which professed to value talent over birth or wealth. In its modest, barely perceptible way Zhukovsky's text reveals some of the discontinuities that would become gaping fissures in Russian literary life and in the novel, another genre marginal to the rituals of polite society.

Vague as they are, these quotations from Zhukovsky and Pushkin offer a set of interrelated characteristics—Enlightenment, cosmopolitanism, honor, taste—that help to distinguish members of society from nonmembers: the totally uneducated, those literate only for ecclesiastical or bureaucratic purposes, those recently ennobled through state service but lacking in cultural graces, and the lower levels of the provincial gentry "unenlightened" by a Western-oriented education. Nikolai Karamzin, using appropriately non-Russian costumes, sketched an ideal set of poses for the gentry: "I love to imagine the Russian gentry not only with sword in hand, not only with the scales of Themis, but also with Apollo's bays, with the staff of the God of the Arts, with the emblems of the Goddess of Agriculture."[31] A male member of the gentry could play a variety of roles in Russian life of the early nineteenth century—among them state servant, Orthodox Christian, landowner, serfowner, fashionably scientific farmer, paterfamilias, amateur poet, and member of polite society. But it was the mastery of this last role with its requisite language and behavior that counted most in society and was most likely to prompt the performance of the other roles.

Discursive Inclusions and Exclusions

> It is high time for us to mock *les précieuses ridicules* of
> our literature, people who are always talking about fair
> readers they have never had, about high society where
> they are not welcomed, all of this in the style of Professor
> Tred'iakovsky's valet.
> Pushkin, letter about Gogol's *Evenings on a Farm Near
> Dikan'ka,* 1831

The ideology of society, at once pervasive and evasive, insisted on society's wealth, liveliness, and openness. Yet it could be remarkably constricting. The terms of these paradoxes become apparent when one tries to specify society's physical loci (balls, salons, familiar gatherings—but at times also offices, estates, barracks, and studies), its membership (ostensibly open to people of talent and education, but for all practical purposes limited to a section of the gentry), and the rules for the language it favored—in literature, social gatherings, and occasionally even in the chancelleries—a discourse that has at various times been called "the new style," "the salon style," "the foppish dialect" (*shchegol'skoe narechie*), the "ladies' language," and "high society jargon."[32] This language fostered a lexicon free of technical and chancellery terminology, which it avoided through periphrasis; a less convoluted, shorter sentence than the one cultivated in the ecclesiastical literature of earlier ages; and a carefully studied casual manner—the style of a person of fashion and culture of the sort that flourished in the French salons of the seventeenth and eighteenth centuries.

Nikolai Karamzin, who brought into focus over fifty years of attempts to make such a language the norm for Russian literature and whose influence would still be a cultural issue in the 1830s, formulated a crucial project for adapting literature to society: the writer should be able to write as he speaks, as the French do, using a language whose pleasantness would not offend the sensibilities of "society women" because it had been learned in their company. Karamzin realized that this was not yet possible for Russian culture when he published the program in 1802, because society women tended to use French in letters and conversations, and so he advised the writer to "create expressions, divine the best choice of words, give old ones a certain new meaning, offer them in new combinations, but so artfully as to deceive the readers and hide from them the singularity of the expression."[33] In short, Karamzin proposed a program of reciprocal influence—society would offer the writer its taste and interests, while the writer would repay this with a style of Russian that could replace French as the language of society, even surpassing it in the range and mellifluousness that polite society cultivated:

> Let our dear society ladies assert that the Russian language is rude and unpleasant; that *charmant* and *séduisant, expansion* and *vapeurs* cannot be expressed in it . . . Our language is expressive not only for lofty oratory, for resounding descriptive poetry, but also for tender simplicity, for the sounds of the heart and sensibility. It is more rich in harmony than French; more capable of expressing the soul's outpouring in tones [of emotion]; it offers more *analogous* words, that is, words consistent with the expression of an action—an advantage that only root languages enjoy![34]

Such was the attractiveness of this exchange that critics would still be continuing to defend it and propose it anew into the 1840s, although what was acceptable to polite society would, for ideological reasons, always be a matter of debate.

For purposes of describing society's ideology, and because Pushkin, Lermontov, and Gogol would thematize this exchange in their novels, it is important to note both the freedoms that it granted and the exclusions it licensed, for this new standard—the ideal oral usage of a social elite—could both free literature from previous limitations and serve as a social barrier to full participation in Russian culture.[35] The former language of literature, Church Slavonic, could be known from texts available to the whole of Russian Orthodox culture. Lomonosov, for example, the son of a fisherman, had credited three books written in this language with opening the world of literature to him.[36] The "salon style," drawing as it did upon the wealth of European culture, no doubt enriched the Russian language immeasurably and made it capable of expressing much that had been inaccessible to it, but at the same time its grace, subtlety, casualness, and harmonious heterogeneity were unavailable to the illiterate 95 percent of the population, to those trained in such inelegant institutions as ecclesiastical seminaries or in tutorials with the village deacon, or to bureaucrats and tradespeople who exercised their minimal literacy in the performance of their occupations.[37]

A Russian gentleman was generally an Orthodox Christian, however unenthusiastic or swayed by fashionable foreign faiths, and a subject of the autocrat, holding officerial rank in the military or civil service. Nevertheless, the special languages associated with these aspects of his being, Church Slavonic and the chancellery language, were generally barred from the intercourse of polite society, or were permitted to enter it under special circumstances—in ironic illumination, for example, or, in the case of Church Slavonic, to give a lofty coloration to written or oral discourse, much as one might use the language of the King James Version in modern English. This linguistic program could make social gatherings seem a place of relative liberty—from the restrictions of rank, from the ritual piety of the Church, and from financial concerns—a place for wit, fantasy, brilliant exaggeration, and verbal improvisation. It could make the literature devoted to and inspired by these gatherings remarkable for its attentiveness to the emotions and to fine points of social interaction. But it also permitted its members to exclude those whose experience bound them to less acceptable linguistic practices. During the years covered by this study, for instance, the socially contemptuous term "seminarist" was applied to critics who were reluctant to witness the fall of Church Slavonic from literary eminence. In *Eugene Onegin* the author-narrator would defend his French-writing heroine in these terms:

> Send me, Almighty, I petition,
> In porticoes or at a ball
> No bonneted academician,
> No seminarist in a yellow shawl! (3:28)[38]

A contemporary critic, P. I. Makarov, dismissed the seminarist's language even more bluntly: "The style of ecclesiastical books has no resemblance to what is demanded of society writers."[39]

Sometimes the linguistic exclusions sound reasonable enough, as in Pushkin's advice to a young journalist: "Avoid scholarly terms, and try to translate, that is, to paraphrase them; this will be both pleasant to the ignorant and useful to our still infantile language" (XIV, 9, 4 April 1832, to I. V. Kireevsky). At other times, the social divisiveness of these stylistic strategies stands out in sharper relief, as when Pushkin ironically distances himself from his merchant publisher's "technical [financial] language" (XIV, 27, 11 July 1832, to M. P. Pogodin).

Ideology's strategies of linguistic enrichment and exclusion appear most strikingly in the working of fashion and taste, on which Zhukovsky's essay properly centers its definition of society. Fashion, because of the arbitrariness that he mentions, and taste, because it was not subject to such objective formulations as could be found in the rhetorical manuals and prescriptive grammars that held sway in the eighteenth century, served as constantly shifting barriers to those who might wish to storm society from the outside.[40] Zhukovsky's well-chosen terms "ruler" and "reigns" precisely capture the power of taste and fashion, comparing them to the government's autocratic power, as would *Eugene Onegin* in the words "unbridled fashion, our tyrant" (5:42). In ways that I shall address in the next chapter, the government could arbitrarily intervene in the creative process at almost any stage; so, imply Pushkin and Zhukovsky, could fashion. This became particularly true when two additional strategies were engaged to fortify the shifting boundaries of polite society's ideology of exclusion: confusion or mixing of categories and convenient shifts between the observable and the ideal.

Philologists have been able to get a very good sense of early nineteenth-century linguistic taste by reading the many contemporary statements about usage—such was the general concern with style that it was a constant topic of discussion, and such was its prestige that good conversation was quickly recorded in letters, diaries,memoirs, and notebooks, and in special collections, like Pushkin's *Table-talk* (title originally in English). However, there was no small fluctuation between emphasis on the empirically ascertainable and the desirable here, just as definitions of "society" fluctuated between the "high society" that could be observed and the ideal "good society" that might or might not be coextensive with it. Thus earnest journalists of the 1820s–1840s would continue to reproach writers for not following the linguistic decorum of polite society, while Pushkin, waxing both empirical and conscious of social distinctions, would ridicule their efforts, as he defended the linguistic wealth and range of society:

> Is it not ridiculous for them to pass judgment on what is acceptable or not acceptable in society, on what our ladies can and cannot read, on what expressions belong in the salon [*gostinaia*] (or *boudoir*, as these gentlemen put it)? Is it not amusing to see them as the protectors of high society, in which they probably have no time or need to appear . . . Why should they know that in the best society mincing manners and pomposity are even more intolerable than commonness (*vulgarité*) and that it is precisely this which reveals ignorance of society? Why should they know that the unashamed, original expressions of common people are repeated in high society without offending anyone's ear, while the prim circumlocutions of provincial politeness would only arouse a universal, involuntary smile . . . This desire to pass themselves off as members of high society has led our journalists to commit amusing blunders. One of them thought that it is inadmissible to speak of fleas in the presence of our ladies and delivered a stern reprimand about this—to whom? To one of our brilliant young courtiers . . . Not long ago an historical novel attracted universal attention and for several days turned all our ladies from their *fashionable tales* [English in the original] and historical memoirs. So what happened? A newspaper let the author know that in his scenes from the life of the common people could be found the dreadful words *son of a bitch*.   (XI, 98)

Shortly thereafter Prince Viazemsky would defend Gogol's pungent prose in similarly exclusive terms: only an insider could know society's liberties, liberties that could include Gogol's flights of linguistic fancy and swift descents from the sublime to the scatological.[41]

Still another example shows how difficult it could be for an outsider to master the style of society:

> I met Nadezhdin at Pogodin's. He seemed quite common to me, *vulgar*, boring, presumptuous, and without any manners. For instance, he picked up a handkerchief that I had dropped. His criticisms were very stupidly written, but with liveliness and sometimes even with eloquence. There

was no thought in them, but there was movement; his jokes fell flat. (XII, 159)

This cruel reaction to a seminary-trained critic, recorded in Pushkin's *Table-talk*, moves between Nadezhdin's social and linguistic styles, his speech, and his writing, noting in each case his ineptness and measuring his performance in these areas according to the elusive criteria of wit, distinction, grace, movement, liveliness, measure, and manner. Although it is important for historians of literary style to isolate statements on verbal style from these other considerations, it is no less important that the student of ideology mark the interweaving of concerns here. Gestures and manners—surprising norms for one writer to use in evaluating another—become as significant as words in a culture that adopts oral communication as a model for writing and literary life.[42] Since they could only be learned and perfected in society, they served to secure society's control over the identification and promotion of talent.

Ultimately the need for a versatile literary language that had led Pushkin to assert the richness of society's talk brought him to question the preeminence of the conversational norm that Karamzin's generation had proposed and that polite society had accepted:

> Can the written language be completely similar to the conversational one? No, no more than the conversational one could be completely similar to the written one . . . The richer the language in expressions and turns of phrase, the better for a skilled writer. The written language becomes livelier every minute through the use of expressions born in conversation, but it should not renounce what has been acquired in the course of centuries. To write only the conversational language means not to know the language. (XII, 96)

Yet there is no question in this journalistic piece of abandoning a century's efforts to make the vernacular of the educated Westernized gentry the *basis* of the literary language. Pushkin's terse, elliptical syntax, conversational manner, and graciously conciliatory tone manifest, in fact, the development of that vernacular. In this essay, while defending the use of nonspoken lexical and morphological features (certain demonstratives and participles), he nevertheless assimilates them somewhat to the ideals of the spoken norm; he does this by giving several examples of colloquial expressions that preserve (in petrified form) the bookish demonstratives (for example, *seichas*, "now") and by suggesting that the bookish participles can lend "expressive terseness" to the language. Moreover, Pushkin takes pains to distance himself from the linguistic conservatives of his time, and he couches this essay in epistolary form, which Russians had associated with the conversational norm since the early eighteenth century.[43] Thus, while probing one aspect of society's ideology—its exclusion of certain linguistic practices—he remains faithful to its sense of freedom and inclusiveness, "liveliness" and "richness," as he puts it here.

The way in which Pushkin conducts his moderate defense of bookish, traditional elements in the written language suggests the extent to which the syntax, lexicon, and general manner of society's cosmopolitan language—along with its embedded ways of thinking—could become second nature to the small fragment of the population that enjoyed the possibilities of this syncretic culture and brought forth the "golden age" of Russian literature. It is appropriate in this regard to recall Mérimée's recognition of the eighteenth-century French cast to Pushkin's prose, N. A. Polevoi's comment that all of Pushkin's work bore the yoke of society and of a Karamzinian upbringing, or Sękowski's obsequious letter to Pushkin that praises "The Queen of Spades" for its "bon goût," "langage civilisé," "langue qu'on parle et qu'on peut parler entre les gens comme il faut," and "langage de la bonne société."[44]

Linguistic analysis, both contemporary and modern, has not only identified this Europeanized Russian as the basic substratum of Pushkin's language or Karamzin's, it has also found examples in the speech of the new style's opponents, such as Admiral Shishkov, who campaigned against it for decades. One striking example finds Shishkov calling to order his Colloquium of Lovers of the Russian Word (Beseda liubitelei russkogo slova), ostensibly a gathering of linguistic conservatives, with the following piece of salon *politesse* that reiterates Karamzin's proposed exchange:

> Women, this most charming half of the human race, this soul of conversations, these dear consolers, instill in us the language of kindness and politeness, the language of feeling and passion, women, I say, are those lofty inspirations which enflame our souls to song . . . Industrious minds invent, write, compose expressions, and define words; women, reading them, learn purity and correctness of language: but this language, passing through their lips, becomes clearer, smoother, more pleasant, and sweeter.[45]

Shishkov prefers the Russian word *zhenshchiny* ("women") to the French loan word *damy*, but otherwise this passage is shot through with usages quite alien to the pre-Enlightenment, pre-Westernized Russia that he idolized. "Charming" (in a positive sense), "soul" with a noun object (*dusha besed;* compare *l'âme des conversations*), or "language" (in a narrow sense, as "discourse") demonstrate the extent to which the new style could penetrate the Russian gentry's way of thinking. Shishkov protested against such penetration and railed at extreme examples of it, yet could not escape it in his own language when forced to deal with such phenomena as the role of women in literary life.[46] Moreover, Shishkov's impressionistic criteria here (clarity, smoothness, pleasantness, sweetness) are fully consonant with the ideology of polite society, as is this treatment of gentlewomen, who, "free" from commercial and governmental duties, to say nothing of a productive part in ecclesiastical literature, provided an ideal touchstone for the new style's exclusiveness.

Stylistic Imperialism

Our language . . . which was not without purpose
forgotten for a time by our best society.
Gogol, *Selected Passages from Correspondence with Friends,* 1847

So far I have measured the potency of the ideology that Pushkin, Lermontov, and Gogol would confront by its ability to exclude other discourses (bureaucratic, ecclesiastical, commercial) and social groups bound to them. But the spread of polite society's discourse, together with its attendant modes of behavior, into the home regions of other discourses, most notably the church and the bureaucracy, is only slightly less remarkable in light of the previous impermeability of these cultural activities.

By the 1790s the elegant "new style" had begun to win entrée into the chancelleries, which had once cultivated a particular language (*prikaznyi iazyk*) of their own. Thus Ivan Dmitriev—poet, Karamzin's principal correspondent, future Minister of Justice—came to be praised for the polite qualities, purity and pleasantness, of his official writings.[47] Pushkin would later parody the chancellery language in a familiar letter (XIII, 210–211, 14–15 August 1825, to V. L. Pushkin); otherwise, he tended to conduct his official correspondence in French, and he wrote a memorandum on education to Nicholas I (1826) in a style practically free of official formulas. The future statesman M. M. Speransky, who rose far above his clerical origins, drafted a stylistic manual which modern scholarship finds remarkably similar in its prescriptions to the "new style."[48] Henceforth the provincial and low-ranking clerks who practiced the chancellery language could be dismissed as "semiliterate" by officials who had developed other alternatives, such as Speransky.[49] And membership in the salons or other familiar associations that cultivated the new style could serve as a channel for advancement in the service.

Bureaucratese would remain the mark of outsiders, since society's ideology encouraged its members to forget the recent historical origins of their social group, which had been reconstituted in the early eighteenth century as a class of state servitors.[50] Admission to the modern Russian nobility had thus depended upon reaching a certain rank in the hierarchy that Peter I had established with his Table of Ranks in 1722. Although the nobility had been emancipated from obligatory state service in 1762 and given the Charter of the Nobility in 1785, and although eighteenth-century developments made it possible for noble status to be inherited and held by nonservitors (a fact recognized by the 1833 Code of Laws), service still provided an avenue to ennoblement. Nevertheless, the educated Westernized gentry developed attitudes toward service that would assimilate it into a sense of honor, civic duty, and privilege more appropriate to the longer-established, landed nobility of England or France; scorn for the chancellery language represents a clear manifestation of these attitudes.

Most noblemen, to be sure, continued to serve in the military or bureaucracy and to regard service to the autocracy as their chief privilege. Indeed the gentry obstructed measures, such as university reform or compulsory education, which made it possible for non-nobles to enter and rise in state service.[51] Russians and foreigners of noble origin dominated the civil service, especially in the capital, throughout the period covered by this study.[52] Ranks, decorations, and other signs of autocratic approval continued to attract members of the gentry to such an extent that Gogol saw them, not love, as an "electric charge" for dramatic plots (V, 142).

But society persistently sought to perform this service on its own terms. Griboedov's Chatsky in *Woe from Wit* (II.ii) captures this spirit in his famous pun, "Sluzhit' by rad, prisluzhivat'sia toshno"—"Glad to serve, sickened by servility." A sense of civic duty or the presence of national crisis, such as the War of 1812, made service a point of honor. But honor also required independence of character. Nicholas I's chief gendarme A. Kh. Benckendorff, although of noble origin and high rank, was snubbed in Moscow and Petersburg high society for his official position and despicable behavior.[53] Karamzin, who twice refused governorships in order to pursue his preferred position as Official Historiographer, demonstrated a more acceptable mode of civil service behavior, one marked both by a spirit of independence and by a sense of national responsibility.[54] A demonstrative resignation from the service could also maintain a gentleman's sense of personal superiority to the official hierarchy, and the punitive reaction of Nicholas I to Pushkin's and Lermontov's attempts to resign shows how well he understood this device. Duelling, an alternative system of justice for the nobility, provided, as Lednicki has suggested, an even more extreme evasion of the bureaucracy and its procedures.[55] The high sense of civic responsibility that led nobles into government service could at times lead them to exchange service for debates in their salons or other familiar groups, or for the reorganization of their country estates, or even (as was the case with the Decembrists) for political conspiracy.

The ideology of society could also license a nobleman not to take his state position very seriously or to regard it as merely one of the many roles that an *honnête homme* might choose to play. It was not uncommon for gentlemen to retire from active civil or military service after a few years, as did Gogol and as Pushkin and Lermontov tried to do. By 1811 statistics show that 112,200 members of the gentry, like the heroes of *Eugene Onegin* and *Dead Souls*, lived in Russian towns without serving.[56] By 1843, despite Nicholas I's insistence on service as a lifelong obligation, over one-third of the nobles in his capital city did not serve.[57] Those who did serve and had reached a certain level, such as the hero of Lermontov's novel, did not find their duties particularly time-consuming. At the turn of the century an officer's day began early—muster at six o'clock—but was finished by noon; a civil servant would appear later at his chancellery and be finished by one o'clock.[58] During the somber reign of Nicholas I, working days of three or four hours were still common, although a more conscientious office might demand eight.[59]

Society could dictate not only whether or how long or how well a gentleman served, but also where. Fashion established hierarchies of regiments (for example, cavalry over infantry, guards regiments over regular ones) and of civilian duties (diplomacy over the others). The "archival youths," a group of young littérateurs, enjoyed a prestigious sinecure in the Moscow Archives of the Ministry of Foreign Affairs. And, while influencing the language and membership of the state service, society reserved the right to name its own membership, as we have seen in Benckendorff's case. Society's ranking did not always agree with the state's; glancing at a crowd of senators, Karamzin reportedly told Pushkin that not one of them belonged to "good society."[60]

In addition to the bureaucracy, a second cultural-linguistic zone, the Russian Orthodox Church, also proved permeable to the language and manners of society despite the barriers of education, Westernization, and nobility which, by the late eighteenth century, had locked the Church's servitors, the clergy, into a separate "caste-estate" and subculture within Russian society.[61] It is useful to recall in this context, for comparative purposes, that parish preferments in the Church of England often went to the younger sons and poor relations of the landed gentry, such as Edmund Bertram in *Mansfield Park;* members of prominent families could fill important positions in the Roman Catholic Church. But in Russia the gentry very rarely entered the parish or monastic clergy, for this entailed loss of noble status and a host of attendant legal, eonomic, and social hardships. Candidates for the Russia clergy studied in seminaries reserved for the children of the clergy, while the gentry—until universities became socially acceptable in the 1820s—were educated at home, in military schools, or in private pensions. The clergy studied Church Slavonic, which society tended to avoid, and, in the upper grades, Latin, a relic of the beginnings of Russia's Westernization in the seventeenth century. The educated Westernized gentry learned the modern languages, especially French, but also (in estimated order of frequency) German, Italian, and English. Latin could not stick to their ribs, at least the solemn oratorical Latin that the seminaries fed their pupils. *Eugene Onegin's* author-narrator makes the point in a blunt chiasmus:

> Chital okhotno Apuleia
> A Tsitserona ne chital.   (8:1)

The bluntness is captured in Nabokov's translation:

> would eagerly read Apuleius,
> while Cicero I did not read.[62]

The novel's eponymous hero, finding Latin out of vogue, does no better (1:6).

Once finished with schooling, the clergyman's sons themselves entered the clergy or minor positions in the provincial chancelleries; occasionally they obtained further education in order to take up the legal, medical, and teaching professions that the gentry disdained.[63] The gentry gravitated toward the military, civil service posts in the capital cities, or the country estate. Later, when systematic aesthetics and German idealism began to attract littérateurs during the 1820s, university professors of clerical origin (such as Raich or Nadezhdin) proved important cultural mediators and began to find their way into the Moscow salons and literary circles. But these were exceptional cases, and, as we have seen from Pushkin's malicious treatment of Nadezhdin, their path was far from smooth.

Yet even earlier the considerable barriers between the subcultures of the gentry and church did provoke breaching actions. Certain churchmen, aware of the growing isolation of their group, sought to align themselves with the gentry by adapting their speech and manners. The remarkably enlightened (in any sense of the word) Metropolitan of Moscow, Platon Levshin (1775–1812), spoke French and insisted that the seminarists under his supervision learn table manners, civility, "noble ambition," and—cornerstone of society's ideology—the art of conversation; other seminaries taught their pupils some French and German to help them gain entrée into the homes of the gentry.[64] The success of this program in giving the seminarists a place in the salons of society may be surmised from the three novels that this study investigates: the only priests who appear in them do so to bury Eugene's uncle and to tip a hat to the passing carriage of Gogol's protagonist. Neither has a speaking part.

When, however, Eugene Onegin attends a fashionable "rout" in St. Petersburg (autumn 1824) and his fellow guests suspect that he is sporting the "mask" of a Quaker or religious fanatic (8:7), the novel fathoms two of the powerful anti-Enlightenment currents, Protestantism and Orthodox extremism, that fed Russian culture during the later years of Alexander's reign, at first merging and then, in early 1824, colliding to create a whirlpool of political intrigue. With varying proportions of theatricality—the novel's image "mask" is most appropriate here—and genuine fervor, Russians had been supplementing the largely sacramental nature of their Orthodoxy with a succession of Western religious movements since the late eighteenth century (Freemasonry—the most important—then Roman Catholicism, Pietism, the Bible Society). While a few Orthodox clergymen were learning to emulate the manners of society, many members of society—the Emperor Alexander I foremost among them—were swept up in a tide of religious syncretism. Prince Viazemsky's notebook records a conversation on the subject that nicely catches the eddying cultural and linguistic crosscurrents:

When the Bible Societies, Shishkov's [heavily Slavonicized] manifestos, and the misuse of scriptural texts were in flower, Dmitriev (the former minister and poet, Karamzin's brother-in-arms) said: "Ever since our society writers have begun to enter the clergy, the clergy have been trying to adapt their language to society's." One Moscow priest used to visit him; he was rather well educated and so versed in the French language that when he passed the ladies in church with his censer, he would say to them: "Pardon, mesdames."

He didn't like the Metropolitan Filaret and criticized the language and style of his sermons. Dmitriev was not a great supporter of Filaret, but in this case he defended him. "Forgive me, Your Excellency," the priest once told him, "But is it in this language that your [verse tale] 'The Fashionable Wife' is written?"[65]

This priest's fondness for the new style, even in the conduct of his pastoral duties, demonstrates its prestige and influence. Although society itself did come in the late 1810s to couch Bible Society speeches and reports in pompous Church Slavonic rhetoric, its own language made considerable inroads into Russian religious life through this organization.[66] The Bible Society, British in origin, founded a branch in St. Petersburg with the blessings and financial backing of the Emperor and then established other societies throughout the Empire until forced by political in-fighting to close in the mid-1820s. Alexander I, who considered Church Slavonic a barrier to understanding the Bible, urged its translation into "the new Russian tongue." The Bible Society implemented this request with bilingual (Russian–Church Slavonic) editions of the Gospels (1818), then with Russian Psalters and New Testaments that were produced in large editions.[67] Nor was the religious use of the vernacular limited to the Bible, the private reading of which had not been so central in the Russian church as in the Protestant denominations that caught the Emperor's fancy. In 1823 the Metropolitan Filaret issued an Orthodox Catechism in Russian and was awarded the Order of Alexander Nevsky for it. Princess Meshchersky, a wealthy benefactress of the Bible Society, published at her own expense some 420,000 copies of religious tracts, translated from English and Church Slavonic writings. Robert Pinkerton, a member of the British and Foreign Bible Society who was active in Russia, wrote of these works:

> Their publication formed a new era in Russia with regard to religious books; for the standard dogmatical or religious works of the Russians are all in the Slavonian character and tongue, so that when these tracts made their appearance in the modern character and language, and written in a style of simplicity and elegance, instead of the stiff scholastic manner of the ecclesiastical writings, religion, seeming to have put on a more attractive dress, was brought nearer and made more intelligible to readers of all classes. And it is only since these works appeared that the New Testament has cast off its ancient Slavonic dense veil of the tenth century.[68]

Pinkerton's book, more ingenuous than penetrating, is valuable here for the traces of society's ideology in its imagery ("attractive dress," "dense veil") and stylistic criteria ("simplicity," "elegance").

The Ideology of "Talk"

The most important vehicle of reality-maintenance is
conversation.
Peter L. Berger and Thomas Luckmann, *The Social Construction
of Reality*

Examining this ideology in terms of its linguistic and stylistic preferences—these aspects of language use are frequently confused in
the writings of the early nineteenth century—I have mentioned certain fundamental tendencies: the orientation of written communication toward the "talk" of the educated, Westernized gentry at the
expense of other discourses; insistence on the wealth and harmony
of this talk; the preservation in written form of artful good talk; the
promotion of "taste," not fixed rules, as a cultural arbiter; fluctuation
between practice and ideal as cultural norm; the intermingling of
stylistic and social evaluations; and a tacit assertion of the universal
validity of this cosmopolitan norm. Other important features of this
ideology—the behavior, moral ideals, modes of social association,
political activity, and literary life that it favored—may be seen to
derive from its orientation toward talk. But in order to examine these
features it is necessary to understand "talk" not only in terms of its
selection of linguistic styles, as I have been doing so far, but in a
broader social-psychological sense.

"Talk," as Erving Goffman has brilliantly illuminated it, is not geared
to extensive projects, but rather to passing or past moments. Its casualness and generally loose connections can foster a weak referential
relationship to the topic of conversation and can condone inconsistencies and polymorphous performances in which the speaker appeals for sympathy, understanding, and other expressions of audience
appreciation while screening himself and his performance from over-
close scrutiny. Quotations (direct and indirect), proverbs (as collective
wisdom), wit, asides, changes in intonation, and gestures are some
of the devices that aid the talker to accomplish such screening and
performing, unless by their violation of norms they accomplish the
opposite effect (as Nadezhdin's intonations and gestures did in his
conversation with Pushkin).[69]

This rather negative conception of talk might seem more applicable
to some of society's activities than to others. To be sure, ballroom
chatter and memorable salon discussions differ significantly from each
other in profundity, but the difference could be more a qualitative
than a structural one. The heroine of Pushkin's prose fragment "Ros-
lavlev" inadvertently suggests this, anyway, as she attempts to

distinguish between Muscovite table talk and the salon conversations to which the visiting Mme. de Staël must have been accustomed:

> How insignificant our high society must seem to this unusual woman! She is used to being surrounded by people who understand her, on whom a brilliant remark, a powerful movement of the heart, or an inspired word is never lost; she is used to fascinating conversation of the highest culture. But here she saw what they needed, what these apes of enlightenment could understand, and tossed them a pun.   (VIII, 151)

The inability of Polina to imagine structural alternatives to society's talk is already evident when Mme. de Staël figures in her outburst not as the author of novels and extended critical studies, but as a salon interlocutor. Polina's sense of salon discourse emphasizes its brevity ("a remark," "a word"), theatricality (the performing hostess before her rapt audience), and variety (intellectual brilliance, emotional force). Conversation "of the highest culture" would seem to require inspired wit—the Russian *slovo* ("word") here suggests a calque from the French *mot* (compare bon mot).[70] And it is precisely these qualities—wit, theatricality, brevity, variety—that the hapless "apes of enlightenment" were trying to provide.

Talk's brevity, fragmentariness, and polymorphousness came to shape not only such individual events as salons, literary circles, or routs, but the social whirl as a whole—a round of dinners, visits, theatricals, casual gatherings, balls, and early-morning suppers. This plethora of Westernized Russia's cultural possibilities is scarcely more detailed in the scintillating first chapter of *Eugene Onegin* than in memoir accounts of the time, including Sergei Aksakov's reminiscences of Admiral Shishkov, who would return from brief appearances at the Admiralty to pore over the Tasso translations and ancient Slavonic manuscripts in his study, then dine on foreign foods with his Protestant wife and her French-speaking relatives before engaging the dinner guests in linguistic discussions and departing to visit friends or gamble at his club.[71]

In the next chapter I will discuss in detail the institutionalization of talk in Russian literature of the early nineteenth century and the important role that this institutionalization played in contemporary education, cultural politics, and government service. For now suffice it to remember Iurii Tynianov's point that an orientation toward talk (as opposed to other uses of language, such as oratory) helped shape the generic preferences of the period.[72] Familiar letters and essays, verse epistles, satires, album verse, and other genres of limited length that could represent the discursive practices of polite society, advanced to the fore of Russian literature. The author-reader relationships in literary texts changed in conformity with this orientation toward sociable talk, as the didactic tone of earlier works yielded to the familiarity that characterizes the prevalent narrative manner of our three novels. Pushkin's prescription for the novel—that it should possess "all the freedom of a conversation or letter"—summarizes this development (XIII, 245, 30 November 1825, to A. A. Bestuzhev).

The Social Self

A person is not absolutely an individual.
C. S. Peirce, "The Essentials of Pragmatism"

The particular ideology that I am examining, with its orientation toward the talk of polite society, might strike the modern student as an exception to Louis Althusser's theory that it is the function of all ideologies to constitute individuals as subjects.[73] From external or subsequent perspectives—religious or post-Romantic, for example— the ideology of polite society seemed to impose a fragmentation of the personality upon its members that prevented them from becoming unified subjects.

This, anyway, I take to be the thrust of the future Metropolitan Filaret's letter to his father, a priest: "The first lesson of *living in society* is learning to become more or less a chameleon."[74] Vladimir Solov'ev's analysis of Pushkin makes a similar point about the writer who, more than any other, realized the aesthetic potential of this ideology: "Pushkin never had such a dominant central content to his personality [as did Byron and Mickiewicz]. He had simply a lively, open, unusually receptive soul that responded to everything—and nothing more."[75]

From this and a host of similar comments about Russia's national poet and the time in which he lived, we may isolate an important aspect of the cultural wealth that society claimed as its own: participation in the social whirl required considerable adaptability and a large repertoire of roles. Not only were members of society expected to maintain a variety of costumes, properties, personae, and linguistic styles for different events and occasions, they were further required to tailor their talk and letters to the characteristics of their different interlocutors and correspondents. An idée fixe was a serious conversational flaw, as Sękowski noted in his essay on enlightened conversation.[76] The potential of this behavioral norm for encouraging imposture soon became a prime generator of literary plots, especially for Gogol, but at least initially this multiplication of "selves" could be seen not as insincerity, but as an essentially moral activity, one necessary for social harmony.[77] Nevertheless, Zhukovsky's apt characterization of society—"a vast theater where each is at once actor and spectator"—finds relevant amplification in Erving Goffman's thesis that casual talk provides a social arena for performances that differ from theatrical ones not so much in absolute terms as in degree of fictionality and preformulation.[78]

To be sure, every diverse culture requires a variety of behavior and "selves" from its individual members. As William James suggests, an individual has as many different social selves as there are distinct groups of persons about whose opinion he cares.[79] Yet Russian life of the period, with its whirl of activities, ever-changing fashions, abundant foreign models, and orientation toward talk, developed this multiplication of selves to an extraordinary degree, largely because the subject that the ideology of polite society constituted was an insistently composite one: the *honnête homme* (*chestnyi chelovek*, as Pushkin translated it, X, 132, and XI, 57)—a person of balanced humors, emotions, and interests, capable of playing a variety of roles. This norm could encompass any attitudes, beliefs, or occupations that might otherwise have overwhelmed its multiplicity—political radicalism, Romantic nationalism, Byronic "spleen," a cult of the sentiments, Evangelical Christianity, or an authorial vocation—and reduced them to discrete roles, thereby discouraging any form of specialization. Many examples demonstrate the allegiance of contemporary Russians to this composite norm. Karamzin's favorite review called him "l'honnête homme avant le savant."[80] Faddei Bulgarin, the notorious police spy and journalist, argued for the rise of a profession of letters in Russia, yet took care to place this occupation last as he identified himself in a letter of denunciation as a "man, gentleman, and writer."[81] The Slavophile Aleksei Khomiakov appears in Koshelev's memoirs as a nonspecialist who could converse with any specialist.[82] Well into the 1830s this social-psychological norm would inhibit not only the development of a literary profession, but even the persistent cultivation of letters. One recalls, in this regard, Zhukovsky's fear that authorial vanity might render a writer unfit for society.

As with other social patterns of the time, this one was translated into aesthetic programs. A gentleman-poet was expected to practice a variety of genres and to parcel out the expression of different emotions and mental capabilities among the different elements of the genre system: patriotic fervor in odes, melancholy in elegies, trenchant wit in epigrams, friendly concern in familiar epistles, and amorous feeling in madrigals. Vil'gel'm Kiukhel'beker's account of humor reveals a more thorough acquaintance with German aesthetics and with Schiller's notion of the harmonious individual than was usual among the amateur poets of his time. Nevertheless, his vision of the humorist is compatible in its variety, balance, and independence with the norm of the *honnête homme:*

> What is *humour* [English in the original]? Concepts that are not completely clear are best defined in negative terms. Thus humour is not simply mockery, nor wit alone, nor the *vis comica* without any admixture; humour is not expressed exclusively either by direct satire or by irony; the mocker, the wit, and the comic are cold; their obligation, their craft is to distance themselves and to avoid feeling; the sarcastic satirist is limited to the feeling of anger or indignation. The humorist, on the contrary, is open to *all* possible feelings, but he is not their slave. He rules them and not they him, he *plays* with them—this is how he differs from the elegiac or lyric poets, who are utterly carried away and enslaved by feeling; the humorist amuses himself with feelings and even at their expense, but not the way the vulgar amuse themselves, imagining their superiority with rude and unpleasant arrogance; but rather as a kind elderly man amuses himself with children, or as sometimes in a familiar circle one makes fun of the small failing of a friend whom one loves and respects. The humorist is by no means afraid of a momentary burst of emotion; on the contrary he willingly pursues it, but he never loses sight of his power over it, his individuality, and his personal freedom. Humour can enter into all genres of poetry: tragedy itself does not exclude it.[83]

As Kiukel'beker was writing this in 1832, the system of verse genres that had organized Russian literature in the 1810s was already yielding to the more general lyric verse genre that was characteristic of European Romanticism.[84] Nevertheless, Russian writers continued to dedicate their talents to an unusual variety of forms, including the previously disreputable novel. Our three novelists, for example, produced not only lengthy narratives, but also verse and drama. Both Gogol and Pushkin also wrote history and literary criticism, as Karamzin had done before them. Each of these writers, in different ways, combined a sense of personal freedom, licensed by the ideology that I have been discussing, with an openness and commitment to aesthetic innovation as they explored the possibilities of the Russian language and their cosmopolitan, secular culture.

To violate the *honnête homme*'s norm of nonspecialization, whether in social life or in literary activity, was to risk ridicule, which—while less severe than subsequent Russian tools of cultural control—was nevertheless a powerful inhibiting force in an aristocratic milieu, as the pioneer sociologist Mme. de Staël has noted.[85] In practice, society interpreted violation of this ideal versatility as ineptness, comic excess, strangeness, or—in the extreme—madness.[86] Admiral Shishkov, obsessed with his etymological research and defense of Church Slavonic, became a figure of fun, not only to his literary opponents, but even to his family circle.[87] When Zhukovsky seemed to be writing ballads (already a suspect enterprise) to the exclusion of other genres, he became the stuff of parody to his friends and opponents alike, even on the public stage in A. A. Shakhovskoi's comedy *A Lesson for Coquettes, Or the Spa at Lipetsk* (*Urok koketkam, ili Lipetskie Vody*, 1815). Indeed, the comedies and satires of the time reinforced the ideal of the *honnête homme* by exposing any emotional, intellectual, behavioral, and stylistic excesses to ridicule. Even activities acceptable to an *honnête homme*—poetry, scientific farming (based on European farming), military service, or dedication to French culture—became laughable when carried to excess. Twenty years after the staging of Shakhovskoi's play, Gogol would, in a programmatic essay, continue to call for drama to address "contemporary passions and eccentricities" (*strasti i strannosti*, VIII, 182).

The reception of Griboedov's brilliant *Woe from Wit* (*Gore ot uma*, 1823) documents the power of this norm. When the play's version of Moscow high society declared the intelligent but obsessed protagonist "mad," the rhetoric of the play turned upon that society to accentuate the hypocrisy, viciousness, crassly material interests, and vulnerability to imposture of its members. Yet Pushkin, reading the play in manuscript, persistently evaluated it according to the social-psychological norms of polite society and faulted Griboedov's hero for lacking "the first attribute of an intelligent man—to know at first glance with whom he's dealing" (XIII, 138) and to tailor his conversation accordingly. Prince Viazemsky's notebook records a similar evaluation of the hero in social-psychological terms: "a person in society like Chatsky on stage would be, for all his wit and grandiloquence, unbearably ponderous and boring."[88]

Not only comedy and satire, but other aesthetic forms that were produced by society members depended upon the norm of the *honnête homme*. Epigrams seized upon incidents that revealed departures from this norm, and the ability to write them figures as a social skill in both *Eugene Onegin* and *A Hero of Our Time*.[89] In *Dead Souls*, epigrams appear as the inevitable accompaniment of a ball. Although generally unpublishable, they circulated among society. Verbal caricatures that isolate contemporary obsessions, excesses, and imbalances grace the letters and diaries of the period.[90] The visual art of caricature, meanwhile, came to adorn notebooks, manuscripts, and albums; and *Eugene Onegin* pays tribute to one of Petersburg's masters of this art, Count Saint-Priest (8:26). The novel's hero, adept at the other social arts, limits himself to mental caricatures of the heroine's birthday guests (5:31). In each case, the text suggests that the objects of these caricatures find themselves so treated because of their *behavior* and not merely because of their physical appearance.

This approach to character, measuring it according to a composite behavioral norm, not only fragmented the social subject but also precluded examination of the inner life, to say nothing of the depths of the psyche as more recent periods have come to know them. Lidiia Ginzburg concluded from the study of the "documentary" prose of Viazemsky, Pushkin, Griboedov, and other contemporary writers that the inner life, the soul, remained a matter of such privacy that it could not be fixed in any mode of writing.[91] In different ways Pushkin, Lermontov, and Gogol present this silence in their novels, and intellectuals of the 1830s and 1840s begin to fill their letters with intense passages of psychological self-examination. In the introduction to his translation of Constant's *Adolphe* (1831), Viazemsky can comment on the striking departure that the protagonist's self-analysis constituted.[92] But those Russians of the early nineteenth century who concerned themselves with the inner life did so largely in terms of moralistic generalities and discrete, passing emotions. The ability to account for an essential inner self remained largely beyond the limits of language and culture. Belinsky, a leader of the first intellectual generation to follow this one, would insightfully remark that "with us the personality [*lichnost'*] is just beginning to break out of its shell."[93]

The Amelioration of Manners

Language and literature are not merely means of mass
enlightenment, they are the *principal* means.
N. M. Karamzin, "Speech Delivered at the Solemn Assembly of
the Imperial Russian Academy," 5 December 1818

The rules of polite sociability and talk that shaped the art forms, behavior, and self-image of this culture became as well the cornerstone of a secular moral system dedicated to social harmony and the amelioration of manners. That fragmentation of the personality that appalled outside observers, such as Solov'ev or the Metropolitan Filaret, appeared to those inside society as a necessary condition for such harmonization. In an article on "politeness and *bon ton*" that Karamzin published in his *Messenger of Europe,* an excessive concern with self, egoism, figures as "the one true enemy of society and all its institutions"; this piece, translated from the French, warns its readers, "fear to be different from other people and do not desire to be better than they are."[94]

Literature—understood as the active practice of letters—was assigned an important role in this process of social harmonization, through comedy and satire and, indirectly, through the infectious civility of its manner. To inspire civility and to inculcate good taste became the moral purpose of literature and literary criticism. Consequently, such writers as Karamzin and Zhukovsky took pains to avoid the slightest offensiveness in their criticism. Karamzin ultimately refused to criticize contemporary works altogether, for fear of discouraging the amateurs who produced them and renewing the vulgar squabbles that had marred the literary life of the previous century, in Russia no less than in France or England.[95] Zhukovsky, assuming the editorship of Karamzin's journal several years later, cautiously justified a return to the criticism of specific works by enlisting criticism under the aegis of moral philosophy: criticism helps form moral feeling since it calls attention to beauty in art, which is analogous to the good (moral beauty) in nature.[96]

Perhaps no work of the time pays greater tribute to the ameliorating role than does an essay by the Decembrist Aleksandr Kornilovich, "On the First Balls in Russia" ("O pervykh balakh v Rossii"), published in the almanac *Polar Star* (*Poliarnaia zvezda*) in 1823 and reissued a year later in another almanac, *Russian Antiquity* (*Russkaia starina*). An army officer who would later bravely try to rally the rebels on Senate Square, Kornilovich couched his celebration of balls in a form ideologically consistent with his refined topic, an elegantly conversational letter to a young lady.[97] His epistle presents an all-inclusive vision of ritualistic conjunction. Social distinctions, economic status, civil service ranks, even differences of sex and nationality disappear or undergo transformation, as the eighteenth-century balls join their participants in harmonious community. Commoners dance with the imperial family, forgetting their rank; Russians, taught to dance by Swedish prisoners of war, later invite captured French officers to join them on the dance floor; the empresses dance both the Western minuet and Russian folk dances; women disguise themselves as men and vice versa. Competitive games, such as cards or draughts, figure in the festivities, but the division into winners and losers that these produced did not (at least in Kornilovich's idealization) undermine the sense of universal pleasure and harmony.[98]

Such balls, instituted in Russia by Peter the Great as instruments of his Westernizing policy, appear less and less subject to official regulation as Kornilovich's chronicle advances and increasingly overcome hierarchal distinctions in a carnivalesque manner, especially when the balls began to be given privately. Pushkin's biography reminds us, however, that the court did not fully surrender the ordering potential of these ceremonies; as the convicted Decembrist Kornilovich was living out his short life in prison and exile, the poet was being reprimanded for not appearing at court functions in his humiliating Kammerjunker's uniform. Nevertheless, Kornilovich's epistle, unlike Zhukovsky's essay on the writer in society, does not include disparate ideological viewpoints, as the discourse of polite society weaves its seamless fabric of manners, beauty, and morality.

Rebellion in Society

At Ryleev's littérateurs and many of his acquaintances and friends often gathered. In addition to the above [A. A. Bestuzhev, Kornilovich, Grech] there were Kiukhel'beker, Bulgarin, Fedor Glinka, Orest Somov, Nikita Murav'ev, Prince Sergei Trubetskoi, Prince Aleksandr Odoevsky, and many others . . . The talk was enlivened by subjects that were not always purely literary; not infrequently they moved to the vital social questions of that time . . . Natal'ia Mikhailovna, the hostess, was attentive to all.
Memoirs of Prince E. P. Obolensky

The inclusion of Kornilovich's article in an almanac of two no less prominent members of the period's most important political conspiracy, A. A. Bestuzhev and K. F. Ryleev, demands mention of that complex movement's proximity to the everyday life and ideology of polite society. In geographical and architectural terms nothing reveals this proximity more strikingly than the magnificent Laval mansion, where the Decembrists gathered. The interrelationship between their political activities and their other social commitments during the decade that ended with the failure of the uprising in December 1825 was from all accounts a fluid one, and one on which there was no unanimity within the movement. To the extent that members of the conspiracy and its sympathizers were scattered from the Baltic to the Caucasus, held a variety of political opinions ranging from republican to constitutional monarchist, adhered to a spectrum of Enlightenment and Romantic literary views, advocated in turn such disparate tactics as open propaganda and regicide, and represented both the impoverished provincial gentry and the enlightened Westernized gentry that I have been calling "society," such a fluid relationship to the daily life of polite society is not surprising.[99] However, the Northern Society, headquartered in St. Petersburg, was more aristocratic in composition, more restrained in its program for political transformation, and more involved in the social-aesthetic life of the fashionable world than was the Southern Society. Consequently, the Northern group's dynamism depended more upon a relationship with society. Its members, descended from the best families, belonged to important literary groups (Arzamas, the Green Lamp, and the Free Society of Lovers of Russian Literature);[100] frequented the theater, salons, and balls; conversed on such fashionable topics as political economy and history; and with few exceptions belonged to prestigious regiments or branches of the civil service. The Constitution of the Union of Welfare (*Soiuz blagodenstviia*, 1818–1821), which preceded the Northern Society (1822–1825), committed it members to public involvement in spheres familiar to society and its notions of enlightenment: philanthropy, education, justice, and the national economy.[101] These legal activities did not merely screen clandestine work—as would be their primary function with subsequent revolutionary organizations—but were considered generally conducive to social improvement. As such, public action (or at least talking about it) was one role that a gentleman's ideology would license him to play. Indeed, the Northern Society's commitment to ameliorating governmental harshness, limiting the power of the autocrat, and educating the broader public at relatively little expense to the status of the gentry expressed the same independence vis-à-vis the government that marked the very language of polite society.[102]

At times the logic of this independence swept the Decembrists and those close to them beyond the conventions of polite social interaction. Speaking bluntly (instead of using polite periphrasis), cultivating mild scabrousness and later obscenity (in Arzamas and in the Green Lamp), sacrificing the company of women for serious study, or refusing to play cards and dance at balls were some of the ways in which the Decembrists chose to challenge the status quo and to make changes beyond those involving the gradual amelioration of manners.[103] Writers close to the movement, such as Griboedov, redirected satire toward society itself; other writers publicized heroic images more militant than the *honnête homme*, the man of feeling, or the dandy, as odes and historical meditations [*dumy*] challenged the priority of elegies and madrigals.

Yet the Decembrists in the capital needed the social conventions and ideology of polite society in order to mount challenges through this process of cultural estrangement (*ostranenie*). After all, they had to appear at balls in order not to dance at them, take cognizance of social fashions in order to oppose them diametrically, and, ultimately, contribute to the theatricality of society's behavior by staging scenes of latter-day Roman virtue in ways that did more to intensify the *honnête homme*'s image of Stoic virtue and self-control than to contradict it.[104] Marc Raeff's summary of the Decembrists' orientation suggests that, if anything, they projected the enlightened gentleman's idea of independence onto all levels of Russian society:

> It is now clear that the criticism of the Decembrists was focussed on one single basic feature of the Russian situation, the source of all evil: lack of security and respect for the individual, his dignity, his honor, his property, his work, and even his life. The main cause for this situation was the autocracy and the arbitrariness and whims of its agents. This was naturally [!] the case for the peasant serf; but it was equally true for the townspeople. More important, it was also true for the nobility and the educated elite.[105]

This ideological projection becomes particularly apparent if we reverse Raeff's last sentences to read down the hierarchy: educated elite, nobility, townspeople (not yet a bourgeoisie in a Western sense), peasantry.

Society, meanwhile, played its part in this relationship by providing a stage for demonstrations of civic virtue and by adapting the Decembrists' interest in history and economics, and by licensing a measure of rebelliousness. To these ends Pushkin's Eugene Onegin would dutifully read his Adam Smith, memorize some appropriate historical anecdotes, and learn to chat about Juvenal (1:6–7). Gogol's Chichikov would worm his way into the hearts of provincial polite society by passing himself off as one who had "endured much in the cause of justice" (VI, 13), and the traveling author-narrator of Lermontov's novel would drop similar hints.[106] Another of Pushkin's characters would subsequently be reminded by a correspondent: "your speculative and solemn arguments belong to the year 1818. At that time strictness of behavior and political economy were in fashion. We appeared at balls without removing our sabers—it was unbecoming for us to dance at balls, and we had no time to attend to the ladies" (VIII, 55, "Roman v pis'makh," 1829).

These intellectual interests—often superficial—passed soon enough. This same fictional correspondent continued, "I have the honor to inform you that now all this has changed. The French quadrille has replaced Adam Smith" (VIII, 55). This flighty comment might well caption the cruel scene in which a party of fettered Decembrists were conducted from St. Petersburg past the Kochubei residence, from which echoed the music and happy sounds of a ball.[107]

Nevertheless, the Decembrists' ties with polite society hardly ceased with the failure of the conspiracy. The swift trial of nearly six hundred young men, all but several under the age of forty, astounded the capital. Few members of society did not discover that a son, husband, relative, or friend had been among the conspirators.

The new emperor, Nicholas I, himself interrogated the prisoners, skillfully employing the heavy armaments of polite conversation— polymorphousness, concealed viciousness, shrewd character analy- sis—against the Decembrists. Anatole Mazour's presentation of Nich- olas as the "royal chameleon" recalls the Metropolitan Filaret's metaphor for society people in general.[108] P. E. Shchegolev expands upon this analysis of the emperor's behavior:

> The Tsar waited in his cabinet, selecting masks, every time a new one for a new person. For one he was a severe monarch offended by a loyal subject; for another—a citizen of the Fatherland equal to the one who was arrested and stood before him; for a third—an old soldier who had suffered for the honor of the uniform; for a fourth—a monarch ready to proclaim constitutional covenants; for a fifth—the Russian lamenting over the evils of the Fatherland and passionately striving for their cor- rection. But in reality he was not the first, nor the second, nor the third; he simply feared for his existence and indefatigably sought all threads of the plot with the purpose of unraveling these threads and gaining his peace of mind.[109]

This performance—worthy of Eugene Onegin in the art of seduction (1:8–12) or of Gogol's Chichikov among the townsfolk of N (VI, 17– 18)—was no less effective than those of his fictional parallels. Many Decembrists, softened by the harsh conditions of imprisonment, re- called themselves to the social roles they had never fully abandoned— father, son, friend, civil servant, loyal Russian officer—and gave in to the tsar's hypocritical performances and to those of their other interrogators and judges, to whom they were bound by a variety of personal, social, and service ties.

The legends that soon enveloped the captured Decembrists have generally passed over their behavior under interrogation, the point at which their vulnerability as members of society became most evi- dent. The five executions, the ruthless sentences to hard labor and suicidal military missions, and the behavior of the exiled Decembrists in Siberia—their mingling with and service to the people of that region—have earned them the title of "martyrs," both in the popular consciousness and from historians of the movement.[110] To the extent that the Christian martyrs were often depicted as young patricians with seemingly everything to lose by adhering to their faith, this term has considerable appeal.

But the title "martyr"—which Russians have so generously bestowed throughout their history—should not obscure the extent to which the Decembrists embodied the ideology of polite society with its vision of independence and social amelioration. An English traveler who met a group of Decembrists after they had endured decades of hard labor, physical privation, and psychological harassment paid the following tribute to the polite society that they had raised along the banks of the Angara:

> At the time of my visit to Irkutsk there were six of the exiles still living in town, viz. Prince Volkonsky, Prince Trubetskoi, and Colonel Poggio with their families; the others were P. A. Mukhanov and the two brothers Borisov. These formed the best society in Irkutsk, and some of the most agreeable days which I spent in Siberia were in enjoying the intercourse with them. They are now living in comfort, mixing in society, and gathering around them all the best that Irkutsk afforded. The Princess Trubetskoi has spent several of her youthful years in the Kingdom [of Great Britain]. She was a clever and highly educated woman, devoted all her energies to the education of her three daughters and young son, and was the first lady who followed her husband into Siberia.[111]

Here, on the brink of death (Princess Trubetskoi), insanity, and suicide (Andrei Borisov), and three thousand miles from the Laval mansion, the Decembrists kept alive the conversation, cosmopolitanism, and educational ideals of polite society.

The Decembrist uprising represents the most intense and principled political manifestation of society's ideology, an expression so direct that many other members of society recoiled from it, shocked by the bloodshed and talk of regicide. Karamzin's wife, an important salon hostess, voiced this shock and revulsion most vividly: "Que le ciel nous préserve de ces benefacteurs de l'humanité qui passent sur le corps de leurs mères, de leurs femmes, pour parvenir je ne sais à quelles chimères!"[112] Nevertheless, the connections, social and intellectual, between polite society and the crushed conspiracy continued to excite the suspicion of Nicholas I and his subordinates during the decades following the uprising. The religious experimentation, political speculation, and cosmopolitanism made possible by society's discourse found direct and conscious opposition in the ideology of "official nationality" ("Orthodoxy, Autocracy, Nationalism") that the advisors of Nicholas I would formulate during the years that Pushkin, Lermontov, and Gogol were writing their novels.[113]

At the same time, the ideology of polite society would be challenged even more powerfully on other fronts, as it failed to answer the cultural needs of a new generation of Russian intellectuals: aspiring professional writers, university students, low-ranking civil servants, and children of the clergy—most of whom had been barred from full participation in society. Nevertheless, the ideology embedded in the language, behavior, self-image, art, and ethics of Russia's cultural elite could not be eradicated overnight. For the negative forms of government control—censorship, restriction of academic freedom— made a cultural life oriented toward talk, salons, and familiar circles even more of a necessity. Russian literature would still be bound, even in the 1830s, to the ideology of polite society, and this did much to shape the institutions of literature through which, and in opposition to which, that literature was produced.

II

Institutions of Literature

In every society the production of discourse is at once
controlled, selected, organized and redistributed
according to a certain number of procedures, whose
role is to avert its powers and its dangers, to cope
with chance events, to evade its ponderous, awesome
materiality.

Michel Foucault, "The Discourse on Language"

L ITERATURE has been perceived as an *institution*—an objectified
social activity with established roles and functions—since classical
antiquity.[1] Plato's concern over regnant interpretive practices or Ar-
istotle's account of tragedy's impact on its audience or Aristophanes's
parodies in *The Frogs* are examples of such awareness of precedent
and predictable interaction. Since that time few commentators on
literature have willfully ignored the literary work's participation in
social processes. Early nineteenth-century Russia provides no exception, and a representative list of titles suggests the widespread obsession with literature as an actual or potential institution: Karamzin,
"Why There Are Few Authorial Talents in Russia" (1802) and "On
the Book Trade and On the Love for Reading in Russia" (1802); Zhukovsky, "The Writer in Society" (1809); Pushkin, "A Conversation
between a Bookseller and a Poet" (1824); Gogol, "On the Movement
of Journalistic Literature in 1834 and 1835" (1836); Lermontov, "Journalist, Reader, and Writer" (1840). Essays and works of literature by
these and other writers addressed every conceivable aspect of literature as an institution: the status and role of the writer; the reader's
role in the literary process; the proper subjects and language for literature; literature as a mode of association; literature and social concerns (education, leisure, morality); literature and the marketplace;
censorship.

These concerns are so persistent and so frequently voiced that one
might well doubt whether early nineteenth-century literature could

be called institutionalized at all. Intelligent complaints by Russian writers that their country lacked a literature (or, alternatively, responsible critical attention to its scattered works) span the period.[2] Such perceptions are, of course, important conveyors of contemporary awareness, and they express a common human tendency to be dissatisfied with institutions.[3] But the publication history of *Eugene Onegin*—which was recited in salons, published in fragments in an elegant almanac, and pirated for a disreputable journal—suggests another way of looking at the problem, one which would notice not an absence of institutions, but a vexing multiplicity of them. I will follow the latter course because, as the recollections and insights of contemporaries will show, however small the reading public may have been and however unsatisfactory its relationship to belles lettres, this public did present the Russian writer with sets of expectations, and the writer did have to make choices within several frameworks that can truly be called institutionalized. But before pursuing this argument, I must develop a notion of "literature as an institution" that will facilitate comparisons and permit the synthesis of many valuable insights by contemporaries and subsequent scholars.

In recent decades literary critics and sociologists have articulated an awareness of institutionalization in important ways. Harry Levin has stressed the power of tradition and convention, necessary differences between the work and the world, which the work does not so much reflect as refract.[4] Wilhelm Vosskamp has treated genres, especially the novel, as "literary-social institutions," focusing on problems of selection, institutionalization (and deinstitutionalization), prototypes, and functional changes.[5] Robert Escarpit has outlined the institutional roles of various agents in the modern "business of letters" (writers, educators, publishers, critics, booksellers, consumers) and has linked them together into two broadly defined circuits of literary dissemination, "cultured" and "popular."[6] Hugh Dalziel Duncan developed an ingenious model for differentiating institutions of literature that is based on the nature of author-public-critic relationships in which critics are the pivotal element (Do they orient themselves toward the author? the public? Do they exist at all?).[7] Peter Bürger, in turn, distinguishes between institutionalizations of art (courtly, bourgeois, avant-garde) on the basis of their social functioning.[8] Raymond Williams founds his treatment of cultural institutions on shifts in commercial relations (patronage, artisanal, market, and postmarket).[9] Although Boris Eikhenbaum did not use the term "institution," his understanding of literature's "social being" resulted in the concept of "systems of literary environment" (*literaturno-bytovye sistemy*) that anticipated many of the roles and relationships later detailed by Levin, Escarpit, and Williams.[10] Important structuralist and post-structuralist essays have reflected upon a more limited, but no less important, aspect of literary life: conventions of reading and interpretation.[11]

Each of these valuable studies has its own aims and develops its concepts accordingly. Considered as a whole, however, they reveal a vexing problem for the enterprise of literary sociology: how to account for literature as a social institution that responds to historical forces and situations without ignoring the dynamics of the literary text and the compelling force of literary tradition. Those studies that are most sensitive to the intricacies of literary texts and to the power of tradition, such as Levin's, tend to neglect the social functions and conditioning of literary art, while models for the analysis of the literary process in its multiplicity of roles and functions tend to neglect individual instances altogether (Escarpit) or to underestimate the challenge that literary traditions present to individual creativity (Duncan). Meanwhile, any discussion of literary institutionalization encounters the concrete historical problem that different periods face crises that affect different aspects of the literary process, crises such as the absence or recalcitrance of a reading public (including critics), the insufficiency of literary codes, or conflicting models of a writer's role.

A Model

In general any work of art is created as a parallel and
a contradiction to some kind of model.
Viktor Shklovsky

Language—at once the material of literary art and a medium of social power that is affected by social processes—suggests a link between the social and literary phenomena that seem to elude each other in literary sociology, particularly if one views language as, in Jürgen Habermas's terms, a meta-institution on which all social institutions are dependent.[12] But language, to serve this purpose, must be seen not as an abstract system of rules, but as discourse—realized in time and possessing a subject, interlocutor, and context.[13]

A well-known communication model that was developed by Roman Jakobson possesses these discursive elements. It offers a convenient tool for identifying the roles and functions that constitute literature as an institution, for recording changes in the institutionalization of literature, and for comparing different ways of literary life. I shall use it for such analytic, mnemonic, and comparative purposes. I make no claim that it has the power fully to explain changes, differences, and cultural constraints. These and the communicative static that they occasioned will be discussed in the institutional studies which follow the presentation of the model, as will the social functioning of particular institutions. Likewise, the interrelationships between the elements in Jakobson's model—or absence of these elements—will need to be discussed in each case.

According to Jakobson, any speech act involves the presence (explicit or implicit) of six factors: an *addresser*, who sends a *message* to an *addressee*, a *context* referred to in the message, a *code* that the addresser and addressee hold in common, and a *contact* (a physical channel and mental connection between them).[14] In schematic representation:

CONTEXT

ADDRESSER   MESSAGE   ADDRESSEE

CONTACT

CODE

In a modern literary situation these terms translate into familiar roles and situations (although creative ingenuity is continually testing the definition of each factor—multiple authorship, nonfiction novels, new contexts, and others): the addresser, a professional author whose addressee is some segment of the reading public, contacts it through the medium of the printed page. The modern author's context spans a seemingly inexhaustible range of subject matter (including, of course, literature itself), selected and shaped, however, according to the relatively enduring codes of language, genre, and culture together with the temporary codes of fashion, codes which the author and the competent reader will share, if not always respect. Special realizations of these factors and relationships account for various complexities of the literary situation: readership, for instance, will include a general public as well as those privileged readers (critics, editors, publishers, censors) who have the opportunity to provide various sorts of feedback through the communicative channel, thereby altering the printed text. And we do have a variety of institutional situations; poetry published in small magazines, entertainment literature on the drugstore revolving racks, postmodernist fiction—to name just a few instances—feature different writers, readers, modes of dissemination, and generic codes. Writers who wish their works to be available in small town or high school libraries might not find the range of subject matter inexhaustible, after all.

Moreover, as Jakobson clearly notes, literary texts, which (according to postmedieval Western reading conventions) orient the reader's attention primarily toward the message, feature a sort of communication quite different from that of face-to-face interaction: namely they render the message, addresser, addressee, and context of the work ambiguous.[15] Who, to give one example of such ambiguity, is the addresser of a modern novel—the "real" person whose name appears on the title page, the "personality" that a reader might choose to extrapolate from the work, a narrative "voice," or some other possibility? Such ambiguities demand distinctions that recent narrative theory has drawn between author-reader communication, implicit narrative communication (the "implied author" and the "implied reader" that readers extrapolate from a text) and inscribed narrative communication between narrators and narratees (for example, the author-narrator of *Eugene Onegin* and the cynical readers he addresses in the text, with whom actual readers are encouraged by the text not to identify themselves).[16] Such refinements of the Jakobsonian model make it more suitable for analyzing relationships between literature and society because literary texts can be "boundary art," to use Saul Morson's fruitful concept, not just in generic terms, but also in institutional ones;[17] that is, texts can probe distinctions between the modes of production and reception that different institutions present by proposing (in their implicit and inscribed communications structures) alternatives to the communicative patterns that existing institutions of literaure have established. *Eugene Onegin, Dead Souls,* and *A Hero of Our Time* each object, for example, to the then regnant interpretive practice—carried over from conventions of reading Byronic poetry—of identifying the hero of a work with its author, and each novel presents a multiplicity of authorial or narrational voices to frustrate this reading habit.

Meanwhile, creative ingenuity has challenged the familiar modern realization of this institutional model at every point: various forms of collective or anonymous authorship; devices to make the reader an active participant in literary creation (or, conversely, its puzzled dupe); unconventional formats; the crossing of generic and linguistic boundaries within a work ("the nonfiction novel," *Finnegans Wake*); the treatment of "forbidden" topics. Language itself, to quote one recent account, possesses a "creative nature" that makes the uttering of new sentences in new contexts possible.[18] More flamboyantly, Gogol asserted that the Russian language itself is a poet (VIII, 408–409). In many of these cases, however, challenge is itself institutionalized. The frequency with which it has been noted that the *novel* by its very etymology is expected to provide something *new* illustrates this point. It could, indeed, be argued that these challenges to "authorship," passive reading, standard formats, generic schemata, decorum, and linguistic norms confirm the accepted definitions of literature in modern Western societies. Such challenges render the "message" ever more arresting, intriguing, or duplicitous. They recall attempts to define literature as messages dominated by the "poetic function," as "hypothetical verbal structures," or as a largely self-referential and self-generating system.[19] Thus, these challenges to discrete features of the institution may be simply absorbed, as enrichments. Moreover, human ingenuity, mounting such challenges, finds that an awesome array of weaponry defends the institutionalization of literature: the guidance implicit in an institution's own predefined roles and patterns of thinking; generally accepted legitimating notions ("individual creativity," "the organic unity of the work," or, more recently, "the plurality of the text" and "the death of the author"); related institutions, such as education; the mechanisms of legal control (copyright and libel laws, the censorship); last, but by no means least, the marketplace.

This nexus of roles, functions, and precedents will not vanish tomorrow at the stroke of a pen, although some strokes will have crossed out more than others. Yet no ancient cosmogonic myth convinces us that "competent" readers arose from the primordial clay, took their seats in armchairs, and lost themselves in a triple-decker novel, produced by a godlike author. The institutionalization of literature has a history, and it entails the possibilities for evolution and rupture, action and inertia that attend the histories of other human processes.[20] This social structure, which may seem an impregnable fortress to an aspiring author, will appear a crumbling ruin to an avant-garde critic and an architectural palimpsest to a literary historian. Moreover, the architectural associations of the words "institution" and "structure" should not be permitted to convey a sense of stasis. Each new text, writer, and reader in some sense restructures the institution, however slightly, and thriving institutions can impose their patterns on different areas of social life, as we have seen with polite society, the government, and the church.[21]

Early nineteenth-century Russia contributes to our understanding of these vicissitudes not merely because it witnessed the beginnings of a modern institutionalization of literature, but because these beginnings took place in close interaction with two other institutionalizations, which may be labeled, approximately, a patronage system and a system of familiar associations. A relatively distinct version of the roles and functions arranged in our communications model may describe each of them, and each was buttressed by other institutions, by ideological legitimations, and by material factors. A writer could encounter all three, and his wishes to fulfill the authorial roles suggested by one institutionalization could find powerful barriers in the modes of reception and dissemination presented by other institutionalizations.

Patronage

Trediakovsky happened to be thrashed more than once.
Pushkin, 1827

A writer who never commits his manuscript to print or circulates it, never hears a critical voice save the one implicit in his literary models, and remains his only reader has but little part in an institution of literature. In *Eugene Onegin* the author-narrator imagines himself such a writer, haplessly seeking the attention first of his unlettered nanny, later of the ducks on his remote estate (4:35). Yet early nineteenth-century elegiac poets, such as Pushkin imagines in these lines, could at least draw upon a native elegiac tradition and a refined verse language. They would have learned to weave their plaints in Russian schools or in familiar literary groups and by reading works of several decades of Russian sentimentalist writing as well as French examples of the genre. Furthermore, someone wealthy enough to have been reading Pushkin's elegantly printed lines when they first appeared in 1828 would have known that the opening chapters, published separately, had won critical attention in the periodical press and a good measure of commercial success. Fragments of the novel had been read in the salons and literary circles, published in genteel almanacs by Pushkin's schoolfellow Baron Del'vig, and stolen for a less reputable medium by the notorious police informer and journalist Faddei Bulgarin. Favored by these modes of literary dissemination—Russia's rudimentary profession of letters, the familiar associations, and the disreputable journal—the solitary elegist had also momentarily won the favor of the two tyrannical forces that could intervene at any point in the literary process: the autocracy, which had recently released Pushkin from exile and permitted him to return to the capital, and polite society, whose taste and fashion-consciousness shaped not only reading habits but also authorial personae, literary codes, and the field of representation for imaginative literature.

As isolated as Pushkin's unheeded elegist appears to be, his genuine predecessors in the early eighteenth century found themselves in far more straitened circumstances, for they lacked not only authorial status and readership, but even the linguistic and literary codes appropriate for such newly encountered Western genres as the elegy. The better educated and better traveled Russians—Kantemir, Trediakovsky, Lomonosov—soon found various aspects of Russia's ecclesiastical heritage inadequate to the writing they sought to contribute to Russia's incipient secular literature.

Under these circumstances, which make the complaints of Pushkin's contemporaries seem ludicrous by comparison, only a system of patronage could offer any support for literature, and it remained the dominant mode of literary institutionalization throughout the eighteenth century. Westward-looking, "enlightened" despots, the Academy of Sciences, and highly placed aristocrats protected—with varying degrees of constancy and fairness—a number of writers that included, toward the end of the period, Pushkin and Gogol. Under this system, at least in its earliest and purest moments, the protégé's primary audience was his protector, whom he might address orally (at court fêtes, in the drama), in manuscript (letters), and occasionally in print (with an appropriate epistle dedicatory). Patronage placed particular value, as might be expected, upon the lofty genres of neoclassicism (odes, tragedies, epics), upon the informative (history, the sciences), and upon the monumentally useful (grammars, dictionaries), in other words, upon those modes of writing which served to magnify, illuminate, and improve the protector and the state. The dominant linguistic code remained the liturgical language, Church Slavonic, transformed—as is the language of the King James Bible in modern English—into a signifier of loftiness. In terms of our model:

EMPIRE

PROTÉGÉ   ODE, LOFTY WORK, LARGE PROJECT   PATRON

COURT OCCASION, MANUSCRIPT, EXPENSIVE EDITION

CHURCH SLAVONIC (AS "HIGH STYLE")

Fugitive or entertaining genres of less prestige led a precarious existence, as the publication history of Trediakovsky's verses clearly illustrates—many were inserted into his translations and treatises. And, subject to the caprice of the powerful, the publishing industry itself could hope to be nothing more than the victim of "chance," to borrow Kufaev's fortunate term.[22] The bankruptcy of such nineteenth-century publishers as Smirdin was merciful by comparison with the torture and exile that their eighteenth-century predecessors had faced.

At best, the patronage system gave writers the opportunity to work on lengthy projects, such as Karamzin's *History of the Russian State* (1816–1826), and to produce the dictionaries, grammars, rhetorical manuals, and disquisitions on poetry that in turn helped to develop the linguistic and literary codes necessary for the flowering of a national literature. In the hands of such talented writers as Lomonosov and Derzhavin, the occasional ode could, and did, become a work of lasting aesthetic value and a victory over servitude, political and linguistic.[23] If nothing else, timely odes saved each of these writers from immanent arrest.[24]

At its worst, the situation is summarized in the brutal frankness of Dr. Johnson's definition of a patron: "A wretch who supports with insolence and is paid in flattery."[25] Patronage vested in its addressees the power to interfere capriciously in every aspect of the literary process, imposing a crippling subservience upon writers, preventing the institution of a stable publishing trade, dictating the themes and forms of imaginative literature. "The baseness of Russian writers is incomprehensible to me," wrote Pushkin, referring to the age of Catherine the Great (XI, 17), and he could later recount a story that Trediakovsky was caned for his failure to deliver an ode on schedule (XI, 53). A periodical that Pushkin helped to edit subsequently published two letters by an eighteenth-century poet, Aleksandr Sumarokov, to help make such "baseness" comprehensible to a public that was only beginning to enable a new institutionalization of literature. The first letter complains to the treasury that the Academy of Sciences had unjustly withheld from Sumarokov's salary the price of printing his works, an act which he attributed to Lomonosov, who "often went mad from drunkenness" (a malady from which Sumarokov was himself not immune).[26] This letter is important because it reveals some of the meanness that characterized literary life and because it shows a writer playing one patron (the Academy) off against another (the empress), but the second letter, to Prince Potemkin displays even more of the literary, economic, and social dynamics of the patronage system. Sumarokov writes in connection with the impending foreclosure on his house:

I most humbly request that Your Excellency, who honors philanthropy, write to Mr. Demidov [Sumarokov's creditor], that he should, being mindful of philanthropy, demand nothing but the sum given to me and that this sum should be withheld from my salary, which I receive every year at the beginning of May. I have only one home in this world and thus would have nowhere to find shelter and would be obliged, in my old age, to wander the earth . . . Instead of interest and a forfeit, I will repay your Excellency with the composition of a new unrhymed tragedy, which You were so kind as to order. I await, at your decision, either my salvation or despair; and there already remains but little time for your decision. Imagine my condition . . .   (10 July 1775)

As Viazemsky notes in his sardonic preface to the letters, the nature of Potemkin's "order" (a blank-verse tragedy) should give him an "honorary place in our Romantic school."[27]

A brief memorandum follows the second letter, in which Sumarokov gives an even more detailed account of his financial and literary troubles. Among these we see a typical situation: Sumarokov could not even get free tickets to the performances of his plays, from which the theaters enjoyed exclusive profit. With other genres, it was the publishers who made the profits. Authors and translators did not generally receive royalties, nor did they hold any legally binding copyright. Remuneration for writing came in the form of membership in the Academy of Sciences; a precarious position at court; and such grants as rings, sums of money, or snuffboxes, of which Sumarokov mentions two in his memorandum.

Fifty years after Sumarokov wrote these letters, another highly placed connoisseur of literary genres, Nicholas I, would also seek to accelerate the movement of literary history, this time by suggesting to Pushkin that his *Boris Godunov*, another tragedy in blank verse, be rewritten as "an historical tale or a novel, in the manner of Walter Scott."[28] Pushkin declined to produce the requested form, although his personal fate was no less in the hands of the government than Sumarokov's had been. The difference between the two writers in this case was not one of social class or personality. Both writers were proud members of the gentry and are legendary for their independent-mindedness, although Pushkin's would have been better supported by the ideology of polite society, which was only beginning to coalesce in Sumarokov's time.[29] The main difference between the two lay in the institutionalized possibilities open to a Russian writer. By Pushkin's time, although the imperial family continued to reward writers with snuffboxes and grants, the institution of literary patronage had diminished in several of its aspects. The Academy and high nobles no longer played so important a part in it.[30] And contact between the writer and the government was less likely to be as direct as it had been in the eighteenth century. Pushkin was still under the direct supervision of the court, but he generally contacted the tsar through

Benckendorff, the chief of gendarmes. Only occasionally were his works addressed to Nicholas—as in the special memorandum that he sent to the tsar along with his *History of the Pugachev Rebellion* (1835). Gogol was given a three-year grant to work on his last large project, but it was obtained for him indirectly, through the agency of his friends at court, and not through a personal communication with the tsar. Both writers sold their works to booksellers and derived income from the sale of them. Both writers held copyrights. In short the development of other institutions (universities, schools, journals, literary groups) during these years had reduced patronage to a form of sponsorship.[31] A writer could seek broader audiences, for profit as well as for literary satisfaction and constructive criticism. And, while limiting in other ways, the codes of the new institutions licensed more than the panegyric, the lofty, and the informative.

Familiar Associations

The circle of poets gets narrower by the hour—soon we
will be forced for want of listeners to read our verses aloud
to each other. And that's not bad.
Pushkin, 1820

Alongside the patronage system, satisfying some of its insufficiencies and fulfilling different functions in Russian culture as it became secularized and Westernized, a literature practiced in and by familiar groups developed slowly throughout the eighteenth century, then came to dominate Russian literary life during the decades spanned by this study. Salons, circles, soirées, also—but later and less frequently—bookstores, editorial offices, and coffeehouses became the locus of an institutionalization of literature that differed in almost every respect from the patronage system, although it was far from free of its own social and economic problems.[32]

Differences between these associations and the patronage system may be approximated in terms of our model:

"SOCIETY"
GENTLE (WO)MAN-AMATEUR BOUTS-RIMÉS, LETTERS INTERLOCUTOR
FAMILIAR GROUP
"THE CONVERSATIONAL LANGUAGE OF POLITE SOCIETY"

Instead of a subservient relationship to his patron, the writer now enjoyed by convention a position of social and cultural equality with his (or her, we may now add) immediate audience, and, indeed, the roles of addressers and addressees ideally coalesced in this institutionalization of literature.[33] Friendly criticism from the group could lead the poet to revise his work, which was generally written to be recited for the group in the first place. Perhaps the most vivid example of this coauthorial relationship (although hardly one conducive to enduring interest or poetic excellence) is provided by *bouts-rimés*, a popular salon game in which poems were composed to fit given rhymes.[34] Familiar verse epistles were composed in imitation of the style of their recipients' verse. Familiar letters were also tailored to the interests of the addressee. To be sure, a patron had been able to dictate themes and genres to his protégé, as we saw in Potemkin's request for a blank verse tragedy, but now the addresser and addressee relationship became a more reciprocal one, shaped by friendly intercourse, shared experience, and shared values. The epistle dedicatory of *Eugene Onegin*—addressed to Pushkin's friend Pletnev, not to a patron—exemplifies this development.[35]

As this suggests, an author established contact with his audience orally or through the medium of the neatly hand-written page, although literary circles did gather works for journal publication, and the authors permitted their works to be printed. "The spoken language of good society" served as the dominant linguistic code of this literature, although controversies over the linguistic, aesthetic, social, and political ramifications of this norm never ceased until the 1840s. The genres that this institutionalization of literature privileged were those that could most appropriately embody this elusive language: familiar letters and essays, verse epistles, and bouts-rimés, also elegies, madrigals, commonplace books, epigrams, and sentimental lines penned in the omnipresent albums of young ladies. Pushkin, looking forward to a more public (and financially profitable) mode of literary life, devoted an impatient four-stanza disquisition to these albums in *Eugene Onegin*. Yet his proposed solution consists merely in replacing one element of this generic repertoire, a madrigal, with another, an epigram:

> When glittering hostesses come purring
> With quarto tome and "would you care,"
> I'm seized with panic and despair
> And feel an epigram astir in
> The dark recesses of my soul—
> When all I'm asked is to pay toll! (4:30)

He would remain, in short, within the same institution of literature.

Consistent with the stylistic and generic preferences of this literature, its institutionalized field of reference ("context") was the everyday life of the educated, Westernized gentry, constructed according to the ideology of polite society. Tolstoy, who belonged to this social group and who carried some of the values of this period into a later one, outlined the process of selection with a breathtaking bluntness that was made possible by the subsequent development of other perspectives and representational possibilities:

> The lives of officials, merchants, seminarists, and peasants do not interest me and are only half comprehensible to me; the lives of the aristocrats of that time, thanks to the documents of that time and to other reasons, are comprehensible, interesting, and dear to me.[36]

When texts strayed from this field—into the fantastic, into the past, into madness, into the life of nongentry groups—these excursions were encoded in terms of the comic or allegorical (the minutes of the Arzamas society, Pushkin's *Ruslan and Liudmila*), or the psychology of the sentiments (Karamzin's "Isle of Bornholm," Zhukovsky's ballads, Batiushkov's "Song of Harold the Bold"), or the satirical (Pushkin's "Undertaker"). Or they served as swift counterpoints, as with Pushkin's introduction of bustling artisans into *Eugene Onegin* (1:35), which accentuated the frivolity of Eugene's social whirl ("making midnight out of dawn"). Readers were quick to point out the slightest transgression of decorum and were quick to read new literary phenomena in terms of these encodings. Thus a number of Gogol's salon readers either viewed him as an outsider, a Ukrainian, or else recuperated his cosmic humor into the playful-allegorical comic traditions of the familiar circles.[37] Likewise the critics of *Eugene Onegin* hastened to indicate failures of social discrimination in literary casting, such as the introduction of servants and peasants at seemingly inappropriate moments, indications which Pushkin sardonically recorded in the notes to later editions.

A brief analysis can hardly do justice to the variety of the groups, their energy and cultural productivity, especially since one account lists more than four hundred of them.[38] A study of several memoirs might, however, capture something of their purpose and organization, as the participants understood them. The first account, by A. F. Merzliakov, a professor of Russian literature at Moscow University and Lermontov's tutor, describes (with conversationally paratactic syntax) the internal dynamics of the student groups at the turn of the century. Such gatherings, supported by the Masonic tradition of self-improvement through collective and friendly self-criticism, gave beginning writers useful criticism at a time when public criticism was not a widespread phenomenon:

> In many private student literary assemblies, united by ties of acquaintance or friendship, they wrote, translated, and criticized their works and translations, and thereby improved themselves in the difficult ways of literature and taste. Such groups existed in Petersburg and Moscow. They thought neither of repute nor of profit, but lived solely on self-contained satisfaction, that is, on the *pleasures* of learning . . .
>
> How captivating it was to us, who were still youths, to see, amidst our peaceful and isolated conversations, our elders, celebrated for their excellent services to the fatherland, and figures, standing at the helm of state, who listened to our youthful conversations with a smile, heard our first essays in composition, and rejoiced in our dreams as in the dreams of children not knowing either the world or their future lot. They moderated our bursts of ecstasy without killing them completely, gave us stern counsel without leading us into despair, closing before our eyes the sorry future with a curtain of promising remoteness. How pleasant for us was our own way of life! A flaming love for literature, a simple sincere disposition toward each other, freedom, sweet lightheartedness, amiable dreaminess, mutual trust, love of *humanity* and all that is refined, striving for the good—innocent, willing, disinterested, even frenzied. This was the life in our assemblies, our conversations, and our activities.
>
> We strictly criticized each other in speech and writing, analyzed the most illustrious writers, whom we considered our models, discussed almost all the most important subjects for Man, argued much and noisily at our learned board, and went home good friends.[39]

This account, published in 1817 in the proceedings of a literary society at Moscow University, stresses the literary and scholarly orientation of the groups, predictably enough, but not inaccurately. Surviving speeches and other works show, nevertheless, that philosophy, history, and political issues also shared the attention of the best known of these groups, the Friendly Literary Society, in which Merzliakov played a leading role. During the 1820s and later, such groups of students and recent graduates met to discuss philosophy and political problems excluded from university curricula and inaccessible to the heavily censored periodical press. Merzliakov's account hints at such interests ("the good," "freedom") but shows more clearly the institutionalized interactions of the groups with their precedents (model writers, translations) and their coauthoring, critical audience. *Friendship* served the crucial, harmonizing function, here described in the ecstatic accents of Schiller, a favorite author of these circles.

Such circles might seem remote from the salons that flourished in high society, and distinctions may be drawn between these two forms of familiar association. The salons were more long-lived as a rule than the student groups; the salons, unlike the groups, were organized around a hostess (sometimes a host) who was not necessarily a writer herself; the salon featured none of the formal accouterments of the circles (speeches, minutes, by-laws), and the conversations in them were, it seems, more free and easy than those in the literary circles.[40] Particular circles, such as the Friendly Literary Society, expressed occasional dissatisfaction with the frivolity and sentimentality of salon literature.[41] Nevertheless, the amateurism ("disinterestedness"), moderating function, and friendly exchanges that Merzliakov lauds are important similarities between the two forms, similarities consonant in turn with the ideology of polite society. And at times the distinctions between salons and circles fade—as, for example, when Ponamareva's salon decided to publish a journal. Similarly, the terms in which the relatively unproductive, but famous, philosopher-poet Stankevich (the head of a circle) is remembered recall the obligatory paeans to salon hostesses.[42]

It was not, in fact, uncommon for members of society to attend both circles and salons, sometimes several different ones in the course of a day. Baratynsky remarked, for example, that "an argument begun at the Odoevskys continued at the Karamzins and was the chief subject of conversation."[43] A former student of Merzliakov, the Slavophile and social reformer A. I. Koshelev, was one of many who frequented both types of gathering. His memoirs record the interests and interactions of one of the most celebrated and long-lived Russian salons, that of the Karamzins. The paterfamilias, who did more to establish the salon aesthetic than any other Russian writer, died in 1826, but the salon flourished under the direction of his widow and eldest daughter until the widow's death in 1851 and numbered among its visitors two of our novelists, Pushkin and Lermontov. As in the early nineteenth-century literary circles, a variety of topics commanded the salon's attention, literature (broadly defined) foremost among them:

In the Karamzin salon the subject of conversation was not philosophical matters, nor was it hollow Petersburg gossip and old wives' tales. Literature, Russian and foreign, important events in Europe—especially the activities of the then great statesmen of England, Canning and Husquisson—comprised most frequently the content of our lively talks. These soirées . . . refreshed and nourished our souls and minds, which was especially healthful for us in the stifling atmosphere of St. Petersburg. The hostess always directed the conversation toward interesting subjects.[44]

Elsewhere Koshelev elaborated upon this description:

At E. A. Karamzina's gathered littérateurs and intelligent people of various orientations. Bludov was often there, and he entertained everyone with his stories. Zhukovsky, Pushkin, A. I. Turgenev, Khomiakov, P. Mukhanov, Titov and many others also frequented it. The soirées began at ten and lasted until one or two o'clock; the conversation rarely flagged. Karamzina herself was an intelligent woman, of firm and always even character and a good heart, although her heart seemed cold at first meeting. These soirées were the only ones in Petersburg where one spoke Russian and did not play cards.[45]

Koshelev's account does not merely reflect the familiar European ideal—an inspiring hostess, refined and elevating literary conversation, catholicity of interests, informality without superficiality. His account is largely produced by that ideal, for such tributes to the hostess as Koshelev's were one of the salient forms of salon literature. Pushkin and Lermontov had already paid their tributes to the Karamzin women in verse, and Pushkin had included a similar description of a salon in chapter 8 of *Eugene Onegin* by the time that Koshelev was writing these memoirs.[46] Thus, Koshelev's insistence on the uniqueness of the salon in encouraging the use of Russian is more faithful to a rule of salon discourse—singling out one's salon for special praise—than it is accurate in evaluating the place of other important salons in Russian culture of this time: those of the Olenins, Smirnova-Rosset, V. F. Odoevsky, Khitrovo, Rostopchina, and Sollogub in St. Petersburg; those of Volkonskaia, Elagina, and the Aksakovs in Moscow, to name just a few. These other salons played no less important a part in bringing such writers as Pushkin, Lermontov, and Gogol together with willing listeners and in providing a forum for the discussion of Russian literature.

Other accounts of the Karamzin salon could complete the paradigm—information on the graceful manner in which the hostess and her stepdaughter attended to the guests; descriptions of the comfortable surroundings, conducive to good talk; assertions that its visitors included the flower of the Russian literary world and that the salon "distributed diplomas of literary talent" (as one disgruntled—and diplomaless—memoirist put it); even a description of how Karamzin himself achieved a prominent place in high society through his literary talents.[47]

Any institutionalization of literature, even one as seemingly limited and self-sufficient as this, engages literary life in some way with other cultural processes and, in turn, responds to them in keeping with its own structuring capabilities. The literature of familiar groups had assumed educational recreational, and entertaining functions. Literary composition that observed the conventions of polite society was, like dancing, a valued social skill, and a member of society acquired it both in school and at home.[48] Beyond its role in the upbringing of the gentry, however, the practice of literature found functions less "disinterested" than the memoirs would sometimes lead one to believe, first of all as an avenue of social mobility. Beyond this, literary people also sought a second public function: to play a role in the development of Russian society by contributing to the spread of civility, the amelioration of manners, and (by means of periodicals) the formation of public opinion. As a vehicle for the language and ideology of polite society, the literature of familiar groups demonstrated its vitality by entering the areas of the government and the church, as we observed in the last chapter. Consequently, an analysis of this institutionalization of literature would be incomplete without a discussion of these two extramural aspirations, each of which had its important and acknowledged precedents in Western culture.

The European salons which served as models for their Russian counterparts of the early nineteenth century insisted no less upon their openness to talent than upon the charms and brilliance of their hostesses. As examples, it is customary to mention how Vincent Voiture, the son of a wine merchant, or Mlle de Lespinasse, a foundling, rose to prominence in French polite society of the seventeenth and eighteenth centuries by taking advantage of such opportunities for advancement.[49] "The ideology of the salons," as Caroline Lougee has noted, "rested on this substitution of behavior for birth; their prized *esprit* at times even denigrated mere aristocracy."[50] Or, as Prince Viazemsky put it, "Even in literature there is an aristocracy, an aristocracy of talents."[51] For France of the ancien régime, statistical analyses confirm ideology's self-advertisement; within Parisian polite society there did occur considerable social fusion of families with "disparate ranks, diverse occupations, and heterogeneous lineage," thereby infusing the newly rich and recently enobled with the values of the traditional nobility.[52] The salons came not only to promote this sort of social mobility, but also to make literary reputations. In this sense they assumed the supportive function of the patronage system without, in theory, the repugnant aspects of that system, as well as the function of mediating between writer and public that public criticism would come to play in more recent institutionalizations of literature.

In Russia the familiar literary associations seemed to offer (at least initially) somewhat similar prospects to people of wit and talent. By the beginning of the nineteenth century, a number of writers and cultural figures occupied prominent positions in society and government. The poets Derzhavin and Dmitriev served as government ministers; A. N. Olenin (president of the Academy of Arts) and Admiral A. S. Shishkov (president of the Russian Academy) held high government posts. All liked to surround themselves with young literary people; thus, a knowledge of literature and the ability to produce it—together with a measure of charm and some sort of introduction—became an entrée into social and governmental circles for ambitious young gentlemen without wealth or position. N. I. Gnedich, a serious poet who devoted much of his adult life to translating the *Iliad*, saw through the "disinterestedness" of their literary pursuits: "our youth labors little for literature in particular and tries to fall in with littérateurs merely for some special ends and maybe out of having nothing else to do."[53]

Gnedich himself offers an example of the second sort of mobility that the familiar associations provided, nonpatronizing patronage for a serious writer. Although of undistinguished Ukrainian origin, he received a sinecure in the Imperial Public Library and a government pension through his participation in the salon of the Olenins, whose informality a niece of the hostess, Mme Kern, has dutifully proclaimed: "we supped at small tables without ceremony and, naturally [!], without ranks. And what ranks could there have been, where the enlightened host appreciated and valued the arts and sciences?"[54] During the early decades of the century, the salons and circles included a number of literary figures of less than gentle birth. Zinaida Volkonskaia's Moscow salon (1824–1829) welcomed M. P. Pogodin, the son of a serf, and S. E. Raich, a priest's son, as did other Moscow literary groups, which fulfilled, on the whole, the salon ideal of openness to talent better than their Petersburg counterparts. N. A. Polevoi, scion of a merchant family, visited various groups of predominantly gentry membership and collaborated on a journal with Prince Viazemsky, subsequently a leader of the so-called aristocratic party of writers.[55] Stankevich befriended a number of writers of humble origin, including the cattle dealer Kol'tsov.[56] Nikitenko, later a professor and censor, began his rise from serfdom by attracting the attention of influential circles. Indeed, self-made littérateurs (*samorodki*) became something of a fashion in the post-Napoleonic era.[57] Even in the 1830s, when the doors began to close, and *raznochintsy* (people of less than noble rank) began to form their own circles, a few provincial littérateurs, such as Gogol, won entrée to the salons of the two capitals, and a few high society hosts, such as Sollogub and Vielhorsky, tried to keep alive the openness of their gatherings.[58]

This "openness" of the familiar associations to talented representatives of other social groups is evidenced, as well, by Pushkin's attempt to collaborate with Vissarion Belinsky, a *raznochinets* and the first of the great radical journalists who were to shape Russian literary life during the coming decades (and, it has been argued, up to the present day).[59] Through a Moscow intermediary Pushkin seems to have sought Belinsky's participation in his quarterly, *The Contemporary* (*Sovremennik*).[60] But the possible terms of that involvement may be surmised from Pushkin's comments on Belinsky in a "letter to the editor" that he published in his own journal: "He shows talent which gives great hope. If he would join to his independence of opinion and his wit greater learning, greater erudition, greater respect for tradition, greater circumspection—in a word, greater maturity—then we would have quite a remarkable critic in him" (XII, 97). Pushkin describes both Belinsky's strengths and weaknesses in terms of the civilized values of polite society, values to which the other contributors would expect him to conform. When "furious Vissarion," as his friends called him, did come to work for the *Contemporary* a decade after Pushkin's death, any qualities of "respect" and "circumspection" that he showed were in response not to the ideals of polite society, but to the demands of the censor. Observing such decorum was no longer a means to literary advancement, even if Belinsky had been capable or desirous of it.

The second social function to which the literature of familiar groups aspired was to create and shape public opinion. In this, too, the experience of the ancien régime proved irresistible, as one senses from a passage in Viazemsky's essay on Zhukovsky's prose (1827):

> The role which writers, the so-called *gens de lettres*, played in France, especially during the reigns of Louis XV and Louis XVI before the start of the Revolution, is so far from our *moeurs* and regnant concepts that we poorly understand the omnipotent influence that they had, not only on the general educational level of the people, but also on the private opinions and habits of society. Parisian society was a republic then, ruled by an oligarchy of a new sort, consisting of intelligent people and littérateurs.[61]

Viazemsky's pessimism about the Russian situation may be understood in the context of the failure of the Decembrist uprising (1825), the "cast iron" censorship code (1826), and the apparent policy of

Nicholas' reign, which preferred obedience to talent and intelligence. It conveniently ignores the recent success of Karamzin's *History of the Russian State* (1816–1826), Pushkin's Southern poems (1821–1827), the almanac *Polar Star* (1823–1825), and Viazemsky's own journal, *The Moscow Telegraph*, in which this article appeared.

If a literature of familiar association was incapable of reaching a public outside the studies and drawing rooms of Moscow and St. Petersburg—and Merzliakov's memoir has suggested that it enjoyed some success—then it was due to no lack of good intentions and effort on the part of Russian literary people. The first twenty years of the century witnessed a proliferation of journals unprecedented in Russian culture; sixty appeared during the first decade alone, most of them published by the literary circles and societies of the two capital cities.[62] Even the most playful of the circles, the Arzamas Society, planned to publish a satirical, literary, and political journal that would wage war against "prejudices, vices, and absurdities" in defense of "common sense and taste" and would force an opening in the "wall of China" separating Russia from Europe.[63] Increased censorship during the last years of the reign of Alexander I rendered the political section virtually unthinkable, but the Decembrist conspirators in the society were willing to influence public opinion through literature and literary criticism in the circles and their periodicals.[64] Even without the political section, the project came to naught, but a literary-philosophical circle, the Lovers of Wisdom (*Liubomudry*) managed to publish four issues of a periodical, *Mnemosyne*. Even after the advent of a commercially viable press in the 1830s, the surviving members of these two earlier groups continued their journalistic efforts. A former Arzamasian and member of the Friendly Literary Society, A. F. Voeikov, exacted unpaid contributions for his hapless journal from the participants in his literary evenings.[65]

Although Pushkin's *Contemporary* paid its contributors the relatively handsome honorarium of two hundred rubles per signature, it has been fairly regarded as a continuation of the earlier, nonprofessional approach to literary life:

> All the collaborators—especially Pushkin, Viazemsky, and Zhukovsky—remained littérateurs of a single circle, joined by memories of long friendship, the psychologically vital tradition of the Arzamas brotherhood, and a common social position. Pushkin's statements testify that he remained true to the tenets of the gentry enlightenment. It was precisely this literary platform that united him with Viazemsky, Zhukovsky, A. I. Turgenev, P. B. Kozlovsky, and other collaborators of the *Contemporary*.[66]

Indeed, the journal's table of contents for the early years offers a nearly complete roster of the surviving members of the groups and salons that I have mentioned: the Friendly Literary Society (Zhukovsky, A. I. Turgenev), Arzamas (Pushkin, Viazemsky, Zhukovsky, A. I. Turgenev, Davydov), the Raich circle and the Lovers of Wisdom (V. F. Odoevsky, Pogodin, Titov, Tiutchev), the Volkonsky salon (Odoevsky, Pushkin, Viazemsky), and the Karamzin salon (Zhukovsky, Pushkin, Viazemsky, Titov, A. I. Turgenev, Odoevsky). Gogol, accepted into these circles and interpreted by them (mistakenly) as an Arzamasian writer, contributed actively to the journal. Indeed, Pushkin, the editor, anxious not to enmesh his journal in squalid quarrels, seems to have felt it necessary to step back from Gogol's polemics against the commercial press. Lermontov, also a habitué of the salons, wished to found a journal, but, like many such projects conceived in the familiar groups, it was never realized.[67]

By the 1830s, the shortcomings of this institutionalization of literature had become plain, to those whose literary activity it precluded, but also to writers whom it had nurtured. In many cases these latter turned the wit, exaggeration, and sense of paradox that the familiar groups had fostered in them against this way of literary life, although they continued to take part in it even as they sought alternatives. Viazemsky's dismissal of the early nineteenth-century periodicals— "all our journals are school archives of pupils' essays"—is a case in point.[68] He is to some extent correct, but his statement does little justice to the drive for enlightenment that such essays represented, and it neglects the intelligent essays, notable not only for their good sense, but for the grace and civility of their style, that the familiar groups inspired. Nevertheless, in each of its crucial aspirations—to promote talent and to create enlightened public opinion—this institutionalization of literature failed.

The conduits that the familiar literary groups had provided to governmental careers and to literary repute were drying up by the late 1820s. Several minor literary figures (among them the former Arzamasians Bludov, Uvarov, and Dashkov) did reach ministerial rank, but they did not attract and promote young people of outstanding literary talent, as earlier cultural figures of high rank had done. To be sure, they still might help secure loans, pensions, or a professorial position for a writer sponsored by Zhukovsky, who had himself become tutor to the imperial family.[69] But a number of important ties in the network of literary associations and friendship were severed in the aftermath of the Decembrist uprising, which left—to continue with the example of Arzamas—one member in Siberia, one in foreign exile, several under government surveillance, and others distrustful of the few members whose careers did flourish. In Moscow this turn of events left the salons to function as forums for such older literary figures as Chaadaev and M. F. Orlov, whose promising careers had been forever halted, or for the Slavophiles, whom the government distrusted.[70]

Nor did government service remain so attractive to people of talent as it had been in the first years of the century, when the Enlightenment ideals of education, cosmopolitanism, and the rule of law had attracted people of talent to the Ministries of Education, Foreign Affairs, and Justice, ministries that were in turn staffed by people of literary interests. If anything, the government sought to discourage people of talent. Uvarov, who had made a brilliant career with his skill at letters and the connections it won him, came eventually to defend the rank system of advancement, arguing that inclusion in the upper classes should depend on state *service*, not on "birth, wealth, or even gifts."[71] In this, Uvarov (always the cunning courtier) was merely echoing principles that Nicholas had himself asserted at the beginning of his reign, in responding to a memorandum on popular education that he had solicited from Pushkin.

> His Highness deigned to note that the rule you have adopted, that enlightenment and genius should serve as the exclusive basis for perfection, is a rule that threatens public tranquillity and one which has drawn you yourself to the edge of an abyss and has cast so many young people into it. Morality, diligent service, and zeal must be preferred to inexperienced, immoral, and useless enlightenment. Well-ordered upbringing must be based upon these principles.[72]

Benckendorff, the infamous chief of gendarmes and head of the third section (secret police), who conveyed this chilling message to Pushkin, embodied the virtues that earned advancement under Nicholas I: a military background, loyalty proven during the Decembrist uprising, and a resolute commitment to the status quo. Given these virtues, his notorious absent-mindedness, his lack of intelligence, his ignorance of grammar, his disinterest in literature, and his lack of a position in polite society proved no hindrance to a brilliant career.[73]

Under Nicholas I, there were few upper-level bureaucrats whose recruiting policies matched those of the Minister of the Interior, L. A. Perovsky (appointed 1842), as the novelist P. I. Mel'nikov recalled them: "Perovsky liked to surround himself with literary people and he recognized and openly argued that it was necessary for any truly enlightened minister to conduct himself in such a way. Without any entreaties or solicitations he transferred from the provinces into his ministry young men who had shown some particular talent in scholarship or in literature, assigning them to positions that were being sought in vain by candidates with powerful patrons."[74]

Generally, however, people of talent now entered the service merely to help support themselves. Their talents won them little respect or advantage, and the emperor's notion of service made it difficult to accommodate civil or military service to the *honnête homme*'s ideal of noble independence. Pushkin served briefly, but without interest or distinction, as did Gogol, who remained in the civil service only long enough for the experience of mindless paper-pushing, petty venality, and a soulless hierarchy of ranks to fertilize his imagination. Lermontov marred his military career with a studied disregard for dress codes.[75] Prince Viazemsky, whose literary activities encompassed all aspects of the literature of familiar associations and who survived to become its archivist and apologist, served under both emperors: in Warsaw during a time of political ferment, in which he recklessly participated (1818–1820) and, under Nicholas I, in Petersburg, where his request for an assignment to the Ministries of Education or Justice was not honored. In fact, Viazemsky, who had spectacularly squandered a huge fortune, found himself assigned to the Ministry of Finances. His notebook entry on this piece of logic records insights that were probably often thought, but not so well expressed, by talented Russians in the 1840s:

28 October 1846. Strange is my fate: from a publican I am made into a pawnbroker, from vice-director of the Department of Foreign Trade I shall become manager of the State Loan Bank. What in these positions, in the sphere of these activities is compatible or sympathetic with me? Absolutely nothing. All of this is unnatural to me, and so it must be, according to Russian custom and order. Our government thinks it indulgence, ruinous permissiveness, to take a man's natural capabilities and inclinations into account in assigning him to a position. A man is born to stand on his feet; precisely for this reason he must be stood on his hands and told, "Walk!" Otherwise, what meaning would authority have, if it were subordinate to the general order and course of things. Moreover, another danger lurks here: a man in his proper place becomes a certain force, independent, and authority wants to have mere tools, often crooked or inconvenient, but, for that reason, all the more dependent on its will . . . What was given to me by nature has been crushed and swept aside in the service; it is my shortcomings that are summoned and put into action. I have no capability for the *effective conduct of affairs;* accounts, bookkeeping, and figures are mere gibberish to me. My head spins from them, and all my capabilities grow faint, all my mental and spiritual powers. If this were an accident, an exception falling to my lot, what could I do? It would be my misfortune and nothing more. Thus it would have been preordained for at birth. But, in fact, this is the general rule and my misfortune is at once the misfortune of all Russia.[76]

Viazemsky's drawing-room esprit was not so crushed, however, as to preclude an appropriate pun on the situation: "Menia germeticheski zakuporivaiut v banke"—"They are sealing me hermetically in a bank / a jar."

As the familiar groups were ceasing to sponsor advancement in the service, they were also failing to advance the literary careers of new writers. The Odoevsky salon in St. Petersburg illustrates this development with unusual clarity because it segregated its visitors into two groups: around the hostess in the drawing room congregated her friends from the fashionable world, while her husband's literary acquaintances met in his study, where institutionalized familiarity held its sway. The memoirs of Iurii Arnol'd, a composer and writer, record this failure with a sharpness that would be suspect, were it not shared by other memoirists:

> When I first appeared I naturally felt not quite at ease; among this rather numerous company I knew no one . . . I had to be satisfied that the lackey . . . pronounced loudly: "Mr. Arnol'd." Mutual introductions occurred only in the intimate circle or in extraordinary cases . . . Naturally the first thing I did was to approach the hostess and testify to the obligatory "great respect on the part of her most humble servant" with a most proper bow. Her Excellency vouchsafed me a gracious nod of her head, but did not deign to extend her hand. This, to translate from the mysterious language of *grand monde* ceremony, signified: "Messieurs et mesdames, this one is a plebian or—even worse—a nonentity; consequently, he needn't concern you." I made an even more saccharine face and bowed in a still more distinguished manner to the members of that society which, calling itself "good," has shown and shows itself not infrequently bad. But, smiling at them I thought: "Gentlemen and ladies! It is certainly not for your sake that I have appeared here . . . You are not that 'good' society that I will, without a doubt, find in the next room!"
> Here the prince himself [Odoevsky] had already come out to greet me very affably and, after shaking my hand, led me into the other room . . . Before sitting down on the ottoman, I glanced at the person who was sitting at the other end. It was Belinsky, and I bowed to him.[77]

Prince Odoevsky's friendly greeting and the presence of Belinsky in the study suggest a partial observance of the salon ideal of literary life, but the behavior of the hostess and her aristocratic friends shows that the salon no longer fulfilled two critical social functions: bringing writers and readers together and helping young writers to learn the manners and language of polite society from inside its drawing rooms. When Pogodin writes that Gogol "appeared on the scene of the *grand monde*" in this salon, or when Sollogub notes that Gogol "eavesdropped on the speeches of society" here, their vocabulary ("scene," "eavesdropped") betrays an awareness of the writer's growing marginality.[78]

I. I. Panaev, who rejected his noble family's tradition of amateur letters to become a professional journalist, presented the Petersburg salons he had once visited as closed and aristocratic when he came to publish his memoirs in the radical *Contemporary* of the early 1860s:

> The majority of the so-called society people of that time . . . knew of the existence of Russian literature only through Pushkin and through others who belonged to their society. They supposed that all of Russian literature consisted of Zhukovsky, Krylov (whose fables they had been made to study in their youth), Pushkin, Prince Odoevsky, Prince Viazemsky, and Count Sollogub . . . In order to earn a reputation in the circle of high society, it was necessary to land in the salon of Mme Karamzina . . . There diplomas were distributed for literary talent. This was a real high society literary salon, strictly selective, and the [Mme de] Récamier of that salon was S. N. Karamzina, to whom all of our well-known poets considered it their duty to write epistles.
>
> Thus the caste spirit, an aristocratic spirit, was introduced into our "republic of letters." Aristocratic littérateurs [grew?] apart from their remaining fellows with relentless pride, now and then treating them with the patronizing manner of a grandee.[79]

This nicely captures the divisions that occurred as the institution of familiar associations began to fail. But Panaev's memoirs neglect to mention that his own home provided a gathering place as late as the early 1840s for writers of all groups, including two of the aristocrats he mentions, Prince Odoevsky and Count Sollogub.[80] Moreover, Panaev's first published story, the melodramatic society tale "Boudoir of a Woman of Society (An Episode from the Life of a Poet in Society)" (1834), takes much of its plot—impoverished amateur poet meets society woman, he introduces her to German literature, she lends him social graces, they fall in love—from the ideal patterns of salon interaction. The final catastrophe is occasioned only in part by a breakdown in the conventions of familiar literary association (the poet's friend, a social lion, betrays this friendship by attempting to renew an affair with the hostess); the love between poet and hostess remains firm, as does the ideal of the salon's opennness to talent, an ideal whose realization a radical journalist of the 1860s could no longer acknowledge.[81]

As the social ambition of the familiar associations, to assimilate and promote talent, was encountering obstacles both within and without the polite society whose ideology had made it a legitimate activity, the second aspiration—to influence and even create public opinion—was suffering frustrations even more severe. The periodicals that groups produced turned out to be, at best, short-lived and of narrow circulation. Four brave projects for an Arzamasian journal (1818–1824) did not proceed past the stage of tentatively assigning responsibilities to the society's members.[82] Government discouragement played some part in this (the censorship was reluctant to license new periodicals), but much of the fault lies with the group's naive and condescending attitude toward the material aspects of literary dissemination, without which literature remains a matter of oral recitation and hand-written texts. Viazemsky's project testifies both to the nobility of their aims and to their amateurish vagueness about the means of realizing these aims:

> The journal's earnings, should there be any, are to be used for charity for abused children of Apollo, to publish at our expense good translations or good original compositions and in this way to tear from the greedy claws of the booksellers their poor victims, who sell and abase their gifts. In time we should start a printing-house, available at no cost to our impoverished brethren.[83]

Viazemsky at the same time joined his fellows in mocking the society's secretary, Zhukovsky, for publishing a collection of his verse, *Für Wenige* (1818), in a limited edition for court circles, but the title could have served for nearly all of the group's efforts.

The other groups that have been mentioned fared somewhat better. The Lovers of Wisdom avoided the ban on new journals by passing their periodical off as an almanac, *Mnemosyne* (4 issues, 1824–25). Its advertisements promised "satisfaction of the various tastes of all readers," and its coeditor, Kiukhel'beker, boldly attacked the literature couched in "un petit jargon de coterie" that such elegists as Zhukovsky seemed to be producing.[84] The other coeditor, V. F. Odoevsky (whose salon has already been discussed), also tried to transcend the limits of "society's" attitude toward literature. These attempts won them a mere 157 subscribers, and, even taking into consideration the extra four hundred copies that were printed and sold, they could not have reached far beyond their friends and relatives in the two capital cities. A journal that this Moscow group founded, *The Moscow Herald*

(*Moskovskii vestnik*) lasted but three years (1827–1830) while losing over half of its initial six hundred subscribers and the most valuable contributor, Pushkin.[85] The seriousness—indeed, the solemnity—of the group's philosophical interests would not permit it to make such concessions to taste (color plates of Paris fashions, material on contemporary life) as won its encyclopedic competition, Polevoi's *Moscow Telegraph*, greater longevity and a profit-making list of 1,200 subscribers.[86]

Perhaps the most shocking failure befell the *Literary Gazette* (*Literaturnaia gazeta*, 1830–31), which was edited by Pushkin and Del'vig. Despite contributions from prominent littérateurs (Viazemsky, Davydov, and Shakhovskoi), early works of promising young writers (Gogol, Khomiakov), and translations from Western literatures (E. T. A. Hoffmann, Tieck, Scott, Stendhal, Paul de Kock, Manzoni), it lasted a mere eighteen months and attracted less than one hundred subscribers.[87] Not all of the contributors stood on a uniformly high level, the indolent Del'vig's editing left much to be desired, and later issues failed to appear regularly. But these typical shortcomings of the amateur periodicals tell only part of the story. The commercially skilled journalists—Bulgarin, Grech, Polevoi—joined forces to promote their own periodicals at the expense of the new one. The government, rewarding Bulgarin for his loyalty and espionage, not only permitted him to wage unscrupulous war on Pushkin, but tied the hands of Bulgarin's rivals, refusing permission to the *Literary Gazette* to publish political news and even closing it down for several weeks. The former Arzamasian Bludov, now highly placed in the ministry of internal affairs, obtained permission for it to resume publication, but no such intercessions could win it a public, the continuing interest of its contributors, or a professional level of editing.

By 1842, S. P. Shevyrev, a veteran of the salons and circles who had condemned the new commercial trend in Russian literature with more vehemence than logic or success, wrote an epitaph for this institution of literature as a public force, couching it in appropriately financial terminology:

> The entire Russian reading public now lies in the hands of commercial literature . . . Meanwhile, the capital of the Russian intellect and imagination, the treasures of thought, knowledge, and language lie in the lands of talented people who are, for the most part, inactive. Contenting themselves with peaceful, friendly conversations, squandering their vital capabilities on a game for small stakes, growing ever more disused to labor, weaned by frequent refusals from inspiration, they release virtually none of the capital of their gifts into general circulation and concede in

their idleness and apathy, the leading roles to literary entrepreneurs—
and this explains why our contemporary literature has grown rich in
money and bankrupt in thought.[88]

But Shevyrev's bitter characterization of the literary scene, although
it won Viazemsky's speedy approval, cannot be left unqualified as a
history of the years 1830–1842.[89] During these years the amateur writers had continued their attempts to establish journals; new writers of
unquestionable talent (Gogol, Lermontov, and Belinsky among them)
had won wide attention; the profession of letters had continued to
lure such proud members of the gentry as Pushkin, and a number of
brilliant new works of narrative art—including the three novels that
are the object of this study—had been completed. Nevertheless, a
punitive censorship, police surveillance of and by literary people, the
death of both Pushkin and Lermontov, and Gogol's self-imposed exile
did seem to leave the reading public "in the hands of" unscrupulous
editors. Shevyrev's view of literary life is, however, most valuable as
a reminder that during these years of growing commercial possibilities, the familiar groups constituted a separate institution of literature
with its predictable patterns of interaction ("talk"), topics of interest,
and attractiveness to talented people.

Rescued from the oblivion that Shevyrev feared by the continuing
efforts of archivists, literary scholars, and other agents of cultural
transmission, this institutionalization of literature remains a fact of
modern Russian life. To cultured Russians the creative energy, critical
orientation, and particular independence of the familiar groups, fixed
in canonical publications and no longer buttressed by the ideology of
polite society, constitute a treasured and living legacy, if not always
of great individual works of literature, then of vital and determined
cultural activity.

But, returning to the early nineteenth century, we can see (as the
most perspicacious of contemporaries saw it) that the widening gap
between the ideals of mobility, openness, and enlightenment and the
often perceived state of exclusiveness and triviality had opened the
way, by the late 1820s, for a new institutionalization, a profession of
letters.

Professionalism

I am beginning to respect our booksellers and to think that
our trade is no worse than any other.
Pushkin, 1824

The profession of letters, like the patronage system and the literature of familiar groups, begins to find a place in Russian culture during the eighteenth century. Like the other modes of literary life, it sought to respond to specific needs of Westernization and secularization, in this case by producing (or, more frequently, by translating) works that were in various proportions educational and entertaining for readers eager to make their way in a world of new languages, careers, social relations, and values. To this end, ambitious Russians took notice not only of individual foreign texts, but of the technology, marketing techniques, literary forms, and cultural functions that would ensure the survival of a profitable public literature on their native soil. The journals, letters, biographies, and bureaucratic memoranda of eighteenth-century cultural figures reveal awareness of and a longing for nearly all the aspects of the modern public institution of literature that I outlined at the beginning of this chapter—broad dissemination of literary texts, principled criticism to mediate between reader and writer, remuneration for the writers that would permit them to pursue their vocation, a demand for writing on the part of a public. One even finds, by the end of the century, laws permitting the establishment of private presses (1783), a censorship code (1796), and university instruction in Russian literature.[90] Once Catherine permitted the publication of journals, a number of merchants rushed to finance them. By 1769, Fedor Emin, an enterprising foreigner who practiced the commercially attractive genres of prose fiction and journalism, could claim to write not merely to pass the time of day, but to earn his daily bread.[91]

Novikov, who sold inherited estates to finance a series of publishing activities, best represents these aspirations of the Russian Enlightenment. He had perhaps the most comprehensive view of the literary process, the most altruistic, and, at the same time, the most commercially sound. He sought to expand the reading public for serious writing by engaging the marketing services of provincial merchants and clergymen, by extending credit, and by offering discounts.[92] Several decades later, Karamzin would write that Novikov had increased the newspaper circulation from 600 to 4,000. In ten years, his company published 900 editions, or 28 percent of the entire Russian book production.[93] His concerns spread beyond the dissemination of literature to its production and consumption, and he founded two schools for poor children, seminars at Moscow University for teachers and translators, Russia's first children's magazine, and Russia's first student society.[94] His treatment of the translators whom he helped to train stands out in bright relief against the background of the relationship between other booksellers and translators.[95]

If Novikov represents the best aspirations for a commercially viable, socially responsible literature that would engage the interest and participation of people from a variety of social classes and regions, his fate shows that such an independent public institution could not be tolerated by the "enlightened monarch," Catherine II, who ruled over three crucial decades in the development of Russian literature (1762–1796).[96] Just as systematically as he had engaged the entire literary process, the government attacked his project: it threatened to confiscate his publications, harassed him with special investigations, seized control over his schools, deprived him of the right to publish textbooks and religious works, and refused to renew his lease on the Moscow University press. Financial ruin followed. The government disbanded the Masonic circles in which he played a leading role and exiled some members to their estates to remain there under surveillance. There remained only the "addresser" from our communication model. In secret proceedings his *person* was sentenced to fifteen years in the dread Schlüsselburg Fortress. Nor did the government neglect the carefully wrought *persona*—honest, enlightened, public-spirited—that Novikov had presented to his public in over twenty years of literary activity. In an official pamphlet he was branded an ignorant, perverted rogue, infected with the spirit of ambition and self-interest.

The thoroughness of this punishment and Catherine's vindictive desire to destroy her one-time journalistic rival explain in large part why a patronage system could survive while a modern profession of letters might founder. Novikov's intelligent, comprehensive, and at times well-financed efforts had attempted to circumvent, even to confront, the very force that had made a secular Western literature conceivable in Russia, the autocratic government. Nicholas Riasanovsky has made this crucial point in a comparative analysis:

> The modern Russian educated public was created by the reforms of Peter the Great and his successors. Its very *raison d'être* was the turning of the country towards the West and Western light. In Russian conditions, the government completely dominated that process. In contrast to Western states, Russia in the eighteenth century lacked an independent caste of lawyers, advanced private education, and a powerful church balancing the state or competing for the minds of men in the modern world. More fundamentally still, the development of Muscovy based on the service gentry and serfdom deprived the country of a middle class of any prominence, of precisely that Third Estate which was crucial to the Western Age of Reason. Russian Enlightenment remains the despair of those who must link that phenomenon to a new state in the development of a market economy, to a victorious rise of the bourgeoisie, or to a diffusion of literature and learning among broad layers of the population.[97]

By the beginning of the nineteenth century the literature of familiar associations, supported in its independence by the ideology of polite society, might try to escape this dependency. But any professionalization of literary life would have to reckon with the will of the autocrat, and with the very direct interest that the rulers of the eighteenth and early nineteenth centuries took in literature's impact upon its readers. Forty years later, Faddei Bulgarin would boast that the development of a commercially viable literature had freed writers from the departments of the bureaucracy.[98] This was at best a half-truth, as Bulgarin well knew, for his own profitable literary activities depended upon the support of the Third Section of His Majesty's Imperial Chancery, which helped finance Bulgarin's newspaper, protected him from other censorship organs, restrained his literary competitors, and even sought promotions for him from the Ministry of Education, to which he was formally attached.[99] Pushkin, in turn, depended upon the tsar (his self-appointed personal censor) for financial support and for access to the archives that were essential for his serious historical studies.

Thus, a discussion of the profession of letters must take cognizance of this godlike force that had not only peopled the literary process but also stood poised over it, capable of interfering with any stage in that process at almost any time, and thereby hindering its institutionalization. The laws, such as they were, changed rapidly. During the period 1780–1848, for example, private presses were permitted, banned, and reestablished; ambiguous passages in a text were held against the author, then disregarded, and—de facto—held against him; the importation of foreign books was banned, permitted, then severely curtailed. And censorship agencies proliferated, supervising and often contradicting one another; there were no less than twelve by the end of this period.[100] But this confusion and rapid change in the legal process was not, in itself, the chief problem facing the would-be professional writer, his publisher, and his reading public. Laws, however rapidly they changed, at least could enable people to predict the consequences of their actions. Nor was censorship, in itself, necessarily a principal retarding force. Much of the censoring was performed, as Donald Fanger has aptly noted, by professor-littérateurs who shared the best aspirations of writers and public.[101] The central problem was surely the unpredictability, arbitrariness, and vindictiveness of the government, from the tsar to the "very important people" in its agencies—ecclesiarchs, army officers, bureaucrats. Although the censorship examined works prior to publication, writers and publishers could be punished subsequent to publication, even when the laws ostensibly protected them, if the published work incurred the displeasure of someone in high places. When Bulgarin was incarcerated briefly in the guardhouse for panning a novel that the tsar admired, many could not help rejoicing, but the censor Nikitenko sadly noted "no one took into account the blow to one of the best paragraphs of our censorship code."[102] The censors were themselves vulnerable. An article that displeased higher authorities could result in severe reprimands, loss of position, or brief jail sentences. It is not surprising, then, that they passed their own uncertainties on to the writers. No less an authority than the most notorious "mystifier" in Russian literature, Nikolai Gogol, complained of the censors' "strange mystifications" in their work on *Dead Souls* (XII, 40).

To be sure, the punishments that censors, writers, and publishers endured were less severe than they had been or would be at other times in Russian history. Monas notes, for example, that not a single case of literary treason was prosecuted during the reign of Nicholas I.[103] Nevertheless, the banning of periodicals (even temporarily), the intimidation of censors, and the humiliation of writers made it difficult for honorable, independent people to overcome other problems that confronted them—the lack of public criticism and a predictable reading public, for example—as they sought to earn a living through their literary vocations.[104]

The would-be professional, then, had to confront two tyrannical powers: the autocratic system, as we have just seen, and the fashion-oriented capriciousness of polite society, with its norm of the *honnête homme*, which held any professionalization in contempt. Despite these unpredictable and shifting barriers, two sorts of professionalism had, in fact, taken hold in Russian culture by the first decade of the nineteenth century, each of them unsatisfactory, however, in terms of the ideal institution of letters that the West continued to hold up to Russians of talent. These remunerated activities revolved around the publication of chapbooks, broadsheets, and adventure narratives, first of all, and, second, around various literary collections (almanacs, and some periodicals). It will focus this discussion to recall the publication history of *Eugene Onegin* that I mentioned at the outset of this chapter; the first fragments of Pushkin's verse novel reached the public through representatives of these two conduits: an unscrupulous editor with no respect for the rights of authorship (Bulgarin), and a gentleman-editor who could rely on poetic friendship fostered in the familiar associations (Baron Del'vig).

The chapbook industry (*lubki*) thrived from the mid-eighteenth century to the Revolution, providing the only literature that the majority of Russians encountered: relatively inexpensive illustrated pages with captions or texts.[105] The market stalls distributed them to urban readers; wandering peddlers (*ofeni*) took them to areas and to a public that "high literature" rarely reached. Sometimes printed books were appropriated for this form of publication or distributed together with them, so that the adjective *lubochnaia* came to apply not just to these primitive sheets, but to popular literature of dubious quality, particularly adventure and fantastic novels that were "translated" (that is, freely adapted) from foreign models and produced for an indiscriminating audience.[106] I will use the term in this broad sense here.

Writers who belonged to "society" and shared its ideological aversion to commerce and specialization regarded these productions with predictable contempt. Batiushkov, a gentleman-poet of genius, reported to his genteel readership that chapbooks were sold in the Moscow market like fish, furs, and vegetables, and that the authors or translators of this commodity were paid according to the quantity, not quality, of their production.[107] Pushkin addresses the dissemination of these literary products in the provinces by showing the source of his heroine's dream interpretation manual:

> This fountain of unfathomed learning
> Had come to her secluded nook
> When a stray peddler was sojourning
> Nearby; from him she bought the book.
> She had to throw into the barter,
> Besides three rubles and a quarter,
> *Malvine*, Part Two, then had to add
> Two grammars and a Petriad,
> A fable-book of vulgar diction
> And Marmontel (just Volume Three).   (5:23)

The stanza laconically captures many features of this literary situation—the casual attitude of readers and distributors toward the integrity of a literary text (the broken edition of Mme de Cottin's novel) or of an author's oeuvre (the broken set of Marmontel); the indiscriminate mingling of imaginative literature and how-to books ("two grammars and a Petriad"); outmoded and indiscriminate taste.

But what most distressed the serious, ambitious writers of the 1820s and 1830s, who were seeking wider scope than the familiar associations allowed, was the author's insignificant or defenseless position in this mode of literary life. The gentleman writers, anxious to preserve their good names, and romantic votaries of the poet's sacred mission—the two positions were ideologically quite compatible—found much to deplore in this commercial situation. Anonymity, such as befalls the epic poets in this passage (there are two Petriads and one grammar in the Russian original) suggests one way that this institution neglected the author: casual disregard.[108] Another was the flagrant misuse of his name. In connection with this passage on Martin Zadeka's dream-book, Pushkin commented, "Dream-books are published in Russia under the imprint of Martin Zadeka, a respectable man who never wrote any" (VI, 194) and who, adds Nabokov, may not have even existed.[109] Finally, until 1828, no copyright laws protected the author's text from unauthorized publication or mutilation. Thus, profiting from the casual recitation of verse in the familiar groups, Bulgarin was able to hear bits of *Eugene Onegin* and to publish the first fragment of it without Pushkin's knowledge or permission.[110] Bulgarin later distanced himself from these and related practices with hypocritical statements and by obtaining considerable support from the government, not by tempering the ruthlessness of his own commercial activities. Nevertheless, he does capture the bleak prospects that this institution offered to the educated public:

> In Moscow now they publish novels one after the other for delivery to the fairs and villages. Who writes all of this? It's anyone's guess. But they write and print quite a lot in Moscow. There they have a special kind of literature, special principles, a special class of littérateurs, whose chief representative is the well-known Mr. Orlov, the author of a multitude of parodies on Petersburg novels. Books of this manufacture are not even reviewed in the journals. They slip by to a special category of the reading public, spreading bad taste and destroying all traces of grammar and common sense in it. For the common good littérateurs should have thought of damming this flood of illiteracy, so harmful to the progress of letters and enlightenment.[111]

As we shall see, Bulgarin had special reasons for wanting to suppress this form of literature, particularly the narratives of Mr. Orlov. The "special principles" of this institution, meanwhile, may be schematized as follows:

FOLKLORE, POPULAR RELIGION, CURIOSITIES

ANONYMOUS SCRIBE   TALES, SONGS, NOVELS   VIEWER, READER

CHAPBOOK, BROADSHEET

MIXED STYLE (ECCLES., BUREAUCRATIC, LANG. OF COMMERCE)

Great literature, indeed, this was not, but it slavishly answered the demands of a huge public and filled the coffers of its publishers. Until the 1820s, patronage was the only alternative for those littérateurs who wanted to gain a living from their authorial pens and not from their editorial blue pencils; and the poor scribblers (such as A. A.

Orlov) who produced chapbooks, songbooks, and translated novels had no choice but to accept such conditions. To serve as a cog in this machine, moreover, was a prospect that haunted the professional authors with gentry status, most of all Bulgarin, to whose very successful Vyzhigin novels the enterprising Orlov wrote seven sequels.

When Pushkin, another aspiring professional, found it necessary to combat Bulgarin's monopolistic hold on the dissemination of literature, he fired a devastating pseudonymous critical essay at Bulgarin, "The Triumph of Friendship, or the Vindicated Orlov" (1831). Here Pushkin savaged Bulgarin by comparing the self-styled "gentleman and writer" with the chapbook novelist, to the latter's disadvantage. Both have something to sell, the article argues: the poor but honest Orlov—his modest sequels; Bulgarin (a turncoat and police spy)—his honor and credibility. Both emerge from Pushkin's account as commercially motivated, but with different degrees of honesty. Adding insult to injury, Pushkin couched the essay in a parody of the refined language with which Bulgarin sought to become acceptable to the more competent reading public. This intricate literary equivalent of the children's game of "king of the hill," played here by Pushkin and Bulgarin, illustrates the social and psychological importance of the boundaries between the chapbook trade, the familiar associations, and the next institutional possibility that I shall discuss.

The second mode of remunerated literary activity that Russian culture accepted by the 1820s centered on the almanacs, for which there flourished a French precedent, the annual *Almanach des Muses* (1765–1833).[112] This institution derived much of its appeal to reputable writers from its dissimilarity to the productions of both the patronized odists and the *lubok* industry. Established as a commercial venture by Karamzin in the 1790s (*Aonidy, ili sobranie raznykh novykh stikhotvorenii*, parts 1–3, 1796–1799), the almanac was an elegant pocket-sized volume that generally sought to meet the literary interests of a reading public that pretended to refinement. The chapbook publishers provided prose narratives and manuals; the almanacs, lyric poetry. When the almanacs offered prose, it tended to be short fiction (lyrically oriented toward the sentimental outpourings of the narrator), familiar essays, or fragmentary travel accounts, as opposed to the plot-oriented adventure romances of the chapbook press. Here the bright old illustrations of the chapbooks yielded to precious vignettes (lyres, urns, wreaths, portraits).[113] The typical almanac delivered a wide selection of short works, often in time for the new year (as the name of the genre implies). They furnished people of fashion with material for salon conversations, and one might well regard them as the portable, commercial equivalent of a lady's album. The almanacs cultivated the fugitive themes, the generic trifles (*bezdelki*), and the mellifluous style of album verse from the very outset, when Karamzin had consciously sought to avoid the "superfluous pomposity" of the odic tradition.[114] Later almanacs, most notably *Poliarnaia zvezda* (1823–1825), edited by the Decembrists Bestuzhev and Ryleev, might choose to include material on more civic themes, and Bestuzhev made the annual survey of Russian literature a fixture of the serious almanacs, but readers nevertheless expected the almanac to proffer a wealth of different works and to address a genteel reader in the polite style which Karamzin had done so much to institutionalize in Russian letters and which was the fundamental expression of polite society's ideology.

This adherence to the codes and interests of polite society made it possible for gentlemen (and lady) writers to give their works to these commercial ventures. But at first only the gentlèman editor (such as Karamzin, Bestuzhev, or Del'vig), the bookseller, and the printer profited from the enterprise. The editors' friends would contribute short pieces out of friendship and for the pleasure of seeing their works in print. But one almanac, *The Polar Star*, soon became so profitable that Bestuzhev and Ryleev proposed honoraria for their contributors. Their publisher, Slenin, fearing an inroad into his profits, countered by withdrawing his support from them. Not wishing to abandon this profitable territory altogether, he then persuaded Baron Del'vig to accept the handsome sum of four thousand rubles for founding a rival almanac, *Northern Flowers, Gathered by Baron Del'vig*, to which Pushkin dutifully donated a fragment of *Eugene Onegin*, the first (excluding Bulgarin's pirated one) to appear in print. A competition for contributors ensued, but the editors' acquaintances provided sufficient fragments for each, and friendship between the editors survived, which suggests that proprieties had not been severely violated.[115]

This polite mode of literary commerce incorporated a set of participants and relationships significantly different from those of the chapbook trade:

LIFE OF POLITE SOCIETY

WRITER, EDITOR	LYRICS, SHORT FICTION, ESSAY	READER
	ALMANAC	

"CONVERSATIONAL LANGUAGE OF POLITE SOCIETY"

By the late 1820s the almanacs had come to dominate Russian literature. Pushkin, ignoring, like most subsequent commentators, the chapbook trade, could write: "the almanacs have become the representatives of our literature. In time its movement and successes will be judged with reference to them" (XI, 48).[116] Judged according to the almanacs, Russian literature of the late 1820s offered intelligent criticism, lyric poetry of high quality, promising beginnings of longer works, little prose of merit, and much that is best forgotten. The literary situation that produced and consumed these elegant tomes offered little hope to those writers, such as Pushkin, who aspired to support themselves by their writing, not by publishing activities. Gogol, whose plans to edit an almanac with Pushkin and Prince Odoevsky came to naught, by 1833 dismissed almanacs as "trash" (X, 259). And they seemed an unlikely nursery for the serious, intellectual prose that Pushkin had long seen as one of Russia's most pressing cultural needs.[117] Almost as quickly as they came to literary reputability and prominence, the almanacs slipped into the commerical realm that controlled the production and dissemination of translated novels and chapbooks. Pushkin, frustrated by the haphazard professional prospects that this medium offered and by its increasingly crass exploitation of amateur poets, drafted a perceptive comedy on the institution of literature that the almanacs "represented." Its characters include: an impecunious graduate of Moscow University (the would-be editor), who introduces himself to potential contributors in appropriately precious phrases ("a youthful disciple of the muses, taking my first steps on the field of glory"); his drunken collaborator, Shameless, who will rail at the aristocratic poets in the obligatory critical survey, then sign the initials of Pushkin and Viazemsky under his own poems; one amateur poet, whom the editor finds engaged in a dice game, another amateur poet, whom he discovers asleep at midday. The last two roles could have easily been played by Pushkin himself, whose gambling losses included several manuscripts and whom a reverently romantic young Gogol discovered playing cards. Pushkin was himself a victim of an alcoholic almanac-editor's play with initials and of scurrilous reviews.[118] By 1831, the almanacs could fall below chapbooks in a serious writer's esteem, as Pushkin pays a backhanded compliment to Bulgarin's novelistic exertions:

Well, write a *Vyzhigin*.
A *Vyzhigin?* My God! It's no joke to write a *Vyzhigin;* I could probably

knock off four volumes no worse than Orlov's and Bulgarin's in four months, but I would croak from hunger in the meantime.

Know what? Publish an almanac.   (XI, 133)

Just as the mores of the chapbook industry infected other media—the more unscrupulous journals, translated prose narratives—so the publishing conditions of the almanacs characterized other forms of literary endeavor: certain periodicals not directly controlled by familiar groups, and the book trade for "high literature." Like the almanacs, these showed gentlemen-amateurs acceptable—if circuitous and poorly marked—paths toward remunerated literary work. But, like the almanacs, these often channelled most of the proceeds to the editor, not to the poet. Karamzin's *Herald of Europe* provides an unusually successful instance of this polite journalistic activity: its translators and contributors received no honoraria, but the gentleman-editor who secured and arranged these contributions—a number were his own—derived a regular income from them. The journal's publisher paid him three thousand rubles a year for editing it, a salary between three and four times that of the average government functionary.[119]

Similarly, a gentleman-poet could publish his works in book form, but often indirectly (his friends would solicit the subscriptions) and with an air of studied carelessness consonant with the persona of the poems themselves. Derzhavin sold his Anacreontic lyrics to satisfy his wife's request for a relandscaped garden; Pushkin surrendered the manuscript of his youthful lyrics in payment of a gambling debt; Zhukovsky and Batiushkov permitted their verse to be published by friends. In the last instance, it was the friend, Gnedich, who reaped the windfall profits from the poet's verse, as he would later do in publishing Pushkin's early narrative poems.[120] In none of these cases was the author paid by the signature, as were the translators of foreign novels for the mass market.

While these remunerated and sometimes highly profitable activities could help gentlemen poets out of an occasional bind, none provided a steady, dependable source of income. Leaving aside the problem of government interference, commercial and ideological problems made these literary ventures—like such other aristocratic pursuits as gambling and duelling—a matter of high risk and frequent failure. In the first place, the regnant salon institutionalization of literature licensed these activities only for brief periods, and only under the validating stamp of friendship or "enlightenment." Thus none of the almanacs appeared more than eight times, and editorships revolved as quickly as journals failed. Moreover, these commercial activities—again like gambling or duelling—were oriented toward the quick kill, rather than toward the establishment of lasting concerns. Thanks to the relatively low cost of paper and typesetting and to the underdeveloped (therefore inexpensive) marketing networks of early nineteenth-century Russia, considerable profits could be realized on the highly priced small editions (typically 1,200 copies) that satisfied the tastes of well-to-do readers and handsomely filled the shelves of their fashionable libraries.[121] But this inspired neither the gentlemen-littérateurs nor the ever-growing number of booksellers in the capital cities to invest adequate capital in expanding the public and educating it to overcome the whims of fashion, as Novikov had once done, and as the major English publishing houses would accomplish with notable success, starting in the 1830s.[122] Pushkin spoke admiringly of European rewards to successful writers (XIII, 92); Polevoi decried the lack of Russian *gens de lettres;*[123] Bulgarin envied the French, German, and English the quantity and quality of their literary production.[124] Yet the high, immediate prices that Pushkin commanded—five rubles for each separate chapter of *Eugene Onegin,* for example; Bulgarin's treacherous mistreatment of his publisher, A. F. Smirdin;[125] and Polevoi's fatal vulnerability to government oppression, aristocratic scorn, unscrupulous competition, and his own bad judgment all underscore again and again the commercial reasons they could not hope to enjoy the continuing success of their European confrères: unstable, antagonistic relationships in the marketplace and an institutionalized lack of economic foresight among all parties, even those, such as Pushkin, who welcomed the professionalization of letters that offered hope to serious writers of the 1820s and became a pressing cultural issue in the 1830s. But throughout the decades that concern us in this study, book production remained, as Kufaev put it, a cottage industry.[126]

Synthesis and Crisis

Pushkin and Bulgarin: "The two leading lights of our
literature."
Citation by the Moscow Society of Lovers of Russian
Literature, 1829

In very complicated ways writers, public, and critics sought to transgress these institutional boundaries to constitute something of synthesis during the late 1820s, the 1830s, and the early 1840s, *an incipient profession of letters* that could function under constraints imposed by the autocracy and by polite society, could provide a living for a limited number of writers, publishers, and critics, and could foster the development of longer narrative forms (history, historical fiction, novels addressed to contemporary Russian life). The copyright, instituted in 1828; attempts to codify the censor's role in literary life (1826, 1828); new possibilities for windfall profit (from narrative poems, novels, and journalism); the willingness of some literary people to engage in monopolistic activities; and more active agents of literary dissemination, such as the bookseller Smirdin—all these developments no doubt encouraged the possibility of synthesis. But even more striking than its possibility are its *fragility*, the controversies that it occasioned, and the gaps that it revealed.

The mounting professionalization of literature has been described as a process of transferring the practices of the pulp fiction trade into "high literature"—payment by the signature, provincial distribution, and orientation toward a nonaristocratic reader.[127] To be sure, journals began to purchase material by the signature, some of the newly prominent journalists (Bulgarin, N. A. Polevoi) chose to wage war on the "aristocrats," and the most successful periodical of the 1830s, *The Library for Reading (Biblioteka dlia chteniia)*, did reach a provincial reader through the perseverance of its publisher, the omnipresent Smirdin, who had once been apprenticed to a Moscow mass literature merchant. But to view the professionalization of literature in the 1830s as a simple transfer of the roles of the one institution into the other does not adequately account for the problems that this volatile mixture encountered, nor for any reciprocal interaction of the two practices, which, as we have seen, involved different styles and genres, different attitudes toward the author, different readers (at least in the city), different modes of publication, and different systems of remuneration. Between them stood high barriers of contempt and ignorance that were scaled by a few desperate and determined individuals.[128]

The major cultural controversies of the 1830s illustrate the difficulties that Russian littérateurs faced in establishing a new institution of literature from the existing ones: the fading patronage system, the chapbook trade, and the familiar groups with their limited commercial opportunities and their increasingly unsatisfactory opportunities for advancement. In the remainder of this chapter I shall focus on two particular controversies: the debate over the "literary aristocracy" (1828–1831) and the general concern over literary "commerce" (1835–1836). These controversies reveal the reciprocity that I have just mentioned, in that, when challenged, many of the participants in commercial undertakings attempted to justify their commercial or public activities with respect to the values of the enlightened Westernized gentry, or polite society, with its familiar literary associations.

The documents of the first controversy—satires, reviews, crude personal attacks in the major periodicals, anguished notebook jottings, and denunciations to the Third Section—use a terminology ("aristocracy") that invites naive sociological analysis, neglectful not merely of ideological considerations, but even of the noble status of participants on all sides and of their readership.[129] By the time that Pushkin's threat to write a picaresque novel about Bulgarin had scared that worthy into striking his colors, and an uneasy truce had settled over Russian literature, a kaleidoscopic series of alliances had formed. Pushkin and Viazemsky (gentlemen) had defended Polevoi (merchant) against the sallies of Bulgarin (gentleman of sorts) and Grech (likewise), only to have Bulgarin, Grech, and Polevoi form one front against them, while a number of Moscow scholars of various origins (Nadezhdin, priest's son; Pogodin, house serf's son; Artsybashev, gentleman) had opened and ceased other offensives, mainly around the enduring value of Karamzin's historical studies. To sort out the personal, social, and philosophical *causi belli* would require several monographs.[130] For my purposes here, it is most important to note that the term "aristocrat" aroused these passions and conflicts because, like the phrase "dead souls" in Gogol's novel, it suggested a confusing wealth of existentially charged meanings that, for want of a single clear meaning, touched to the quick all who came across it. It excited their particular fears, ambitions, antipathies, resentments, or greed with its pejorative cultural, social, political, and psychological connotations and—at least once Bulgarin and Grech had entered the fray—threatening to dismantle the delicately balanced profession of letters which Karamzin had seemingly bequeathed to Russian culture upon his death in 1826. Indeed, the synthesis which Karamzin (official historiographer, salon figure, salaried editor) was seen to have achieved seems to have been more important in this controversy than his actual writings.

Although the contestants sought to define this legacy in different ways, each to his own advantage, there is considerable agreement in the categories that shape their definitions, categories that address aspects of a literary institution more than the particular merits of Karamzin's works. Karamzin wins credit for astounding feats: for having created the reading public;[131] for having created and defended the writer-scholar's calling;[132] for having created the language of Russian literature;[133] and for having given the first example of large-scale commercial operations in Russian literary life.

The term "feat," however, is Pushkin's, and the passage in which it appears gives Karamzin credit, in effect, for synthesizing positive aspects of the patronage system (freedom from censorship at the emperor's orders), the salons (status in society), and the literary trade (commercial success) while avoiding their pitfalls: compromise with the truth, insufficient dedication to major projects, and loss of dignity:

> The appearance of *The History of the Russian State* caused much commotion and made a powerful impression (as well it should have). Three thousand copies sold out in one month, which not even Karamzin himself had expected. Society people rushed to read the history of their fatherland. It was a new discovery for them. Ancient Russia, it seemed, had been discovered by Karamzin, as America had been by Columbus. For a time nowhere did anyone speak of anything else. I must confess, it is impossible to imagine anything more stupid than the judgments of society that I heard; they were enough to break anyone of the desire for fame . . . In the journals they did not criticize him; none among us was in a position to analyze and evaluate Karamzin's huge creation . . . Almost no one said thank you to this man who had closeted himself in his study during the period of his most flattering successes and had devoted twelve whole years of his life to silent and tireless labors. The notes [equal in length to the text] bear witness to Karamzin's broad learning, acquired by him at that age when for ordinary people the circle of education and knowledge has long been closed and occupational cares replace striving for enlightenment. Many forgot that Karamzin published his *History* in Russia, in an autocratic state and that the tsar, having freed him from the censorship, imposed upon Karamzin by this sign an obligation to be as modest and moderate as possible. I repeat, *The History of the Russian State* is not only the work of a great writer, but the feat of an *honnête homme*.[134]

Succès de marché, an enlightening impact on the public, and personal independence—to name them in the order in which they appear— join in this lonely and heroic achievement. Lest the reader miss the point, Pushkin places the passage toward the end of a series of fragments that show the disadvantages of patronage:

> It happened that Trediakovsky was thrashed more than once . . . Volynsky had ordered an ode for some festival from the court poet Vasily Trediakovsky, but the ode was not ready, and the fiery State Secretary punished the negligent versifier with his cane.   (XI, 53)

The disadvantages of the salons and their hostesses:

> Notice how they sing fashionable romances, how they distort the most natural lines, thwart the meter, and destroy the rhyme. Listen to their literary judgments and you will be amazed at the distortedness and even crudeness of their concepts . . . Exceptions are rare.   (XI, 52)

And the disadvantages of literary commerce, including publicity-conscious professionals, who rely on their advertisers' ignorance of Russian:

> The traveler Anselot speaks of some grammar [Grech's], yet unpublished, that ratifies the rules of our language; of some novel, [Bulgarin's] still in manuscript, that has made its author famous . . . What an amusing literature! (XI, 54)

The exaggerated fragmentariness of Pushkin's essay itself pays tribute to the magnitude of Karamzin's achievement, realized, Pushkin insists, at no cost to Karamzin's dignity as an *honnête homme*.

The question of independence and dignity was central to Pushkin's interpretation of the Karamzinian legacy, given his own financial difficulties and growing ties to the court. The quarrel with Grech and Bulgarin over the use of the term "aristocracy" touched it in several ways. First of all, because Grech, who had (like Bulgarin) cast his own lot with the regime, sought to portray Karamzin as a creature and favorite of the court in order to pull him, in other words, into the patronage system.[135] The last part of Pushkin's long paragraph argues against this, asking its readers to remember the limits on independence in an autocracy and neglecting to mention the lofty ranks and honors that Karamzin had been granted. It was precisely this direct dependence on the court that defined the Russian aristocracy in Pushkin's eyes. He viewed it as a malignant growth on Russian history, consisting of scheming courtiers elevated to high rank by the post-Petrine emperors and empresses.[136] His disdain for these upper court circles found expression in a series of works starting with his school lyrics, and, in social and political terms, he persistently contrasted these courtiers with the pre-Petrine nobility or with the gentry, to which he, much of the reading public, and many of his fellow writers belonged. For Bulgarin, too, "aristocracy" carried pejorative social and political meanings, but he understood it as the polite society that I defined in the first chapter, and he distinguished it from the "middle condition" [*srednee sostoianie*] of public opinion that was not so thoroughly gallicized, spoiled, and ambitious as the aristocracy, but which consisted largely of the gentry in state service (both well-to-do and not), as well as rich merchants, factory owners, and some non-noble townspeople.[137] For Bulgarin, Grech, and Polevoi to brand their opposition "aristocrats," therefore, infuriated Pushkin, because of the meaning in which he generally used the word. More than this, it constituted a cunning ploy in their competition with the Pushkin Pleiad for the educated reading public. As we have seen, the salons and familiar groups that shaped this public preferred, in theory, talent to mere aristocracy, especially when talent could serve morality and patriotism, in which Bulgarin attempted to cloak himself, and when talent could express itself in the refined Karamzinian language that the educated public used to define itself and exclude outsiders. Even Del'vig, who would be awakened from his poetic lethargy by Bulgarin's tactics and would challenge him to a duel, was forced to concede that Bulgarin's prose language was "pure and correct nearly everywhere."[138]

One of Bulgarin's finest, and most infuriating, exercises in this refined manner was the memoir about Karamzin that he published in 1828. With his keen (and shameless) sense of self-promotion Bulgarin depicted Karamzin—and, by extension, himself—as a man of talent, simplicity, culture, and kindness, who welcomed and inspired these fine qualities in others, unlike the uncultured members of high society around him.[139] Indeed, the memoir rivals any of the ones analyzed above for its understanding of the salon ideal's stress on civility and talent. Pushkin, who caught wind of this impersonation, persuaded Del'vig not to publish it in his almanac *Northern Flowers* and replaced it with his own piece, but Bulgarin's was sufficiently skillful to win the approval of Karamzin's lifelong friend Dmitriev.[140] Bulgarin had, for the time being, captured the authorial persona, the style, the values, and the topics of Karamzin's successful synthesis. Within two years, he could lay claim to its readership as well, when his picaresque novel *Ivan Vyzhigin* prospered as Pushkin's narrative poem *Poltava* suffered a dismal commercial failure.

These initial skirmishes completed, Bulgarin was now licensed by the public's acceptance of his talent and by his new-found fashionability to level the charge of "aristocratism" against his critics, whose number included Karamzin's own brother-in-law (Prince Viazemsky), Pushkin, and other poets of their circle, who had enjoyed a monopoly over the attentions of the 1820s almost as complete as the one that Bulgarin and his colleagues would soon enjoy over Russian literature of the 1830s. The former group had praised and defended each other in their almanacs and journals, inspired in large part by their friendship for each other.[141] Now Bulgarin and Grech would praise each others' works in their newspaper and journals, artfully camouflaging commercial opportunism under the same mantle of friendship that had been woven by the ideology of polite society and by the literature of the familiar groups. Pushkin sought to expose this impersonation and to return the label "aristocrat" to his opponents in two stunning literary satires—"The Triumph of Friendship, or the Vindicated Orlov," which I have already mentioned, and "Some Words on Mr. Bulgarin's Little Finger and So Forth" (also 1831), but he did so in a journal, Nadezhdin's *Teleskop*, that could not hope to compete with the periodicals of its targets.

The temptation to view Bulgarin's success as the opening of a new era of Russian literature must be in large part resisted. *Ivan Vyzhigin* was, it is true, the first nineteenth-century Russian novel to enjoy commercial success with the educated, Westernized public, far surpassing, for example, the earlier Le Sage imitation by Narezhny (1814).[142] But the sequel did not do nearly so well, and the fortunes of his newspaper, the *Northern Bee* (*Severnaia pchela*), rested in large part on its monopoly over political and court news.[143] Its price, and the price of his novels, remained well beyond the reach of the broader public serviced by the chapbook trade.[144] Bulgarin, no less than Pushkin and Karamzin, negotiated his way among the institutionalized possibilities of Russian culture: government patronage, the reading public with its interests and expectations and its ideological susceptibility to "fashion," and the literary market, which could produce high profits on relatively small editions that won fashion's approval.[145] Belinsky, whose philosophical orientation disposed him toward finding regularity in history, saw the success of novels such as Bulgarin's as an accident.[146] And even this success did not surpass that of *Eugene Onegin*, which Pushkin published in separate chapters at a large profit, then in complete editions in 1833 and 1837.[147]

As these parties ferociously contended for possession of the fragile Karamzinian synthesis, its institutional inadequacy revealed itself most clearly in its lack of a critical agency that could mediate between the writer and his public, informing the public of literary developments and conveying to the writer a focused sense of the public's interests and expectations. The dignified authorial persona that Karamzin had bequeathed did not encourage an author to answer his critics or even to engage in the public criticism of published literary works. Karamzin had not only ignored both the critics of his refined style and the scholarly opponents of his history, he had also refused, as editor of the *Herald of Europe*, to criticize contemporary authors, for fear of discouraging their efforts and because in 1802 it seemed a luxury to have criticism when there was so little Russian literature to evaluate.[148] Furthermore, the ideology of polite society, which assigned literature an ameliorating function, discouraged open polemics.[149]

Until the 1820s this absence struck but few Russian littérateurs. A protégé-writer could address his patron-reader directly and be judged by him, although (ideally) he could educate that patron's tastes. In a

circle, writer and reader exchanged roles in a continuing critical dialogue throughout the production of the work. The groups' familiar
letters and the minutes of their meetings have left many examples of
painstaking, hard-headed criticism and response. But the modern
institution of literature presents writer and reader few such
opportunities for personal interaction. Criticism becomes a necessity
with the expansion of the reading public—not yet the case in Russia—
and with the proliferation of different sorts of work reaching that
public.[150] The Russian reader, confronted with the latter situation,
had to select his or her fare from a longer menu of works, whose
dissimilarity to each other called for critical evaluation or fashion's
verdict.

The truism that a work makes its reader ignores this problem of
initial selection. Without intelligent, principled help in the selection
and reception of literature, a reader can remain unaware of much that
is appearing, undisposed toward new developments, and subject to
crudely commercial or ideological manipulation, or else to "accident."
This was precisely the prospect that faced Russian literature of the
late 1820s and 1830s, as representative works of disparate foreign and
native movements filled the bookstores and journals. Mere bibliographical notices in the Russian journals could no longer suffice, as
Pushkin had noted in 1825 (XIII, 178) and would later repeat in the
Literary Gazette (XI, 89), nor could vulgar exchanges of epithets (XI,
151), outright abuse (XI, 123–124), clever jokes (XII, 178), satiric comments, the mutual admiration of friends, proofreaders' comments (XI,
89), "unliterary" ad hominem accusations (XI, 166), and "several separate articles full of bright thoughts and pompous wit" (XI, 167).

As incisive and comprehensive as his list of failings is, it is, perhaps,
more instructive to follow Pushkin's positive attempts to define a role
for criticism. To what could Pushkin turn, given the institutional
possibilities of Russian culture? His notebooks for the years 1830–31,
kept during the debate over literary "aristocracy," are filled with
attempts to create a critical function from these possibilities. No fragment can be taken as his final word on the subject—rather they might
be viewed as a dialogue with himself and with these possibilities.

One possibility that Pushkin entertains is simply to print the debates
of the familiar groups. As one of the parties in an imagined "conversation on criticism" puts it:

> If all the writers who deserved the respect and trust of the public would
> take upon themselves the labor of directing public opinion, soon criticism
> would become something different. Wouldn't it be interesting, for ex-

ample, to read Gnedich's opinion on Romanticism or Krylov's on the present elegiac poetry? Wouldn't it be pleasant to see Pushkin analyzing a tragedy by Khomiakov? These gentlemen are closely connected with each other and probably exchange comments with each other on new works. Why not make us participants in their critical conversations? (XI, 90)

Yet as Pushkin surely knew, much of this conversation involved the exchange of satiric observations, specific comments on turns of phrase, and mutual admiration of a sort that might encourage writers, but could not serve the needs of the Russian reader, especially with these examples, which demonstratively ignore the prose genres that were beginning to capture the public's attention. It takes the reader for granted in ways that the author of *Poltava*, a brilliant poem but commercial failure, could no longer afford to do.

A subsequent attempt to define criticism reads like a somewhat romanticized turn-of-the-century schoolbook:

> Criticism is the science of revealing the beauties and shortcomings in works of art and literature.
>
> It is founded on a perfect knowledge of the rules, by which the artist or writer is guided in his works, on a profound study of models, and on the active observation of remarkable contemporary phenomena.
>
> I am not speaking of impartiality—whoever is guided in his criticism by anything but a true love for art is descending to the level of the crowd, which is slavishly governed by base, mercenary motives.
>
> Where there is no love of art, there is no criticism. "Do you wish to be a connoisseur of the arts?" asks Winckelmann. "Try to love the artist, seek the beauty in his creations."   (XI, 139)

This fragment addresses the vital problem of critical ethics—and here one must recall Bulgarin's confession that he did not always read what he reviewed—and the conjunction of conventions, models, and new phenomena that determines the codes of any institution. Gogol, repeating many of Pushkin's negative comments five years later, expressed the importance of this principled criticism with but little of his wonted exaggeration: "based on profound taste and intelligence, criticism of high talent has a value equal to any original work."[151] But, like Pushkin's preceding fragment this does not allow for the critic's interaction with the reading public. There the reader was permitted merely to overhear the writers' discussions; here a Romantic contempt for the "crowd's" everyday interests promises no attempt to engage those interests and to mediate between them and the poet's artistic choices, yet it was precisely this growing distance between poet and public—physically and psychologically—that criticism was now required to span.

A third approach to the criticism that Pushkin followed in his notebooks reacted more realistically to the shortcomings of Russian literary life in the 1830s, yet permitted the critical dialogue and principled criticism that he sought to define in the other fragments. This involved "anticriticism" or polemics. "Such 'anticriticism,' " wrote Pushkin, "would bring a twofold benefit: the correction of mistaken opinions and the spread of sensible conceptions about art" (XI, 132). Here, in theory, the writer or critic can address both the public and the literary situation. But too often in practice the dialogue became not an exchange of educated opinions, but of harsh personal attacks, necessary and effective with a public that would not distinguish a work from its author and with writers who outwardly "preserved a reverence for concepts sacred to humanity," as Pushkin put it, mimicking Bulgarin's grandiloquence (XI, 129).

Taken together, these notebook fragments frame the problems that Russian literature faced as it became a public institution in a recognizably modern sense; they do not solve these problems. But they do show that existing institutional components of Karamzin's synthesis could not answer the needs of the 1830s. Given these failings of public criticism, it is not surprising that the authors of the most innovative narratives of the period—*Eugene Onegin, Dead Souls,* and *A Hero of Our Time*—each staged a variety of explicit and implicit dialogues with critics of their work within their texts, seeking, in the absence of understanding critics, to mediate between their own fictions and the reader. The earliest of these fictions, *Eugene Onegin,* is the one that does the most to project a familiar, conversational relationship with the reader, a relationship of the sort that characterized the salons and circles which still provided linguistic and literary codes for the incipient profession of the early 1830s. As the quotations from *Eugene Onegin* in this chapter—about mass literature, about young ladies' albums—have suggested, it is also the novel that addresses most directly problems of multiple and competing institutions of literature, modeling in its author-narrator and provincial heroine (who becomes the hostess of a salon) ideals of serious, comprehending, and versatile literary reception, reception competent not only in generic and linguistic codes but also in institutional awareness. The other two novels, as we shall see, strike different stances toward these institutional and critical possibilities. Each addresses the reader directly, wages "anticriticism" against its opponents (real and imagined), asking the reader to accept his novel not as a mere revelation of the novelist's character, but as an innovative work of art, and suggesting appropriate contexts in which it might be understood.

The first institutional controversy—over the "literary aristocracy"—brought to the fore problems of authorial dignity and the shortcomings of Russian criticism; the second ("literature and commerce") not only revealed that these problems were unsolved, but introduced new ones that concerned no less vital aspects of the institution of literature: editing, publishing, and readership. The combatants in the first campaign took part in this one, too, but a new group assumed the leading roles: Smirdin, the bookseller; Sękowski, the editor of the *Library for Reading;* and Shevyrev, Belinsky, and Gogol, commentators for rival journals.

Smirdin's triumphs in the mid-1830s—a new bookstore at a fashionable Petersburg address (1832), a successful almanac that celebrated this move (*Novosel'e* [Housewarming, 1833]), ownership of a virtual monopoly over the print media (including the *Library for Reading*)—are too well chronicled to require a long account here.[152] Belinsky's label for the 1830s, "the age of Smirdin" in Russian literature, captures the impact that Smirdin's well-financed enterprises produced.[153] All Russian writers, including the three on whom this study focuses, had to reckon with Smirdin's editors Bulgarin and Grech and with his commercial network. Pushkin was able to live on Smirdin's honoraria at a time when catastrophes cut off all income from his estates; Gogol refused to deal with him, but could do no better on his own; and some of Lermontov's early verse appeared (without his permission) in the *Library for Reading.*[154] Lermontov elected to publish *A Hero of Our Time* with a rival printer, Glazunov, but received a warm review from one of Smirdin's periodicals when Glazunov bribed the reviewer, Bulgarin.[155] Belinsky, who saluted Smirdin's honesty and reliability, nevertheless noted that books not published by Smirdin and not written or protected by his editors tended not to circulate very widely.[156]

Nevertheless, Smirdin's three years of schooling from a Moscow deacon did not enable him to interact with his authors on an intellectual basis. "Smirdin, naturally, is no Novikov," as Bulgarin gracelessly put it.[157] He differed from the modern publisher who plays the role of a privileged early reader of a manuscript and then works with the author to produce a final version for the public. And his role was not that of the gentleman-editor, such as Gnedich or Pletnev, who helped see a friend's works into print. To call him "Pushkin's friend," as one of his hagiographers has done, ignores the social and intellectual distance between them as well as the distance between this Russian situation and the "republic of letters" that printing had helped produce in Western Europe.[158]

Nor can it be said that he significantly lowered prices in the marketplace and made literature available to a mass public.[159] Annual reading privileges at his bookstore cost fifty rubles, and the availability of monthly rates suggests that it catered to landowners visiting Petersburg for the winter.[160] The almanac *Novosel'e* was an elegantly printed, expensive volume; the *Library for Reading* at fifty rubles per year was among the most expensive periodicals of its time.[161] Smirdin did earn praise, it is true, for publishing relatively inexpensive *second* editions, such as Karamzin's history or Batiushkov's collected works, but these remained elegant volumes, sold at many times the price of the classics that would appear in mass editions only toward the end of the century.[162] The high salaries and honoraria that Smirdin offered his most fashionable writers—even for the mere right to list their names or as bribes *not* to found rival enterprises—and the minuscule reading public precluded mass literature in any modern sense.[163] In turn, these salaries and honoraria—if one examines the matter closely—cannot be given credit for making the practice of letters a profitable profession. To be sure, Smirdin paid his editors unprecedented salaries—Sękowski 15,000 a year, Bulgarin 25,000 a year—and a few established writers received handsome honoraria from him, such as Krylov's 40,000 rubles. But the typical contributor to his journals could not expect to make a comfortable living from his honoraria, as Belinsky noted with common sense unusual in these discussions.[164]

This negative assessment of Smirdin's efforts—necessary to illustrate their differences from more modern ones and from the regnant scholarly descriptions of them—should not obscure his historical role, which was essentially one of consolidation less than one of innovation. Pushkin, Gogol, and Belinsky all noted the reliability and honesty of his commercial dealings: the journals that he owned came out on time and in the promised "thickness"; contributors to his journals received their honoraria promptly.[165] Given the chaotic, "accident"-prone literary marketplace, the gambling instincts of his writers, polite society's adherence to shifting fashions, and other institutionalized drawbacks to literary commerce, such reliability was no mean feat. Indeed, no literary profession can exist without something like it. But Smirdin's efforts were not enough. Smirdin himself was ruined by the 1840s—as unscrupulous writers continued to abuse his extravagant generosity, and as the book trade suffered a general decline. But the commercial principles that his journals established set a standard for the competing "thick journals" that dominated the profession of letters until the last two decades of the century.

Smirdin's success, then, rested not so much upon an intellectual partnership with his writers as upon his ability to distribute their works to a readership that, as we shall see, puzzled the writers who looked beyond their patrons and familiar groups. To some critics of Smirdin's enterprises this meant limiting the reader's choice—hence the justifiable charges of monopolism raised against Smirdin and his journalists, who shamelessly lauded each other in their periodicals.[166] In a complementary sense, this meant giving the readers, participants in an ever more complex, syncretic culture, everything they had demanded of the book trade: both Russian and foreign works; belles lettres, history, and popular science; prose and poetry; works of each and every notable Russian writer of any generation and tendency—an encyclopedic inclusiveness that Smirdin proclaimed in the catalogue to his reading room, on the cover of *Novosel'e* (which showed a multitude of writers raising their glasses to him), and on the title page to the *Library for Reading*, which was subtitled *A Journal of Literature, the Sciences, the Arts, News, and Fashions.* The names of fifty-seven writers appear on this title page, and, when taken out of alphabetical order, they yield confrontations to boggle the literary historian's mind: Pushkin and Bulgarin, Gogol and Sękowski, Prince Viazemsky and Polevoi, Krylov and Zhukovsky, Ivan Kireevsky and Grech, Prince Odoevsky and Kukol'nik, Baratynsky and Masal'sky. No matter that many subsequently asked that their names be removed, that some never published anything in the journal, or that some had been added without their owners' permission. The "trusting public" as Belinsky called it had rushed to subscribe in numbers that amazed all commentators and even the publishers.

Syncretism became the guiding principle for the *Library for Reading.*[167] This in itself was no particular novelty. *Mnemosyne* had promised to satisfy every taste; *The Moscow Telegraph* had addressed a wide range of topics. S. P. Shevyrev's *Moskovskii Nabliudatel'* (*Moscow Observer*), founded in opposition to the *Library for Reading*, would advertise itself as an "encyclopedic journal." But, more than the others, the *Library for Reading* made good on this promise of plenty.

Why, then, did this journal which appeared with unusual accuracy, rewarded its contributors generously, published such brilliant works as Pushkin's "Queen of Spades," and reached an unprecedented five thousand subscribers arouse such a storm of controversy? Just as the word "aristocrat" had evoked a confusing variety of passionate responses, so did "commerce" (*torgovlia*) in the present controversy. Here, as previously, literary phenomena could be understood within a variety of institutional contexts, and thus came to threaten the participants' identity in ways that recall some of Gogol's finest scenes of confusion. It touched the entire literary process—the rights and duties of authors, editors, and critics; the reading public (both actual and implied by the text); style, genre, and areas of representation. The syncretism and success of the *Library for Reading* made it a target both elusive and inviting. That this syncretism was consonant with the ideology of polite society and that its opponents either subscribed to this same ideology or shared certain of its aspects did not make the debate any more rational or their target any less elusive.

Shevyrev opened the charge against the *Library for Reading* in the lead article of the *Moscow Observer*, which seemed founded for the purpose of attacking the *Library for Reading*, just as the *Literary Gazette* had arisen in opposition to Bulgarin's enterprises.[168] Much of Shevyrev's attack on literary commerce, and on the *Library for Reading*, borders on the hysterical—accusations that payment by the signature makes writers long-winded; hyperbolic accounts of the fortunes to be made in Russian letters; fears that commerce would destroy all taste, thought, morality, learning, and honest criticism; and the pious, romantic assertion that only poetry had not fallen into the clutches of commerce.[169] The values that Shevyrev articulates in this essay, its desire for a literature of thought that would lend expression to the age and to society, and its very form (a pseudo-epistolary reply to a friend's question) mark his approach as that of the Moscow familiar groups, of which he was an inveterate member. Their high-minded approach to literature and their hope to form public opinion ran strictly opposite to Sękowski's expressed editorial policy, to entertain the public and cater to its desires. The motives behind Sękowski's approach to the journal had to strike Shevyrev all the more directly as a monstrous profanation because Sękowski had attracted works of high literature. Thus, Belinsky could remind Shevyrev that he had praised the prose of Pushkin and Odoevsky that had appeared in the *Library for Reading* and that he had himself accepted an honorarium for publishing a historical piece there.[170] And Gogol could aptly note that Shevyrev had said nothing about the works published in Sękowski's journal (VIII, 168). More than this, Sękowski had appropriated the codes of high literature, as he professed to base his journal's style on the conversational usage of good society; Shevyrev would profess a similar decorum in refusing to publish Gogol's brilliantly off-color anecdote, "The Nose," which he branded "dirty," urging Gogol to write stories about high society.[171]

Gogol and Belinsky themselves embraced the professionalization of literature, and their analyses of Sękowski, therefore, attacked not commerce per se, but Sękowski's astounding abuses of it. Their quarrel with him, unlike Shevyrev's, took cognizance of the specific requirements of a profession of letters: respect for the author's text, criticism addressed to the public (as well as to the writer—Gogol attacked Shevyrev for not providing this), and awareness of the nature of that public.

Pushkin's struggle with Bulgarin during the years 1828–1831, because Bulgarin hypocritically affirmed much that Pushkin valued (such as the legacy of Karamzin, the writer's dignity), had necessitated personal counterattacks. But Sękowski's practices little resembled the ideals of Belinsky and Gogol, and this made a more intellectually substantial confrontation possible.

By no means the least striking of Sękowski's practices was his unashamed editorial free-handedness, which Gogol, forgetting the traditional deceits of the chapbook publishers, found unprecedented in Russian culture. He could only quote Sękowski in amazement: "we leave no story in its prior form, but redo every one; sometimes we work up one out of two, sometimes out of three, and the piece gains significantly from our alterations" (VIII, 162). Sękowski probably never went this far, but he did add a happy conclusion to Balzac's *Père Goriot*, altered scholarly articles (including Shevyrev's), and inserted his own *idées fixes* into other critics' essays.[172] This was not the mere absence of taste or knowledge that Shevyrev noted, but a blatant assault on the text and, by extension, on the name and unique mission of the poet, which Gogol had outlined earlier in an essay on Pushkin (VIII, 50–55). To Belinsky, it constituted nothing less than a betrayal of the reader's trust.[173]

Measured even by the low standards of Russian public criticism, the *Library for Reading* struck its contemporaries by its irresponsibility, capriciousness, and outright dishonesty.[174] It was, in Lidiia Ginzburg's deft phrase, "unprincipled in principle."[175] Where Pushkin had sought to forge public criticism from an amalgam of rules, models, and taste, Sękowski offered unalloyed, ostensibly ungoverned personal taste, which could not possibly be assayed. The first issue of his journal stated this with Sękowski's usual mixture of desiccated humor, arrogance toward the text, and obsequiousness toward the reader:

I declare my opinion according to my personal view on the subject and ask no advice of Rhetoric or Poetics, about what should please me and what should not. I cannot feel according to given rules, and I confess openly that in my scanty understanding of things there is not a single ready delight for any great literary name. I am so impertinent that I judge even Shakespeare, Corneille, Racine, Schiller, Byron, Goethe, and Pushkin according to my own impressions and not according to their fame. And I marvel at them only in those places, more or less, where they strike me with the greater or less elevation of their intelligence above the zero degree mark, that is, above my mind . . . Thus, for me there are no exemplary works in literature; anything is a model that is excellent . . . My mind rests at the freezing point [of my mental thermometer]. The entire mental atmosphere of our planet is allowed to act upon it, to produce oscillations in it, to raise it or lower it; I am only obliged to indicate the degree on which it stops. In the present state of our literary scholarship, when a terrifying mental revolution has forged into a dagger even that yardstick by which people so conveniently measured fine works of beauty as if they were velvet ribbons, I see no possibility of another critical measure. I call it impartial criticism when in good conscience I describe for those who wish to listen the impression that a given book has made upon me personally. But the degree of my impression is not a rule for others. Criticism in our time has become a picture of the personal feelings [!] of each individual,—each individual who is gifted by nature with a clear feeling for the ways and means by which the beautiful can produce a full and pleasant effect upon the heart and imagination of man. There can be no talk of rules. The only condition for this feeling of ways and means, an à priori condition, is morality. Taste is the whim of the pregnant woman which is society. Consequently, after reading criticism, there is nothing to argue about: the only way is to declare, independently of the already expressed opinion, a second, different opinion, with the same frankness, but without refutations, for to refute someone else's feelings is as ridiculous as it is impracticable.[176]

Aside from its brassy dismissal of literary precedents, this position—fortified by a palisade of noble terms ("heart and mind," "frankness," "morality," "nature")—does not differ in broad outline from the one Karamzin had adopted before the turn of the century, when "taste" had liberated Russian criticism from the sway of the rhetorical manuals and other formularies. Sękowski's success argues that he, like Karamzin, found a personal taste that could be shared by much of the reading public. But three decades after Karamzin's early successes, in the context of the 1830s, such "taste" could not play the liberating role that it had in Karamzin's time, when it emancipated literature from the sway of the rhetorical manuals. Sękowski's practice in the 1830s opposed both the philosophical aspirations of the Moscow critics, such as Belinsky, and the program of public debate that Push-kin had advanced.[177] Given the monopolistic sway that the *Library for Reading* enjoyed, its refusal to engage in open polemics and to ground criticism in anything more stable than whim threatened to debase the already fragile public institution of literature or at least to preserve the institutional status quo, which was ruled by capricious fashion. The journal's refusal to review anything but current literature dis-engaged it from the otherwise universal search for a usable Russian tradition.[178] And its "Literary Chronicle" section, replete with jokes, puns, gossip, and other forms of small wit—sometimes quite funny—nevertheless made it seem a purveyor of mere entertainment. The pseudonym under which much of this appeared, "Baron Brambeus," was itself a provocation to serious critics, derived as it was from the hero of a chapbook tale.[179] While Bulgarin could be shamed into silence by the threat of association with the chapbook trade, Sękowski could confidently taunt his detractors by embracing such an association.

This most popular of Russian journals realized in its policies and practices every failure that Gogol could discover in Russian criticism: (1) contempt for its own opinion; (2) literary infidelity and literary ignorance (that is, neglecting the literature of the past with its insti-tutionally necessary precedents); (3) the absence of pure aesthetic enjoyment and taste; (4) triviality in thought and trivial foppishness (that is, ignoring large questions for petty quarrels and small wit) (VIII, 173–175). As he was writing his article ("On the Movement of Journalistic Literature in 1834 and 1835"), Gogol was also beginning to draft *Dead Souls*. From abuses similar to these, as we shall see, Gogol would weave the language, plot, and characters of his novel, transforming their captivating mindlessness, self-righteous elusive-ness, and legitimated falsehood into an all-inclusive vision, not just of literary relationships, but of the culture that could encompass them.[180] Meanwhile, that Pushkin removed Gogol's name from the article be-fore publishing it in *The Contemporary* and two issues later refused to acknowledge it as a program for the journal could not increase Gogol's confidence in the "movement" of Russian literature.

Gogol could be specific and devastating in his attack on the criticism of his time, but another indispensable aspect of the literary process left him puzzled: "On what educational level does the Russian public stand, and what is the Russian public?" (VIII, 172). The only answer that the journals of his time seemed to give him—apart from boasting of their subscription figures—was their advertisements and their flat-tery of the reader: "it is the estimable public and it should subscribe to all journals and various editions, for they can be read by a paterfamilias and a merchant and a warrior and a littérateur" (VIII, 172). The subscription figure for the *Library of Reading*, 5,000 subscribers, hypnotized all commentators, for it exceeded by several times the figure for any previous journal. Gogol risked no credibility in concluding that the number of readers had increased "significantly" (VIII, 168) because, of course, a single copy might serve a number of readers.

Other statistical information of Gogol's time could barely begin to satisfy Gogol's curiosity about the reader's educational level. The government opposed mass education throughout much of the century and compiled no comprehensive statistics on literacy until the census of 1897. One of the earliest partial samples, taken but two years after the appearance of *Dead Souls*, showed that in the Saratov province—which was well above average in its number of schools and students—only 4 percent of the male population (excluding gentry and clergy) could read.[181] It is, consequently, most premature to talk of a mass reading public for anything more sophisticated than broadsheets and chapbooks. Even at ten readers per copy, the *Library for Reading* would not have reached 1 percent of the population.

Statistics published by the Ministry of Popular Education two years after Gogol raised his questions would have done equally little to inspire faith in the size and competence of the reading public. While the number of students at all levels had increased 75 percent between the years 1800–1834, it was still true that only .5 percent of the population attended any sort of educational institution.[182] Of these, many "attended" village and parish schools, which, as one early researcher put it, "existed mainly on paper."[183] Of Russia's fifty-one million inhabitants, only 1,900 attended the empire's six universities.[184] In short, only .5 percent of the gentry and .03 percent of the "obligated classes" received even a gymnasium education.[185]

Statistics of this sort, while indicative of a society's values and commitment to learning, tell a writer little, if anything, about the reader he most needs to know, the reader who will actually encounter the text, bringing to it literary and life experiences that cannot help but shape his reading. The professional writer cannot deliver his work orally in a salon or throne room; during the writing process, the reader beyond his writing table is, as Father Ong puts it, "always a fiction."[186] But unless some actual reader can find himself in the text's projected ("fictional") reader, there will be no semblance of communication on any level, be it aesthetic, cognitive, conative, or even communication shaped by an adversary relationship, to say nothing of an interaction that the writer can use his text to control. Hence the desperation—and the intelligence—of Gogol's questions. Neither Smirdin, with his bankroll, nor Sękowski, with his shotgun approach to editorial selection, could answer these questions.

Other writers and journalists had tried, if not to define or understand the reader, then certainly to *make* him. Here we can turn to the many expressions of *odi profanum vulgus* in the poetry of the 1820s and 1830s and relate them to the need for a reader. In this context, one could see them less as sociological descriptions of the reading public or conventional posing and more as rhetorical attempts to shape an ideal reader for the poet's lofty and beautiful creations—by holding up mindless, inadequate readings to scorn. Pushkin's masterly dialogic treatments of the theme—"Conversation of a Bookseller with a Poet" ("Razgovor knigoprodavtsa s poetom, 1824) and "The Poet and the Crowd" ("Poet i tolpa," 1828)—make the reader party to a mediation on the production and functions of poetry in social life.[187] And, in so doing, they subject all received opinions (pure poetry, poetry as moral instruction, poetry as reflection of life) to ironic illumination.

The poet's isolation from the crowd found its critical elaboration in a group of essays which offer their own mixtures of description and persuasion. In this vein, Gogol's "Several Words on Pushkin" ("Neskol'ko slov o Pushkine," 1834), as Fanger has noted, made the bold pedagogical gambit of "deploring the state of the reading public to the reading public," a move all the bolder for his rivals' profitable obsequiousness toward these readers.[188]

Meanwhile, the appearance of the *Library for Reading* in 1834 focused these attempts to define and shape the public, and it provoked a social concreteness that earlier attempts had lacked. Nadezhdin, for one, immediately identified the reader of the *Library for Reading* as a provincial.[189] Then Gogol followed, noting with satisfaction that the *"Library for Reading* is already being read less in the capitals, but just as much in the provinces" (VIII, 162). Belinsky set out in the same direction:

> Imagine the family of a steppe landowner, a family reading everything that falls into its hands from cover to cover; it has not yet managed to read to the back cover . . . when another issue is already flying toward it, just as thick, fat, chatty, garrulous, speaking out suddenly in one and several languages. And, indeed, what variety! Daughter reads the verses of Messrs Ershov, Gorniev, Strugovshchikov and the stories of Messrs Zagoskin, Ushakov, Panaev, Kalashnikov, and Masal'sky; the son, as a member of the new generation, reads the verses of Mr. Timofeev and the stories of Baron Brambeus; pappa reads articles about the two and three field systems, about various means of fertilizing the land, and

mamma reads about a new way of curing coughs and dyeing thread; and there's still something left for those who desire criticism, the literary chronicle, from which they can scoop handfuls and handfuls of ready judgments (often witty and intelligent, although rarely just and honest) about modern literature . . . It's true, isn't it, that such a journal is a treasure for the provinces.[190]

Belinsky's analysis of their reading taste is indeed damning, to be sure. But condescending comments about the provinces had been a fixture of Russian intellectual life, from the comedies of the eighteenth century to the cosmopolitan salons of the two capitals. However, unlike Gogol, Nadezhdin, and other critics who branded the *Library for Reading* a journal for the provinces in order to compromise its readership, Belinsky turned back upon the reader in the capitals, making some telling points about the contemporary reception of literature:

But wait, that's not all: variety doesn't hurt even a journal of the capital and cannot serve as the exclusive mark of the provincial. Let's glance at each section of the *Library for Reading*—especially at their order. Verses occupy a large and special place in it: under many of them stand resounding names, such as Pushkin, Zhukovsky; under most stand the names of celebrities who have been invented by the *Library for Reading* itself . . . There's no need for quality in the verse; the names, signed under them, guarantee their merit, and in the provinces this guarantee is more than enough. The same thing must be said about the remaining sections of the *Library for Reading*. Tell me, now, is that not of great benefit to the provinces? You know how many people there are in the capitals whom you would drive to extreme distraction by reading them a poem, concealing the name of the author, and asking their opinion without having expressed your own; how many people there are in the capitals who dare not delight in a piece nor grow angry without having glanced at the signature. It is quite natural that there are even more of such people in the provinces and that people with independent opinions are there by accident and comprise a very rare exception. Meanwhile, provincials, like the inhabitants of the capitals, want not only to read but to judge what they have read; they want to distinguish themselves by their taste, to shine with learning, to amaze others with their judgments, and they do this, they do it very easily, at no risk of compromising their taste, their discrimination, because the names signed under the verses and articles of the *Library for Reading* free them from any danger of running their taste aground and betraying their lack of education, and their ignorance in matters of beauty.[191]

That the *Library for Reading* might have been read less in the capitals than in the provinces, as Gogol speculated, becomes no compliment to the urban reader, who merely has greater access to fashion's verdicts, and certainly no compliment to the *Library for Reading* for dumping trash in the provinces. Once Belinsky has shown that a "provincial" relationship toward literature is to be found not merely in the provinces, the term acquires a moral force, directed against the backward, the counterfeit, the mediocre, the merely entertaining, even when they are clothed in the "good language" of the *Library for Reading*.

Throughout the period that *A Hero of Our Time* and *Dead Souls* were being written and published, Belinsky would continue to express similar doubts about the reading public, distinguishing those who buy literature as a mere entertainment commodity from those for whom literature could be "not relaxation from life's cares, not a sweet slumber in a soft armchair after a rich dinner . . . but a *res publica*, great and important, a source of lofty moral enjoyment and live ecstasy." Such a public would be "a single living personality, historically developed, with a certain direction, taste, and view of things," and it would see literature as *"its own,* flesh of its flesh, bone of its bone and not something alien, accidentally filling a certain number of books and journals." Only such a public could, argued Belinsky, make the titles "writer" and "critic" meaningful.[192] Belinsky found a public to match this organic vision of a literary institution by the late 1840s, a public which would recognize writing and criticism as vocations, even professions. This public comprised university students, *raznochintsy,* and provincials—the "intelligentsia," in short—and Belinsky would exercise a hegemony over this public no less impressive than Sękowski's had been in the 1830s. But this new public was not, ideologically or socially, the polite society that greeted the novels of Pushkin, Lermontov, and Gogol.[193]

Until that day really came, writers such as Pushkin, Lermontov, and Gogol had to contend with the public that Belinsky described in his earlier essay, which he starkly entitled "Something about Nothing." They not only had to play the critic's role within their novels, explaining such elementary concepts as "irony" (Lermontov), "beauty" (Gogol), and "the novel" (Pushkin) to their readers, they had to make model readers for their works *within* those works. Every novelist does this to some extent, but these early Russian ones do it with unusual persistence. The heroine of Pushkin's novel grows in literary understanding throughout the novel, becoming the author-narrator's "ideal" as a reader and cultural force. Lermontov's two prefaces to his novel use the technique of negative inference to create a reader who will not be "like a provincial"; and the preface to the second edition of *Dead Souls* issues a desperate, unprecedented plea to its readers to join the author in creative partnership, a partnership that the familiar associations no longer could provide. Neither *A Hero of Our Time* nor *Dead Souls* invites, ultimately, the familiarity between narrator and inscribed reader that *Eugene Onegin* had modulated and that Sękowski had made his bread-and-butter. Each of the two texts proposes, in place of this intimacy, new conventions (critical and speculative, as we shall see) for its own reception, ones which take cognizance of what Roland Barthes has called the "pitiless divorce" of addresser from addressee that has occurred in public and professional modes of literary life.[194]

It would be highly naive to imagine, however, that the historical human material which encountered Pushkin's ideal reader or the proposed conventions of Lermontov and Gogol presented itself to the novels innocent of ideology, interests, values, and predictable social behavior. Belinsky's essay, negative and unsympathetic though it may have been, did nevertheless characterize a "provincial" reader with all of these indispensable cultural attributes. However mediocre or vulgar the form they took, the reader emerges with a sense of humor, a weakness for happy endings, a variety of interests (Russian, European, practical, aesthetic), and a desire not only to read literature, but to make judgments about it and to perform them for an audience that will in turn evaluate him. Belinsky presents these traits in such qualitatively negative terms that it would be difficult to take them seriously, were they not what the *Library for Reading* won its success by addressing, were they not what the ideology of polite society supported, and were they not repeated in an essay that Pushkin published shortly afterwards, a "letter to the editor" of his own journal.[195]

Here Pushkin appears in the persona of "A.B.," a provincial reader, to comment on Gogol's assessment of Russian journalism. We have already seen Karamzin declare his opposition to the criticism of contemporary works in this manner. The potential for ironic distance between Pushkin's actual feelings and those of the persona is obvious, and the use of the persona has led to speculation about Pushkin's motives in writing it—to protect the *Contemporary* from ugly squabbles with its competitors, perhaps, or to second Gogol's main charges against Sękowski by discrediting only his minor ones.[196] Because A.B. speaks in the first-person plural ("we humble provincials"), it is, however, tempting to see the letter as an answer to Gogol's questions about the reading public. The civilized moderation of A.B., his defense of wit and variety, his catholicity of tastes (the letter praises Gogol, Belinsky, and Sękowski), his thoughtful comments on the literary language, and his insistence on evaluating phenomena of Russian culture within a European context ("many of Sękowski's essays . . . deserved a place in the best European journals," XII, 96), present features of the Russian public that Belinsky noted, but on a higher level of sophistication. As if to emphasize this, A.B.'s praise of Belinsky measures him by the standards of polite society. In a typically Pushkinian game of shifting perspectives, the provincials that polite society, Belinsky, and Gogol may have scorned reappear with the enlightened, urbane values that this small section of Russian society claimed as its exclusive property, and seek to impose those values upon the writers who hoped to transcend them.

The shifting perspectives and ironic reversal notwithstanding, A.B.'s letter—its choice of initials suggesting the fundamental nature of its conclusions—invites us to represent the roles and relationships of the institution of literature that Pushkin, Lermontov, and Gogol encountered as follows:

LIFE OF THE GENTRY, CIVIL SERVITORS, OFFICERS

WRITER,	LYRIC VERSE, SHORT FICTION, ESSAY,	BOOKSELLER, CENSOR,
EDITOR	NOVEL, HISTORY	"CRITIC," READER

ALMANAC, JOURNAL, BOOK, COLLECTED WORKS
"CONVERSATIONAL LANGUAGE OF POLITE SOCIETY"

Writers were not yet the "authors" that they would subsequently become, the "second government" of which Solzhenitsyn has so eloquently spoken; nor, in most cases, were they fully professional, in either ideological or economic terms. They contacted their readers through media too expensive to reach a broad public. The readership included high officials with arbitrary powers, many different censoring agencies, booksellers who might only care about the profit-making potential of the author's name, critics still bound to questions of polite society's "conversational language" and taste, and readers who shared with various degrees of profundity the values and language of society. The novels of Pushkin, Lermontov, and Gogol confronted in different ways this ideology and these institutional features, not only testing and illuminating their boundaries and silences, but provoking and proposing new possibilities.

III

Eugene Onegin: "Life's Novel"

What is a novel? A novel is a theory of human life.
Review of *Eugene Onegin* in *Son of the Fatherland,* 1828

I N MANY WAYS *Eugene Onegin,* Pushkin's most popular work, embodied and brought into focus the disparate, sometimes contradictory and mutually exclusive, possibilities of Russian culture. Written between the years 1823 and 1831, published in various media between 1825 and 1832 as separate parts and fragments, detailing (and willfully ignoring) events in its characters' lives between the late eighteenth century and 1825, evoking a wide variety of critical responses, and addressing the central literary and ideological issues of the time, *Eugene Onegin* could easily strike Belinsky as an "encyclopedia of Russian life."[1] While a sophisticated modern reader may smile indulgently at this naive reduction of a highly intricate piece of verbal art to a mere reference work, it is nevertheless true that Pushkin's novel has inspired two of the twentieth century's most subtle critics, Vladimir Nabokov and Iurii Lotman, to illuminate its art with encyclopedic commentaries on the life and literature of early nineteenth-century Russia. Certainly the novel's inclusiveness has served many times in this study to illustrate the range of early nineteenth-century literary life, which presented the Russian writer so many definitions of his role (protégé, gentleman amateur, journalist, professional), so many genres, and so many historically distinct international styles (classicism, sentimentalism, various romanticisms).

A writer conversant with Russian and European culture and bold enough to question the prejudices of his social group and literary predecessors could exercise considerable choice under these circumstances, and Pushkin did precisely that with genres and styles, following the flight of his imagination across the boundaries of fashion, tradition, and literary history.

As we have seen, Pushkin faced the social problems of this era of changing authorial roles no less boldly. Although his older contemporaries had already taken Russian poetry from the frequently venal panegyrists of the late eighteenth century and made it a refined form of entertainment for the salons, Pushkin was still vitally concerned with this process as he began writing *Eugene Onegin* in the 1820s, and he still felt it necessary to declare his independence as a writer and gentleman from the patronage of the upper aristocracy and from subservience to the government. One of his strongest statements on this problem appears in a letter to A. A. Bestuzhev:

> Among us writers are taken from the highest class of society—in them aristocratic pride merges with authorial self-esteem. We do not want to be protected by our equals. This is what that scoundrel Vorontsov [Pushkin's superior in the civil service] does not understand. He imagines that a Russian poet will appear in his antechamber with a dedication to him or an ode, but the poet appears with a demand for respect, as a member of the gentry with 600 years' standing—a devil of a difference! (XIII, 179, May-June 1825)

The conventions of the familiar letter and the ideology of polite society encouraged such assertions of noble independence, but Pushkin hardly issued them automatically. Behind this assertion stood the bitter reality of exile, hostility within his family, police surveillance, debt, and an insignificant rank in the civil service. Behind them also stood Pushkin's growing awareness of his historically marginal position as the descendant both of an ancient noble family and (on his mother's side) of a captive Abyssinian who became a general through the patronage of Peter the Great's daughter.

The contradictions of this heritage—hereditary noble and post-Petrine creature, Russian and foreign—found a parallel in his precarious economic situation. The poet, desperate to maintain the noble independence of a gentleman *(honnête homme)* would find himself increasingly forced by his and his family's lordly irresponsibility to depend both upon the modest income from his writings and upon the humiliating patronage of Nicholas I, who paid the poet's huge debts after his death. Pushkin's behavior—a series of duels, love affairs dutifully recorded in his famous "Don Juan list," ill-advised marriage to a teen-aged beauty, gambling, free-thinking—reveals an obsessive struggle to maintain gentlemanly status. Independence and dignity had to be won, and his membership in the gentry alone was not enough to satisfy his growing need for them. A writing profession, as he understood it from the example of Karamzin and from Western examples, might help make him independent of humiliating government service and give him peace and leisure to write, but that conflicted with the prejudices and norms of the class to which he was proud to belong.

Nevertheless, during the mid-1820s Pushkin declared his independence from the salon concept of literature as the sentimental recreation of amateurs (XIII, 95) and boldly took up his new "trade," as he provocatively called it (XIII, 59, 88, 93). But the problem of reconciling his professional aspirations, his social identity, and his authorial freedom continued to trouble him. As his financial successes of the 1820s gave way to bitter literary quarrels with Bulgarin and journalists of nongentry origin (N. A. Polevoi, Raich, Nadezhdin), the vicious social intrigues which led to his death in a duel, a humiliating position at court, and nearly hopeless attempts to establish himself in journalism, his previous optimism faded. The short story "Egyptian Nights" (written 1835) returns to the problem of synthesizing patronage, the familiar groups, and professionalism that Pushkin had addressed in his notes on Karamzin (1828). This story raises the problem of literature's place in a social setting and arrives at no happy resolution of the conflict between social position, literary commerce, and inspiration. The two principal characters are poets—Charsky (a gentleman amateur) and an itinerant Italian *improvisatore*—who overcome the social distance between themselves to collaborate in a public performance. Both preserve the miracle of talent and inspiration amid the silly clamor of their uncomprehending public, but at considerable cost to themselves as social beings. The seedy improvisor must play a buffoon's role in polite society; Charsky, meanwhile, can maintain his social status and avoid becoming a public plaything only by cutting himself off from the institutional ties that might support his literary vocation (the company of fellow writers, conversation on literary topics, VIII, 264). The narrator underscores the parallel between their situations by calling no less attention to Charsky's dandy outfit than to the improvisor's gaudy costume. Each testifies to the increasingly marginal, self-conscious position of the artist in "society."

Pushkin did not finish the story, but his review of Voltaire's correspondence (1836) suggests a possible conclusion. Pushkin, reflecting on Voltaire's humiliating life at the court of Frederick the Great, resolves: "The writer's real place is in his study and, ultimately, only independence and self-esteem can lift us above the trifles of life and the storms of fate" (XII, 81). Yet even this conclusion—itself ironic within the review—would be insufficiently bleak for the story; for Charsky's social role so overwhelms him that he purges the books from his library, lest his social acquaintances think him too much a writer.

The historical awareness and keen sense of class antagonism which characterize some of Pushkin's final works and final thoughts on the writer's social position do little, however, to illuminate *Eugene Onegin*. The subtitle of the novel ("a novel in verse") and its dedicatory piece (addressed to Pushkin's friend and publisher, Pletnev) proclaim the author's intention to fuse the widely disparate resources at his command.[2] As a free and audacious blending, reworking, and violation of literary conventions, the form of the novel is thus analogous to Pushkin's desired fusion of the various social images of the writer that the ideology and institutions of his time offered him: the Russian gentleman amateur, the professional European man of letters, the inspired and autonomous poet of the Romantic movement. In this chapter I will argue that a similar attitude toward convention, choice, and autonomy informs the ontological levels of the novel—the level on which the characters act and the level on which the self-conscious author-narrator makes them act for a distant reader. To this end, I will discuss these levels closely, examining the range of possiblities for human action that the novel presents, and analyze the choices that the author-narrator and characters make within this range.

Two Realities or One?

Maintenant je n'écris pas de romans—j'en fais.
From a letter by Lermontov to A. M. Vereschagina,
spring 1835

Pushkin's "Journey to Arzrum during the Campaign of 1829" (written 1829–1835) offers an excellent point of departure for discussing his consideration of autonomy in life and art. At the outset of his journey, after denying his personal reliance upon the patronage of the authorities, Pushkin underscores his independence by making his first visit to General Ermolov, who had fallen under suspicion for his ties to the Decembrist uprising. Pushkin immediately touches upon another sort of dependence, art's reliance upon convention, as he describes Ermolov:

> At first glance, I found not the slightest resemblance to his portraits, which were usually drawn in profile. A round face, fiery grey eyes, grey hair standing on end. The head of a tiger on a Herculean torso. His smile is unpleasant because it is unnatural. But when he grows thoughtful and frowns, he becomes handsome and strikingly reminiscent of the poetic portrait, drawn by Dawe. (VIII, 455)

Pushkin's first impression makes the hardly novel point that art and reality differ; the convention of drawing portraits in profile merely increases the distance between them. But as Pushkin looks more closely at Ermolov, his irony turns to the delusion that we can communicate our perceptions without recourse to conventions, not merely linguistic ones, but those of our culture as a whole: art, literature, social behavior. But to place Ermolov before the reader, the narrator finds that he must become more conventional, not less. His figures become as hoary as his subject's head—an animal metaphor as venerable as mythology itself, a reminiscence from classical mythology, a facial expression (fiery eyes) from the lexicon of romantic demonism that Pushkin had by this time so often parodied. The last two sentences of the passage strike a similar balance, this time adding the problem of the beautiful to that of the real. One conventionally significant social gesture (a smile) is rejected because it is forced and unnatural; but another (the thoughtful frown), no less conventional, pleases the narrator. As the perceived object (Ermolov) assumes his final pose, he suggests that life, art, nature, and beauty *can* coincide, if only the participants in the creative act—the writer, his subject, the reader—have sufficient command of the conventions that their culture provides. The oxymoron, "poetic portrait," combines two different types of artifice to underscore this possibility. Conventions— the necessary instruments of art and perception—can imprison the artist (portraits in profile), serve as probes for investigating reality (the narrator), or join beauty and truth (Dawe). As Pushkin's travel account progresses, he continues to use and test the conventions of his culture. The freedom from domination by any one of them, the genre of the romantic travelogue for example, serves as an analogue for his asserted freedom on the social plane to accept or decline his patronage of the powerful. And yet he remains within the purview of conventions, just as he will never escape the expanding borders of the Russian empire on his journey.[3]

From its generically provocative subtitle to its concluding metaphor ("life's novel"), *Eugene Onegin* raises similar problems: the relationship between art and life, the limits imposed upon social action and artistic expression by a culture's grammar of conventions. Life and literature intersect at every turn, they are not merely analogous to each other. The author-narrator disconcertingly steps into his fictional world to befriend Eugene. The narrator's muse shades into the novel's heroine, Tatiana. She, Eugene, and Lensky (a poet of sorts) try to act out the patterns of the literature which they read in their daily lives— they become what they read, to alter Feuerbach's formula, not merely what they eat. Both Eugene (a dandy) and Tatiana (the hostess of a salon) play roles which unite the social and the aesthetic. And, as the reader tries to focus on this fictional world, the narrator discusses his own craft and its reception so frequently that he generates what Leon Stilman has called the "second reality" of *Eugene Onegin*, the "reality of the creative process."[4]

Pushkin's oscillation between these two realities has created among his critics a situation analogous to the problem of ambiguity in the psychology of visual perception. It has been posited that we cannot simultaneously hold two interpretations of an ambiguous picture— for example, an interpretaton which is conscious of the artist's formal materials (shapes, colors and the like) and one which accepts his illusion of reality.[5] Such has certainly been the case with critical studies of *Eugene Onegin*, which tend either to concetrate on the represented world of the characters as a reflection of Pushkin's social milieu[6] or else to focus on the novel's constructive (formal) aspects.[7] Taken to extremes each reading, the mimetic and the formalistic, seriously reduces the range of Pushkin's genius—his artful manipulation of styles and devices on one hand, and, on the other, his ability to lend such striking verisimilitude to characters and their situations in a few swift lines, producing individuals who became literary stereotypes for the rest of his century. Meanwhile, *Eugene Onegin*—twirling its two realities in a kaleidoscope of narrative viewpoints, parodies, literary reminiscences, and generic fragments—forces any monistic reading to run aground on its ontological complexity.[8]

This complexity suggests that even more readings of the novel are possible—and necessary—than the many useful ones which Pushkin scholarship has already given us. Especially necessary are approaches that will relate the novel's formal and socially mimetic structures, its fiction-making and fictional levels, granting each its brilliance and regarding neither as a mere pretext for the other. Pushkin's perception of Ermolov suggests one basis for such a plural reading: the idea of culture, with its related social, intellectual, and aesthetic aspects. Important areas of early nineteenth-century Russian culture—literature (written/oral, gentry/folk, Russian/Western, traditional/fashionable) and social customs (urban/rural, Moscow/Petersburg, gentry/folk)— present the characters of *Eugene Onegin*, including the author-narrator, with sets of precedents for their actions, social or literary.[9] Sometimes the patterns can be reconciled; sometimes they clash. At times a pattern may be successfully transferred from one area of culture (fiction) to another (social activity), at other times the attempt is foolish. How the characters command these conventions defines them, establishes the contrasts that shape *Eugene Onegin*, and, in turn, constitutes the novel's response to the ideological and institutional problems of its time.

The Range of Culture in Eugene Onegin

> The body of intellectual and imaginative work which each generation receives as its traditional culture is always, and necessarily, something more than the product of a single class . . . A culture can never be reduced to its artifacts while it is being lived . . . A culture is not only a body of intellectual and imaginative work; it is also and necessarily a whole way of life.
>
> Raymond Williams, *Culture and Society*

For Pushkin's most prominent twentieth-century social critics, Blagoi and Gukovsky, an individual's possibilities within a culture are narrowly determined by his class and historical position. *Eugene Onegin*, however, invites the reader to consider whether an individual can assimilate the achievements of more than one social class or historical period and can view them not as the artifacts of a bygone age or remote social class, but as models with some analogous relationship to his own life. The possibilities within one historical period or class situation will, of course, differ from those of other periods and social classes, but the range of conventions, codes, and social patterns within a plural European culture is likely to be a broad one. Georg Lukács speculates that Pushkin can depict the events of his novel with lightness and deftness because they arise from the structure of society and are socially determined; individual pathology, on the other hand, would require detailed analysis.[10] Yet Pushkin does analyze Eugene's approach to the duel and Tatiana's infatuation with Eugene in some detail, although neither character is demonstrably "pathological." Pushkin's analysis is necessary because his culture presents the author-narrator and his characters with many possible definitions of a situation, definitions arising from a variety of class and national sources.

Such hypotheses about culture come easily—perhaps too easily— to a member of a modern academic community, who is likely to compress entire historical periods and national cultures into a day's reading and lecturing. Yet they would find support in the sense of openness and cultural plenitude that early nineteenth-century Russian polite society claimed for itself and in the period's definition of the *honnête homme* as a person of general culture and varied interests. Nevertheless, it remains for me to show, before I discuss *Eugene Onegin* in terms of its characters' choices within their broad cultural framework, that such a framework is established in the novel and that it circumscribes the lives of its characters.

The extent to which Pushkin's characters are creatures of culture, not nature, is readily ascertained by briefly comparing them with the characters of other authors whom Pushkin mentions in *Eugene Onegin*. Because many readers, prompted by Pushkin's use of nature imagery (moons and deer, à la Chateaubriand), associate Tatiana with the state of nature, she provides an excellent starting point.[11] She may love "artlessly" (3:24) with her entire being, not from the flirtatious calculation of high society, but the inspiration for that love is provided by a combination of social (the gossip of neighbors), literary (the influence of epistolary novels), and socially significant natural elements ("The time had come, she fell in love," 3:7). In this combination of natural urges, susceptibility to literary models, and social being, she unites the areas of human existence which Byron assigns, broadly speaking, to three separate women in *Don Juan:* Haidee, the child of nature; Aurora Raby, "who looked more on books than faces" (15.85); and (as Tatiana's social hypostasis matures) Lady Adeline, the perfect hostess.

A second comparison which *Eugene Onegin* invites, Pushkin's Tatiana with Rousseau's Julie, suggests that Pushkin has done considerably more to place his heroine in a persistently cultural setting, most obviously by making Tatiana's French love-letter to Eugene the result of exposure to Rousseau's *Julie, ou la nouvelle Héloise*.[12] Tatiana is altogether more of a reader than Julie and much more of a participant, if not always willingly, in society. The Switzerland of the Wolmars approximates the state of nature—lakes, mountains, Julie's wild garden. Tatiana's Russian "nature" is a cultivated estate, the winter she loves is closely associated with the rituals and tales of the folk, her solitary walks (book in hand!) take her toward new social encounters and literary awareness. When she contemplates nature, it is from her balcony or through the windows of her family home, with its customs, books, and social obligations, at times inspiring, at times constricting.

It is even easier to use such comparisons to show the extent to which Pushkin inserts cultural mediation between his other characters and nature. The hapless poet Lensky only has eyes for the inevitable graveyards of elegiac verse; he learned no *Naturphilosophie* during his stay in Germany. Likewise Eugene lacks even the occasional feeling

for nature of Childe Harold, to whom the narrator suggestively, par-
odistically, compares him. Childe Harold, satiated by social pleasures,
can turn to direct communion with nature:

> Where rose the mountains, there to him were friends;
> Where roll'd the ocean, thereon was his home;
> Where a blue sky, and glowing clime, extends,
> He had the passion and the power to roam;
> The desert, forest, cavern, breaker's foam,
> Were unto him companionship; they spake
> A mutual language, clearer than the tome
> Of his land's tongue, which he would oft forsake
> For Nature's pages glass'd by sunbeams on the lake.   (3.13)

But books and language in Pushkin's fictional world are man-made.
When Eugene leaves society and ventures into nature, he has a literary
precedent:

> Eugene lived in a hermit's heaven:
> In summer he arose at seven
> And lightly sauntered to a rill
> That washed the bottom of the hill;
> In tribute to Gülnare's singer
> He swam his Hellespontus too . . .   (4:37)

Winter comes, but Onegin dutifully follows his Byronic script:

> Childe Harold-like, Eugene subsided
> Into a state of pensive sloth.   (4:44)

By reducing the vast dimensions of Byron's romantic settings, meanwhile, to those of a country estate, Pushkin places further emphasis
on the culturally circumscribed life of his hero.

The narrator's powers of perception and expression by far surpass
those of the other characters in *Eugene Onegin*, and he comes closer
than they do to achieving a direct experience of nature—in the famous
stanza on the coming of winter, for example (4:40). But even here, in
one of his most starkly "objective" and unconventionally "prosaic"
passages, he will not escape the pressures of his culture. Through
metaphor he remains part of the human world, with its aesthetic and
social patterns: "But our Northern summer is a *caricature* of Southern
winters"; "a clamorous *caravan* of geese" [my italics]. Pushkin's natural setting is ultimately inseparable from human work (farmers,
herdsmen; a maiden at her spinning wheel) and, simultaneously,
from the creative work which a poet must perform in communicating
perceptions to an audience with its aesthetic and social expectations.

Thus the poet faces a conflict of rhyme and decorum in describing the girl: *deva* ("maiden," a poetic form) fits the demands of his rhyme, but *devka* ("wench") would lend it greater social verisimilitude. The poet chooses the former, and, in a footnote, records the displeasure of his critics (VI, 193).

Reminded by his critics that he not only creates worlds but lives in a world which views the created one as an analogue of its own, the narrator resumes his description. His dual awareness, of both the natural setting and the cultural position of his readers, choreographs an intricate pas de deux with his audience (stanza 42) that involves the social nature of perception and communication. In the first four lines he repays his readers for their objection to his diction by calling attention to the dreary predictability of their expectations; winter's frosts *(morozy)* inevitably evoke roses *(rozy)* for the dead metaphor "rosy-cheeked":

> At last a crackling frost enfolded
> Fields silvered o'er with early snows:
> (All right—who am I to withold it,
> The rhyme you knew was coming—rose).   (4:42)[13]

At the same time the irony falls upon the narrator as well—in making fun of the reader's expectations, he had not, after all, surpassed him very far in originality. But in the next two lines the poet's dual awareness serves to render the winter scene in all of its brilliance:

> The ice-clad river's polished luster
> No stylish ballroom floor can muster . . .

Instead of attempting a plain description, the poet has drawn on the reader's experience of a cultural setting, one which unites social patterns and the arts of dance and music, to communicate his perception of nature's beauty. The gaiety of the ballroom provides a point of comparison and departure for the remaining lines of the stanza as the sound of skates cutting the ice replaces the music, and the whirling snow, playing boys, and a clumsy goose replace the dancers.

> A joyous swarm of urchins grates
> The frozen sheet with ringing skates.
> A cumbrous goose on ruddy paddles
> Comes waddling down the bank to swim,
> Steps gingerly across the rim,
> Slithers and falls; in swirling eddies
> Descends the virgin snow and pranks
> And showers stars upon the banks.

Again the poet has violated decorum, and another footnote records a critic's apparent objection to the joining of a subliterary subject (skating urchins) and a periphrastic, literary style *(mal'chishek radostnyi narod)*, as Pushkin has creatively conveyed the merry confusion of the scene with an unconventional blend of literary and social conventions. But even for this sort of scene, which some of Pushkin's contemporaries found most original,[14] Pushkin will eventually indicate a cultural precedent: "the motley rubbish of the Flemish School" (VI, 201). In short, Pushkin cannot divorce a natural setting from the humans who work and play in it (on the representational and expressive planes of the novel); and so in the process of conveying his perceptions, the author-narrator finds that nature is best rendered by confronting, not avoiding, the culturally conditioned aspects of perception—social hierarchy, aesthetic codes, life and literary experience. Byron showed his Childe Harold reading the pages of nature; Pushkin ironically shows himself, a poet in need of an audience, reading his own pages to nature (4:35).

As the novel unfolds, all of the characters—urban and rural, gentry and folk—take their places within a cultural framework that includes both social and artistic patterns. Literature, music, dance, and play are as inseparable from the lives of serfs as they are from the gentry way of life. Pushkin's servant girls are inevitably singing (3:39–40, 4:41). Although few critics would mistake *Eugene Onegin* for an abolitionist tract, it does not conceal the harshness of social inequality. The berry-picking girls are forced to sing so that they will not be able to consume the fruit. But the conditions of their work do not restrain the frolic charm of their "private song," which the narrator allows to be theirs, not their masters'. Its unashamedly playful attitude toward the battle of the sexes stands in refreshing contast to the other culturally conditioned attitudes which frame it—Tatiana's abstract and lachrymose sentimentality, the stultifying cynicism of Eugene and the narrator, the nurse's quiet resignation.[15] As so often in Pushkin, culture's ludic facets ameliorate the harshness of social and economic patterns, making them bearable or even transforming them, as we shall see in Tatiana's case.[16]

Culture, not the property of any single class in *Eugene Onegin*, is also syncretic, and not the autochthonous product of any class or national group. The novel presents culture as a sum of patterns of various times and places, superimposed one upon the other in the lives of his characters. This is clear enough for its cosmopolitan gentry, less so for the few serfs who appear in the novel. But their very names testify to the "foreign" component in their culture. As Pushkin reminds us in a footnote, "the most euphonious Greek names . . . are used among us only by the simple people" (VI, 192). By giving his heroine Tatiana a name that was more popular among the folk than among the gentry, yet was taken from the Greek calendar of saints' days, Pushkin simultaneously tapped a source of beauty outside the narrow limits of sentimentalist diction, underscored the folk component in her cultural background, and suggested the breadth and inclusiveness of even the most "primitive" representatives of Russian culture, the peasantry.[17]

This syncretic culture, manifest even in the circumscribed lives of the serfs, overarches *Eugene Onegin*, from the dedicatory piece, which promises chapters both "plain-folk and ideal" (*ideal'nyi*, a foreign loan word in Russian) to the final parts, in which Pushkin allows his heroine both the aristocratic manner of the Europeanized gentry and an enduring fascination with folklore. Seeming to argue against this syncretism is the emphasis which the narrator places on the upbringing of his hero and heroine: Eugene is educated by "Madame" and "Monsieur l'Abbé" (1:3); Tatiana voraciously absorbs the horror stories and superstitions of her peasant nurse (2:27, 5:5–10). This has, predictably enough, led the novel's socially aware critics to view Eugene and Tatiana as representatives, respectively, of the capital's deracinated aristocracy and of the countryside's backward, traditional gentry which was outside the bounds of polite society. This is true in relative terms only. For dissolved in the innermost being of each, as it is depicted in dreams and in the most intense emotional outpourings, are other elements of the novel's syncretic cultural matrix. Tatiana's soul may be "Russian" (5:4), but she expresses its longings to Eugene in French, to the narrator's mock dismay (3:26). Her actions, not merely at the beginning but throughout the novel, are guided by literary models.

Tatiana's dream shows most completely the range of her cultural resources, and, as such, it has been the subject of some controversy among Pushkin's commentators. A few argue that the dream is entirely folkloric in origin, or at least mostly so.[18] Others have looked to Murillo (Pushkin had a copy of that painter's "Temptation of St. Anthony" at his Mikhailovskoe estate), Nodier's Jean Sbogar, Mme de Staël's plot summaries, comic operas, chapbooks, Khemnitser's fables, the playful rituals of the Arzamas society, Zhukovsky's ballad "Svetlana," and Griboedov's *Woe from Wit*.[19] One can but admire these displays of erudition, but at the same time notice that for once it may be more critically fruitful to disregard for a moment the creative reality of the author-narrator and look to his fictional world and to the cultural forces which press upon Tatiana herself—her foreign epistolary novels as well as her nurse's horror stories and songs. The narrator himself encourages us to do this throughout the dream (5:11–21) by refraining from his frequent comments on literature as a creative process and by merging his voice as closely as the intricate *Onegin* stanza permits with the voice of Tatiana's subconscious mind.

In this chaotic world Tatiana blends the images and patterns of her sentimental readings, her folk heritage, and her social situation as the novel has established them in previous chapters. For example, Tatiana's dream features a folkloric bear, an inevitable mummer's costume in holiday festivities, but her mind's eye views that bear through the mediation of her gentry background and dresses it up as a "shaggy footman"; hierarchy is thus established, and the dread object is momentarily transformed by a mollifying periphrastic construction, typical of the sentimentalist manner. The dream itself—as a repository for fears, forbidden desires, punishment fantasies, and premonitions—was an integral part of both the epistolary novel and of some Russian wedding songs. Tatiana's dream, with its dangerous journey and arrival at a terrifying house, echoes the plot of the ritual laments which a Russian bride delivers as part of her preparation for the wedding ceremony.[20] But when Tatiana's imagination places Eugene in that folkloric house, it does so with help from her epistolary novels. The narrator has already described the process by which literary patterns have overwhelmed her:

> With what unwonted fascination
> She now devours *romans d'amour*,
> With what a rapturous elation
> Yields to their treacherous allure!
> Creative fancy's vivid creatures
> Lend their imaginary features—
> He who adored Julie Wolmar,
> Malek-Adhel and de Linar,
> Young Werther, by his passion rended
> And Grandison, the demigod
> Who causes you and me to nod—
> Our tender dreamer saw them blended
> Into a single essence warm,
> Embodied in Onegin's form.
>
> Her fancy-fed imagination
> Casts her in turn as heroine

Of every favorite creation,
Julie, Clarissa, or Delphine.   (3:9–10)

And her reading of Rousseau's *Julie* has dictated her letter to Eugene.
But readers who share the fashionable contempt for epistolary novels
which Pushkin records in the line, "Moral' na nas navodit son" ("Moralizing puts us to sleep," 3:11), will miss the pun in that famous line
on *son* (sleep/dream).[21] The didactic patterns of the epistolary novel
offer not only sleep to insomniacs, they can also inspire dreams and
nightmares, and this is what happens to Tatiana two chapters later.
In its images of violence, strife, and degradation, Tatiana's dream
bears remarkable similarity to one of Clarissa's:

> "Methought my brother, my Uncle Antony, and Mr. Solmes had formed
> a plot to destroy Mr. Lovelace; who discovering it, and believing I had
> a hand in it, turned all his rage against me. I thought he made them all
> fly into foreign parts upon it; and afterwards seizing upon me, carried
> me into a churchyard; there, notwithstanding all my prayers and tears,
> and protestations of innocence, stabbed me to the heart, and then
> tumbled me into a deep grave ready dug, among two or three half-
> dissolved carcasses; throwing in the dirt and earth upon me with his
> hands, and trampling it down with his feet."
>
> I awoke in a cold sweat, trembling, and in agonies; and still the frightful
> images raised by it remain in my memory.[22]

And it is not surprising that Tatiana's dream imagination finds less
in common with a peasant bride at this moment than with a young
woman who, like herself, seeks refuge from an unhappy family situation by placing herself at the mercy of a potential seducer, whom
she regards with a mixture of emotions, including fear and curiosity
(5:18). Each heroine, preparing to violate taboos, is warned by her
subconscious, which blends images of death and vileness with the
desires that her waking mind does not so boldly admit.

But just as the folk pattern, which guided the first part of the dream,
fades into the background, so does Clarissa's terrifying precedent,
affecting and didactically effective as it may be. For Tatiana's position
does not precisely coincide with Clarissa's. Clarissa is caught between
Lovelace, the dangerous outsider, and Solmes, the repulsive "mons-
ter" whom her family has chosen for her;[23] Tatiana's family has, however, welcomed Onegin as a suitor. Thus Tatiana breaks with custom
not in choosing the wrong object for her infatuation and defying her
parents, but in choosing an unconventional, and potentially compromising, way of approaching him. Another important difference is that
Clarissa's feelings toward Lovelace are hopelessly complex, but Ta-

tiana is unashamedly in love with Eugene. And so it is appropriate that the final developments of Tatiana's dream break the patterns of Clarissa's: Onegin takes Tatiana away from the monsters, he is not one of them. His murderous wrath turns not toward Tatiana, but toward those who interrupt her tender scene with him, who are (a wish fulfilled) among the very people whose company Tatiana shuns in her waking life. As Eugene lays Tatiana down on his bench, her dream vision remakes him in the mold of the passionate Werther, who has dreamed of Charlotte in a similarly erotic position:

> In vain do I reach out my arms toward her in the morning, when I awake from troubled dreams; vainly do I seek her at night in my bed, when a happy, innocent dream has deceived me, as if I had been sitting beside her in the meadow and had held her hand and had covered it with a thousand kisses. Ah! Then when I grope about for her in the half delirium of sleep and awaken, a flood of tears breaks from my oppressed heart, and I weep disconsolately over my gloomy future.[24]

But this moment in the dream cannot last, sustained as it must be by the murder and illicit desire which Tatiana's imagination borrows from Clarissa's dream. As Eugene murders Lensky the folkloric house in the forest reels and disappears, together with its novelistic hero and the representatives of Tatiana's depressing family and neighbors. The English epistolary novel (2:29), the book for interpreting dreams (5:23), and the mirror for folkloric fortune-telling (5:10) which crowd Tatiana's bed give no ready answer to her fears and desires. They are, rather, emblematic of the cultural elements from which, as she matures, she will assemble and make sense of her life.

In this Tatiana is not unique among the novel's cast of characters. Eugene, too, must structure his life with a mixture of literary, folkloric, and social materials, as we see at the end of the novel, when his dream imagination boils a brew similar to Tatiana's:

> To what end? While the letters tumbled
> Across his sight beyond control,
> Desires, dreams, regrets were jumbled
> In dense profusion in his soul.
> Between the lines of printing hidden,
> To his mind's eye there rise unbidden
> Quite other lines, and it is these
> That in his trance alone he sees.
> They were dear tales and droll convictions
> Alive among us as of old,
> Weird, disconnected dreams untold,
> And threats and axioms and predictions,

A spun-out fable's whimsy purl,
Of letters from a fresh young girl.

And while a drowsy stupor muffles
All thought and feeling unawares,
Imagination deals and shuffles
Its rapid motley solitaires.
He sees on melting snow-sheet dozing
A lad, quite still, as if reposing
Asleep upon a hostel bed,
And someone says: "That's that—he's dead . . ."
He sees old enemies forgotten,
Detractors two-faced and afraid,
A swarm of beauties who betrayed,
A circle of companions rotten,
A rustic house—and who would be
Framed in the window? . . . Who but She!   (8:36–37)

The printed page, a girl's letter, folklore, love, friendship—balanced by guilt, unfulfilled desire, foreboding, obsession, violence, deception, and socially sanctioned murder—this is the stuff of culture in *Eugene Onegin*. Pushkin allows his characters no lasting refuge from it in the favorite retreats of the romantic imagination: nature, dream, and primitive society. Creativity, beauty, intelligence, truth, and emotional authenticity—all that is valued in this novel—must be won within the broadly defined limits of culture.

Creative Conventionality

Pushkin loved to test himself in skirmishes with restrictions.
Lidiia Ginzburg, *O lirike*

The mind is as inexhaustible in its grasp of concepts as language is inexhaustible in its joining of words. All words may be found in the dictionary, but the books which are continually appearing are not mere repetitions of the dictionary.
Pushkin, 1836

In cataloguing the multifarious elements of culture in *Eugene Onegin*, I have been treating the individual's relationship to that culture as a passive one. But this is largely because my examples so far have displayed the characters in their least controlled moments—in love, in delirium, in dreams—when the text has allowed elements of their national past, social situation, or cosmopolitan literary experience that they have ignored in their conscious lives to assert themselves. The cultural framework which the novel constructs is the instrument of a determinism, to be sure, but a very special one. By establishing its limits and suggesting determinisms which the novel does not engage, one may at the same time understand the possibilities for autonomy within its fictional world.

The deterministic power of this world is perhaps best discussed by examining *Eugene Onegin* as a historical novel,[25] a genre which Pushkin himself perfected in prose in the elegant symmetries of *The Captain's Daughter* (1836). In *Eugene Onegin,* as it stands, the shaping force of history manifests itself in the characters' lives not in the guise of a rapacious Cossack horde, seeking vengeance for generations of social, economic, and cultural oppression—but as change in cultural possibilities and, most importantly, as "fashion," the power so important in setting the boundaries of polite society. Fashion raises Eugene (1:23), seems to exhaust his lexicon (7:24), builds Tatiana's Petersburg home (8:46), and curls her hair, literally and figuratively (7:46). Lensky professes to hate the fashionable world, yet his poetry is nothing more than fashionable, with all the negative connotations of automation and superficiality that the word bears. The narrator himself, the most conscious character in the novel, flees the fashionable Byronism. Yet for all its ability to pervade the corners of human life, the "whirlwind of fashion" (4:21) does lack the iron finality of a Cossack noose or the long-accumulating force of social and economic oppression. The violation of conventions and customs, as Max Weber has noted, may involve psychological pressure and inconvenience—but these are, in most cases, less terrifying than execution, imprisonment, and exile.[26] Tatiana will learn to ignore fashion and will later dictate it. The author-narrator can boldly reject it, or, better still, lend it a profundity which it lacks in common currency: the word "ideal," which is merely "fashionable" in Lensky's verse (6:23) becomes infused with significance in the author-narrator's farewells (8:50–51). It is not surprising, because of his competitive attitude toward fashion, that the author-narrator inevitably colors the word with a certain contempt.

The concept of historical distance—antiquity, olden times *(starina)*—receives similar treatment. Just as "fashion" can be overcome, so can "olden times" in literature and social custom be preserved and renewed. Indeed the noun and the adjective derived from it are inevitably used for the past which survives—in folklore (3:17), social customs (3:35), architecture (2:2), Eugene's subconscious mind (8:36), and in the poet's conversations with his muse (8:1). What fashion abandons, the imagination can recover for its own purposes. Richardson's novels were once so popular that Tatiana's mother did not have to read them to feel their influence; now Tatiana must pore over them, but they still retain their power to impose their patterns upon the behavior of a willing reader.[27] And disparate historical periods impinge not only upon the imaginative mind; the narrator insists that Eugene's boredom ovewhelms him amid both fashionable and ancient halls (2:2). In this way, although ironically for the moment, two modes of conventionality, "fashion" and "olden times," are set up as an opposition that can be overcome.

The ability of the novel's characters, including the author-narrator, to appropriate the cultural achievements of historically distinct situations stands in marked contrast to the inability of the characters of Pushkin's conventionally historical works. These pieces, unlike *Eugene Onegin*, are based on unresoluable clashes: Counterreformation Poland versus medieval orthodox Muscovy *(Boris Godunov)*, the westward-looking supporters of Peter the Great versus the old nobility *(The Moor of Peter the Great)*, the Westernized gentry versus the Cossacks with their folk culture, which the gentry cannot comprehend *(The Captain's Daughter)*.

There is one sense, however, in which *Eugene Onegin* shares in the generic features of historical fiction: in Pushkin's use of historical personages (himself and, in cameo appearances, his friends Kaverin and Viazemsky, 1:16, 7:49). Such use of historical personages imposes a special responsibility upon a writer, as Herbert Lindenberger has noted: he or she must coordinate the depiction with the reader's "factual" knowledge of the personages' historical existence.[28] To give a rather obvious example of this sort of responsibility in historical fiction, Pushkin could let Pugachev shape the destinies of the fictional characters in *The Captain's Daughter*, he could make Pugachev an eloquent folk bard, but it is doubtful that Pushkin would have wanted to, or dared, let his fictional Pugachev succeed in overthrowing the empress.

And so Pushkin, as the primary historical personage in his own novel, establishes himself with biographical details familiar to his readers. And few of these relate to the historical, political, and economic causality of realistic fiction. The poet hints at his exile (1:2) and, it is generally thought, at the fate of his exiled and executed Decembrist friends (8:51). The position of these biographical elements, in the second and final stanzas of the novel, gives them special emphasis, but they are balanced, even at these points, by the poet's sense of himself as a maker—of the effervescent *Ruslan and Liudmila* (1:2) and of the "free novel" *Eugene Onegin* (8:50). Between these two bookends the author-narrator (the persona of a living, contemporary poet) can exercise considerable freedom in making his life, yet at the same time he observes his historical responsibility, for the importance of that life to his audience resides precisely in its creativity, which history has not yet terminated. Indeed, Pushkin uses his historicity to delimit for his characters a period in which sweeping events, such as the Napoleonic wars or the Decembrist uprising, did not intervene to prevent him from treating society in terms of conventions, rituals, festivals, and the aestheticization of polite society. And the class from which Pushkin takes his main characters, the gentry, was precisely the one which had the greatest access to the generous resources of Russian culture, with its folk and European heritage. This class situation, like the historical period, is more an invitation to relatively autonomous action than a deterministic barrier. Georg Lukács has very aptly conceded, in this regard, that "Pushkin knew it was no longer possible . . . to characterize a figure or integrate him into the plot simply by stating his position in society or his class."[29]

While the author-narrator presents himself as even less oppressed by the regime of Alexander I than by literary fashions, he seldom forgets that writing is a social act—reviewed by critics (1:60, footnotes), interrogated by the censor (1:60), and presented to an audience with its social patterns and expectations about the literary decorum which will accompany life into literary form. The urbane, cosmopolitan audience which the author-narrator envisions for his work (1:2, 3:22, 7:5, etc.) causes him little anxiety, and he treats it with the familiarity of a correspondent, occasionally singling out specific addresses from among his friends and fellow writers. But the presence of an audience (or reader) provides, together with conventional codes, a necessary component of any social act, and Pushkin incorporates it into both the fiction-making (author's) and fictional (characters') realities of his novel. The characters, like the poet, must reckon with their audience and reach that audience through, and only through, the conventions of their culture. As determining factors, these conventions are considerably more elusive than the historical, political, and economic constraints of literary realism or the laws of the organism, in which literary naturalism would later seek to enclose human existence, but in the few social situations which *Eugene Onegin* presents (the duel, the love quests of Tatiana and Eugene) conventions provide such tension, such problems of timing and understanding, that one may with little hesitation speak of it as a social novel.

Conventions assume many guises in *Eugene Onegin:* norms and rules; fashions, which bear arbitrary temporal limits of applicability; and customs, which have greater permanence. At times they are the property of different social groups. Conventions, basically, are repeated actions which enable members of a group (with or without having to think about it) to define situations, to predict the results of their actions, and to understand the actions of others by a process of decoding and anticipation. Conventions allow Eugene with his fashionable haircut, perfect French, and unforced manner of talking— scant information, indeed, but essential to the *honnête homme*—to be accepted in high society as "intelligent and very nice" (1:4). When, on the other hand, he refuses to meet with his rural neighbors, use the particles of their polite speech, and kiss their wives' hands, his behavior corresponds to none of their conventional expectations, and, in their anxiety, they imagine him an ignoramus, a madman, or a "Farmazon" (illiterate rendering of "Freemason," 2:5), since only these types would so ignore the conventions which hold society together. But merely by appearing at the home of an unmarried girl, he reintegrates himself into their conventional expectations and can be inserted, inaccurately it turns out, into the role of a suitor. Meanwhile, Tatiana, who also ignores social conventions, but whose understanding of life is shaped by literary ones, views this silent newcomer as a hero like those in her sentimentalist novels and acts upon this assumption.

Eugene Onegin presents no simple attitude toward conventions because there are so many ways of observing and not observing them, and because different ones (literary and social, for example) may have relevance to the same situation. One may observe conventions in a blindly childish fashion (Lensky, Tatiana initially), with resignation (the narrator giving us an expected rhyme), or with creative energy. Indeed, many of the most elegant passages in the novel, those expressing the poet's longing for Venice (1:48–49) and his love of pastoral pleasures (1:55), for example, echo familiar traditions of Western literature.

Disrespect for conventions in *Eugene Onegin* covers a similarly broad range of possibilities, from the creative mixing of genres (a novel in verse) to the fashionable and socially acceptable eccentricity of Eugene (an accomplished dandy) to insultingly casual disregard (Eugene's use of his valet as his second in the duel) to potentially dangerous violation (Tatiana's letter to Eugene).

Clearly these attitudes toward conventionality can be translated into understanding or action with varying degrees of success, depending on the knowledge and intelligence of the characters, author, and reader who use them. In a letter that I have already quoted in describing the ideology of polite society, Pushkin reminded Griboedov that "the first sign of an intelligent man is to know at first glance with whom he is dealing" (XIII, 138), and, this novel sugests, not only with whom but in terms of which cultural code, fashionable or traditional, literary or social. Lest this seem trivial or easy, Pushkin illustrates the difficulties by showing how Petersburg society tries to define the Eugene who returns after a long absence. What is the significance of Eugene's mysterious silence (8:7–8)? Which "mask" is he sporting? Is it literary (Melmoth, Childe Harold, Byron's spleen and suffering arrogance), social (a bigot, an eccentric, a good fellow), or one drawn from the wardrobe closet of sectarian fashion (a cosmopolitan, a patriot, a Quaker)? The narrator's "Do you know him?— Yes and no" provides little help. The next stanza (8:9), in which we might expect some elucidation of that remark, distances Eugene even further by intoducing romantic traits that may have even less applicability—a "fiery soul," a "mind which loves room." The narrator's subsequent accusation simultaneously addresses both the reader and the people at the social assembly. Yet the narrator himself, behind his blustering rhetoric, comes no closer to an understanding. Indeed, the roles of the narrator, created characters, and Pushkin's inscribed reader merge as they measure Eugene with their culture's many conventional definitions.[30] For here, as elsewhere in *Eugene Onegin*, the text conveys an illusion of the characters' reality not directly, with Tolstoyan analysis, but indirectly, by emphasizing the elusiveness of character and our conflicting, inadequate methods of defining it. Indeed, in all three novels that are the subject of this study, the hero's social self, the *honnête homme* or the dandy constituted by the ideology of polite society, is bereft of its solidity and presented as an enigma.

Perhaps the conventions which *Eugene Onegin* most persistently offers for examination are those which relate literary and social facets of culture. Here, consequently, one encounters central aesthetic problems of Pushkin's time: the nature and responsibilty of literature. Should literature as an institution use language in a *referential* fashion—representing reality according to some standard of verisimilude? Or *emotive*—expressing the poet's feelings and attitudes? Or *conative*—supplicating and exhorting the reader, issuing moral imperatives?[31] Among Pushkin's contemporary readers and critics one finds reproaches on all of these grounds: *Eugene Onegin* has represented reality in an improper or insufficient manner (Nadezhdin, Raich, Baratynsky, Bulgarin); *Eugene Onegin* devotes too much space to the author-narrator or has too much borrowed material, the tone is By-ron's, not Pushkin's (Nadezhdin, Baratynsky, Raich, Bulgarin); *Eugene Onegin* lacks moral seriousness (Raich, Nadezhdin).[32] Or, finally, could literature be language in its *aesthetic* function, language which calls attention to itself as an aesthetic object divorced from instrumental functions? Perhaps the tersest expression of this formalistic attitude in Western literature was issued by Pushkin himself in a polemical note to Zhukovsky: "The goal of poetry is poetry" (XIII, 167; April 1825).

These four conventional attitudes toward the relationship of literature and reality were, of course, represented in various admixtures in the literary movements of Pushkin's time, and by embodying them in his characters he was able to play not only with the literary devices of these movements, but with their critical orientations as well. His own comment to Zhukovsky is no less an object of the novel's irony than the other attitudes, for the only unalloyed formal view of literature is provided by Tatiana's father, who neither cares nor knows anything about literature:

> Her honest father, though old-fashioned,
> Last century's child, grew not impassioned
> About the harm that books might breed;
> He, who was never known to read,
> Regarded them as empty thrillers
> And never thought to bring to light
> Which secret volume dreamt at night
> Beneath his little daughter's pillows.   (2:29)?[33]

Meanwhile, of course, his daughter is about to mistake the didactic imperatives of her moralizing novels by offering herself—in epistolary form, naturally—to Eugene, whom she mistakes for a hero à la Richardson and Rousseau:

> With rapturous delight she savored
> Rousseau's and Richardson's deceits.   (2:29)

The irony of this is that the imperatives which one extracts from a work need not be those that the author may have intended to project—a particularly pertinent point in connection with these two authors, whose imagination lent more fascination to vice than to their rather dreary pictures of virtue. Pushkin emphasizes this by making the didactic epistolary novels more seductive than the lurid gothic thrillers that replaced them on fashion's reading table.

The plot of the novel follows Tatiana's maturation in terms of her use of literature. Here, at the first stage of her development, she unconsciously takes it to be the direct representation of reality, a direct command to act, and the direct expression of her self. Childishly, inappropriately, she locates its stereotypes in her life, acting and speaking through them. In her dreams, as we have discussed, the darker side of the epistolary novel manifests itself as a nightmare. Tatiana's total immersion in her culture makes the world a forest of symbols to her:

> And any object could impress her
> With some occult significance.   (5:5)[34]

But, unconscious of herself as a cultural being and trapped with a limited arsenal of conventions, she lacks the key to decode these symbols.

Gradually, however, she learns to distinguish a variety of conventional relationships between literature and reality. The patterns of her reading might suggest ways of understanding the world and even controlling it. The narrator now speculates that had she known of Eugene's impending duel with Lensky, she would have stopped it (5:18). Why? It was a convention of the epistolary novel (*Clarissa, Sir Charles Grandison, Julie*) for the heroine to oppose duelling. In this case the moral imperative of the epistolary novel would not have been a "deceit" (3:9, 3:29) but a sure guide to action. Here, as elsewhere in *Eugene Onegin*, literary patterns, no matter how old-fashioned, are not necessarily distorting or misleading.

The culmination of this development comes when Tatiana visits Eugene's study and reads not only his books, but his reading of them, in his fingernail impressions and penciled words, crosses, and question marks. She finds her own attitude toward literature (guide to action, representation of reality, expression of the self) in Eugene and is supported in this by comparing his reading with his behavior toward her. The questions which pass through her mind are suggested by his reading of Byron and of the two or three novels which he has exempted from his general disinterest in literature and which depict "rather accurately the age and contemporary man":[35]

> And step by step my Tanya, learning
> His mind, at last begins to see
> The man for whom she has been yearning
> By willful destiny's decree
> More clearly than in face and feature:
> A strangely bleak and restless creature,
> Issue of Heaven or Hell,
> Proud demon, angel—who can tell?

> Perhaps he is all imitation,
> An idle phantom or, poor joke,
> A Muscovite in Harold's cloak,
> An alien whim's interpretation,
> Compound of every faddish pose . . .?
> A parody, perhaps . . . who knows?   (7:24)

Here Tatiana understands from observing Eugene that life can be an embodiment of literary stereotypes, as she could not when she was unconsciously following them herself. Her new approach to the relationship of literature and life is a mature one, for she is now aware that such imitation is not a matter of mere reproduction, but can be distorted by parody or inappropriate in its context ("poor joke, a Muscovite in Harold's cloak").

The final step in Tatiana's cultural maturation occurs when she becomes the hostess of a Petersburg salon and, as a "legislatrix" (8:28) and "goddess" (8:27) imposes what her age considered an aesthetic order upon reality.[36] This role, it must be remembered, was the highest form of creativity open to a woman at this time; it gave her the chance to unite, if not "magic sounds, feelings, thoughts" (as the author-narrator defines his poetic aspirations, 1:59), then thoughts, feelings, and good conversation:

> The party talk is soon enlivened
> By the crude salt of worldly spite;
> But with this hostess it is light,
> Gay nonsense, free of priggish preening,
> Or grave at times, is never brought
> To fatuous themes or hallowed thought,
> But brims with undidactic meaning;
> And its high spirits and good sense
> Are powerless to give offense.   (8:23)

Lest we underestimate this achievement, almost equal in its emotional range to the novel as a whole, the narrator catalogues the materials from which Tatiana has crafted her harmonious assembly: fools, malicious-looking ladies, a faintly ludicrous and superannuated wit, a nasty epigrammatist, a caricatured social climber, and an unfashionably overstarched traveler (8:24–26).[37] She has taken the less than inspiring materials of her social situation and shaped them in brilliant fashion into one of the conventional forms of her culture. It is a creation at once aesthetically pleasing and, in its civility, morally effective. The author-narrator underscores the parallels between her creation and his by applying similar epithets to them—"unforced" and "free." And just as Pushkin realizes his freedom to play with literary conventions within one of the most intricate stanza forms in Russian poetry, Tatiana achieves her greatest level of creativity within the sphere of polite society, with all of its norms, patterns, limitations, and potentially corrupting fashions.

It is instructive, however, to study the drafts of these stanzas, which show two different approaches to the salon: the first more laudatory, the second more satiric than the final version, which places greater emphasis on Tatiana's role.[38] The excellence of Tatiana's salon now depends more on her talent and upon her audience's willingness to play their part than on the inherent qualities of this conventional social-literary form. The drafts' wavering in their evaluation of the salon clearly echoes the controversy over the "literary aristocracy" and, perhaps, their author's own uncertainty over his status as an author.

Nevertheless, the versatility with which both Pushkin and his "ideal," Tatiana, are able to select, discard, and order the materials of their culture draws them together. Tatiana, of course, cannot command the narrator's entire range of emotional shadings, especially irony, and her freedom is ultimately more a freedom of awareness than a freedom of action; but she, like the author-narrator, can both partic- ipate in her creation and critically distance herself from it, calling attention to its artificiality. She dismisses the social success which she has fabricated as readily as the author-narrator takes leave of his novel in the final stanzas. It seems initially that she has firmly entered her social role and has adopted the ways of her constricting rank (8:28), yet her awareness of the conventions, her other interests, and her other human capabilities (such as love, memory) give her the per- spectives necessary for personal integrity, critical evaluation, and creativity:[39]

> "To me, Onegin, this vain clamor,
> This tinsel realm appears inane,
> My triumphs here, the modish glamour
> In which I dwell and entertain,
> All void . . . I would be happy trading
> All this pretentious masquerading,
> This whirl of vapor, noise, and glaze,
> For my few books, my garden maze,
> For our country dwelling lowly,
> For those dear places that I knew
> When first, Onegin, I met you,
> And now, for that enclosure holy

> Where cross and swaying branches grace
> Poor Nanny's final resting place." (8:46)

In these and in the lines in which she dismisses Eugene, all of her cultural heritage and all of the ways in which she relates to that heritage merge. The books in which she sought to live join with the artifacts of pastoral retreat (garden, humble dwelling); her memories unite the graveyard of a sentimentalist poem with the nurse who taught her folklore. But literature is more than a consoling, entertaining object to Tatiana, it becomes the expression of her soul and values. Meanwhile, in Eugene's letter and behavior, to which I shall presently turn, she has read the destructive, confused desires of an Adolphe or Lovelace. Having used literature in this way to know Eugene, she turns to it again as a moral imperative:

> I love you still (yes—why deceive you?).
> But I was pledged another's wife,
> And will be faithful all my life. (8:47)

These lines, it has long been established, are adopted from a song found among the folk, thought in Pushkin's time to have been written by Peter I, and translated into French by Pushkin's uncle ("littérateur russe très-distingué," as the *Mercure de France* charitably put it). Tatiana could have read the song in M. D. Chulkov's collection of various songs, in A. S. Shishkov's collected works (1824), in an old issue of the *Mercure de France* (1803), or else heard it from her nurse.[40] As such it represents the wealth and syncretic nature of Russian culture and Tatiana's ability to draw upon that culture to create and understand her life.[41]

Tatiana in her movement toward mastering the conventions of her culture finds no equal in Eugene or Lensky, both of whom also try to impose aesthetic patterns upon social reality. Lensky begins where Tatiana does—naively viewing literary stereotypes as the equivalent of reality (2:6–10)—but, unlike her, he ends there. Tatiana at least has the sense to fantasize according to the conventions of a genre, the novel, which claims the everyday as its field of representation; Lensky ineptly tries to stage various romantic *tableaux vivants* in the Russian countryside: the medieval knight playing chess with his beloved (4:26), the poet fleeing the fashionable world (3:2), the German student bearing rebellious dreams (2:6), the poet's beloved visiting his premature grave. But the fictional world of *Eugene Onegin* will not respond to inept authorship, and everything his imagination touches becomes the stuff of parody: his friend prefers the viciousness of society to the delights of friendship and kills him in a fashionable duel; his beloved, despite the moralizing novels which he has bowdlerized for her (4:26), marries the first officer to come along; a shepherd, such as Lensky never imagined in his elegiac verse, plaits his bast shoe by the poet's grave, which is soon forgotten by his beloved anyway. In all of this there is no convention—of social behavior, of literature, or of the social appropriation of literature—which Lensky can use with any wit or intelligence.

Between Tatiana, whose creative use of conventions comes closest to the author's, and Lensky, whom the author-narrator will not permit to escape from the literary technique of parody, stands Onegin, whose mysteriousness lends him as much reality as is possible within the novel. The problems which the novel's characters face in creating their lives—timing, the pressure of fashion, conflicting conventions—weigh most heavily upon Eugene because unlike Lensky he has sufficient intelligence and maturity to face them, yet unlike Tatiana and the author-narrator he lacks the ability to solve them creatively.

Eugene begins, like the others, by shaping his life along a literary pattern: that of the dandy—cold, scornful, amorally destructive (as the novel's master epigraph suggests).[42] While his education has prepared him for this role, he plays it with a pedantic perfection that is his own—eating the right foods, wearing the right clothes, being seeen in the right places. His life is, on the social plane, analogous to a work of art understood as an end in itself, an object of aesthetic contemplation. The dandy glorifies form and, in Baudelaire's famous definition, dictates it. In this he is the male parallel to the hostess of a salon, such as Tatiana becomes in the final chapter. But while Tatiana's creation, the salon, issues a polite society's moral imperative (civility) to those who join it, Eugene's text, himself, unites the members of society into adulterous triangles, held together by Ovid's science of love, aristocratic fear of ridicule, and Eugene's mastery of at least thirty conventional disguises (1:10–2).[43]

The addition of outfits cut from literary patterns to Eugene's wardrobe closet (Byronic spleen, boredom) rescues him from his round of social activities only to enclose him within a narrower circle: himself. He cannot find alternatives to social boredom, as did Byron and the author-narrator, in writing or nature (1:43, 56). And he becomes the "contemporary man" of the few novels he reads:

> Where shown upon the current stage,
> Man moves with truth and animation:
> Unprincipled, perversely bent

Upon himself, his powers spent
In reverie and speculation,
With his exacerbated mind
In idle seething self-confined.   (7:22)

Eugene's Byronic redaction of dandyism, which makes his life an aesthetic object, finds an audience in the country which is unprepared to appreciate it or even to accept it, except for Tatiana and Lensky, who try to fit Eugene into their own aesthetic patterns. They in turn challenge Eugene with the two tests to which Russian nineteenth-century fiction, following Pushkin's lead, was to subject its protagonists: love and the duel. Tatiana, who might have seemed silly in declaring her love for Eugene after she had seen him only once, nevertheless touched him to the quick. She fit none of his conventional categories, just as he was a mystery to her. So just as she had done in similar circumstances, he tries to understand her and predict their relationship through his reading. He answers her "artless" love, expressed in the words of Rousseau's Julie, with an "artless' reply, drawn, as the reader subsequently learns to suspect in chapter 7, from one of the few novels which he has read, *Adolphe*. The prayers and charity for the afflicted that she includes in her letter, scenes she drew from Rousseau's novel, could have reminded him of similar activities by Constant's heroine, Ellenore. And identifying himself with Constant's bored, restless, vain hero, Eugene envisions their relationship in terms of that novel—boredom, torment, tears, rage (4:14)—and he coldly cuts it off before it can go further.[44] This is the best understanding and the most moral action that Eugene can summon from his limited literary and social existence.

The duel with Lensky presents problems of a different sort, but Eugene is still unable to deal with the conventions of his culture, and he remains "conventions' playball," as the author-narrator aptly puts it (6:10). Upset because Lensky brings him to a large gathering of the people whom spleen has led him to avoid, Eugene punishes Lensky by carrying out a conventional flirtation with Lensky's fiancée. Lensky had no choice but to call Eugene out, as Nabokov has observed.[45] Onegin, who has previously discussed "good and evil" with Lensky (2:16) and who knows that he is wrong (6:10), lacks even the relative independence it would have taken to place conventional friendship (one of the most salient values of his time)[46] above the more compelling conventions and to seek a reconciliation. His aesthetic constructions, the amoral dandy and the Byronic rebel, turn out to have a conative, audience-directed function after all: the dandy implores admiration, the rebel—outrage. Moreover, as Baudelaire noted, the dandy needs social convention as a backdrop for his revolt.[47] But Eugene in either costume, dandy or rebel, would evoke more mockery from his imagined audience and from Zaretsky, the pedantic duelist, by refusing to fight ("whispers, the laughter of fools," 6:11), as Eugene is well aware. But even if fashion forbade a sentimental reconciliation, it still offered two courses of action: shoot to kill or fire into the air (as Pushkin seems to have done in duels with his friends Kiukhel'-beker and Ryleev). But Eugene choose to defy convention in a petty manner; he offends Lensky by bringing a valet as his second, instead of a gentleman, as custom demanded. At the same time Eugene ignores the convention (firing in the air) which might have eased his conscience, spared his friend's life, and earned him society's admiration.[48]

The author-narrator contrasts this helplessness throughout the rest of the novel with his own creative use of conventions. Onegin knows only one way to finish Lensky off, and it haunts him during the ensuing chapters; the author-narrator imagines two ways (6:37–39) to destroy Lensky as a literary character: a literary parody (the premature death of the poet) and a social travesty (the gouty, cuckolded landowner). Onegin's nonchalant rebellion—bringing a valet as his second and showing up inexcusably late—runs parallel to the author-narrator's invocation of the muse in the last stanza of chapter 7. But whereas Eugene stands trapped by a convention (the duel), the author-narrator makes creative, meaningful use of conventions: he goes beyond the standard postponed invocation of mock-epic to begin chapter 8 with an evocation of the muse that is at the same time his own authorial biography (8:1–7).

Eugene's development, then, reverses Tatiana's. As she matures in her ability to relate literature and life in a variety of ways, he loses control over the materials of his culture. Nowhere is this more obvious than when the two characters again face each other at the novel's close. Eugene may have become a good fellow, as several commentators have suggested, and as such he may now be able to love and appreciate Tatiana.[49] In his delirium he does, in fact, see her as a country girl, not as a grand lady who would make a worthy specimen for his amatory science (8:37). But Eugene must, in Pushkin's novel, express this through the codes of his culture, and he has only his experiences in "love" and a few novels, such as *Adolphe,* to help him. Tatiana's firm rejection of him is her only possible response, now that she has read *Adolphe* and can see that it dictates almost all of Eugene's actions—his barrage of letters, his desire to kneel at her feet, his difficulty in controlling himself yet unwillingness to dissemble, his vague threat of suicide.[50] No doubt these phrases are as old as love itself, but their similarity to what Tatiana had read in Eugene's book seems to suggest further correspondences with *Adolphe* to her—that Eugene desires not love, but satisfied vanity, the triumph of conquering and shaming the wealthy, noble mate of a distinguished man (8:44). Eugene's silence, which clearly parallels both Tatiana's earlier response to his rejection of her and the author-narrator's inability to write while loving (1:58), suggests that he may indeed love her; but he fails to communicate it in the only possible way, through the appropriate conventions of their culture.

The concluding stanza of *Eugene Onegin* offers the key metaphor, "life's novel."[51] "Life" and "the novel" are not, it would seem, a combination to inspire confidence, given the rhyming of "novel" *[roman]* with "deception" *[obman]* in *Eugene Onegin* (2:29, 3:9). One can, after all, revise a novel, not arrest or turn back the flow of time and biographical maturation. One can correct a novel's galley proofs; life gives few such second chances. And, most important, the novel as a genre depicts its events much more completely—their causes, consequences, and the thinking of their agents—than does "real life."

The proper reply to these objections lies in the particular conception of social existence which structures *Eugene Onegin*. There life and the novel come to share a common "reality" because the characters make them do so, bridging the space between the literary and social areas of culture with conventional definitions of literature: literature as the representation of reality, as self-expression, as moral guide, and as entertainment or consolation.

While the characters are constructing their lives along literary lines, the author-narrator meets them halfway by deconstructing the complete picture of life the traditional novel purports to give. He never finishes the old-fashioned novel with its happy ending which he playfully promises in chapter 3 (3:13–14) because he arbitrarily and unexpectedly married his heroine off to someone the reader hardly knows.[52] Pushkin severs the coincidental ties which lace conventional fiction together: Tatiana, for all of her good intentions and her reading of epistolary novels, cannot stop the duel if nobody tells her that it is going to take place (6:18). Conventions permit novelists to exercise considerable license in probing the minds and describing the authentic selves of their characters, but Pushkin's author-narrator chooses to offer conflicting evaluations of his hero, as he (like the other characters and like his inscribed reader) tries to interpret Eugene's silence with the codes of society's syncretic culture.

Circumstances and the independence of others can impede even the most brilliant of creators in *Eugene Onegin*. The author-narrator dominates the novel because he creates and dismisses the other characters and because he most successfully threads his way through the culture which he shares with them, separating the wheat from the chaff of that culture, engaging more powerful human resources—intelligence, heart, delight, knowledge—than any one of his creatures. Yet *Eugene Onegin* makes its narrator—as both author and character—party to the risks, failures, and limitations of life. As a character the narrator cannot travel with Eugene (1:51) or write and love at the same time (1:60). As author he cannot integrate Eugene's journey into the novel or satisfy the critics whom he mentions in his footnotes. By not significantly altering the early chapters, written and published separately nearly a decade before the first complete edition appeared, Pushkin made his text share the characters' experience of time's movement.

Finally, life and the novel merge in *Eugene Onegin* because each is a process of creation that allows no recourse to the fantastic or improbable except in dreams and reported legends. Each is a process that uses conventions to organize the materials of everyday life. Because there are many areas within a culture and many conventions relating these areas to each other, the possibilities for creativity are often immeasurable, but so are the chances for entrapment, confusion, and failure of communication. The richness of culture's conventions, its ideology, and its institutional patterns can inspire a novel as original and intricate as *Eugene Onegin,* or they can occasion human disaster as surely as the most crushing events and processes of history.

IV

A Hero of Our Time:
The Caucasus as "Amphitheater"

> We regard the roles that we adopt as means of im-
> posing ourselves on society. It is only gradually that
> we come to realize the extent to which the role can
> impose itself upon the "self" which plays it.
>
> Elizabeth Burns, *Theatricality*

KILLED in a duel at the age of twenty-six, Lermontov wrote or inspired few of the documents by which posterity might confidently chart his relationship to his literary milieu and antecedents: a few autobiographical jottings, a tenth of the letters that Gogol and Pushkin left (few of them concerning literature), other people's memoirs of his appearances in several literary salons, dim memories solicited decades later by diligent biographers and possibly scripted by the informants' understanding of Lermontov's fiction. His contemporaries were even less well supplied with Lermontoviana. He flashed across the literary scene with a fiery poem on Pushkin's death (1837), which circulated widely in manuscript, but he published comparatively little; a few lyrics and narrative poems, a collection of verse (1840), and two modest editions of *A Hero of Our Time* (1840, 1841) were all that appeared during his lifetime.[1] Unlike subsequent critics, who have the opportunity to read hundreds of youthful verses, a handful of plays, and a half-dozen unfinished prose works—few of them intended by Lermontov for publication—and, consequently, to witness a process of maturation, Lermontov's contemporaries could have had no sense of his literary career, except to the extent that several of them speculated about its future development.[2]

Lermontov scorned the student literary groups that his tutor Merzliakov had celebrated. He dismissed the philosophical circles as "literary masturbation."[3] Writing was such a private activity for him that few of his school fellows or guardsmen messmates knew that he wrote serious poetry.[4] Unlike Pushkin or Gogol, he left no public or private literary criticism. He did not seek out publishers for his work. And he most certainly did not seek patronage, expressing his independence from the government by wearing a toy sword to parade and by appearing at a Petersburg ball (upon his return from exile in the Caucasus) before he had reported to his commanding officer.

Dissatisfied with these images of alienation, Lermontov scholars have spent nearly a century and a half trying to determine what Eikhenbaum would call Lermontov's "literary position."[5] In large part, this attempt at contextualization has involved a search for literary influences. Inspired by Lermontov's youthful copying of others' verse, scholars have demonstrated that his texts reveal thorough familiarity with French, English, Russian, and German literature, or at least striking parallels.[6] Foreign precedents have even been discovered for the Maksim Maksimych of *A Hero of Our Time*, a character whose "Russianness" won him the affection of Lermontov's harshest critics, such as Nicholas I.[7] More recently, considerable scholarly effort has been devoted to the question of Lermontov's "realism," "romanticism," or "romantic realism."[8] Such essays in filiation find a certain support in Lermontov's ingenuous confession: "lorsque je me surprends à admirer ma propre pensée, je cherche à me rappeler: où je l'ai lue!" (IV, 385; letter to M. A. Lopukhina of 23 December 1834).

Other studies have sought concrete institutional homes for the poet at his Moscow school, among the politically aware aristocrats of St. Petersburg (the mysterious "Circle of Sixteen"), and among the exiled Decembrists in the Caucasus.[9] Indeed, critics' attempts to link Lermontov and his texts with the aspirations and failure of the Decembrists have at times come to sound like a litany.[10]

However unconvincing such attempts to "place" Lermontov may sometimes be, Lermontov was certainly implicated to some extent in the institutional upheavals of his time, sometimes as victim, sometimes as would-be agent. His first publication, "Khadzhi Abrek," appeared (without his permission) in Sekowski's *Library for Reading*. And, memoirs report, he himself planned to open a journal and to write a trilogy of novels,[11] both activities which characterized Russia's incipient literary professionals.

Nevertheless, Lermontov remains in the most reliable accounts a "man of the salons," as Belinsky put it, a dedicated amateur littérateur and a social lion.[12] His first years in St. Petersburg had been marked by scandalous attempts to storm the citadels of high society, to which membership in a distinguished Moscow family and in a guards regiment did not automatically admit him. And the scandals, such as a quarrel with the French ambassador's son at the Laval mansion, continued.[13] Soon before finishing *A Hero of Our Time*, however, Lermontov had earned sufficient literary reputation to gain entrée into "society" proper as Pushkin had once defined it, "honorable, intelligent, and educated people" (XI, 98). Many distinguished literary figures of the Pushkin period—Zhukovsky, Prince Viazemsky, Aleksandr Turgenev, Prince Odoevsky, Countess Rostopchina, and Baratynsky among them—made his acquaintance, as did Pushkin's widow. At the Karamzins' home, where he became an almost daily visitor between periods of exile in the Caucasus, he struck up a close friendship with the late historiographer's daughter, Sofiia, and he became a member of the Karamzin salon.[14]

Eventually, Lermontov paid the obligatory verse tribute to Sofiia in her album, announcing a new aesthetic commitment, a change from the frenetic enthusiasms of his youth to the civilized conventions of polite society:

> Liubil i ia v bylye gody,
> V nevinnosti dushi moei,
> I buri shumnye prirody,
> I buri tainye strastei.
>
> No krasoty ikh bezobraznoi
> Ia skoro tainstvo postig,
> I mne naskuchil ikh nesviaznyi
> I oglushaiushchii iazyk.
>
> Liubliu ia bol'she god ot godu,
> Zhelan'iam mirnym dav prostor,
> Poutru iasnuiu pogodu,
> Pod vecher tikhii razgovor,
>
> Liubliu ia paradoksy vashi,
> I kha-kha-kha, i khi-khi-khi,
> Smirnovoi shtuchku, farsu Sashi
> I Ishki Miatleva stikhi . . .[15]

I loved in former years, in the innocence of my soul, both the noisy storms of nature and the quiet storms of the passions.

But of their ugly beauty I soon learned the secret, and their incoherent, deafening language came to bore me.

I love more each year, giving play to peaceful desires, clear weather in the morning, quiet conversation in the evening.

I love your paradoxes, and ha-ha-ha, and he-he-he, Smirnova's sally, Sasha's farce, and Ishka Miatlev's verses . . .

Written during the poet's last visit to Petersburg, the poem appeared in a collection shortly after his death, without, however, the final quatrain, in which he characterizes members of the salon—Sofiia Karamzina, her brother, A. O. Smirnova (herself a salon hostess for whom Lermontov wrote album verses), and Ivan Miatlev (a macaronic versifier). The fluid iambic tetrameters elegantly contrast the poet's youthful storms of passion with the "quiet conversation" that he found in the salon, dutifully capturing the hostess's paradoxes and laughter, as well as the light amusements of the other habitué(e)s.

Lest one think, however, that this new commitment to the salon aesthetic suggests a satisfactory explanation of Lermontov's literary development, Sofiia Karamzin's account of the poem's prehistory fractures its ideal of calm conversation, throwing into question Lermontov's harmonious engagement with the traditions of salon interaction and the salon's ability to answer his creative needs:

> We had the Smirnovs, the Valuevs, Count Shuvalov, Repnin, and Lermontov for tea. My evening ended *disagreeably* with the last one; I must tell you about it to ease my conscience. Some time ago I had given him my *Album* to write in. He announced to me yesterday, "When everyone has left, I will read something and you will give me your opinion." I guessed that it was about my Album, and when everyone had left, he gave it back to me and asked me to read aloud and, *if the verses didn't please me, to tear them up, and he would write me some others.* He couldn't have guessed better! These bad, feeble verses, written on the *last* page, expressed the execrable commonplace that he feared to write where there were the names of so many famous men, most of whom he was unacquainted with, that among them he felt like an awkward beginner who enters a salon where he is not up on the ideas and the conversation, where he smiles at the jokes in order to have the air of understanding them, and where, at last, troubled and confused, he sadly goes off *into a little corner.* And that was all. "Well?"—"Really, this doesn't please me at all; it's *quite common,* and the verses aren't much."—"Tear them up." I didn't make him say it twice. I ripped out the leaf and tore it into little pieces which I threw onto the floor; he gathered them up and burned them in the candle, while he became quite red and did not laugh, I must confess, except with the ends of his lips. Maman told me that I was mad, that this behavior was silly and insolent, and finally she did so well that I repented and tears overwhelmed me at the same time, although I maintain (which is *true*) that I couldn't have offered a stronger proof of my friendship and of my *esteem* for the poet and the person. He also said that he was grateful to me for it, that I had been just toward him in believing him above childish vanity, and that he would ask for my Album in order to write something else, for his *honor was now touched.*

Finally he went away rather upset, leaving me very ill at ease. I am anxious to see him again in order to dissipate this disagreeable impression, and I hope to go horseback riding this evening with him and Voldemar.[16]

This troubled scene shows us not the critical interaction between poet and hostess that we studied in the section on institutions of literature, but, quite literally, a moment of fragmentation: the hostess tears up the cliché-ridden verse (which, with its place on the last page of her album, seems almost the sort of thing that Pushkin mocked in *Eugene Onegin*, 4:28). "The writer proposes, the reader disposes." But this saying, appropriate to a commercialized public literature, here comes to apply to the salon as well. Sofiia's mother, steeped in the old traditions of coauthorship and polite criticism, reproves her daughter for this behavior and understandably so, for Sofiia's account suggests that there was no moment of real criticism or discussion between hostess and poet.

Meanwhile, the rejected poem, trite as this narrative makes it seem, did try to express a lyric theme that obsessed Lermontov in his verse and prose: a feeling of otherness, of not belonging to the world. In the crafted, symmetrical stanzas which eventually replaced it, no such anxiety appears, as the poet distances his audience from his inner life. At one with the polite society that surrounds him, he celebrates its traditional harmonizing, creative functions. Romantic psychological commonplaces, in short, yield to polite commonplaces more flattering to the hostess.[17]

Sofiia Karamzina's letter, unlike the final poem, records this process of distancing. It captures the theatricality of Lermontov's gestures (burning the fragments of the unacceptable poem), his masklike laughter (only the ends of his lips show it), and his withdrawal into "honor." The fourth stanza of the poem to the contrary, her narrative allows us to see that for Lermontov creativity has become something to be accomplished not even backstage, when the other habitués had departed, but away from the salon altogether.

Some aspects of this scene—the confrontation in a drawing room, the tearful resolution of a conflict, the grand gestures, the hero's guarded laughter, the concealment of feelings, and the succession of polite social forms (tea, horseback riding)—will seem familiar to readers of *A Hero of Our Time*, especially of its "Princess Mary" section. I am not, however, suggesting a line of influence; Sofiia's Karamzina's story may, if anything, have been shaped by the novel, which was then being written and published and which was read aloud to the

Karamzins at least once that summer.[18] Nor need we assume that Lermontov became capable of writing society tales only upon entering the salons of Petersburg. His unfinished novel *Princess Ligovskaia*, clearly a precursor to the "Princess Mary" section of *A Hero of Our Time*, was begun (1836) and broken off (1837) before he had full access to the highest cultural levels of Petersburg "society."

The incident of the torn album verse will serve here, then, not as a bridge to biographical or influence study, but as a paradigm for my analysis of Lermontov's highly complicated novel, just as Pushkin's visit to Ermolov raised a set of issues (conventionality in art and in social life) for the discussion of *Eugene Onegin*. The passage in Sofiia Karamzina's letter lacks, of course, the exotic women, smugglers, crazed Cossacks, desperate gamblers, and mountain tribesmen who play important roles in the novel's abduction, attempted drowning, murders, and duel, although I will argue that these actors and incidents can be accommodated to the reading that the failed salon interaction provokes. And it does not directly account for the generic variety of the novel's two introductions and five stories—travel sketch and adventure novella ("Bela"), physiological sketch ("Maksim Maksimych"), comic adventure novella ("Taman' "), confession and society tale ("Princess Mary"), *conte philosophique* ("The Fatalist"). We have seen, nevertheless, that such generic virtuosity was consonant with the salon aesthetic and with the *honnête homme*'s ideology of nonspecialization.[19] But the epistolary account concisely emphasizes the element of conscious self-presentation (theatricality) that marked contemporary discussions of polite society, it implicitly questions the ability of this society to deal with an inner world and to foster literary life, and, in Sofiia Karamzina's justification of her conduct (esteem for the poet), it raises the problem of the potential—be it aesthetic, moral, or psychological—that might not find expression in the constricting social patterns of everyday life. In this chapter, referring to earlier chapters on ideology and institutions and using *Eugene Onegin* for comparative purposes, I will use the problems that the letter only adumbrates—cultural conflict, theatricality, constriction, uniqueness, literary production, and implied human potential—to examine *A Hero of Our Time*, less as "Russia's first psychological novel" (its usual designation) than as a refraction of specific cultural issues, which included the problem of identity, but which were by no means limited to it.[20] This analysis cannot, of course, neglect the "hero" of the novel's title, but I shall focus on how it produces that hero and his "time," making him at once a part of that time and potentially apart from it.

Cultural Constriction

The abandonment of the world by God manifests itself in
the incommensurability of soul and work . . . there are,
roughly speaking, two types of such incommensurability:
either the soul is narrower or it is broader than the outside
world assigned to it as the arena and the substratum
of its actions.

Georg Lukács, *Theory of the Novel*

Pushkin's verse novel has often been compared to Lermontov's novel-as-collection-of-stories in terms of character development, the nature of the hero, and narrative technique.[21] The comparison between protagonists is most strongly invited by Lermontov's echo of the Push-kinian phrase "contemporary man" (*EO* 7:22) in the introducton to his own novel (IV, 184). Beyond this, as Belinsky was quick to note, the surnames of the two heroes are derived from the names of Russian rivers: the Onega and the more turbulent Pechora. Yet *A Hero of Our Time* provokes still another comparison to *Eugene Onegin* with four fragmentary quotations from its great predecessor: a bit of nature description (IV, 202, from *EO* 2:28), a characterization of a woman's gaze (IV, 232, from *EO* 5:34), a comment on the size of Russian women's feet (IV, 231, from *EO* 1:30), and two lines from the epistle dedicatory (IV, 278)—"The mind's dispassionate notations, / The heart's asides, inscribed in tears." Pechorin quotes, as well, a hussar whom Pushkin had celebrated in chapter I of *Eugene Onegin* (IV, 271). From these passages one sees that the traveling narrator of the "Bela" section and the hero-diarist of "Princess Mary' can casually draw upon Pushkin's text to salt their conversation and to decorate their depictions of a Caucasian scene, a young woman, or the female sex in general. But the verse novel's full range of cultural levels (folk, Western, gentry) is neither reflected by these quotations nor embodied in Lermontov's novel as a whole.[22]

Eugene Onegin's intricate interrelationships between social and literary life likewise find little place in Lermontov's novel. The traveling narrator and Pechorin drop a modest number of quotations, enough to signal their membership in the "enlightened Westernized gentry," but not enough to suggest the multilayered cultural world of, say, Tatiana. Pechorin does, it is true, describe other characters in literary terms: Werner is "always a poet in deeds, and often in words, although he has not written two lines in his whole life" (IV, 242); Grushnitsky's "goal is to become the hero of a novel" (IV, 238). And

Pechorin persistently uses theatrical vocabulary to organize the entries in his diary, as I shall explain below. But such generic references serve sooner to disjoin literature from social life than to illustrate how they parallel or shape each other: Werner, after all, has written no verse and his actions within the novel seem largely dictated by sober reason; Grushnitsky is not yet a hero and, we learn, will never become more than a supporting actor or conjuror's dupe (IV, 284). *A Hero of Our Time* demands that the reader infer important distinctions between these characters and Pechorin, but in neither case is the difference founded, as it was in *Eugene Onegin*, on differences in reading habits. Here temperament and the arts of self-presentation provide, as we shall see, the grounds for comparison.

One exception to this superficial or nonexistent interpenetration between literary and social patterns may be the novel's persistent references to Byron: the traveling narrator can recognize Pechorin's disenchantment in these terms (IV, 210); Princess Mary's knowledge of Byron and algebra (IV, 246) perhaps suggests to a reader that she will be able to break the code of Pechorin's behavior. But Byron appears in the novel less as an aesthetic phenomenon, as the traveling narrator notes, than as a phenomenon of everyday life, a pose long familiar in Russian society: "I replied that . . . disenchantment, like all fashions that had begun with the highest layers of society had descended to the lowest, which were wearing it out" (IV, 210).[23]

A second important exception to the novel's limited invocation of literary precedents is Sir Walter Scott. On the eve of his duel Pechorin reads *Old Mortality* and finds solace or distraction in it (IV, 290–291). But Scott's ideology of moderation does nothing to influence Pechorin's subsequent actions and thoughts. Henry Morton's resolute political independence, principled religious faith, and devotion to Edith Bellenden stand in marked contrast to Pechorin's invovement in petty social intrigues, his suicidal gamble in the duel, and his equally suicidal test of fate against the murderous Cossack. If anything in Scott's novel has an impact on Pechorin, it is not the moderate hero Morton but the aristocratic, socially polished and murderous Claverhouse, who, like Pechorin, challenges fate, wondering about the memories he will leave behind.[24] Here the literary reference may facilitate the reader's understanding of Pechorin; however, it does so indirectly, by associating Pechorin not with the ideals of Scott's novel but with their antithesis.

A Hero of Our Time not only limits the role that literature plays in shaping the lives of its characters, even those of the traveling narrator and of Pechorin, who are in some sense writers, it also constricts the forms of literary life that appear in the novel. In contrast to *Eugene Onegin*, which reflected upon almost all of the institutional possibilities of Russian literature (including no institutionalization at all), *A Hero of Our Time* deliberately suppresses almost all sense of writing as a public activity.

The drafts of the novel amply illustrate this process of suppression in at least two places. The first is the "Author's Introduction," which was added to the novel for its second, 1841, edition.[25] As it stands, the introduction takes cognizance of certain institutional problems: the functions of a foreword, the habits of the reading public (unawareness of irony, identifying the author with his protagonist), the credibility of fictional heroes and plots, the uses of fiction (diagnostic or curative) (IV, 183). The introduction thus helps determine the categories in terms of which the novel might be read, as I have already discussed in Chapter 2. But by comparison with the draft of the introduction, which lists specific heroes that readers have found credible (Melmoth, the vampire), which refers specifically to a journalistic attack, and which distinguishes between the novel's reception by journalists and by the reading public, the final version gives a simpler, more homogenized view of the literary scene.[26] It reduces all of the novel's readers, journalists and nonjournalists alike, to a single "our public," it excises the titles of its romantic predecessors, and it removes the mockery of its journalistic adversaries. In a clear challenge to its readers, the final version abuses them in terms of the values of urbane "society," branding them "provincials" and accusing them of not understanding how conflicts are conducted in decent company. In place of Pushkin's epistle dedicatory, which advertised culture's multiple resources and proclaimed the poet's allegiance to the salient values of polite society, such as friendship and poetry, Lermontov's introduction prepares its readers for a constricted cultural framework, in which "decent society" is notable mainly for its subtle forms of abuse.

The second passage in which the institutional possibilities of literature are suppressed comes in the "Maksim Maksimych" section of the novel, where the traveling narrator is given ten notebooks filled with Pechorin's writings. In the draft, this narrator justifies publishing the journals by reference to Pechorin's authorial intentions: "he had prepared them for publication, without which, naturally, I would not have decided to abuse the staff captain's trust. Indeed, Pechorin in several places addresses the reader." He goes on to note, in a swipe at the editorial practices of the *Library for Reading*, "I, despite the bad example set for us by certain journalists, decided not to correct anything, nor to finish someone else's work."[27] The final version eliminates this poke at the period's most popular journal, and it eliminates Pechorin's public aspirations. Instead, the privacy of Pechorin's reflections functions as a guarantee of their sincerity:

> Reading over these notes, I became convinced of the sincerity of someone who so mercilessly exhibited his own weaknesses and vices. The history of a human soul, even the most trivial, is scarcely less curious and useful than the history of an entire people, especially when it is the consequence of the self-observations of a mature mind and when it is written without the vain desire to arouse sympathy or amazement. Rousseau's confessions have this very shortcoming, that he read them to his friends.   (IV, 225)

Eliminating Pechorin's explicit sense of audience may guarantee the "sincerity" of his journal, or at least have the rhetorical effect of predisposing the reader to sympathize with Pechorin's account. But it also eliminates any thought of public literary life, thereby constricting the circle of possible activity in which the novel's action can take place and, specifically, closing this circle ever more tightly around Pechorin. At the same time, the traveling narrator, deprived of his reference to the period's journalistic practices and of his initial justification for publishing the journals, is transformed by the final draft into another vicious member of society: "I recently learned that Pechorin had died . . . This news delighted me considerably: it gave me the right to print these journals" (IV, 224).

A Hero of Our Time, unlike *Eugene Onegin,* takes for its settings a series of exotic places—a mountain road through the Caucasus, a Russian outpost among the Circassians ("Bela"); towns along the Military Georgian Road ("Maksim Maksimych"); a smuggler's den on the Black Sea ("Taman' "); resort towns in the Northern Caucasus ("Princess Mary"); and a Cossack settlement ("The Fatalist"). In the first story, "Bela," the location inspires memorable descriptions of nature, but by the "Maksim Maksimych" section the traveling narrator has abandoned this exercise, itself already exhausted by Bestuzhev-Marlinsky and parodied by Pushkin's *Journey to Arzrum:* "I will spare you the descriptions of mountains, the exclamations which express nothing, the pictures which depict nothing, especially for those who have not been there, and the statistical remarks, which certainly nobody will read" (IV, 216).[28] By "Princess Mary," the longest section of the novel, the Caucasus has become a vacation spot for the Russian gentry, an occasional place of refuge for Pechorin, and an "amphitheater" for his performances (IV, 236, 254); and in the last section, "The Fatalist," its starry skies serve primarily to inspire metaphysical speculation. This gradual disappearance of the natural setting as a place apart from cosmopolitan civilization, then, parallels the novel's movement toward constriction of the cultural sphere. At least one contemporary reader, S. P. Shevyrev, denied Pechorin any love of nature at all.[29]

As the novel ceases to highlight its exotic natural settings, it simultaneously comes to pay less attention to the customs of the non-Russian or non-"civilized" peoples of the Caucasus. The exotic tribesmen of "Bela" are replaced by the ethnically indeterminate and socially marginal smugglers of "Taman' " and the Slavic Cossacks of "The Fatalist." Even more important in this regard, however, is the way that Maksim Maksimych, the traveling narrator, and Pechorin limit the categories according to which they represent the culture and social patterns of the Ossetians, Kabardians, Chechens, and others. Inevitably, these categories are limited to ones of deceit, theft (abduction), or violence (murder, vengeance), which is more or less socially acceptable, as Maksim Maksimych notes with an attitude of cultural relativism (IV, 201). From the traveling narrator's first contact with the Ossetian drivers, who cheat him, to Pechorin's last view of the smuggler Ianko, who, coldly abandoning his confederates, carries off Pechorin's weapons, to the drunken Cossack Efimych, who indiscriminately bisects pigs and officers, the novel's passages dealing with these noncosmopolitan societies present a virtually unmitigated succession of destructive acts. The art that arises from these milieux, as opposed to the serf girls' playful song in *Eugene Onegin*—Kazbich's paean to his horse or the "undine's" song—celebrates such "uncivilized" activities. The noncosmopolitan peoples have their ceremonies, hierarchies, and customs, none of which militate against the violence of the relatively "free" Kazbich or Ianko. Yet both of these ostensibly unbridled characters nevertheless are implicated in patterns of economic exchange with the societies in and out of which they move. The two women who figure prominently in these sections of the novel, Bela and the nameless "undine," stand somewhat apart from the other characters in their capacity for passionate devotion. But this, in turn, brings them to participate or to contemplate participating in the deceit, theft, or violence of their immediate social groups, the "undine" by attempting to drown Pechorin, Bela by flashing with anger at the sight of her father's murderer (IV, 208).

The civilized traveling narrator, recording Maksim Maksimych's reaction to these non-Russin mores, salutes the staff captain's relativism: "I was struck by the Russian's capacity to adapt himself to the customs of those peoples among which he happened to live; I don't know whether this mental trait merits blame or praise, only that it demonstrates his incredible flexibility and the presence of that clear common sense which forgives evil everywhere that it sees the inevitability of evil or the impossibility of destroying it" (IV, 201–202). Examining the behavioral patterns of the novel's polite society, however, as it is presented fragmentarily in "Bela" and "Maksim Maksimych" and then thoroughly in "Princess Mary," the longest section of the novel, one is strongly invited to interpret the traveling narrator's comment as an example of that "irony" that was announced in the book's introduction. Deceit, theft, and violence are no less the dominant principles of the novel's polite society than they are of the Caucasian tribes. Pechorin's manipulation of the other characters, his successful attempt to lure Mary from Grushnitsky, Grushnitsky's desire for vengeance, and Pechorin's duel with Grushnitsky may show the effects of a superficial refinement of manners, but the parallels between "civilized" and "uncivilized" society are clearly established by the novel's structural patterns.[30] Indeed, the spa society accepts Grushnitsky's death in the duel as calmly as Bela's people accept Kazbich's vengeance for the theft of his horse.

"Princess Mary" features many of the genteel gatherings that might, according to the ideology of polite society, set the quests at the spa in harmony with each other, providing an aesthetically pleasing and ethically effective outlet for the antagonisms of these civil service dandies, officers of the guards and of the regular army, and visitors from the capitals and from the steppes. The opening pages of the story, which establish these distinctions quite clearly and which immediately reveal Pechorin's antipathy toward Grushnitsky, create the initial situation for a narrative of harmonization, such as the account of Tatiana's salon in _Eugene Onegin_, chapter 8. Instead, the promenades at the spa, the picnic, the two balls, the horseback-riding parties, the musical soirée, and the drawing-room gatherings merely serve as the loci for vicious competitions among the characters. The initial social distinctions (urban/provincial, Petersburg/Moscow, guards/regular army) are preserved. And new distinctions based on the ability to humiliate, to conceal information, and to give false information are produced at the same social occasions that were believed to generate personal and collective harmony. Where _Eugene Onegin_ had presented polite society as a marginally viable social-aesthetic possibility, if not as a manifestation of transcendent value, _A Hero of Our Time_ strips it of all value, transcendent or relative. But at the same time as the novel so constricts the aspirations of polite society, it presents none of the ideological alternatives that contemporaries entertained: the autocratic Russia of the official nationalists or the Russian Orthodox community of the Slavophiles.

Pechorin has already involved the other characters in such a network of hostile relationships when Princess Ligovskaia reminds him (and the reader) of the harmonizing function of polite society: "I hope that the air of my salon will dispel your spleen . . . won't it?" (IV, 259). The question with which she ends her invitation should probably be interpreted as a sign of politeness, not uncertainty or lack of confidence. But unlike Mary's mother, the reader of Pechorin's diary can readily appreciate how little store the hero sets by the genteel social conventions of his time: "I said to her one of those phrases, which everyone should keep ready for such occasions" (IV, 259).

A Hero of Our Time, then, does not offer the multiplicity of aesthetic, cultural possibilities and contrasts that *Eugene Onegin* had set before its characters, author-narrator, and readers. But for those who have read the novel, I need hardly add that this is not an aesthetic deficiency. On the contrary, *A Hero of Our Time* organizes its novelistic resources no less rigorously than *Eugene Onegin*. But its extraordinary interest lies elsewhere, in its contradictory hero and in the relentlessness with which it presents a world held together by nasty intrigues, not by a productive commitment to enlightenment or the amelioration of manners.

This impression of cultural and social constraint that *A Hero of Our Time* projects by its treatment of literature and by its representation of social interaction is, in turn, rigorously reinforced by other narrative aspects, such as plot, setting, and patterns of characterization. One feature of the novel's plot, the ordering of its sections, has challenged its readers to a narratological parlor game since it was first published: how, if at all, can one account for the order of the novel's stories? Belinsky and many subsequent critics have noted that the reader's progress through the novel leads to increasingly intimate views of Pechorin.[31] But this narrative of revelation—a journey into Pechorin conducted by Maksim Maksimych, the traveling narrator, and Pechorin himself—gives few clues to the progress of Pechorin's own journey through the Caucasus, which might permit the reader to chart a narrative of becoming, Pechorin's maturation as a character.[32] Most critics agree that "Taman' " comes first, followed by "Princess Mary," with "Maksim Maksimych" coming before the two introductions. Controversies arise over the relative positioning of "Bela" and "The

Fatalist" between these two groups.[33] Rather than continue this line of critical discussion, however, I think it would be more useful to ask what effects this double chronology produces. One salient effect is surely to keep the reader moving back and forth between sections, evaluating Pechorin's actions and statements in terms of what was learned earlier but may have happened later. Such double movement, for example, undercuts the boldness of Pechorin's resolution in "The Fatalist" to act as if fate held no power over him (IV, 193). It does so because in stories which come chronologically later in Pechorin's life we see him inevitably using "fate"as an excuse for his callous actions and moral passivity (IV, 222, 235, 272, 290). The book ends on his note of triumphant self-assertion, but it is difficult to accept this place-ment of the declaration as a final "triumph of art over the logic of facts, or, in other words, a triumph of plot over story."[34] Plot and story, rather, constantly challenge each other, enmeshing text, reader, and hero in an unresolvable set of patterns and problems. That the reader's enounter with Pechorin is framed both by the theme of "fate" and by the fortress setting, moreover, helps to make even more per-ceptible the plot-generating pinciple of constriction.[35]

No persistent references to historical time, meanwhile, help the novel's readers to orient themselves among its various parts.[36] Such indefiniteness makes the novel "timeless," not in the superficial, ide-ological sense of "eternal, outside of history," but rather in a sense that challenges the reader to meditate upon historical possibility, the sense implied by Musset: "Tout ce qui était n'est plus; tour ce qui sera n'est pas encore."[37] There is, after all, much more to historical awareness than the mere mention of dates, names, and events. Ler-montov's violation of the general European tendency of the 1830s to date fiction, a tendency he observed in his earlier fiction, underscores the novel's sense of constricted, even absent possibilities.[38] Belinsky, surely, was not alone in finding that such indefiniteness charged *A Hero of Our Time* with unexpressed meaning.[39]

The novel's double chronology, one of them unclear, contributes to its sense of constriction not only because it helps to render actions pointless and conclusions inconclusive, but also because it impels the reader to question the possibility of character development. The sec-tions of the novel—each of short duration and several of them ori-ented toward action, not the analysis of character—do not permit the subordinate characters (young women/more mature women, Russian women/"native" women, the rational Dr. Werner/the impulsive Grushnitsky) to do more than act as foils for its hero, illuminating him by contrast or similarity. But the hero himself figures in both chronologies, and while the "chronology of the narration" orders a set of incidents which help make Pechorin's character more familiar to the reader, the chronology of events" (inferred by the reader from the novel's references to the passage of time, to gaps between stories, and to Pechorin's own consciousness of past and present) provokes the reader into considering what has become of him during the course of these years. Pechorin himself invites such questions with his confessional tirades to Maksim Maksimych (IV, 209–210) and to Princess Mary (IV, 268), in which he describes his life as a series of disillusionments and crippling conflicts with society. Having raised the question of development or biography, however, the novel leaves it unanswered. Pechorin arrives once from Petersburg ("Princess Mary"), and arrives again ("Maksim Maksimych") on his way to Persia. Of his background we learn only that he came from the best society, and of his subsequent fate we learn only that he died.[40] The points between the arrivals from Petersburg, although they encompass at least six years, permit one to chart no satisfactory course of development. Neither do the frequent references to "memory" in Pechorin's diary, which are remarkably unspecific in bringing forth details of his past and thereby giving a sense of biographical development (IV, 230, 232, 247, 252–253, 310); he neglects the distant past, and the novel makes him incapable of remembering incidents from one section to the next. Indeed, critical attempts to see development in Pechorin's character have come mainly from modern Western scholars more accustomed to biographical novels and more susceptible to Western conceptions of the unified self than were Lermontov's contemporaries, for whom such a self was, as I have discussed in connection with the ideology of polite society, still in the process of formation.[41]

That *A Hero of Our Time* renders attempts to create a biography for its hero ultimately fruitless shows the workings of its mechanism of constriction on still another level. Pechorin remains locked within a character, no less than his presentation locks him within an eventless time and within a relatively narrow set of themes, behavioral patterns, plot movements, and cultural possibilities. That the novel has provoked such attempts to read between or beyond its lines, however, demonstrates its power to enlist its readers in challenging the limitations of the world it presents. In presenting Pechorin's enclosure within a set character, as was the case with its presentation of an historically undefined period, *A Hero of Our Time* reproduces an element of the ideology of polite society in such a way that this element—universality, static character—not only becomes perceptible, but invites the reader to look beyond it. That the novel in turn frustrates this search only increases its reader's activity, just as frustration goads Pechorin himself into action in the novel. In his case, the author-editor's and the traveling narrator's articulation of their project, to give a "portrait" of Pechorin (IV, 184, 220), recalls not only Lermontov's remarkable skill as a painter, but also a favorite word game of the salons, the *portrait moral*, in which the participants would try to capture someone's moral essence as tersely as possible.[42] But *A Hero of Our Time* with its several narrators and double chronology involved and involves its readers in a search for something more dynamic and changeable than the static characterizations this kind of writing offered.

Theatricality

> . . . a vast theater, where each is at once both
> actor and spectator.
> Zhukovsky, "The Writer in Society"

To this point I have emphasized the novel's processes of cultural constriction by indicating the limited impact of aesthetic forms upon the characters' lives and by suggesting that an ultimately uniform set of behavioral patterns shapes all of the novel's social settings, civilized and uncivilized: deceit, theft, and violence. Yet careful reading of the novel's stories and introductions shows that one aesthetic source of metaphors, the theater, pours forth more generously as the narration passes from the uncultivated Maksim Maksimych (who uses the relatively neutral "scene" once, IV, 199); to the traveling narrator, who refers to the theater four times in describing nature, people, and a story; to Pechorin, who uses approximately forty theatrical terms to organize his presentation of social dynamics in "Princess Mary," the section of the novel most directly concerned with the cultural elite. Pechorin transforms the very mountains around Piatigorsk into an "amphitheater," repeating the image, lest a reader miss the point (IV, 236, 254). Sequences of human actions move from "initial situation" (IV, 245) to "dénouement" (IV, 245, 272, 276, 288) and the "fifth act" (IV, 245); such sequences in turn assume the shape of "farce" (IV, 240), "melodrama" (IV, 240), "comedy," (IV, 245), or "bourgeois tragedy" (IV, 272). The "actors" (IV, 241) strike "poses" (IV, 240), don "tragic mantles" (IV, 239) and other "costumes" (IV, 254), "assume airs" (IV, 241, 250, 258, 264, 268, 274, 293), play "roles" (IV, 261, 272, 281, 289, 290, 304), and "declaim" (IV, 238) in order to produce "ef-

fects" (IV, 238, 248) in particular "scenes" (IV, 241, 248, 260).[43] Even
when Pechorin's diary does not explicitly use the metaphor, his theatrical consciousness is likely to be present in his awareness of dress,
gesture, and oral mannerism or in his arrangement of the narrative
by scenes (which quantitatively overwhelm the number of confessional, psychological passages). Incessant mention of the characters'
eyes recalls, of course, the traditional window-of-the-soul motif. But
when the characters use those eyes to keep each other under constant
surveillance, to catch each other off guard, and to conceal emotion,
the eyes become less a sign of romantic insight and more an indicator
of a theatrically organized society in which each character becomes,
in Zhukovsky's words, "both actor and spectator." The novel's constant use of eavesdropping and spying becomes not proof of artistic
limitation, as Nabokov has seen it, but an appropriate presentation
of the novel's constricting theatricality.[44] Pechorin's spying is, let us
recall, not just the formal necessity of a first-person narrative; it acquires explicit thematical motivation when Grushnitsky naively re-
quests that the more experienced man observe Princess Mary for him
(IV, 261).

The theater is, of course, a venerable metaphor for social life, and
one that was readily available to Lermontov from numerous literary
sources, among them *Eugene Onegin* (8:28, 8:46) and the "society tales"
of the 1830s, Russian and French. "Theatrical" was, moreover, an
adjective already used in early nineteenth-century Russian in its transferred sense, to characterize composed, artificial, or exaggerated behavior.[45] It is hardly surprising that a recently Westernized elite should
perceive its actions in this way, especially since the *honnête homme*
was expected to play so many different social and cultural roles.[46]
Amateur theatricals became a common diversion for the nobility. Indeed, they were trained to act in schools and even in military academies.[47] The masquerade, a special type of performance in which
the participants were at once actors and spectators, figured regularly
among the entertainments of "society," and almost as regularly in its
literature, providing settings, plots, and even titles for a play by Lermontov ("Masquerade," 1835) and a story by N. F. Pavlov ("Masquerade," 1835–36). The enlightened, Westernized gentry had, as
usual, the greatest access to these cultural possibilities, but other social
groups were also exposed to forms of theatricality: the clergy had the
school drama of the theological academies; the folk and the soldiers
had their puppet shows and other stage entertainments.

Nevertheless, even against the background of this theatricality for
which the gentry was trained, which Zhukovsky saw as the governing

principle of the fashionable world, and which Sofiia Karamzina recorded, consciously or unconsciously, in her letter, Pechorin's attentiveness of self-presentation stands out in very sharp relief. His *portrait moral* of Grushnitsky immediately reveals the extent to which the theater has become his model for analyzing those around him. Pechorin begins by examining the impressions that his rival for Princess Mary and his duelling adversary gives and inadvertently "gives off" by his dress, appearance, and physical mannerisms:[48]

> Grushnitsky is a cadet. He has only served for a year but wears, out of a particular sort of foppishness, a thick soldier's greatcoat [to make himself seem an officer demoted to the ranks for duelling]. He has the Cross of St. George. He is well built, swarthy, and dark-haired. He seems twenty-five at first glance, but has hardly reached twenty-one. He throws his head back when he speaks and he constantly twirls his moustache with his left hand, for he leans on his crutch with his right.

The description passes to Grushnitsky's delivery of his lines:

> He speaks quickly and ornately: he is one of those people who have prepared, pompous phrases for all of life's occurrences, whom simple beauty does not move, and who solemnly drape themselves in unusual feelings, elevated passions, and exceptional suffering. To produce an effect is their delight.

Pechorin then speculates on the ideal audience for such performances and on the subsequent careers of such actors, dismissing both in terms of the urbane values of polite society,

> They please provincial romantic girls to distraction. In the old age they become either peaceable landowners or drunkards, sometimes both. In their souls there are often many good qualities, but not a pennyworth of poetry.

He returns to Grushnitsky's talk, the excessive theatricality of which likewise violates good taste and social conventions:

> Grushnitsky's passion was to declaim: he showered you with words just as soon as the conversation passed out of the sphere of ordinary concepts: I could never argue with him. He doesn't answer your objections, he doesn't listen to you. As soon as you stop talking he begins a long tirade, evidently having some connection with what you have said, but which, in fact, is only a continuation of his own speech.

Finally, in rapid succession Pechorin evaluates Grushnitsky's other social-aesthetic skills and mentions the remaining roles that he plays:

> He is rather witty; his epigrams are often amusing, but they are never well-aimed or vicious: he will not kill anyone with a single word; he does

not know people and their weak points, since he has been absorbed in himself alone his whole life. His goal is to become the hero of a novel. He has so often tried to convince others that he is a being not made for this world, doomed to some secret sufferings, that he himself almost believes it. For this reason he wears his thick soldier's greatcoat so proudly. I understood him, and consequently he does not like me, although outwardly we are on very friendly terms. Grushnitsky is reputed to be an exceptionally brave person; I have seen him in action: he waves his sabre, shouts, and hurls himself forward with narrowed eyes. This is somehow not Russian courage! . . . By the way, in those moments when he casts off his tragic mantle, Grushnitsky is rather nice and amusing. I will be curious to see him with the women; there, I think, he will really put out!   (IV, 237–238)

The dramaturgical flaws that Pechorin captures in this portrait—being carried away with one's own performance, having the wrong script for the wrong audience, miscasting (Pechorin as friend)—only increase in number as the story progresses, so that Grushnitsky violates and is made to violate virtually every principle of impression management that modern sociology would subsequently discover: preparing for emergencies, segregating audiences from each other (Pechorin watches every move in his play for Princess Mary), loss of control over impressions given, unawareness of impressions given off.[49]

Perhaps even more important than what it says about Grushnitsky, however, is what the passage can tell its reader about Pechorin. Superficially, it is shaped by the values and behavioral patterns of polite society: good talk, love, friendship, and mastery of such aesthetic forms as epigrams provide the measure according to which Grushnitsky is found wanting. As it reproduces these values and patterns, however, the passage transforms them radically, so that they become not forces of harmonization, but weapons in what must be seen as a competition, the goal of which is to ruin the performance, to penetrate the interlocutor's defenses, to discover his or her secrets.[50] Pechorin, as the "hero" of his time, surpasses the other characters in "Princess Mary" in the ability to play this game, but not only he may be counted upon to join in destroying performances that appear vulnerable. As the characters become spectacles for each other, they inevitably read, expose, mock, or somehow exploit each other's impressions "given off," be this Mary laughing at the too earnest Grushnitsky (IV, 272), Werner noting Pechorin's agitation over Vera (IV, 247), or the captain of the dragoons washing his hands of the exposed Grushnitsky (IV, 298). If for heuristic purposes one momentarily accepts Goffman's abstract description of a viable society, one in which an individual with certain characteristics has the moral right to expect treatment appropriate to these characteristics and in which the individual ought to be what he claims he is—riotously problematical conceptions, to be sure—then one can readily appreciate the power and itensity of "Princess Mary," in which the characters incessantly dedicate their energies to compromising and deceiving each other.[51]

With its persistent references to theatricality, *A Hero of Our Time* invites its readers to consider further aspects of the theatre trope. In particular, two important questions arise: who writes the script for these performances, if there is one, and are there ever moments of relaxation from the destructive theatrical contests that organize this society?

The question of scripting is not as easily answered as it might have been in *Eugene Onegin*, where the characters' reading to a large extent governed their behavior. *A Hero of Our Time* may have been shaped by generic and specific precedents, as a century of influence studies have sought to demonstrate, but it does not foreground the life/literature problem as did Pushkin's verse novel. Yet something makes speech and behavior boringly predictable to Pechorin, at least, who foresees his final conflict with Grushnitsky (IV, 238), that Grushnitsky will seek an introduction to Mary (IV, 248), that Grushnitsky will eventually bore Mary (IV, 250), that he himself and Vera will part (IV, 253), and that Mary will come to love him (IV, 263). "Upon making a woman's acquaintance, I have always unerringly guessed whether she will love me or not" (IV, 263). Indeed, in this constricted little world all of his conjectures do come true, as was not always the case in his dealings with the book's other social groups, such as the smugglers.[52]

The script is, in part, provided by the conventional activities of "society"; it is more or less inevitable that Pechorin will visit the Ligovskaia family once they discover that they have mutual acquaintances or that he will fight a duel with Grushnitsky once he hears Grushnitsky publicly implicate him in a sordid affair. But *how* such sequences of actions are realized is another matter, involving not simply norms and conventions, but the novel's particular reworking of these as tools of vicious competitions, its transformation of harmonizing rituals into disjunctive contests.[53] Thus Pechorin will visit the Ligovskaia salon both to seduce Mary from Grushnitsky and to conduct his affair with Vera. He will orchestrate the duel with Grushnitsky so that it will not heal anyone's wounded sense of honor but, on the contrary, will force Grushnitsky to admit his dishonorable participation in a plot to brand Pechorin a coward. In these cases the social occasion becomes a point of departure for competitions in deception and exposure. The characters who take part become differentiated from each other as winners from losers and as those able to improvise upon a script from those less able.

The concept of "script" not only applies to the actions of the characters but is extended by the novel to their analyses and reflections. Pechorin repeating fragments of tired worldly wisdom (on female psychology, for instance, or on the passions), Grushnitsky delivering his tragic tirades, or Vera stating her jealous fears all adhere to a standard discourse on the emotions and on love that must have been as familiar and predictable to the novel's readers as it was to Pechorin, whose comments on predictability not only signal his intelligence to the reader but also convey a sense of dreary constriction. As Pechorin puts it after his most theatrical confession to Princess Mary has produced the desired effects: "I know all this by heart, that's what's so boring!" (IV, 269). The theatricality which might have liberated the Russian gentleman from subservience to the tyranny of set behavior and made him a "personality," not the function of his social position—according to Lotman—has become in this novel's production of that theatricality a new source of tyranny because the available scripts are so limited.[54]

In a more immediate sense, "script" may include not simply the conscious or unconscious pursuit of social conventions, but the direct imitation of other characters. No character embodies this reliance upon the actions of others more fully than does Pechorin in his love affairs. It may be argued that in almost every case the object of his affections has been proposed to him by another. Pechorin decides to abduct Bela after learning of Kazbich's attraction to her; Pechorin begins his flirtatious teasing of the "undine" after seeing her concern for Ianko; Pechorin, however deep his affection for Vera, cannot help crudely remarking that each time he has pursued her she was married to another (IV, 65). Lest these interpretations of Pechorin's behavior be dismissed as a case of reasoning *post hoc ergo propter hoc*, one could point to his obviously mediated desire for Princess Mary, a mediation of which Pechorin takes passing cognizance in his diary (IV, 242) before blaming such behavior on "high society" (IV, 242), noticing it in Vera, then elevating it to a universal principle of feminine psychology: "What wouldn't a woman do to distress a rival? I remember one who loved me because I loved another" (IV, 277). Such self-forgetfulness on the part of the novel's most self-aware character nicely demonstrates the power of unwritten scripts in *A Hero of Our Time*, be they the conventional behaior patterns of polite society or the actions and desires of concrete individuals. Negative proof of this power appears in the final story, "The Fatalist," where in the absence of a mediator the Cossack girl arouses no interest in Pechorin.

Because the theatrical metaphor, the theatricality of the characters' behavior, and the script of "society's" ideology do so much to shape Pechorin's narrative, the question of off-stage behavior must inevitably strike the novel's readers. Does the tightly bound world of the novel permit any "intermissions," to borrow Lotman's term, or, using Goffman's more discriminating spatial analysis (front, backstage, and outside regions), can a character in this fictional world ever retreat backstage or even leave the theater altogether?[55] Close examination suggests that "Princess Mary" offers its characters little, if any, respite from the need to perform, and that when it is offered they are unlikely to take it. Pechorin, for example, may gallop out into the countryside for relief:

> Whatever grief weighs on my heart, whatever anxiety wearies my mind, all are dissipated in a moment; my soul becomes light, my body's exhaustion overcomes my mind's disquiet. There is no woman's gaze that I would not forget at the sight of the shaggy mountains, lit up by the southern sun, at the sight of the dark blue sky, or at the sound of a torrent falling from crag to crag.

But even here, presumably offstage, he cannot resist immediately considering the impression that he makes:

> I imagine that the Cossacks, yawning on their watchtowers, after seeing me galloping without need or goal, must have long been tormented by this riddle, for truly they would have taken me for a Circassian from my clothes. I have, in fact, been told that on horseback in my Circassian costume, I am more like a Kabardian than many Kabardians. And properly so, for concerning this noble fighting dress, I am a perfect dandy.   (IV, 253–254)

Following a long dissertation on his costume and manner of riding, the spa society, out for a picnic, catches up to Pechorin, and he takes prompt advantage of an opportunity to disrupt Grushnitsky's brave performance for Princess Mary with a better show of his own (IV, 255).

Not only are the characters incessantly on stage, the plot (and subplots) frequently put them on more than one stage at a time. Disaster attends those (such as Grushnitsky) who forget this or never knew it. The June 4 entry in Pechorin's journal precisely sums up the principle characters' multiple parts and degrees of dramatic circumspection. It begins with Princess Mary going backstage with Vera, not knowing that Pechorin and Vera have staged Pechorin's visits with her so that they will be able to see each other at her house:

> I saw Vera today. She tormented me with her jealousy. The princess took it into her head, it seems, to confide in her the secrets of her heart: a fine choice, I must confess!

Vera, forgetting why Pushkin and Mary have been put together, offers some conjectures about Pechorin's script (inaccurate, it turns out) before proposing that the stage be narrowed still further:

> "I can guess what all this will lead to," Vera said to me, "it would be better simply to tell me now that you love her."
> "But if I don't love her?"
> "Then why persecute her, trouble her, excite her imagination? . . . Oh, I know you well! Listen, if you want me to believe you, come next week to Kislovodsk; we are going there the day after tomorrow. The princess will stay here longer. Rent an apartment next door; we will live in a large house near the source, on the mezzanine. Princess Ligovskaia will be below us, and next door there is a house of the same proprietor, which is not yet taken . . . will you come? (IV, 269)

This exchange, which may be considered a backstage one, is immediately followed by one in which Grushnitsky offers some backstage information to Pechorin on his costume and on the ball, information which Pechorin will shortly thereafter exploit in foiling Grushnitsky's plans (IV, 270).

The journal entry ends with an intimate gathering which is, small audience and relative relaxation notwithstanding, a dramatic tour de force. First Pechorin lists the audience, recording his power to deprive Mary of her expressive resources:

> I finished the evening at the princess's; there were no guests, save Vera and one very amusing old man. I was in good spirits and improvised various unusual stories; the princess sat across from me and listened to my nonsense with such deep, tense, even tender attention, that I felt guilty. Where have her vitality, her coquetry, her whims, her arrogant mien, scornful smile, and distracted glance gone?

This is not the only audience that Pechorin sweeps away with his talk:

> Vera noticed all of this: deep sadness appeared on her sickly face; she sat in the shadows by the window, sunk in a borad armchair; I felt sorry for her.
> Then I told the whole dramatic story of my acquaintance with her, of our love—concealing all of it, naturally, with invented names.

> I depicted my tenderness, my anxieties, my ecstasies so vividly, I
> showed her actions and character in such advantageous light, that in
> spite of herself she had to forgive me my flirtation with the princess.
>   She got up, sat close to us, became animated . . . and only at two
> o'clock did we remember that the doctors had ordered her to go to bed
> at eleven.   (IV, 270)

The same improvisation moves at least three different audiences, each
with a different relationship to the performer: the witty old man, the
infatuated princess, and Pechorin's consumptive lover. Where Mary
and Grushnitsky had failed to distinguish between front region and
backstage, Pechorin artfully manages to segregate his audiences, captivating all of them.

Theatricality and the idea of "being on stage" are so much a part
of Pechorin that when he is alone he must posit a conscious spectator
for his actions and speech acts. That a journal not written for publication presupposes an audience of the diarist himself, is, of course,
basic communication theory.[56] And Pechorin makes the presence of
the second, observing self explicit for Dr. Werner: "Within me there
are two persons: one lives in the full sense of the word, the other
reasons and judges him" (IV, 292). The division of the self into heart
and head, acting and observing aspects, was at least as old as Plato
and as recent as *Adolphe*, where the judging capacity is presented in
theatrical terms: "cette portion de nous qui est, pour ainsi dire, spec-
tatrice de l'autre."[57] Such theatrical metaphors shaped important
eighteenth-century discussions of moral philosophy.[58] Where Lermontov's treatment of this psychological structure stands out is in
the energy that he makes Pechorin invest in trying to captivate Princess Mary and the other visitors to the spa. Brief confessional phrases—
"I felt guilty" or "I felt sorry" in the long passage just quoted—seek
to preempt the judging self's potential objections, as do many ra-
tionalizing passages, which generalize Pechorin's actions as universal
flaws ("Who has not concluded such agreements with his conscience," IV, 295); or which deflect the judging self's potential accusations onto other characters. Pechorin's parting from Dr. Werner—
who is clearly upset by the duel and who has externalized the judging
self for Pechorin by offering alternatives, by reminding him of the
consequences of his actions, and by provoking ideas and confes-
sions—illustrates Pechorin's ability to overwhelm and deflect moral
objections:

> He stopped on the threshold, he wanted to shake my hand . . . and if
> I had shown the least desire for it, he would have thrown himself on
> my neck; but I remained as cold as a stone, and he left.
>   That's people for you! They know in advance all the bad sides of an

action, they help, they counsel, they even approve it, seeing the impossibility of any other means, and then they wash their hands and turn
with indignation from him who had the daring to take upon himself the
full weight of responsibility. They are all alike, even the best, the most
intelligent!   (IV, 302)

Werner was neither washing his hands nor turning in indignation.
Pechorin's need to overwhelm the consciousness that Werner represents, however, occasions this extraordinary tirade.

Pechorin's fear of that consciousness and his sense of the categories
with which it operates are tersely captured in the statement, "I have
become incapable of noble impulses; I am afraid of appearing ridiculous to myself (IV, 283)." Pechorin's internal spectator, for which
he performs his journal with its self-analytical and confessional passages, here shares the worst values of the society in which Pechorin
moves.

"Hero" and "Time"

To write the history of oneself is to write the confession of
the deepest part of our neighbors' souls as well.
Jacques Lacan, "The Insistence of the Letter in the Unconscious"

So far I have discussed *A Hero of Our Time* in terms of its constricted
cultural and social world, a world presented largely in theatrical terms,
in which the public stage on which its hero acts so successfully is
morally quite similar to the internal stage on which he performs in
the privacy of his reflections. At one in this way with the values and
behavioral patterns of the society that he represents and superior to
the other characters in his ability to realize these values and patterns,
Pechorin is indeed the "hero" of his "time." "Accustomed to good
society" (IV, 248), he has mastered its refined talk and aesthetic forms
(epigrams, "portraits," polite phrases), its "logic" (IV, 257), and its
"signs" (IV, 268). There is no contest in which this mastery does not
bring him victory.

Yet few readers of the novel, contemporary or modern, would be
fully satisfied with a critical account that left Pechorin so enmeshed
in the values and patterns of his fictional "time." No matter that
Pechorin replicates the vicious behavior of the world that surrounds
him, no matter that his improvisations on the script do not funda-
mentally change the play, for a century and a half readers have felt
compelled to tip the scales back and forth between hero and world,
seeking an excess of potential in one or the other and trying to defend

one or the other as if these were a living person and a real world.

The history of the novel's reception is too long to repeat here, but it might (allowing for those who slid between the world of the text and the world that they brought to it) be outlined according to the critics' emphasis on the relative value of "hero" or "time."[59] Some early critics who were intellectually close to the positions of the Slavophiles or government propagandists, Shevyrev or Burachok for example, responded to the novel by condemning Pechorin as improbable or un-Russian or criminal and by trying to rehabilitate the world of the novel. Their criticism focused largely on questions of representation, and the fidelity of the novel to Russian reality as they themselves saw it. Belinsky initiated another line of criticism by giving the greater weight to the hero, stressing the "contradiction between the profound nature and wretched actions of one and the same person."[60] To support this he could draw upon such passages as Pechorin's declaration of frustrated greatness (IV, 265) and Vera's paean to her lover's spiritual capacity (IV, 300), neither of which is very well substantiated by Pechorin's thoughts or deeds in the remainder of the novel. Lermontov, meanwhile, entered into a dialogue with both positions in the second edition to the novel with his "Author's Introduction"; there he invited the reader to approach the text with a sense of "irony," a point that had already been made in the "Introduction to Pechorin's Journal," where the reader was likewise asked to evaluate the novel, the hero, and the title in terms of "irony."[61] Beyond this ambiguous resolution he left no explicit statements, except the novel.

Some of the novel's readers and critics agonized not only over its representation of the hero and his world, but also over the effect that the hero might have on its readers. Nicholas I, in particular, worried about the novel's conative force: "Morals are ruined and character is embittered by such novels . . . What result can it give? Contempt or hatred for humanity! . . . People are too inclined to become hypochondriacs or misanthropes anyway, why excite them to develop such inclinations with writings like these?"[62]

The novel's capacity to inspire such intense, diametrically opposed reactions, and such limited ones, recalls us to the dynamics of its text, which, as has already been discussed, offered and withdrew the possibility of a biography for the hero and suggested two chronologies, the interplay of which offers conflicting views of Pechorin as heroic thinker and as forgetful casuist. From a closer perspective it is possible to see that *A Hero of Our Time* sets against each other many passages which contradict each other, forcing its reader to infer contradictory conclusions about Pechorin. Thus, callous laughter at the death of Bela is offset by the possibly psychosomatic illness he suffers as a consequence of it (IV, 214–215); his arrogantly casual and superficial politeness toward his old comrade in "Maksim Maksimych" must coexist with the reader's knowledge that this same Pechorin has left ten notebooks of sensitive diaries (IV, 221–223); his inept scheming in "Taman' " is balanced by his daring challenge to predestination in "The Fatalist." His desperate chase after Vera erases—at least momentarily—the cold staging of the duel and his manipuation of Mary, especially since Pechorin's comments on the theatricality of Vera's last letter were eliminated from the drafts of the novel.[63] Accounts of his theatrical contests are tempered by passages of "lyric" meditation.[64] Not just the sophisticated traveling narrator, but also the artless Maksim Maksimych note contradictions in Pechorin's appearance and behavior (IV, 189, 220).

These explicit invitations to contradictory understandings of Pechorin keep the reader moving back and forth in the text, seeking a resolution which never satisfactorily presents itself. Pechorin fits into the novel's polite society too well and dresses too unremarkably (IV, 200) to stand apart as a principled dandy, yet is too strange (IV, 260, 293) and disharmonious to be an *honnête homme*.[65] He participates too willingly in society's competitions to speak very convincingly of "fate," yet the other characters and cultures of the novel offer no convincing alternative courses of action either. He writes of social oppression and presents persuasively destructive analyses of the polite society in which he moves, yet he acts out his antagonism to that society by playing the same games, only better.

In the passage that served as an epigraph to an earlier section of this chapter, Lukács distinguished between two types of novel, those in which the hero is broader than the world in which he moves, and those in which the hero is narrower.[66] *A Hero of Our Time* by its very title invites commentary in these terms, difficult as they may be to define and apply. Its success, in its own time and subsequently, rests on its power simultaneously to constrict both hero and world and to intimate that each might surpass the other and surpass itself. Its continuing vitality has surely been advanced by the rigor of its constriction, and the ineffability of its intimations.

V

Dead Souls: "Charmed by a Phrase"

> The world clusters and unclusters. The need to order
> and stabilize, the "centripetal" forces of social life,
> leads to the accumulation and hierarchization of rules
> and practices—i.e., to grammar and the relatively sta-
> ble patterns of institutions and ideologies. But a va-
> riety of "centrifugal" forces insures that clusters will
> never cohere, once and for all, into systems . . . ,
> whether stable or dynamic. These centrifugal forces
> include the random and unpredictable events of
> everyday life . . . and our need to create what is
> genuinely new; to parody, to invent, to play.
>
> G. S. Morson, "Dialogue, Monologue, and History"

SET IN THE algebraically labeled town of "N" and in a landscape
of lunar desolation, which is dotted by the verbal particles that
Sergei Bocharov has aptly called "imaginary numbers which unclearly
measure some imaginary reality," unfolding in a period Gogol
vaguely specified as "shortly after the glorious repulsion of the French"
(VI, 206), and featuring the comic misadventures of a bumbling confidence man among a world of ludicrous monomaniacs, *Dead Souls*
would hardly seem the stuff of cultural controversy and recurring
national identity crises.[1] Yet Gogol's longest prose fiction, first published in 1842 in a moderately sized, expensive edition (2,500 copies,
10 silver rubles) and reprinted four years later, set off a storm in
Russian culture which has never ceased to rage. Few aspects of the
book have escaped continuing controversy, starting with its very title,
which struck the censor as an impossibility (the soul was officially
presumed immortal), and ending with its final image of Russia as a
flying troika (which some readers took to be a note of optimism and
others have taken to be a conjuror's trick, a rhetorical puff of smoke
into which the novel's principal rogue might conveniently disap-

pear.)[2] Within a few months Gogol's self-styled "narrative poem" (*poema*) had managed to fragment the Russian readership as thoroughly as Pushkin's Southern poems or Bulgarin's *Ivan Vyzhigin* had once united it. Salons and circles frequented by Gogol continued to praise *Dead Souls*, as they had done after the private readings of the previous six years; in other salons it was damned as a Ukrainian's calumny on Russia, or worse. Konstantin Aksakov captured these reactions for the anxious author:

> We haven't had such movement for a long time as we now have with *Dead Souls*. Decidedly, not a single person has remained indifferent; the book has touched everyone, aroused everyone, and everyone says his piece. Praise and abuse resound from all sides, and there is plenty of each, but also a complete absence of indifference . . . Without this book it would be impossible to presuppose the variety of opinions that has now arisen in society. Some say that only here can they see a Gogol which until now has not struck them nearly so much, only here can they sense his colossal quality; others would have proclaimed that this book was Gogol's downfall, the death of his talent, but soon, deafened by the general uproar that rose up about their heads, they had to fall silent; they now limit themselves to pointing out your previous works, on the Ukraine. For others Russia stands out in colossal fashion here, running through the first part and stepping forth at the end of the book; tears well up in their eyes as they read the last lines. Others read it and say that they must suffer and cry. "Look," they say to me, "what a heavy, terrible mockery at the end of the book." "What?" I asked, goggle-eyed . . . Some say that *Dead Souls* is an epic, that they understand the meaning of this title [the book's subtitle, "a narrative poem," in fact]; others see in it a joke, completely in the spirit of Gogol: "There you are, gnaw on that word." Many landowners are seriously angry and consider you their mortal, personal enemy. It goes without saying that all of this includes attacks on you for indecency . . . The journals can't stop writing about *Dead Souls*.[3]

That Gogol had fragmented the reading public became a commonplace. Sergei Aksakov, Konstantin's father, divided Gogol's readers into three groups: those who had been delighted by *Dead Souls*, those whom it had puzzled, and those whom it had embittered.[4] Another analyst, charting the intellectual currents of the early 1840s, would divide Gogol's public supporters into pseudo-aristocrats, Hegelians, and those who made a Homer out of Gogol.[5]

Indeed the journals were writing about Gogol's novel, and they showed no more uniformity in their reactions and only a little more artistic awareness than did the social lions of Moscow and St. Petersburg. Unfriendly journalists (among them Grech, Sękowski, and

N. A. Polevoi) meticulously combed it for flaws in language and for offenses against the good taste of polite society. Friendly journalists appropriated it for their favorite causes, and new storms arose. Pletnev, one of Masal'sky's "pseudo-aristocrats" and the friend to whom Pushkin had dedicated *Eugene Onegin*, used *Dead Souls* as raw material for an essay on aesthetics, challenging as he did so any claim that the text might make to "serious social interest."[6] As the philosophical circles squared off against each other in the battle of Slavophiles versus Westernizers, *Dead Souls* provided heavy weaponry for each side. Thus, the Westernizer Belinsky found it a useful occasion for comments on Russia's shortcomings, while the young Slavophile Konstantin Aksakov patriotically claimed it Homeric or Shakespearean in its grasp of life's fullness.[7] Nor was each critic necessarily in agreement with himself: Belinsky, during the course of his reviews of the novel and his polemics with Konstantin Aksakov, managed first to salute, then to question the novel's epic and lyric aspects.[8]

Critical and cultural controversies over Gogol and his comic epic in prose have lost none of their intensity since the early 1840s. It has never been allowed to rest peacefully in the library or professorial study, dusty and neglected like the books and journals described in its own pages. This is not to say that Gogol's pages were always read, or that his novel's significance for many of its Russian readers derived from their contemplation of its artistry. "No matter how great the artistic merit of Gogol's works," a Russian historian of the intelligentsia later pointed out, "it alone cannot explain all of his fascination and all of his power over people's minds."[9] On the contrary, much of its value for readers throughout the remainder of the tsarist period resided precisely in its appropriability as a vehicle for social commentary on the institution of serfdom or on the corruption of the imperial bureaucracy or on the nature of Russia herself. Even now, when collective and state farms have replaced the landowners' estates and when a new bureaucracy has taken over the duties of the old one, *Dead Souls* is officially venerated for its historically critical role, as if to legitimate the new regime by keeping alive the memory of a historical "other."[10] Indeed, examining its oft-divided readership, one cannot help but note that far more than *Eugene Onegin*, which celebrated the confusing wealth of Russia's cosmopolitan culture, more even than *A Hero of Our Time*, which constricted so severely those possibilities, *Dead Souls* allowed—and allows—its readers to raise the question of "Russia."

While the best of recent Pushkin scholarship has been devoted to pursuing his many cultural references, and while Lermontov's academic readers have become unfortunately bogged down in deciding whether he was a realist or a romantic, the study of Gogol's novel remains fruitfully charged by the problems of art and representation raised by its first readers. To chart every step in the division of Gogol's subsequent readers is not necessary here because it is readily available elsewhere.[11] More important for my purposes is the nature of the continuing division. At virtually each stage in the history of Gogol criticism, readings which insist on the artfulness, idiosyncrasy, or mimetic malfeasance of *Dead Souls* have countered the dominant readings which have presented the text as a piece of reportage and civic responsibility.

Doubts and qualifications about the lifelikeness of Gogol's plots and characters were voiced sporadically throughout the nineteenth century. Early critics as disparate as Pletnev and Belinsky, however, blamed this on the insufficiencies of Russian life which might have produced stunted people and stillborn actions.[12] Other readers wisely hedged their bets on this issue by claiming that Gogol had given them the occasion for thinking about their surroundings, which is, of course, not the same thing as saying that he had in some sense showed them a photograph.[13] But it was Vasily Rozanov and a brilliant array of modern critics who followed him—Briusov, Bely, Nabokov, the formalists, to name a few—who most sharply criticized the tradition which had found Gogol's characters, situations, and depiction of Russia lifelike.[14] This modern countertradition in Gogol criticism could look back at Gogol through the experience of high literary realism, with its meticulously developed characters, its attention to historical and social conditioning, and its intricate plots; and when it did, it found that the magic of Gogol lay elsewhere—in his hyperbolic style, his alogical connections, his grotesque collisions of perceptual categories, his ability to create a universe at once horrifyingly evil and seductively banal.[15]

The modernists challenged the institutionalized social readings in a variety of ways, providing their formal, psychoanalytic, religious, and mythological alternatives as they reminded the public of moments in Gogol's life and texts which provocatively embarrassed the view of Gogol as a progressive critical realist: that Gogol was more attached to polite society than to Belinsky and his fellows, that Gogol was generally more interested in art and language than in political or social progress, that Gogol looked not to the intelligentsia but to the government and to religion for the transfiguration of Russian life, that Gogol's comically puppet-like characters are largely incapable of change and improvement, that the critical voices in Gogol's texts are attrib-

uted to the greatest rogues, that the rhetoric of *Dead Souls* seems not
to challenge serfdom as a system, that Gogol's plots are merely anecdotal and that nothing much really happens in them. These prov-
ocations have become particularly infuriating to the official Gogol
criticism after the 1920s, because, with a few important exceptions,
they have been issued outside the boundaries of the Soviet Union or
by critical currents (symbolism, formalism) that had fallen into official
disfavor.[16]

The Gogolian text, then, has lost none of its power to fragment its
publics and to participate in the cultural, social, and political controversies that have convulsed Russian life. But its continuing ability to
stir up the publics of Russian literature hardly stops at mere fragmentation. No less fascinating than the intensity of the debates it sets
off is its ability—and this holds particularly for *Dead Souls*—to set the
ostensibly opposed parties at cross purposes, transforming an align-
ment of "either/or" into one of "both . . . and." Thus, in the course
of treating the novel as a piece of critical reportage, some of the most
rigorously social readings have managed to contribute important insights into its structure and style. V. F. Pereverzev's highly reductive
attempt to read all aspects of Gogol's oeuvre in terms of the author's
petty landowning background offers, nonetheless, detailed studies of
style, characterization, and composition; amidst his chapter on *Dead
Souls* as a piece of social satire, G. A. Gukovsky became one of few
readers to comment adequately on its complicated narrative presentation; A. A. Elistratova intersperses useful, systematic comparisons
with Western novels with virulent attacks on Western and modernist
Gogol scholars, then refines with her comparative analyses the conclusions about the Gogolian universe and its denizens that her opponents had already reached.[17] Meanwhile, those who have challenged
the sociological tradition have, no less paradoxically, begun to clear
the way for socially and historically aware readings that might address
the shortcomings of earlier sociological analyses: their inattention to
institutions of literature; their imposition of alien social formations,
such as a "bourgeoisie," on Russian life; and their attempts to dress
Gogol in a literary uniform, realism, into which only the most obsti-
nate terminological tailoring could make him fit.

These beginnings point toward the aestheticization of social life and
the concern with style and "talk" which characterized the ideology
of polite society in the early nineteenth century. Boris Eikhenbaum's
essay on "The Overcoat" took issue with the sentimental view of
Gogol as a humanitarian social critic, but in so doing it called attention
to the story's contrapuntal imitations of oral performance, a mode of
dissemination crucial to Gogol's interaction with his audience.[18] Vla-

dimir Nabokov's famous seven-page disquisition on "poshlust" [the Russian *poshlost'*, vulgarity] points toward an ideologically aware reading of *Dead Souls* in terms of its manipulation of the everyday patterns, exclusions, and aspirations of polite society.[19] Finally, A. de Jonge's suggestion that the positive hero of the book may be "the Russian language" in its livelier manifestations leads the novel back toward a social reading by recalling the ideologically loaded linguistic controversies of the 1830s, although the Gogolian logic of "both . . . and" must move one to ask whether that language could be the villain of the piece as well as its hero, since language generates the characters' reality as well as the author-narrator's.[20]

In this chapter, taking my cue from readings which have insisted on the uniqueness and vitality of Gogol's language, yet refusing to isolate the continuing fascination of *Dead Souls* from its historical and social beginnings, I will examine the novel's interaction with the literary institutions of its time, then pursue its elusively devastating reproduction of the ideology which had shaped those and other institutions of early nineteenth-century Russia, crystallizing, playing with, travestying, and ultimately fragmenting that cluster of values, social patterns, and styles.[21] *Dead Souls*, a deceptively simple account of a macabre attempt to purchase and then to mortgage serfs who were biologically dead but legally still alive on the census rolls, has turned out to be not only a comic epitaph for an entire way of life, but also a continuing invitation to measure other forms of existence, real and possible, against its conglomeration of disasters or pseudo-disasters. I will treat, however, the means by which the novel undertakes its process of comic subversion, its fragmenting and its irrepressible ambiguity, not as literary universals, abstracted from the controversies of their time, but as themselves part and parcel of those struggles.

Astride Institutions

> I need to know with whom I am dealing . . . I need to sense
> and hear those to whom I am speaking.
> Gogol, letter to P. A. Pletnev, 1846

> People had already spoken this way in some places, but no
> one had yet written like this.
> Andrei Bely, *Masterstvo Gogolia*

A famous early twentieth-century attack on Gogol's reputation as a realistic writer bears the formidable title "Gogol Absolutely Did Not

Know Real Russian Life." The most striking point in its enchantingly positivistic indictment quantified Gogol's "knowledge" as follows:

> The final sum of this direct study of "Russia" comes to: 27 days of travel and 7 days in Kursk before the appearance of *The Inspector General* and 20 days of uninterrupted travel during the interval between *The Inspector General* and *Dead Souls*, in all 47, or, for an even count, let's say *50 days of travel and 7 days in Kursk.*

Vengerov was even more scandalized by Gogol's negligent behavior during his longest layover, in a posting station not far from Moscow: "To speed the time, he writes letters to Prokopovich and Pogodin and reads Richardson's *Clarissa*. *And these 8–10 hours are . . . the only stay by the author of 'The Inspector General' in a Russian provincial city.*"[22] That Vengerov expects the writer to function like an anthropologist in the field betrays, of course, an understanding of the possibilities and duties of imaginative literature different from those which reigned in Gogol's time or which prevail in ours. Yet his polemic is hardly naive, parodying as it does the intelligentsia's view of Gogol as a "citizen writer." Through his mockery of this tradition, however, emerges a Gogol who in terms of his own time not only "knew" Russian life but also *practiced* being Russian. For writing familiar letters and reading Western epistolary novels showed more engagement with the ideologically sanctioned "knowledge" of the early nineteenth-century Russian elite than conducting ethnographic research on provincial Russia could possibly have shown. Gogol's engagement with "real" Russian life, however, was indeed ambiguous.

Pausing on his 1837 grand tour in Baden, Andrei Karamzin sent home an account of Gogol's activities which listed the omens attending the birth of *Dead Souls*. For my purposes, it abounds in implications for the study of the novel's place in Russian literary and social life, if not very incisively:

> I dined at the Smirnovs with Gogol, who brought a new, as yet unfinished work to read: it is a long humorous novel about Russia. This is the best thing he has written up to now, but I dare not say anything else, because he read to us sous le sceau du secret. And, incidentally, we laid in a store of this reading, which held us over until late in the evening, because in the sky and in the air such deviltry was running wild that a tale couldn't tell it, nor a pen write it down. Thunder, rain, a whirlwind![23]

The letter reminds us, first of all, that Gogol may have been physically distant from Russia as he completed the first volume of *Dead Souls* (1836–1841), but that he was, if anything, closer to Russian salon life than he had previously been in St. Petersburg. An inepcunious young gentleman of undistinguished Ukrainian descent, Gogol had, to be sure, followed the classical pattern of salon acceptance, finding a place in polite literary life after the success of his first collection, *Evenings on a Farm Near Dikan'ka* (1830–31, 2 parts); he had established working relationships with such littérateurs as Pushkin, Zhukovsky, and Pletnev; his works had appeared in the periodicals of the "literary aristocrats," and he had begun to take an active part in the public literary ventures of the familiar groups with his almanac plans and with his critical essays for Pushkin's *Contemporary*. He had, taking further advantage of the possibilities for advancement afforded by polite literary life, used his connections to acquire a professorship in history at Petersburg University, as he would later use his well-connected friends Zhukovsky and Aleksandra Smirnova to solicit imperial sponsorship for his work on *Dead Souls* (XI, 15, 97–99; XII, 22). He had, in short, begun to play the various roles that constituted the Karamzinian synthesis of institutional possibilities (official encouragement, familiar literary association, remunerated literary work); and he joined in the polemics of Pushkin's associates against such rivals for this synthesis as Sękowski and Bulgarin.[24] At the same time Gogol's hold on this complicated institutional possibility had been, at best, precarious. His stories had so clearly violated the current stylistic conventions that Pushkin and Viazemsky had been forced to relocate the bounds of taste in his defense, and the prophetic-sermonical-didactic essays of Gogol's *Arabesques* (1835) had proposed an author-reader relationship out of keeping with the conventions of the period's refined prose.[25] Pushkin, as we have seen, had felt it necessary to blunt the edge of Gogol's polemics. And fashion, which had embraced his early Ukrainian tales, had turned its back on the far more brilliant fictions of *Mirgorod* (1835) and *Arabesques*. Gogol's flight abroad after the mixed reception and inept staging of *The Inspector General* (1836) had seemed to constitute a break with the institutions of Russian literature. The death of Pushkin, who, however psychologically ornate Gogol's feelings toward him and however different their styles, was nothing less than the embodiment of Russian literature to Gogol, threatened to isolate him further from those institutions.[26]

And yet, returning to Andrei Karamzin's letter, we can see that Gogol had abandoned only a part of the elder Karamzin's synthesis: the public, remunerated literary work at such ongoing activities as journalism or criticism. Gogol's bitter comments on Russian journalism and his steadfast refusal to publish any fragments of his novel in his friends' journals (XI, 77, 332) show how firmly he rejected even that public part of the institutional synthesis which Lermontov had

been willing to countenance. While Pushkin and Lermontov had committed sections of their novels to print, Gogol insisted on placing his
under a "seal of secrecy," preferring a sudden impact on his readers
to a continuing journalistic pseudodialogue. In its place, he chose to
observe and perform for the would-be distillate of the public that he
encountered in the salons.[27]

The available records, much more extensive in Gogol's case than
in Lermontov's, show that while Gogol was dedicating himself to the
writing of his masterpiece he enjoyed and even sought the company
of many of the hostesses and many of the littérateurs who had shaped
the great age of familiar literary associations: Aleksandra Smirnova,
Zinaida Volkonskaia, the Vielhorskis and Sollogubs, Aleksandr Turgenev, Zhukovsky, Shevyrev, Pogodin, Iazykov—to name some who
have already appeared in earlier chapters of this study. His brief
returns to Russia were likewise spent in the company of literary society, as the object of a certain rivalry between St. Petersburg and
Moscow circles.[28] During these years Gogol kept up an active correspondence with a number of society's members. And while it is one
of the aspects of Gogol that modern scholars have ignored, especially
those who would like to celebrate him as Belinsky's fellow-traveler
or as a weird and isolated introvert, Gogol's contemporaries did not
hesitate to view him as a man, however eccentric, of the salons.[29]

While these documents show Gogol to have been very much a part
of this elite world, they also suggest that he was, like Lermontov but
differently, apart from it. Something of this ambiguous position may
be inferred from the tone of young Karamzin's letter, in which the
writer subsequently acknowledged as Russia's most arresting prose
stylist figures merely as humorous provender for a stormy night. The
condescension emerges even more clearly from a slightly earlier passage in Karamzin's letters: "Gogol gagne à être connu, he becomes
talkative and often funny and original in conversation, as he is in his
stories. It is very much a pity that he lacks education, and still more
the pity that he doesn't feel it."[30] A few interlocutors, such as Sainte-
Beuve or Sturdza, testify to the intelligence, pleasantness, and ap-
propriateness of Gogol's talk.[31] As a rule, these were the witnesses
who saw him least or were not members of Russian society. Their
testimony, like the sketch of an elegantly insouciant Gogol who stares
out from the frontispiece of the Academy edition (vol. 6), is belied
by almost all the other memoirs, which, while differing from each
other in detail, net a Gogol who could be counted upon to tell a
riotously funny anecdote to a family in mourning, introduce himself

by commenting on his intestines, become bogged down in trivia, chat ineptly with women, or, alternatively, wax inappropriately sermonical in his letters, to say nothing of dressing pretentiously, falling asleep at dinner, failing to pay social calls, and committing other faux pas less offensive to a modern reader than to Gogol's contemporary society.[32] The memoirists, of course, knew Gogol's fiction well and could recognize in this behavior some of Gogol's finest comic scenes, but they seem not to be so clearly projecting the fiction onto the author here as did Lermontov's verbal portraitists, who had, as a rule, less time to observe their subject than had Gogol's.

Despite Gogol's lapses, something drew the salons to him as forcefully as he was drawn to them, if only the novelty of a "strange phenomenon," as Sergei Aksakov put it.[33] Andrei Karamzin's letter points to the source of this attraction—Gogol's reading, not his conversation or manners. The memoirs of Gogol's appearances in society generally center upon his oral performances—of his stories, plays, and impromptu anecdotes, which he was incessantly asked to provide. Unless his topics of conversation were particularly outrageous—his defense of the censorship to Turgenev, for instance—it was the oral performances of his written work that proved most memorable to his audiences.[34] Sergei Aksakov, who found Gogol's conversations forgettable and sometimes trivial, carefully recorded valuable impressions of Gogol's reading.[35] Consequently, Gogol's marginality in this world may be at least partly described in terms of his verbal behavior: unable to take part in the free-flowing exchange of repartee, gossip, or light verse, he either came with a written text, provided a self-contained oral narrative (an anecdote), or remained a silent observer.

The anomaly of this position notwithstanding, many ecstatic recollections have preserved the excitement with which these chamber audiences listened to recitations of *The Inspector General* or *Dead Souls*. More importantly, a number have described Gogol's manner of reading, inevitably finding it "natural"—not exaggerated, not theatrical, and not particularly shocking, despite its intersecting lexical levels, its uninhibited syntax, and its dazzling turns of phrase. Ivan Turgenev, for example, compared Gogol to Dickens, whose readings he had also attended: where Dickens struck Turgenev as a dramatic, almost theatrical reader, Gogol impressed him with the "extreme simplicity and restraint of his manner, a certain solemn and at the same time naive sincerity."[36] Panaev, too, insisted on the nontheatrical quality of Gogol's reading, and Sergei Aksakov exclaimed that Gogol recited so naturally "that none of those present guessed that he was hearing a composition."[37] Annenkov, who produced a fair copy of *Dead Souls* from Gogol's dictation, recorded a similar impression of "artistic naturalness."[38]

Frequently the "naturalness" of Gogol's reading lulled his listeners into projecting the quality of "naturalness" or "verisimilitude" onto the matter of the works themselves. Apart from those, such as Belinsky, who had a manifestly political need to proclaim Gogol's representational accuracy, those most likely to assert the "naturalness" of *Dead Souls* were those who heard it. Andrei Karamzin's calm assumption that he was hearing a humorous novel "about Russia" is a case in point. The following year in Paris, another man of the salons, Aleksandr Turgenev, recorded a similar, but more extensive, reaction in his diary: "Gogol came to me and read a fragment of his novel *Dead Souls*. It is a true, living picture of Russia, of our officials' and nobles' everyday life, of our governmental and private landowning morality."[39]

Sergei Aksakov, also enchanted by Gogol's reading, described its overwhelming power precisely as an *oral* phenomenon:

> I told Gogol afterwards that hearing *Dead Souls* for the first time, and even not for the first, and having been fascinated by the beauty of its artistic consciousness, no critic in the world capable of perceiving poetic impressions would be in any condition to note any shortcomings; that if he wanted my comments, he should give me the fair copy, so that I could read it at my leisure and, maybe, read it more than once. That would be a different matter. But Gogol did not want to and couldn't do it; the manuscript was hastily recopied and quickly sent off to the censor in Petersburg.[40]

Within the familiar surroundings, read aloud, Gogol's text could sound at once faultlessly artistic and natural according to the simultaneously aesthetic and social conventions of that milieu. Another of Gogol's salon auditors, Pletnev, would subsequently review *Dead Souls* in these terms, adding a point perhaps more appropriate for Pushkin's subtly crafted *Eugene Onegin* than for Gogol's manifestly new and puzzling novel: "he who knows the rules of convention will act successfully; but whoever picks them up and uses them unconsciously will produce a merely mechanical work, creating nothing artistically."[41]

Taken together, these comments by people who *heard* Gogol recite his novel suggest that his account of Chichikov's macabre swindle (and, ultimately, of psychological obsession, social fragmentation, and artistic alienation) had powers beyond even those that subsequent readers have found in it, powers to make itself accepted by and to delight those whose values it may have most thoroughly subverted. Like the greatest of Chichikov's dupes, the vacuously sentimental Manilov, they seem truly to have been "enchanted by a phrase" (VI, 146). Yet their reaction tells only part of the story of the novel's reception, as we have already seen. No less adamant in their opinions were those outside of Gogol's circle who encountered the novel in its written form. In salons which Gogol did not frequent, in the commercially oriented journals of his quondam opponents, and in the writings of those (such as Belinsky) who sought new functions for literature, something very different emerged, with very different powers, if only the power to outrage.

Such a double reaction, depending on different modes of institutional dissemination (oral for the salons, printed for the public of Russia's incipient profession of letters), could have, in theory, befallen many works of the time, given the availability of multiple institutions and, consequently, multiple audiences. Certainly a writer's familiars would be expected to listen to his texts in a more kindly fashion than reviewers and a capricious public might greet its printed version. Yet the intensity of the fragmentation in Gogol's case demands more than this "common sense" explanation. For even among Gogol's friends, there was disagreement on how *Dead Souls* should be presented. For Pletnev, the text was best when heard: "for his works one needs a reciter who has studied him beforehand."[42]

But for Konstantin Aksakov, as ultimately for Gogol himself (VI, 587–590; XII, 144) *Dead Souls* was a text which demanded a reader's prolonged and attentive engagement:

> When I heard *Dead Souls* no sense of a whole was yet awakened within me. I read it; I felt that it was beautiful; I saw the beauty of the composition, the life of each separate trait; but what the composition was, its general meaning in which joined together all of these wonderful, living traits, this I could not understand . . . but later the inner harmony of the whole composition was revealed to me.[43]

Some of the differences between hearing and reading, this last comment argues, resided in the opportunity that contact with the written text gave for reflection, analysis, and construction of an overall design. The orally delivered text seems to have invited a spirit of cooperation from its listeners, a willingness to accept as natural and to overlook or tolerate the comic strangeness, contradictions, and discontinuities of *Dead Souls*.[44] But the experience of reading could more readily open the text to critical scrutiny and make such discontinuities palpable.

Sergei Aksakov's unwillingness to criticize the orally performed text
and his desire to make his comments on the basis of the manuscript
version—"that would be a different matter"—seem to bear this out.

A representative piece of Gogolian syntax which is marked by the
phonetic and semantic associative chains of oral composition shows
how the written and oral invitations to the text might differ from each
other:

> Potom on byl na vechere u vitse-gubernatora, na bol'shom obede u ot-
> kupshchika, na nebol'shom obede u prokurora, kotoryi, vprochem, stoil
> bol'shogo, na zakuske posle obedni, dannoi gorodskim glavoiu, kotoraia
> tozhe stoila obeda.   (VI, 17)

> [Then he was at a soirée at the vice governor's, at a large dinner at the
> tax farmer's, at a small dinner at the prosecutor's, which, by the way,
> was worth a large one, at a buffet luncheon after mass, given by the
> mayor, which was also worth a dinner.]

Although Russian has a rich system of inflections that generally protect its speakers from syntactic ambiguity, in this case the nature of
the mayor's party is no less ambiguous in the original than in English
translation. Did he give a luncheon or a mass? The form "given"
[*dannoi*] could agree with either. In listening to an oral performance,
one is likely to follow the flow of discourse, accepting the semantically
plausible alternative in a syntactically ambiguous passage. As one
reads the printed version, however, this rare mention of a religious
practice can stand out in bold relief. Pleonastically sandwiched between the dinners [*obed*, in Russian], the celebration of the Holy Eu-
charist [*obednia*] becomes just another culinary occasion, another
trivialization of spiritual significance, and a travesty of society's incursion into the religious sphere. Perhaps this was only a "careless"
mistake, but Gogol carried it through the drafts of the novel.[45] A reader
can place it together with other such trivializations, and in so doing
construct a sense of the novel's world and of the relationship between
that fictional world and his or her own "real" one.

Dead Souls in fact, straddles the boundary between oral and written presention, or, for a modern reader, between the written imitation
of oral presentation and oral presentation proper. Gogol made it do
so in his own time by performing the chapters dominated by a chatty
author-narrator who was, culturally and intellectually, on the characters' plane of action, and who could transmit their hilarious ways
of thinking with light, seductive irony and with verbal play.[46] These
are, primarily, the opening chapters, in which Chichikov ingrati-
ates himself into the society of N and into the households of five
nearby landowners, Manilov, Korobochka, Nozdrev, Sobakevich, and

Pliushkin. But in the chapters Gogol read less frequently to his acquaintances, the chapters dealing with the town and its reaction to Chichikov's caper, the author-narrator's position becomes increasingly that of a "writer," a producer of printed works, who is self-consciously isolated from the reading public. Not only did Gogol read these chapters less frequently, he inserted a number of new digressions, lyrical and moralizing, into them just before publication.[47] These digressions, different in tone, different in projected addresser-addressee relationship from the earlier sections of the novel, could and did provoke intense efforts on the part of Gogol's readers to put the radically sundered pieces together. As we have seen, these efforts remain no less intense a century and a half later.

Most immediately, the institutional uncertainty of *Dead Souls*—its ambiguity as a text for oral or written reception, its generic ambiguity (picaresque novel, lyric, epic), and the attendant ambiguity of its author-narrator—could, in turn, inspire the questioning of important ideological processes which might otherwise have remained "natural": the constitution of the *honnête homme*, the harmonization of social antagonisms, the spatial configuration of Russian life (provincial/cosmopolitan), the very functioning of language itself. Stretching the ideological reconciliation of contradictory situations to the breaking point, *Dead Souls* produced a fragmented reception along these very lines. It did so, however, not merely by directing a moralizing discourse against the ideology of polite society, not even by persistent satire or parody, although these appear in fragments throughout, but by a process of playing with that ideology, mimicking its discourse and then confounding it, and intimating alternatives without actually articulating them.

Polite Society Picaresque

> The comic arises when society and the individual . . . begin
> to regard themselves as works of art.
> Henri Bergson, *Laughter*

> The comic is everywhere, but we, living amidst it, don't
> see it. But if the artist brings it into art, onto the stage, then
> we shall fall all over ourselves with laughter and shall won-
> der that we hadn't previously noticed it.
> Gogol, quoted by S. T. Aksakov

Not the least of the many storms set off by *Dead Souls* swirled around the question of genre. And like other questions it has continued to

vex the book's readers and critics. As is generally the case with controversies surrounding *Dead Souls*, the instigator may be the indefiniteness or multifariousness of the literary situation, but also may be
Gogol himself, who, as always, subverted the logic of "either/or"
with one of "both . . . and." In this case, his generic designations
included, at various times, "novel," "novella" [*povest'*], and "epic"
or "narrative poem" [*poema*]. Never one to let the reader have it easy,
Gogol likewise referred to the interpolated "Tale of Captain Kopeikin"
as a "poema" (VI, 199), "povest' " (VI, 199), and "novel" (VI, 205).

It solves many taxonomical problems, of course, merely to accept
Bakhtin's thesis that all genres undergo "novelization" in ages dominated by the novel and, consequently, to call *Dead Souls* a novel,
marked as it is by the generic and linguistic openness which Bakhtin
finds central to that type of writing.[48] Certainly the pages of *Dead
Souls* offer a multitude of generic fragments (verse, letters, portraits,
compliments, essays, parables) and clashing social idioms, jargons,
and languages.

Leaving aside the possible implications of the subtitle "poema"—
epic, mock-epic, Dantesque, Homeric, Fieldingesque, or Pushkinian
(the inverse of a "novel in verse" might be an "epic in prose")—all
of which are illuminating, it might reopen critical perspectives on
Dead Souls to return to Gogol's provisional designation, (X, 375),
"novel."[49] Although it has embarrassed some of Gogol's readers (especially those who imagine that the dialectics of literary history must
always move forward), *Dead Souls* bears strong resemblance to a particular subspecies of that type, the picaresque novels, primitively episodic in their story lines, which had dominated Russian fiction during
the eighteenth century, as they had once prevailed in sixteenth- and
seventeenth-century Spain, and, indeed, throughout Western Europe. Recounting the passage of an orphaned, homeless outsider
through a series of loosely connected adventures, each introducing
him (or her) to a different sphere of life or social stratum, the picaresque fiction would bring its protagonist-narrator to an understanding of life's brutal hypocrisy and to a knowledge of how to make his
or her way toward respectability in a superficial, spiritually empty
world.[50] The episodic structure of the picaresque, meanwhile, would
have facilitated the oral performance of *Dead Souls*, while Gogol's particular elaborations would have, and did, become more perceptible to
the succeeding generations who could pore over the printed version.

Read in these terms, *Dead Souls* becomes a picaresque collection of
interwoven picaresques, with the biographies of the dead and runaway serfs and the tale of the outlaw Kopeikin casting Chichikov's

journeys in sharper relief, cultural and ideological. Certainly the account of the runaway Popov's encounter with the district police (VI, 137–139) or the adventures of the armless, legless veteran Kopeikin with the imperial bureaucracy (VI, 199–205) recall picaresque recreations of Golden Age brutality, replacing the degenerate knights, pardoners, and priests with minions of the state.[51] Chichikov's line of the plot itself may be seen as a double picaresque, in which the author-narrator finally "harnesses" (VI, 223) the rogue-hero in the final chapter by adjoining a conventional picaresque biography (birth, maturation, adventures) to the first ten chapters of the hero's journeys, which began and ended in medias res. As a consequence, the openness of the beginning chapters, their episodic extendability, is partially "closed" by an open, extendable conclusion, which leaves hero, narrator, and reader still moving down the same road.[52]

The picaresque impetus of *Dead Souls*, however, carries even beyond its hero's imaginary serf biographies and the narrator's chronologically backward account of the hero. For in the middle chapters of the novel the narrator, who had interrupted his story for bits of conventionally Sternean play with the reader's expectations and for didactic little essays on Russian *moeurs*, becomes himself a traveling, homeless outsider, first as a child, fresh of perception and imagination, then as a jaded outsider with dulled powers of perception and imagination: "Now I drive up indifferently to every unknown village and I look indifferently upon its vulgar [*poshluiu*] exterior; to my cooled gaze it is inhospitable, and I do not find it funny" (VI, 111). The change from lively child to jaded adult is motivated only by the passage of time, not with reference to concrete episodes, and it has been belied by the scintillating descriptions of the first five chapters; these lines serve, rather, to introduce the decaying landowner Pliushkin and to immerse the narrator, as author, in the comfortless, restless sphere of the picaresque.

At the beginning of the next chapter (7), the homeless traveler's bleak world gradually acquires situational specificity, precisely in literary terms, in the misadventures which befall the comic writer. Long as the passage is, it merits quotation, not only for the insights it offers into the aesthetics of *Dead Souls* (as guides to an ideal reception of the novel), but also for its thematic linking of the hero's and the author's fate. It begins with a lyric interlude on traveling and homelessness:

Happy is the wayfarer, who, after a long boring journey, with its cold spells, slush, mud, sleepy station masters, clattering carriage bells, repairs, squabbles, coachmen, blacksmiths, and all types of roadside rascals, sees at last the familiar roof, with its lights rushing toward him, and there appear before him the familiar rooms, the joyful sound of people running out to meet him, the noise and bustle of the children and the calming, quiet speeches, interrupted by flaming kisses with the power to tear all that is sad from the memory. Happy is the family man who has such a corner, but woe to the bachelor!

The mood now set, the metaphoric stage properties in place, the role of homelessness can be acted out upon the literary scene, where the writer who flatters the public, a successful rogue, plays the family man's part:

Happy is the writer, who, passing characters who are boring, repugnant, and striking in their sad reality, approaches characters who reveal the lofty dignity of mankind, the writer who from the great whirlpool of images which are transformed every day has selected only the few exceptions, who has never once betrayed the elevated pitch of his lyre, nor descended from his heights toward his poor, insignificant brethren, and, without touching the earth, is entirely immersed in his extolled and far-from-earthly images. Doubly enviable is his beautiful lot: he is among them as in his own family; and, meanwhile, far and loud rings his glory. He has burned people's eyes with intoxicating smoke; he has magically flattered them, by concealing what is grievous in life and showing them the beautiful man. Everything [sic], applauding, tears after him and races after his triumphant chariot. They name him a great universal poet, soaring high above all other geniuses of the world, as an eagle soars above other high-flying creatures. At the mere mention of his name, fiery young hearts are already seized with trepidation, tears responsive to him sparkle in all eyes . . . No one is his equal in strength—he is a god!

And the comic author plays the homeless wayfarer:

But such is not the lot, and different is the fate of the writer who has dared to summon forth everything which is before our eyes every minute, but which our indifferent eyes do not see, the entire terrifying, staggering mire of trivia which has bogged down our life, the entire depth of the cold, fragmented, everyday characters, with which our life is teeming. Bitter and boring at times is his journey, who with the firm force of an inexorable chisel dares to exhibit them prominently and strikingly before the eyes of the nation! His is not to gather the applause of the people, his is not to see the grateful tears and universal ecstasy of the souls he has aroused; toward him will not fly the sixteen-year-old girl with her head in a whirl and her heroic passion; his is not to forget himself in the sweet enchantment of sounds he has himself brought forth; his is not, finally, to escape the contemporary verdict, the hypocritically unfeeling contemporary verdict, which will call base and insignificant the creations he has cradled, will allot to him a contemptible corner among the writers who have offended humanity, will attribute to him the qualities of the heroes he has depicted, and will take away from him his heart, soul, and the divine flame of talent. For the contemporary verdict will not admit that the optics which view suns and those which convey the movements of unnoticed insects are equally wonderful; for the contemporary verdict does not admit that it takes much spiritual profundity to illuminate a picture taken from contemptible life, and to elevate it to a pearl of creation; for the contemporary verdict does not admit that lofty enthusiastic laughter is worthy of standing beside lofty lyric movement and that there is a whole chasm between it and the affectation of a carnival clown! The contemporary verdict will not admit this and turns everything into reproach and abuse of the unacknowledged writer; without sharing, without response, without sympathy, like the kinless wayfarer he stands alone in the road. Severe is his calling, and bitterly does he feel his loneliness. (VI, 133–134)

This lyricized account of the author's critical reception reworks, in its convoluted, anaphoric way, the hostile reviews that Gogol's earlier works had, in fact, received.

As its intertwined picaresques unfold, the novel implicates not merely its characters and, at times, its narrator in the fragmented, hypocritical world that the genre has traditionally presented, but also its fictive reader, as it attempts to open eyes which, as in the passage just quoted, do not see what was before them: the disjointedness of their world and the coarseness of their everyday existence.[53] But as the novel approaches its conclusion, the author-narrator, an abused picaro to the hostile readers that he addresses in the text, leaves the picaresque world to become a different sort of wayfarer, a prophet without honor in his own country, a seeker whose severe trials are now interior ones (VI, 243). With this movement he implores the reader also to set off on an inward journey: "And who of us, filled with Christian humility . . . will plunge deeply into his own soul this difficult question: 'And is there not in me some part of Chichikov?' "(VI, 245).

Between the runaway serfs, whose adventures cast Chichikov's in perspective by their physical harshness, and the emerging figure of the author, whose wanderings propel him toward a sense of moral and spiritual mission, there remains Chichikov, trying to capitalize on the physically dead in a morally dead world, which is opened toward further adventures and opened into the reader's own. Chichikov, like the author-narrator, has the ability to change voice and guise, which gives them both an additional measure of openness. Yet, as Guillén remarks, "the roguish novel is formally open . . . and ideologically closed."[54] For *Dead Souls* the closed world in which Chichikov must make his way, once he has finished school and climbed the lowest ranks of the civil service ladder, is one ideologically shaped by the conventions of the enlightened, Westernized gentry, or "society." The "all of Russia" which Gogol had promised Pushkin to present in the novel (X, 375) consists, for the most part, of characters representing groups which might aspire to membership in this cultural elite. With few exceptions—merchants who bribe the police chief, a priest who witnesses a transfer of dead serf souls, some scruffy clerks quickly overridden by the higher ones, and some dead serfs who spring to life in Chichikov's imagination and in Sobakevich's inspired sales pitch—the characters belong to Gogol's fictive gentry and civil service. Their wives, appropriately, play travesty roles in the novel's imagined polite society. The visits in Chichikov's picaresque journey are precisely to these squires and servitors, and the estates offer Chichikov, if not the Spanish picaro's encounters with a broad social spectrum (hidalgos to whores), then encounters on the three officially recognized levels of serfowners (petty, average, and large—*melkopomestnye, srednepomestnye,* and *krupnopomestnye*), and encounters with a broad range of the passions which polite social interaction might have been expected to mollify.

The social occasions which bring the novel's characters together are inevitably elements of the polite whirl: visits between ladies, visits to neighboring estates, dinners, suppers, and, framing Chichikov's visit to the town, the two balls which help to integrate him into the life of N and then to expel him from it. Signs of this process of acceptance and rejection are the series of successful visits he pays in the opening chapter and the parallel series (chap. 10) during which he is not received at all or else received halfheartedly.

The residents of N indulge in such fashions as Lancaster schools (VI, 156) in sufficient measure to link them, if minimally, with the cultural pastimes of the educated, Westernized gentry. Whenever these characters choose something to read, which happens rarely, it is inevitably a sentimentalist text of the late eighteenth or early nineteenth century: a play by Kotzebue, Zhukovsky's mellifluously terrifying ballad "Liudmila," Young's "Night Thoughts," Werther's verse epistle to Charlotte (by V. I. Tumansky), or unspecified works by Karamzin. The last-named ideologue of polite society plays, appropriately, a more prominent role than the others. When, for example, a superannuated local Tatiana writes Chichikov a love letter, its sententiousness parodies Karamzin's "Two Comparisons" ("Dva sravneniia," 1797).[55] The narrator sarcastically notes its typicality: "In the last line there was no meter, but that, by the way, meant nothing; the letter was written in the spirit of the time" (VI, 160). Chichikov's constant companion, a historical novel by Mme de Genlis, also recalls Karamzin's less memorable contributions to the Russian Enlightenment, in that her sentimental, pious fictions crowded *The Herald of Europe* during the years that Karamzin served as its editor, principal essayist, and translator. On the bookshelves and reading tables of this world there is no place for the most questioning works of these writers: Karamzin's history and essays or Zhukovsky's more mature verse. Nothing by Pushkin, Griboedov, Viazemsky, or Fonvizin interrupts the flow of works which offered models of ameliorated manners, periphrastic expression, and pious resignation. The narrator, when he locates his intelligence in this milieu, exceeds the characters in his cultural repertoire only to the extent that he can, for purposes of sarcasm, dredge up a few figures from Greek mythology or drop the names of a few famous authors.

Although specific texts have little place in the town of N, the composed, periphrastic discourse and the manners of polite society have more success, spreading from the salons and ballrooms to the government offices, where friendship and social connections at the highest levels have overwhelmed the petty venality of the penpushers with a more refined venality, as the president of the court graciously explains to Chichikov: "I'll ask you not to give anything to the clerks. My friends don't have to pay" (VI, 146). Manilov takes this manner into the barracks, where "he was considered a most modest, a most delicate, and a most educated officer" (VI, 25). Manilov, more than any character save Chichikov, strives politely to aestheticize the financial and bureaucratic spheres of life. His ludicrous response to Chichikov's request for dead serfs is to wonder whether it is a verbal exercise, offered "for the beauty of its style" (VI, 35). Politely assured that it is all that one might hope for, including an act of civic virtue, Manilov presents Chichikov with a deed of purchase that has been elegantly decorated by his wife (VI, 140).

The fashionable world's incursion into the church, whose ceremonies and texts it has subverted or replaced, is no less striking. The narrator hyperbolically records it in a scene which captures the priorities of N: "during the mass one of the ladies was observed to have beneath her gown such a [colossal] hoop that it made the gown spread out through half the church, so that a local police officer, who happened to be there, gave an order to move the people farther away, that is, closer to the porch of the church, so that no one would wrinkle the toilet of Her Excellency" (VI, 160).

It is, however, the prominence of talk, of polite oral performance, which most persistently makes *Dead Souls* a polite society picaresque. The peculiar reality of N is produced and maintained by conversation:[56]

> One must also say that the ladies of the town of N, like many Petersburg ladies, excelled in their unusual carefulness and decorum in words and expressions. They never said, "I blew my nose, I sweated, I spat," but rather, "I relieved my nose, I made do by means of a handkerchief." Under no circumstances was it possible to say: "This glass or this plate stinks." And it was even impossible to say something that would have hinted at this, but instead they would say: "This glass is behaving itself badly," or something like it. In order further to ennoble the Russian language, almost half of its words were completely cast out of conversation, and, consequently, it was quite often necessary to resort to the French language, since there, in French, it was a different matter; there such words were permitted which were much coarser than the ones I have mentioned.   (VI, 159)

This refined, periphrastic style—as it had been established early in the century and was later defended by such self-appointed heirs to Karamzin as Bulgarin—distances the unpleasant and contributes to the enforcement of social harmony, as the narrator outlines in an extended piece of satirical ethnography:

> The ladies of N were what is called présentable, and in this respect one could have boldly placed them as an example before all others. As far as behaving themselves, preserving ton, maintaining etiquette (a multitude of the most subtle proprieties), and, especially, observing fashion to the latest detail, in this they surpassed even the ladies of Petersburg and Moscow. They dressed with great taste, drove about town in carriages, as the latest fashion prescribed, with a lackey swaying in back, in livery with gold braid. A carte de visite, even if written on the deuce of clubs or on the ace of diamonds, was a most sacred object to them. Because of it, two ladies, great friends and even relatives, fell out completely, precisely because one of them had somehow manqué to repay a visit . . . And so both ladies remained in a state of mutual disinclination, according to the expression of the town's high society. About questions of social precedence, there also occurred many powerful scenes, at times inspiring the husbands to quite chivalric and magnanimous acts of intercession. Duels, naturally, did not take place between them, because they were all civil servants, but in their place one would try to

tarnish the other wherever possible, which, as is well known, is at times more grievous than a duel. In their morals, the ladies of N were stern, filled with noble indignation against anything wanton and against all temptations. They punished unmercifully any weaknesses. If among them "something else" were going on, as they call it, then it was going on secretly, so that there was no sign of it going on; all dignity was preserved . . .

As this and other passages make abundantly clear, the talk of polite society in *Dead Souls* does not so much inspire an amelioration of bad manners as facilitate a precarious concealment of them.

Because he can converse on a variety of subjects while mustering the appropriate emotions and gestures, Chichikov—hyperbolically soaped and perfumed, possessed of French sounds, if not the language—worms his way into this world of appearances and shifting, superficial values. He masters the possibilities of talk that I discussed in Chapter 1 above: casualness, loose syntactic connections, and light fictionality, all mustered in support of polymorphous performances in which he appeals for sympathy and understanding while screening himself and his performance from penetrating scrutiny.

The new arrival managed somehow not to be at a loss for anything and to show himself to be an experienced man of the world [*svetskii chelovek*]. Whatever the talk touched upon, he could carry it: if it was a matter of horse breeding, he even spoke of horse breeding; if they spoke of fine dogs, even here he delivered some very sensible comments; if they were considering an inquest conducted by the provincial revenue office, he showed that judicial frauds were not unknown to him; if the discussion was about billiards, he didn't miss a cue; if they were talking about virtue, he discoursed very well about virtue, even with tears in his eyes; about the preparation of mulled wine—he knew the benefit of mulled wine; about customs overseers and clerks—he passed judgment on them as if he were a clerk and overseer. But it was remarkable that he could cloak all of this in solidity; he knew how to behave. He spoke neither loudly, nor quietly, but completely as one ought to speak. In a word, whichever way you looked, he was a very respectable man.   (VI, 18)

In his initial contacts with the eccentric landowners, Chichikov's performances show no less virtuosity, as his mastery of the arts of conversation brings him to adapt himself to the saccharine Manilov, the kopeck-nursing widow Korobochka, the inspired liar Nozdrev (in whose talk fictionality becomes the dominant principle), the "kulak" Sobakevich, and the miser Pliushkin. Of these, only Manilov belongs to polite society, properly speaking. Yet Chichikov succeeds, at least initially, in adapting his manner to each of their idiosyncracies, except for Nozdrev's, whose unpredictability renders him immune to Chichikov's more pedestrian consideratons (VI, 78).[57]

Consistent with society's constitution of subjects in terms of their ability to take part in such polymorphous performances and in terms of the dominant passions which preclude such virtuosity, the remaining characters of *Dead Souls* are performed by the narrator though their comically dim-witted, obsessed conversations with or about Chichikov, as he becomes the embodiment, first, of their hopes, then, after his catastrophe at the ball, of their fears.

An Ideology in Fragments

> The humorist's soul yearns for a more genuine substantiality than life can offer; and so he smashes all the forms and limits of life's totality.
>
> Georg Lukács on "minor epic forms," *Theory of the Novel*

To this point I have been considering the novel's representation of society's ideology as a passive one, as I have been showing the extent to which that ideology shapes the novel's scenes, characters, and language, thus forming the space through which Chichikov and the lesser picaroons make their journeys. The discussion of this problem would be far from complete if it ceased here, however. For *Dead Souls* does not merely display the values, conceptions, and conventions of the enlightened Westernized gentry; it also manipulates them, turning them back upon themselves and rendering the seamlessness of the cultural fabric they comprised. We have already seen how the ambiguous institutional status of *Dead Souls* (as an object of oral and/or written performance) could both soothe a listener with its seeming naturalness and call a reader's attention to the fundamental triviality of its world—"those minutiae which seem minutiae only in a book" (VI, 222). So, too, the picaresque structure of *Dead Souls*, no matter how elaborated with interpolated biographies, contributes actively to the reader's sense of fragmentation by presenting a minimally connected series of adventures between characters whose contacts with each other are exceptionally brief and superficial.

Beyond this, however, *Dead Souls* plays with the principal categories of society's ideology (the amelioration of manners, the *honnête homme*, the shifting boundaries of taste and fashion), measuring them and their adepts according to a set of overlapping categories, themselves both social and aesthetic, which were familiar to readers from Gogol's earlier works, but which were also spelled out with increasing urgency in the author-narrator's increasingly sermonical interludes: the colossal/the trivial, the whole/the fragmentary, order/disorder, the kinetic/ the static, the living/the dead. The playful and arresting ambiguity of *Dead Souls*, its revaluation of ideological values in terms of these nebulous oppositions, is evident throughout the text, but especially in its treatment of the building blocks of narrative, characters and events.[58]

According to society's aesthetic-psychological understandings, the obsessed, narrow, and unpolished landowners whom Chichikov visits would have been the very stuff of comedy, and Gogol's first listeners, such as Andrei Karamzin, quickly defined *Dead Souls* accordingly. Indeed, the depiction of these characters does, at first glance, recall the psychology of humors which informed such comedies as Molière's.[59] But, for all of the similarities between Gogol's characters and certain recognizable types of comic excess and eccentricity, for all of the author-narrator's use of the vocabulary of "passions" and "types," *Dead Souls* is far from lending its laughter as a corrective to departures from the norm of the *honnête homme*. Instead, it challenges in the most profound and varied ways, the often facile assumptions about human change and identity which supported the coherence of the *honnête homme* and which licensed laughter at departures from the composite norm it offered. *Dead Souls* does this, as its plot unfolds, by emptying the figure of the polite, refined gentleman of all content save the most venal self-interest, by insulating its "provincials" from all human interaction inside nearly impenetrable walls of obsession and materiality, and then by destroying—or trying to—the distance between "provincials" and the capital cities.

The first of Chichikov's visits brings one travesty of the *honnête homme* (Chichikov, who can imitate all passions) together with another travesty (Manilov, who possesses none):

Only God could say what sort of character Manilov had . . . You could not expect to hear from him any living or even haughty word, such as you can hear from almost anybody, just as soon as you touch upon his pet subject. Everyone has his fervor [*zador*]: one man's fervor is directed toward borzoi hounds; to another it seems that he is a great lover of music and feels marvelously all of its profound passages; a third is a master at dining extravagantly, a fourth at playing a role just above the one ordained to him; a fifth, with more limited desire, sleeps and dreams of stepping out with some aide-de-camp to show off before his friends, acquaintances, and even nonacquaintances; a sixth is gifted with a hand which feels a supernatural desire to bend the corner of some ace or deuce of diamonds, while the hand of the seventh itches to give someone a present, to get closer to the person of a stationmaster or coachman—in a word, everyone has his own, but Manilov had none.   (VI, 24)[60]

Manilov's lack is devastating because a "fervor" is, in the Gogolian hierarchy of pseudo-emotions, less intense, less spiritual than a passion. His lack is all the more devastating to a reader's sense of society's norms, because it produces them not as a harmonized totality, but as an absence.

In exchange for an intellectual or cultural life, Manilov, like the other landowners, possesses a minutely detailed speech pattern (a verbal mask, as Iurii Tynianov put it) and is surrounded by layer upon layer of material objects: a clearly individualized landscape and serf villages, gardens, the walls of the manor house, animals and servants, rooms and furnishings, art (or its absence), foods, clothes. Unlike the classical pen portrait, Gogol's is astoundingly dense in physical detail. Sobakevich, the most physically solid of the landowners, has furniture which seemed to talk for him: "Every object, every chair, it seemed, was saying: 'I, too, am Sobakevich!' or 'I, too, am very much like Sobakevich!' " (VI, 96). All the others are surrounded by objects which testify to their moral and mental characteristics: Manilov's macabre little piles of pipe ash, Korobochka's weird clock, Nozdrev's dogs (his children), Sobakevich's portraits of thick-thighed Greek heroes, Pliushkin's shriveled lemon. I have charted the principal aspects of this materiality and their realization in the estates on pages 190–191.[61]

All of this extravagantly detailed materiality bears in relation to its owner an ontological status very much different from that of the congealing, imprisoning environment of subsequent works of literary realism. Gogol, in fact, leaves open the question of causation, strongly implying that these layers of materiality are as much or more the product of the landowner's personality as they are determinants of that personality. This becomes particularly evident as the boundaries come to reflect the mental firmness of the landowner: Manilov, most vulnerable to Chichikov, has an estate on a hill, open to the winds; Pliushkin, slightly less vulnerable, has fences and churches, but they are broken and cracked, and, in a haunting passage, nature returns to take a part in remodeling his garden; Korobochka, who exacts a high price for her dead serfs, has a solid fence; Sobakevich, who exacts an even higher price, has even more solid walls and fences. But Nozdrev, who most frustrates Chichikov, has the most impenetrable boundaries of all, ones established by his own fancy: " 'There's the boundary!' said Nozdrev, 'Everything that you see on this side, that's all mine, and even on that side, all this forest that seems so dark, and all that's beyond the forest, that's all mine' "(VI, 74).

The psychologization of the material world provocatively reproduces ideology's suppression of origins and consequences, an effect which is reinforced by the landowners' general lack of parents (only Sobakevich has a father), their lack of children (only Manilov and Pliushkin have them), their lack of detailed biographies (except for Pliushkin), and their rootedness in an indefinite historical frame.

More provocatively still, *Dead Souls* projects the solidity of these environments back into their owners, giving them a highly diminished capacity for change. Nozdrev remains the same at thirty-five as he was at eighteen (VI, 70); Pliushkin collapses into ruins after his wife's death, but his emotional foundations were never firm anyway (VI, 119). Chichikov's meditations on Sobakevich—meditations possibly too profound to be plausibly attached to Chichikov—challenge the ideology of gradual amelioration with an image of immutable character that is nowhere contradicted:

> Were you born such a bear, or did provincial life, the crops of grain, and troubles with the peasants make you a bear? And did you become what is called a human fist [*kulak*] because of them? But no, I think you would have been just the same, even if they had brought you up according to fashion, and set you loose, and if you had lived in Petersburg, not in the provinces. The only difference is that now you go through a half side of mutton with kasha, having begun with a cream cheese pie the size of a plate, and there you would have eaten some sort of truffled cutlets. Now you have the peasants in your power; you live in harmony with them and don't harm them, naturally, because they are yours, and it would be worse for you; but there you would have clerks, whom you would knock about, having realized that they are not your serfs, or you would rob the treasury! No, you can't unbend a fist into an open palm. And if you just unbend one or two fingers, it'll be even worse. (VI, 106)

No less than Sobakevich, Chichikov himself comes to bear an inexorable passion, as the author-narrator complicates the psychology of the passions beyond easy comprehension and easy manipulation:

> As innumerable as the sands of the sea are the passions of mankind, and none of them is like another. All of them, base and beautiful, are at first obedient to man, but then they become his terrible masters. Blessed is he who elected for himself the most beautiful passion of all; it grows and multiplies with every minute and hour his immeasurable felicity, and it goes deeper and deeper into the boundless paradise of his soul. But there are passions which are not of man's choosing. They are already

The Material World of *Dead Souls*

Paradigm	Manilov	Korobochka	Nozdrev	Sobakevich	Pliushkin
Setting, manor	On a hill, open to the winds, Eng. garden, stagnant pond	Mud puddle, small house, fences	Bog, uncertain boundaries, messy house	Functionally asymmetrical, solid fence	Inanimate, rough road, rotten produce, ruined churches, broken fence, cracked walls, closed windows, irregular
Landscape, foliage	Lilac bushes, few birches, "boring"	Veg. gardens, orchards		Birch, pine forests	Overgrown garden, hopvine, topped birch
Peasant huts	Grey, log, no greenery	Solid, haphazard		Solid, not ornamental	Decrepit, roofless, irregular, no panes
"Souls"	200	80 (18 dead)			800–1,000 (120 dead) (78 runaway)
Owner	Empty	Fussy	Liar	Bear, "kulak"	Spider, "fisherman"
"Zador"	None	Selling	Tricks	Eating	Collecting
Manner	Saccharine, amiable	Vernacular, familiar	Vernacular, hearty	Sceptic	Crabbed, snivelling

Art	"3 Graces"	Bird pictures, Kutuzov, military man	Fake dagger, hurdy-gurdy, pipes	Thick-thighed Greek heroes, Bagration	Horses drowning, still life
Books	Unfinished		None		Ancient book
Color	Grey, pale blue			Brown	
Animal	Rooster	Dogs, flies	Dogs, horses	Bear	Flies
Furniture	Something missing	Clock		"I, too, am Sobakevich"	Broken, disordered
"Wife," family	Amiable, sons		Dogs	Feodulia (cucumber, pickle brine)	"Housekeeper," 2 dead, 2 disowned
Servants	Crooks, drunk	Old woman, little girl	Brutes		Boy in boots
Dinner	Soup, mucus	Pastries	Bad food, bad wine	Whole beasts	Liquor, moldy cake
Leitmotif	Ash, sugar, pipe	Dogs, flies, pig eating chick	Dogs	Bear, stepping on feet	Lemon, dirt, liquor with insects
Image of Chichikov	Sentimental friend	Buyer	Rogue, two-faced	Businessman	Mad benefactor
Reaction to Chichikov's proposal	Gapes: "For stylistic beauty"	Fears being cheated	Chance to cheat, deal	Ordinary venture	Happiness, distrust
Cost to Chichikov	Free	1.2r/"soul"	1.2r/"soul"	2.5r/"Soul"	32K/"soul"

born with him in the instant of his birth into the world, and he is not given the strength to refuse them. (VI, 242)

The only clear possibilities for change—time's dulling passage or sudden possession—bring ruin:

> Everything changes quickly in man; you no sooner look away, than a terrible worm has already grown up within him, despotically drawing off all his life fluids. And more than once it has not been a grand passion, but a paltry, nasty little passion [strastishka] for something petty which has spread in someone born for better deeds and has made him forget great and sacred duties and see the great and sacred in worthless trinkets. (VI, 242)

Polite social interaction, as it is modeled in *Dead Souls*, is not the "great and sacred," but just such an enterprise fixed on "worthless trinkets," be these the ladies' fashionable fabrics, Chichikov's fine soap, or Manilov's dream of the promotion that sentimental friendship might bring him: "then he and Chichikov would enter some society, where they would enchant everyone with the pleasantness of their manner, and the tsar, learning of their friendship, would make them generals" (VI, 39).

Dead Souls, then, undercut society's understanding of human capability by trapping its characters in layers of brute materiality and in a "staggering mire of trivia," rendering them incapable of gradual improvement. But in producing its more composite characters, the text employed a second strategy as well: stretching their comprehensiveness beyond the breaking point. The *honnête homme*, to be sure, was expected to play many roles, to have a variety of interests, and to adapt himself to the concerns of many interlocutors. But the conventionality of the roles and traits, a set of behavioral patterns, a proper name, and a biography could hold the *honnête homme* and the literary productions of him together in a unity constituted by the ideology of polite society. Pushkin became a chameleon to later generations and to those outside society, not to those within it. His creature Eugene may have puzzled the Petersburg society to which he returned in chapter 8, but the poses he seemed to strike (8:7–8) fell within a range sanctioned by fashion. The author-narrator of *Eugene Onegin* produced a wide variety of tones and generic fragments, but these were incorporated into a coherent literary autobiography. Already in the drafts of *Dead Souls*, however, Gogol was striving to articulate a moral-psychological problem which *Eugene Onegin* had begun to adumbrate in the passages of Eugene's greatest passivity and which *A Hero of Our Time* had suggested by narrowing Pechorin's behavioral alternatives to participation in that novel's violent competitions:

> . . . someone starting to grow old is imperceptibly quite encompassed by the almost unnoticably vulgar habits of the *monde*, by the conventions, and by the decorum of senselessly moving society, which finally so ensnare and envelop a person that there no longer remains a self in him, only a heap of the conventions and habits of those who belong to the *monde*. And when you try to break through to the soul, it's no longer there. (VI, 691)[62]

But moving beyond the relentless constriction of Lermontov's novel, Gogol's presents characters whose soullessness appears in the incoherent variety of their roles and personality traits, or else in their indistinguishability from other characters.

One clear example of this loss of identity figures in the encounter of two society women, the "Lady who was Pleasant in All Respects" and the "Pleasant Lady" (who was less enthusiastically labeled because she was made to lack the first lady's "versatility of character," VI, 179). Here Gogol presents their mindless dialogue without many of the tags necessary to identify the speakers. As a consequence, it requires the greatest effort to link lines with a speaker, and the personalities of the two blend into each other, then disappear into the flood of rumors concerning Chichikov's true identity (VI, 180–188).

Chichikov, because of his ability to imitate the speech patterns of all of his interlocutors and his ability to adapt himself to all situations, has struck many readers by his absence of identity. Even the narrator's belated identification of his dominant passion, "acquisitiveness" (VI, 242), clarifies little, given the aimlessness and universality of its exercise. Meanwhile, attributions by which the citizens of N attempt to characterize Chichikov utterly exceed the normal possibilities of the *honnête homme*, to say nothing of plausibility, as he becomes, in turn, a millionaire, the author of satiric verse (VI, 171), the would-be abductor of the governor's daughter, the double amputee Captain Kopeikin, Napoleon, a spy, and (by a suggested extension) the Antichrist (VI, 205–206). This amorphousness, present already within him but also projected onto him by the townspeople, fragments, as we shall presently see, the novel's society.

While Chichikov's simultaneous absence of personality traits and excess of attributes help occasion the ludicrous plenitude of possibilities set in motion by rumor, the author-narrator's multiple guises raise a different challenge to the coherence of the social self constituted by the ideology of polite society. In rapid succession the author-narrator enters the world of N and rises above it, waxing silly and sermonical, worldly and idealistic.[63] Only our habits of inference— that is, our attribution of a single utterance to a single speaker— justify locating the narration of *Dead Souls* in a single "person." But the novel strains a reader's ability to make the inference because it provides no coherent biography for the author-narrator(s), no concrete assurance save the name on the title page that the subject of discourse should be "Gogol," and no uniformity of verbal behavior between the various narrating and commenting figures. Unlike *Eugene Onegin*, *Dead Souls* does not account for its production, for its freshness of language and observation, for its movement between comically trivial commentary and lyric elevation, for its conjunction of travesty and panegyric. Such radically disjoined poses, such persistent ellipses of motivation, have, it is fair to say, opened the spaces that have been filled with generations of wildly divergent readings, as disparate in their way as the townspeople's interpretations of Chichikov.

The ambiguities in characterization, the tensions between constriction and fragmentation, between absence and excess, are no less central to a reader's experience of the novel's plot. For just as *Dead Souls* provokes reflection on the constitution of character, so it calls into question the very nature and connection of events.[64] If one follows Iurii Lotman in defining a textual "event" as the shifting of a character across a semantic boundary, then Gogol's oft-quoted manuscript note on *Dead Souls* reveals his preoccupation with the perceiving of eventfulness and its absence:[65]

> The idea of the town. The emptiness which has arisen in it to the highest degree. Idle talk. Gossip, surpassing all limits. How all of this has arisen from idleness and has assumed the expression of absurdity in the highest degree . . .
> *Details* in the conversations of the ladies. How private gossip mixes into the general gossip, how one doesn't spare the other. How understandings are created; how these understandings reach the height of absurdity. How everyone is unwittingly engaged in gossip . . .
> How the emptiness and impotent idleness of life give way to dull and unspeaking death. How that terrible event takes place senselessly. They are unaffected. Death strikes the unaffected world. Still more powerfully, meanwhile, must the dead insensibility of life be presented to the reader.   (VI, 692)

Here, in Gogol's conception, three perspectives intertwine: that of the note-maker, producing the discourse about the characters; that of the characters, producing a world of talk; and that of the reader, who needs (in the note-maker's opinion) a powerful presentation of the novelistic world (to awaken him or her from insensibility, it is implied). What is an imperceptible state for one of these parties, a non-event, may be a "terrible event" for the others. And the eventful process of making a world (talk, understanding) may, to the others, be the epitome of stasis. "Events," as Lotman reminds us, are not just culturally and historically determinate, they are determined in different ways within the different regions of a culture.[66] Moreover, the "character" crossing a semantic boundary may be a collective ("the town"), not an individual. Finally, the events may move not toward the resolution of an enigma about a character or his actions, but toward the revelation of a state of affairs ("the dead insensibility of life").[67]

Subtle as this note is, and valuable as it is for showing the processes and categories of Gogol's aesthetic thinking, it is, ultimately, more straightforward than *Dead Souls*, which plays with the notion of "event" from a series of still more complicated perspectives, to the extent that the note-maker yields his place to the author-narrator with his shifting positions, the "reader" becomes specific in *Dead Souls* as someone on the intellectual-cultural level of N, and the characters are made to produce the "private" and "general" discourses mentioned in the note.

Moving back to the novel from the note, one sees that other sorts of "plot" in *Dead Souls* intersect its picaresque unfolding, raising the possibility of collective (the town) and individual (Chichikov) action. These come to the fore during the second half of the novel, as Chichikov returns to N and then flees it, but the author-narrator has been careful to prepare the reader with a playful rhetoric of eventfulness, exercised conventionally at the openings and conclusions of the novel's chapters: "an escapade" (VI, 18), "an ending to crown the affair," "moves," "mainsprings" (VI, 19), a major "role" (VI, 70), a "plot" (VI, 191), "events" (VI, 176, 193, 194), and a "consequence" (VI, 177). Figures who promise eventfulness reinforce this rhetoric: a mysterious letter-writer, who might involve Chichikov in a love intrigue (VI, 160–165); and a mysterious lieutenant, who might catch him in the snares of the military-police state. These promises are, of course, unfulfilled. The letter-writer never appears, and her letter remains a sterile exercise in polite sensibility; the potential agent of just retribution becomes obsessively bogged down in the "staggering mire of trivia":

The inn was wrapped in deep slumber. Only in one window was the light still visible, where the lieutenant who had arrived from Riazan' was living. He was, evidently, a great amateur of boots, because he had already ordered four pair and was persistently trying on a fifth. Several times he approached the bed in order to cast them off and lie down, but he could by no means do so. Indeed, the boots were well stitched, and for a long time he would raise a leg to examine the smartly and marvelously turned heel.   (VI, 153)[68]

These figures are surpassed in promise of eventfulness by a third, the governor's daughter, because of her high position and multiple appearances (chaps. 5, 8) in the novel. The very manner of her introduction into *Dead Souls* realizes the metaphor of plot complication, as her carriage passes Chichikov's, and their harnesses become entangled. Moreover, her oval face and transparent whiteness (VI, 90) suggest a total absence of character and, to Chichikov, a fullness of potential (VI, 92–93); he promptly fulfills this potential with imaginary narratives of education and marriage. The novel exploits her availability further when she is made to play the abducted heroine in the townspeople's rumor narratives (VI, 185, 191). Their fictions within the fiction most implausibly give Chichikov the capacity for love, just as Manilov's dream narrative had given him the capacity for another of society's virtues, friendship. There is no "event" in either case, except the one produced by their talk and just as quickly annulled by the overwhelming realities of the novel's world.

It is, finally, the ball scene and its aftermath (chaps. 8–10) which shows the greatest play with eventfulness and, concomitantly, the most thorough fragmentation of society's ideological coherence.

The sequence of events and non-events begins peacefully enough, as all the characters join in a single "disinterested" understanding of Chichikov: "the millionaire" (VI, 156). But already venality threatens to erupt through the polished style of polite sociability, and the fiction generated by this talk turns back upon the society that produced it:

By the way, the ladies were not at all intéressées; the word "millionaire" alone was the cause of it, not the millionaire himself, but just the word. For in the very sound of the word, beyond any money bag, there is something which acts on people who are scoundrels, on good people, and on people who are neither one nor the other, in a word, on all people. A millionaire has the advantage of being able to see baseness which is quite disinterested, pure baseness, not founded on any considerations. Many people know very well that they will get nothing from him . . . , yet they will rush ahead of him without fail, laugh, take off their hats, or forcibly press themselves upon that dinner party to which they know the millionaire has been invited.   (VI, 159)

The narrator's sarcastic presentation of the speech-produced reality is followed by counterposed evidence of the vulnerability of society's talk: the sentimental letter, with its inept versification, and Chichikov's French sounds, which he cannot bring together into words (VI, 161).

Harmony attends Chichikov's arrival at the ball, as all greet him, smiling in obedience to "the immutable laws of reflection" (VI, 162), but the fragmentation of this scene is prepared by the ambitions of the participants, and by their sense of themselves as bodily parts:

> Everything was devised and foreseen with unusual attentiveness; neck and shoulders were uncovered just as much as was necessary, and no more; each one bared those possessions until she felt, by her own conviction, that they could destroy a man. (VI, 163)

This self-absorbed aestheticization of the disparate bodily parts is effected at the expense of social harmonization by precisely those people, the ladies, whom society expected to produce that harmonization. Innocuous as it seems, it captures the fragmentation which finds its fullest expression in the ensuing social catastrophe.

The catastrophe itself makes a mockery of human agency, when the insubstantial Chichikov, who has swept the town off its feet, is in turn swept off his feet by the reappearance of the governor's daughter, a figure of emptiness.[69] In confronting each character, the language of polite society fails to restore equilibrium. The ladies cannot recapture Chichikov with their "pleasant phrases" (VI, 167): Chichikov's "multitude of pleasant things" (VI, 170), breaks down into a mindless list of ineptly dropped names.

In the pages that follow, the polite surface cracks. "Fervors" and "nasty little passions" break through. And the polite society of N disintegrates as its ideology loses all power to organize its subjects and their interactions. The ball itself survives some satiric verse and Nozdrev's drunken ramblings about the dead souls. These (if not Nozdrev's inadvertent truthfulness) were habitual occurrences and, therefore, non-events. It even survives Chichikov's faux pas—not until Dostoevsky's novels would such catastrophes become instantaneous. But the damage done by and to the fragile product of talk (Chichikov the dashing "millionaire") has begun to take effect. Society disintegrates into conflicting parties, each of which supports a different, but equally illogical (VI, 189), interpretation of the enigmatic phrase "dead souls": the male party (focusing on the dead souls) and the female (concentrating on the governor's daughter).

Just as nature came back to assert its rights to the design of Pliushkin's garden, all that society had suppressed rushes back to reclaim its territory. Those excluded from the drawing rooms of N seize upon its discourse and multiply it:

> In Russia the lower societies love to talk about the intrigues which take place in the higher orders, and therefore they began to talk about all of this in such little houses as had never seen nor known Chichikov, sending on supplementary information and still more explanations.   (VI, 191)

while others denied entrée emerge from between the gaps in the now fractured society of N:

> There appeared a certain Sysoi Pafnut'evich and a MacDonald Karlovich, of whom no one had ever heard; a certain tall, tall character with a hand that had been shot through, of a height so great that no one had ever seen the likes of it, began to hang out in the drawing rooms.   (VI, 190)

The refined language of polite society, which had invaded the government offices and churches, has lost its empire. The narrator becomes increasingly colloquial in producing his account. The postmaster couches his "Tale of Captain Kopeikin" in a wildly vernacular mix of slang, folksey particles, and civil service jargon. Liberated from their stylistic prison by the troubling phrase "dead souls," such lexical elements were now free to shatter the bounds of decorum. And together with the language repressed by decorum returned the narratives consigned to oblivion, as peasants and merchants could now be remembered for their recent outbursts of counterfeiting, lechery, mayhem, and murder. The folk religion, also tamed by the discourse of polite society, returns to join in the interpretive orgy, filling the space vacated by fashionable religiosity:

> They began to ask: "What are they writing in the newspapers? Have they let Napoleon off his island again?" The merchants were very much afraid of this, for they believed completely the prophecy of a certain soothsayer, who had been in jail for three years; the prophet had arrived, no one knew whence, in bast sandals and a sheepskin reeking terribly of rotten fish and had proclaimed that Napoleon was the Antichrist and was being kept on a chain of stone behind six walls and seven seas, but that afterwards he would break the chain and gain dominion over all the world. The prophet landed in jail for his soothsaying, and properly so, but nevertheless his affair had completely troubled the merchants. For a long time afterwards, even during their most profitable dealings, the merchants would talk about the Antichrist as they drank their tea at the inn. Many officials and noble gentlemen would also involuntarily think about this and, infected by the mysticism which, as is known, was then in great fashion, would see some special meaning in each letter com-

prising the word "Napoleon." Many even discovered the Apocalyptic numbers in it. (VI, 206–207)

As the ideologically constructed world of N collapses, so does the map of Russia drawn by the ideology of polite society, which had set a boundary between the cosmopolitan capitals and the backward, uncultured provinces. The narrator rooted in N crumples the map of Russia to reduce the distance: "Perhaps some readers will call all of this improbable; the author also would be prepared to call it improbable to please them, but unfortunately everything took place just as it has been told, and it is all the more amazing in that the town was not in the sticks but, on the contrary, not far from both capitals" (VI, 206).

But the author-figure who strives, morally and lyrically, to rise above this world is not hopeful that the readers will abandon the comforting concepts (eccentricity, marginality) which separated them from a world like N: "A self-satisfied smile will appear on your face, and you will add: 'Indeed, one must agree that the people in certain provinces are most strange and most ridiculous, and there are more than a few scoundrels to boot'!" (VI, 245). The calmly bemused re-actions of some readers could have supported such fears; the outrage of others testified to the rhetorical eventfulness of the ideological collapse.[70]

As a last resort for explaining Chichikov, the men of N turn from the salons of their wives to the company of the police chief, an agent of the government, from which polite society had sought to separate itself.[71] But here, too, the comic collapses of N continues, as the public prosecutor comes home from an interrogation and drops dead:

> All of these interpretations, opinions, and rumors for some unknown reason acted most of all upon the poor prosecutor. They acted on him to such a degree that when he had come home, he began to think and think and, suddenly, as they say, for no reason at all, he died. Whether it was paralysis or something else that seized him, he just flopped down off his chair. They cried out, as one usually does, and wrung their hands. "Oh, my God!" They sent for the doctor to let some blood, but they saw that the prosecutor was just a body without a soul. Only then did they learn, with sympathy, that the prosecutor had, indeed, had a soul, al-though he never displayed it out of modesty. (VI, 209–210)

In taking the prosecutor on his last and conventionally most eventful journey, the narrative plays once more and in its most macabre fash-ion with the notion of "event." As the prosecutor crosses the exis-tential and semantic boundary between the realm of the living and the realm of the dead, the narrative in a countermovement shifts the boundary under him. Death and life become confused, as it takes death to signify life, which is now no more and perhaps never was.

Just as suddenly as it lost its equilibrium, the town of N regains it, permitting Chichikov to depart unmolested, and joining without him in the ritual of burial, with its conventional procession and its participants, whose everyday talk about civil service matters, balls, and frills restores the world that had seemed so irrevocably shattered (VI, 219). *Dead Souls*, it turns out, had played a double game with the ideology that had prevailed for decades among Russia's cultured elite, in one movement making a spectacular pseudo-event of its demise, then in a countermovement suggesting that this self-satisfied and ultimately immutable world, like the prosecutor, had been dead all along.

Conclusion

> Our society presents a grievous spectacle: in it there
> are no generous aspirations, no justice, no simplicity,
> no honor . . . Small souls exhaust themselves in petty
> intrigues amid social chaos . . . The words "intelli-
> gence" and "roguery" are synonyms. The words
> "honest man" [*chestnyi chelovek,* cf. *honnête homme*]
> mean "a simpleton," almost a "fool," and a "good
> fellow." Social depravity is so great that the concept
> of honor, of justice, is considered either softhead-
> edness or a sign of romantic exaltation.
>
> A. V. Nikitenko, *Dnevnik,* 15 January 1841

THE DIARY of Nikitenko, the censor of *Dead Souls,* shows that even
before the novel's publication, Russian intellectuals were contem-
plating their moribund ideals not in terms of a comic interplay of
absence and presence, but in terms of the purest desolation.[1] Nevertheless *Dead Souls,* like *Eugene Onegin* and *A Hero of Our Time,* contributed to the process by which the Russian novel and Russian society
discovered each other. The aestheticization of social life and the interpenetration of social and aesthetic conventions during the early
decades of the nineteenth century facilitated this mutual discovery,
and the three novels gave language and understanding to those willing to reflect upon their culture and made great art from the situation
that Nikitenko came to condemn so bluntly toward the end of the
period.

The various institutional frameworks of the 1820s–1840s encouraged different modes of literary production and reception, and, as
we have seen, Pushkin, Lermontov, and Gogol exploited these frameworks in remarkably different ways, overcrowding them (Pushkin),
narrowing them (Lermontov), or exploding them (Gogol), but working from within them with profound and different understanding of
their conventions, aspirations, and failures. Some readers came to

grips with how these novels represented the period's primary social-aesthetic form, polite society, but many readers dismissed the three novels for not measuring up to society's idealized self-image, and a few began to tailor their readings to fit the concerns of the incipient intelligentsia.

Of the three novelists, only Gogol lived long enough to brave the full force of the institutional and ideological turmoil of the later 1840s, and it is instructive to outline his response and contribution to the changing map of Russian literary life. These consist primarily of two long works, neither of which the contemporary public saw in its entirety: the heavily censored *Selected Passages from Correspondence with Friends* (1847) and the unfinished second volume of *Dead Souls*, which Gogol himself destroyed, perhaps inadvertently. *Selected Passages*, despite the title's reference to the polite tradition of familiar letters, proposes a radical restructuring of the profession of letters that was beginning to take shape during the 1820s, 1830s, and 1840s. In place of a conversational relationship with the reader, in place of the language of the educated, Westernized gentry, in place of light poetry and humorous prose, these "letters"—sermonical, confessional, didactic—offered aspects of an institution which may be modeled as follows:

RUSSIAN LIFE (IN PATRIARCHAL,
HIERARCHICAL TERMS)

AUTHOR (TEACHER, SERMONIST)	MORALLY, SPIRITUALLY SERIOUS WORKS	READER-CONVERT, COMMUNITY

THE BOOK, THE LIVING WORD
CHURCH SLAVONIC, POPULAR RUSSIAN EXPRESSIONS

A number of Gogol's selections concern the themes and traditions of Russian literature, and he interweaves these passages with his prescriptions for religion and government. Gogol presents Zhukovsky's translation of the *Odyssey*, for example, as a model work, capable of exercising a profoundly beneficial influence on Russian public morality, on the Russian literary language, and, indeed, on the entire literary population (writers, readers, critics). Gogol selects Russian precedents largely for the dignity of their authorial posture (Karamzin, VIII, 266–267) or for their challenges to the Russian Enlightenment (Fonvizin, Griboedov, VIII, 396). In place of the prevalent author-reader relationship of friendship and equality, Gogol posits one of teacher or sermonist to disciple. Prematurely, and perhaps as an incantation, Gogol asserts the Russian veneration of writers (VIII, 261), as he seeks, through a fabric woven from Patristic readings, modern religious literature, and the Bible to ground Russian literature in a new set of values. Perhaps the most striking moment in this assault, first on polite literary intercourse, then on the ideology of polite society, comes toward the end of the collection, as he dismisses Pushkin (a universal "echo") from his tutelary position, in favor of a "Christian education" for the new generation of Russian poets (VIII, 407–408).

Where *Dead Souls* managed to fragment the reading public, *Selected Passages* reunited it—against Gogol himself. The new book featured positive ideals, where the comic novel had only adumbrated them: a static world of fixed positions and boundaries, social immobility, national identity, meaningful language, and universal state service. Where the comic detail of *Dead Souls* subverted a moribund way of life, the outrageous detail of *Selected Passages* (insults for landowners to deliver to feckless serfs, etc.) was marshalled to solidify that order, or so it seemed to those of Gogol's readers who were able to survive their initial encounter with the book's authorial persona and to finish reading it.[2] Where the gaps and discontinuities of the first book opened spaces for a variety of interpretations, *Selected Passages* seemed only to leave room for one, in which few of Gogol's admirers could find comfort. Beyond these problems, enough of his argument recalled the salon religiosity of the early nineteenth and late eighteenth centuries to merit mockery of the book's radical ambitions.[3]

The surviving chapters of *Dead Souls* (vol. II), over which Gogol agonized during the last decade of his life, are less clear in their position than *Selected Passages*, combining as they do moments of his former humor with new attempts at psychological analysis, at thinking characters, and at biographical narratives of repentence and transformation. From the fragments one sees Gogol weaving a more plotted novel with tighter social and psychological connections between characters than figured in the unconventionally plotted volume I. The estates, which border each other, are joined in a more conventional sense of neighborhood. The characters have parents, children, and other human connections; some have biographies. The static serf-owning economy which Gogol depicted in volume I begins to yield to a cash economy. The notebooks (like the preface to the second edition of *Dead Souls*, vol. I, VI, 587–590) display a Gogol anxious to know Russia not so much through the ideology-filled talk of the cultured elite as through concrete agricultural and bureaucratic details. All of this may have threatened to produce more of the drab fiction of the late 1840s, of the "natural school," as Bulgarin and Belinsky called Gogol's motley heirs-presumptive. Or, say those who heard him read it, it might have indeed represented a new stage in his work. These memoirists, were, however, the sort of listeners who found the first volume "natural." The jury must forever remain out.

Already by 1844 Belinsky could find the work of Pushkin and Lermontov dated.[4] By 1847 he would see that Gogol, too, differed from writers of the "natural school."[5] This gap would come to yawn still more, because for a number of reasons—among them economic (a slowdown in publishing), governmental (in 1847 the head of the censorship wanted to ban *all* novels), and aesthetic (the prevalence of small prose genres, such as physiological sketches)—the development of the Russian novel went into a state of temporary remission during the late 1840s and early 1850s.[6] Meanwhile, important memoir narratives, such as Sergei Aksakov's, added a new biographical dimension to Russian prose, although some novelists, such as Dostoevsky, would not rush to exploit it. And new journals, in which the serialized novel figured as a regular feature, offered a new institutional framework for Russian fiction, a framework exploited in a variety of ways by such novelists as Dostoevsky, Tolstoy, and Saltykov-Shchedrin. Under the impact of these "thick journals" of the 1850s–1880s, new discourses (scientific, political, economic, religious, legal—to name a few) challenged the Russian novel, replacing, or at least supplementing, the literary ones which had played such an important part in early nineteenth-century fiction. Shifts in narrative technique, psychology, and epistemology opened new possibilities for fictional representation, particularly in the previously unexplored realm of interiority (memory, mental disturbance, psychological analysis, subjective time awareness).

Despite these sweeping changes in Russian literary and intellectual life, later nineteenth-century novelists, critics, and readers did not ignore the achievements of Pushkin, Lermontov, and Gogol. The characters and situations of *Eugene Onegin, A Hero of Our Time,* and *Dead Souls* were frequently appropriated and made to serve different literary structures and cultural controversies. Pushkin's Tatiana— wrenched from her institutional, ideological, and fictional settings— could become an emblem of Russian womanhood in Dostoevsky's discussions of Russian culture. Eugene and Pechorin could enter journalistic discussions of the "superfluous man," once their ready participation in the rituals and contests of society was forgotten. Chichikov could become an incipient capitalist as new economic patterns came to the fore. Gogol's landowners could lend their names as labels for a range of negative phenomena in Russian life.

To the extent that ideology is not an easily detachable screen between the text and "reality," traces of the ideology of polite society accompanied the characters, situations, and narrative techniques of these novels as subsequent novelists adapted them to their fictions. But in the context of new values, new discursive confrontations, and new fictional possibilities, the social-aesthetic ideal that had once been replete with the promise of cultural productivity inevitably appeared hollow, constricting, or unproductively quaint. Thus in Tolstoy's *Childhood* (1852), the little boy's training in the arts of polite society (foreign languages, poetry, dancing) becomes a process of confining his powers of observation and his generous impulses. In *Rudin* (1856) Turgenev gives the salon far less cultural power than the intense philosophical circles of the poor Moscow students or the family gatherings of the provincial gentry. Dostoevsky's *Idiot* (1868) features a savage satire on the social and aesthetic pretensions of polite society; in *The Possessed* (1871–72), a festival designed to harmonize conflicting social and political groups unleashes antagonism and violence on a scale unimaginable in the earlier nineteenth-century novels. The central gathering in Chekhov's "Name-Day Party" (1888), which ends in the hostess's miscarriage, is undermined by her growing irritation and illness. The discursive elements—innate or spiritual goodness, intuition, psychologized personal history, the body's internal (physiological) environment—which inserted these fictions into new controversies helped impoverish their readers' memory of the intense cultural struggles in which the novels of Pushkin, Lermontov, and Gogol had once participated.

Something of this process of transformation and impoverishment may be inferred from some Dostoevskian texts of the 1870s. In the April 1876 issue of his *Diary of a Writer*, Dostoevsky, whose brilliantly creative interaction with the texts of Pushkin and Gogol is well documented, took issue with a critic, V. G. Avseenko, who had faulted Gogol for not addressing the concerns of the intelligentsia and for inspiring a literature more interested in artistry than in "inner content."[7] The diarist responded with a sharpness that Avseenko's primitive aesthetics deserved, but the response ultimately replaced this voiding of the text with a dismembering: "Gogol's . . . *Getting Married*, his *Dead Souls* are his most profound works, his works most rich in inner content, precisely because of the literary types depicted in them. These depictions, so to speak, nearly crush the mind with the most profound, unbearable questions, provoking in the Russian mind the most disturbing thoughts."[8] But even in this passionate defense, which most perceptively captures the texts' continuing appeal, one senses a loss of connections, and a dismantling of those texts for appropriable elements ("literary types").

Dostoevsky attributes a different appropriation, a sentimental, reifying one, to the hero-narrator's tutor in *The Raw Youth*. It merits quotation because its nostalgic evocation of the earlier period stands diametrically opposed to the ways in which *Eugene Onegin, A Hero of Our Time*, and *Dead Souls* presented that world:

> If I were a Russian novelist and had the talent, I would certainly take my heroes from the Russian hereditary nobility, because only in this type of cultured Russian is possible even the appearance of a beautiful order and a beautiful impression, so necessary in a novel for effecting a fine influence on the reader . . . Pushkin had already planned the subjects of his future novels in [his lines about] "the legends of a Russian family" [*Eugene Onegin*, 3:13-14], and, believe me, that is really everything that has been beautiful among us up to now, that has been the least bit complete. I am not saying this because I am unreservedly in agreement with the correctness and the uprightness of that beauty; but there, for example, were already the finished forms of honor and duty, which, except among the nobility, have not only never been completed in Russia, but never even started. I say this as a calm man and as one who seeks calm.
>
> Whether that honor is good and whether that duty is true is another question; but more important for me is precisely the completeness of form and just some order, and not a prescribed order, but one ultimately experienced by them themselves. God, how the most important thing for us is some kind of order, our own! In this lies our hope and, so to speak, our rest.[9]

We have seen, and the author of *The Raw Youth* knew perfectly well, that Pushkin never wrote those traditional family novels, lending instead, like Lermontov and Gogol, the openness of form to the novelistic exploration of what Dostoevsky's desperately "calm" character calls "another question."

To be sure, their novels, like other works of the "Golden Age," fulfill a continuing need for beauty and order. Yet the questions they raised and the struggles in which they participated—over the role of literature in a secular culture, the problem of identity and social life, and over possible transformations of society—have helped the novels to retain their power, both over subsequent writers and over their reading publics, in a culture which has rarely made artistic excellence its overriding concern.

My principal task in this study has been to evoke those struggles, which have been a gage of the novels' continuing, if discontinuously manifested, vitality.

Notes
Index

Notes

Introduction

1. V. V. Kozhinov, "K sotsiologii russkoi literatury XVIII–XIX vekov (Problema literaturnykh napravlenii)," in V. Ia. Kantorovich and Iu. V. Kuz'menko, comps., *Literatura i sotsiologiia: Sbornik statei* (Moscow: Nauka, 1977), 167.

2. Ernst Cassirer, *The Philosophy of the Enlightenment*, trans. Fritz C. A. Koelln and James P. Pettegrove (Princeton: Princeton University Press, 1951), 294.

3. On this problem, see Erich Auerbach, *Mimesis: The Representation of Reality in Western Literature*, trans. Willard R. Trask (Princeton: Princeton University Press, 1953), chaps. 15 and 18.

4. M. N. Murav'ev, "Predpochtenie prirodnogo iazyka," *Sochineniia* (St. Petersburg, 1847), II, 265; N. M. Karamzin, "Otchego v Rossii malo avtorskikh talantov," *Izbrannye sochinenii v dvukh tomakh* (Moscow-Leningrad: Khudozhestvennaia literatura, 1964), II, 185–186; K. N. Batiushkov, "O vliianii legkoi poezii na iazyk," in *Sochineniia*, ed. L. N. Maikov and V. I. Saitov, 3 vols. (St. Petersburg: Kotomin, 1885–1887), II, 243.

5. P. A. Viazemsky, *Staraia zapisnaia kniga*, ed. L. Ia. Ginzburg (Leningrad: Izdatel'stvo pisatelei v Leningrade, 1929), 187–188.

6. David J. Welsh, *Russian Comedy, 1765–1823* (The Hague: Mouton, 1966), 49–50.

7. R. V. Iezuitova, "Svetskaia povest'," in B. S. Meilakh, ed., *Russkaia povest' XIX veka: Istoriia i problematika zhanra* (Leningrad: Nauka, 1973), 170. Elizabeth C. Shepard presents an enlightening formal analysis of such fictions in "The Society Tale and the Innovative Argument in Russian Prose Fiction of the 1830's," *Russian Literature*, 10 (1981), 111–161.

8. For Bakhtin's most detailed outline of the novel's possibilities in these terms, see M. M. Bakhtin, "Slovo v romane," in his *Voprosy literatury i estetiki* (Moscow: Khudozhestvennaia literatura, 1975), 72–233. An excellent English translation is available in M. M. Bakhtin, *The Dialogic Imagination: Four Essays*, trans. Caryl Emerson and Michael Holquist (Austin: University of Texas Press, 1981), 259–422.

9. See, in this regard, Roman Jakobson and Iu. Tynianov, "Problemy izucheniia literatury i iazyka," *Novyi lev*, 12 (1928), 36–37; René Wellek, "The-

ory and Aesthetics of the Prague School," in his *Discriminations: Further Concepts of Criticism* (New Haven: Yale University Press, 1970), 291; Iu. I. Surovtsev, "Vozmozhnosti i predely sotsiologicheskogo izucheniia iskusstva," and V. E. Kovsky, "Sotsiologicheskii i esteticheskii kriterii v kritike," in Kantorovich and Kuz'menko, *Literatura i sotsiologiia*, 7–51 and 52–82.

10. On this sort of disciplinary cross-pollination, see Clifford Geertz, "Blurred Genres: The Refiguration of Social Thought," *The American Scholar*, 49 (Spring 1980), 165–179.

11. For important contributions to this argument, see A. G. Tseitlin, *Masterstvo Turgeneva-romanista* (Moscow: Sovetskii pisatel', 1958), chap. 1; W. Lednicki, "O proze Pushkina," *Novyi zhurnal*, 21 (1949), 111–145; and D. E. Tamarchenko, *Iz istorii russkogo klassicheskogo romana* (Moscow-Leningrad: ANSSSR, 1961).

12. On these early twentieth-century processes of canon formation, see Jeffrey Brooks, "Russian Nationalism and Russian Literature: The Canonization of the Classics," in Ivo Banac, John G. Ackerman, and Roman Szporluk, eds., *Nation and Ideology: Essays in Honor of Wayne S. Vucinich* (Boulder: East European Monographs, 1981), 315–334.

I. A Russian Ideology

1. For additional information on the role of the Laval family in the conspiracy, see A. L. Vainstein and V. P. Pavlova, "Dekabristy i salon Laval'," in V. G. Bazanov and V. E. Vatsuro, eds., *Literaturnoe nasledie Dekabristov* (Leningrad: Nauka, 1975), 165–194. For a picture of the Laval mansion, see A. N. Petrov et al., *Pamiatniki arkhitektury Leningrada* (Leningrad: Izdatel'stvo literatury po stroitel'stvu, 1969), 72.

2. V. V. Vinogradov, ed., *Slovar' iayzyka Pushkina* (Moscow: Gos. Izd. slovarei, 1956–1961). For a discussion of the special meanings of the term *obshchestvo* in the period immediately following the one that this book analyzes, see Victor Ripp, *Turgenev's Russia: From "Notes of a Hunter" to "Fathers and Sons"* (Ithaca: Cornell University Press,1980), 98–100, 102–106.

3. "World" in this sense is used in English from Dryden on, without the epithet "fashionable" until the nineteenth century. Lady Mary Wortley Montagu used it with the epithet "great"—See *le grand monde* in *The Compact Edition of the Oxford English Dictionary* (Oxford: Oxford University Press, 1971).

4. N. V. Riasanovsky, *A Parting of Ways: Government and the Educated Public, 1801–1855* (Oxford: Oxford University Press, 1976), 187.

5. For a different mapping, see Fredric Jameson, "Ideology and Symbolic Action," *Critical Inquiry*, 5 (Winter 1978), 417–422. On early uses of the term, see Emmet Kennedy, "Ideology from Destutt de Tracy to Marx," *Journal of the History of Ideas*, 40 (July-September 1979), 353–368. For a survey of the term's changing role in social theory, see George Lichtheim, "The Concept of Ideology," *History and Theory*, 4 (1965), 164–195.

6. The word "ideologiia" began to appear in Russian dictionaries in 1803 in the meaning "the study of ideas," which recalls Destutt de Tracy's

project; M. M. Bakhtin, "Slovo v romane," in his *Voprosy literatury i estetiki* (Moscow: Khudohestvennaia literatura, 1975), 84, 146–147, 157, 169–170, 177. Boris Uspensky, *A Poetics of Composition: The Structure of the Artistic Text and a Typology of a Compositional Form*, trans. V. Zavarin and S. Wittig (Berkeley: University of California Press, 1973), 8, equates the ideological and the evaluative, defining evaluative as a "general system of viewing the world conceptually.

7. For arguments on the immunity of the proletariat and of leftist thought to ideology, see David Braybrooke, "Ideology," *The Encyclopaedia of Philosophy* (New York: Macmillan, 1972), IV, 126; Roland Barthes, *Mythologies*, trans. Annette Lavers (New York: Hill and Wang, 1972), 145–148; and Lichtheim, "The Concept of Ideology," 176–177.

8. Karl Marx, "The German Ideology," in Robert C. Tucker, ed., *The Marx-Engels Reader*, 2nd ed. (New York: Norton, 1978), 153, 159, 173–175.

9. A. Solzhenitsyn, *Arkhipelag GULag, 1918–1956: Opyt khudozhestvennogo issledovaniia*, vol. 1–2 (Paris: YMCA Press, 1973), 181.

10. Geoffrey C. Kabat, *Ideology and Imagination: The Image of Society in Dostoevsky* (New York: Columbia University Press, 1978). Fredric Jameson develops a psychoanalytic approach to ideology further in his *The Political Unconscious: Narrative as a Socially Symbolic Act* (Ithaca: Cornell University Press, 1981), chap. 3.

11. G. W. F. Hegel, *Reason in History: A General Introduction to the Philosophy of History*, trans. R. S. Hartman (Indianapolis: Library of the Liberal Arts, 1953), 88–95.

12. On Marx as a writer of narrative, see Hayden White, *Metahistory: The Historical Imagination in Nineteenth-Century Europe* (Baltimore: Johns Hopkins University Press, 1973), chap. 8; Terry Eagleton, "Ideology, Fiction, Narrative," *Social Text*, 2 (Summer 1979), 71–73; and Jameson, *The Political Unconscious*, 33. Louis S. Feuer, *Ideology and the Ideologists* (Oxford: Basil Blackwell, 1975), analyzes ideology in terms of an "invariant mythic structure" that is shaped by the Mosaic legend.

13. V. N. Voloshinov, *Marksizm i filosofiia iazyka: osnovnye problemy sotsiologicheskogo metoda v nauke o iazyke*, 2nd ed. (1930; rpt. The Hague: Mouton, 1972), 71. V. V. Vinogradov also links language and ideology, *Ocherki po istorii russkogo literaturnogo iazyka XVII–XIXvv.*, 2nd ed. (Moscow: Uchpedgiz, 1938), 188–91; and *Iazyk Pushkina: Pushkin i istoriia russkogo literaturnogo iazyka* (Moscow: Academia, 1935), 349.

14. Barthes, *Mythologies*; Bakhtin, "Slovo v romane"; Iu. M. Lotman, "Dekabrist v povsednevnoi zhizni (bytovoe povedenie kak istoriko-psikhologicheskaia kategoriia)," in Bazanov and Vatsuro, *Literaturnoe nasledie Dekabristov*; Iu. M. Lotman and B. A. Uspensky, "Spory o iazyke v nachale XIXv. kak fakt russkoi kul'tury ('Proisshestvie v tsarstve tenei, ili sud'bina rossiiskogo iazyka'—neizvestnoe sochinenie Semena Bobrova)," *Uchenye zapiski Tartuskogo Gosudarstvennogo Universiteta, Vyp. 358, Trudy po russkoi i slavianskoi filologii, XXIV, literaturovedenie* (Tartu, 1975), 168–222.

15. Althusser's seminal essays on ideology, Lacan, and art appear in

Louis Althusser, *Lenin and Philosophy and Other Essays,* trans. Ben Brewster (New York: Monthly Review Press, 1971). Here Althusser distances himself from Marx's allegedly "non-Marxist" theory of ideology, 158–160. Eagleton, in turn, distances himself from Marx's teleological writings, as well as from the idea that ideology will wither away with class society, "Ideology, Fiction, Narrative," 72–75, 78.

16. Louis Althusser, "A Letter on Art to André Daspre," *Lenin and Philosophy,* 223; Pierre Macherey, *A Theory of Literary Production,* trans. Geoffrey Wall (London: Routledge & Kegan Paul, 1978), 59, passim; Terry Eagleton, *Criticism and Ideology: A Study in Literary Theory* (London: New Left Books, 1976), 15, 54, 81. These, in turn, recall Voloshinov's point that formed ideological systems (e.g., social morality, science, religion) interact with "life ideology," 92–93.

17. Macherey, *A Theory of Literary Production,* 20, 52, 60, 64, 133, 195. Such a view is far from incompatible with Viktor Shklovsky's concept of *ostranenie* ("making strange") or Wolfgang Iser's "depragmatization." Viktor Shklovsky, "Iskusstvo kak priem," *Sborniki po teorii poeticheskogo iazyka,* 2 (Petrograd: Tip. Z. Sokolinskago, 1917), 3–14; Wolfgang Iser, *The Act of Reading: A Theory of Aesthetic Response* (Baltimore: Johns Hopkins University Press, 1978), 61.

18. Eagleton, *Criticism and Ideology,* 85.

19. Lionel Trilling, "Manners, Morals, and the Novel," in his *The Liberal Imagination: Essays on Literature and Society* (Garden City: Anchor Books, 1953), 200.

20. Eagleton, *Criticism and Ideology,* 54–63. On equivocation in literary sociology, see Jeffrey L. Sammons, *Literary Sociology and Practical Criticism: An Inquiry* (Bloomington: Indiana University Press, 1977), chap. 2.

21. Riasanovsky, *A Parting of Ways,* p. vii. Nevertheless, considerable help in defining the gentry and its values is provided by Terence Emmons, *The Russian Landed Gentry and the Peasant Emancipation of 1861* (Cambridge: Cambridge University Press, 1968), 3–18; and Iu. M. Lotman, "Ocherk dvorianskogo byta oneginskoi pory," in his *Roman A. S. Pushkina "Evgenii Onegin": Kommentarii* (Leningrad: "Prosveshchenie," 1980), 35–110. Two further works which complain of the lack of a social history of the period and of a clear definition of its cultural elite also contribute significantly to our understanding of the Russian gentry of the post-Petrine period: Marc Raeff, *Origins of the Russian Intelligentsia: The Eighteenth-Century Nobility* (New York: Harcourt, Brace and World, 1966); and Michaël Confino, "Histoire et psychologie: à propos de la noblesse russe au XVIIIᵉ siècle," *Annales,* 22 (November–December 1967), 1163–1205. I hope that my notion of the "ideology of polite society" will resolve some of the differences between these two outstanding works of historical interpretation.

22. N. M. Karamzin, "Otchego v Rossii malo avtorskikh talantov," *Izbrannye sochineniia v dvukh tomakh* (Moscow: Khudozhestvennaia literatura, 1964), II, 185.

23. A. S. Pushkin, *Polnoe sobranie sochinenii,* 17 vols. (Moscow-Leningrad:

Nauka, 1937–1959), VI, 22; V. A. Zhukovsky, "Pisatel' v obshchestve," *Polnoe sobranie sochinenii v dvenadtsati tomakh* (St. Petersburg: Izd. A. F. Marksa, 1902), IX, 36; N. V. Gogol, *Polnoe sobranie sochinenii*, 14 vols. (Moscow: Nauka, 1937–1952), I, 103. Where convenient, I will give references to these editions of Pushkin and Gogol in parentheses in the text, but see n. 38 below on the verse translation of *Eugene Onegin*.

24. Lotman and Uspensky, "Spory o iazyke," 232.

25. V. A. Zhukovsky, "Pis'mo iz uezda k izdateliu," *Vestnik Evropy*, 37, no. 1 (1808), 3. In a personal communication, Stephen L. Baehr suggests that Zhukovsky's definition is more Pietist than Masonic in its deterministic tone, although the stress on self-perfection is, of course, Masonic.

For a study of the Russian Anti-Enlightenment that traces its Catholic, Russian Orthodox, and Protestant variants, linking them with mystical Masonic traditions in Russian eighteenth-century thought, see James Billington, *The Icon and the Axe: An Interpretive History of Russian Culture* (New York: Knopf, 1966), 269–306. On the range of the Russian Enlightenment, see Riasanovsky, *A Parting of Ways*, 50–51.

26. S. S. Uvarov, "Literaturnye vospominaniia," *Sovremennik*, 27 (1851), book 6, sec. II, 40.

27. Andrei Walicki, *A History of Russian Thought: From the Enlightenment to Marxism* (Stanford: Stanford University Press, 1979), 53.

28. Zhukovsky, "Pisatel' v obshchestve," 37.

29. Marcelle Ehrhard, *V. A. Joukovski et le préromantisme russe* (Paris: Champion, 1938), 73.

30. On the middle-class orientation of Addison and Steele, see Robert J. Allen, "Introduction," *Addison and Steele: Selections from "The Tattler" and "The Spectator"* (New York: Holt, Rinehart & Winston, 1957), x, xiv; Ian Watt, *The Rise of the Novel: Studies in Defoe, Richardson, and Fielding* (Harmondsworth: Penguin, 1963), 54; C. S. Lewis, "Addison" in James L. Clifford, ed., *Eighteenth-Century English Literature: Modern Essays in Criticism* (New York: Oxford University Press, 1959), 149–150.

31. N. M. Karamzin, "Priiatnye vidy: nadezhdy i zhelaniia nyneshnego vremeni (pisano v 1802 goda)," *Sochineniia Karamzina* (St. Petersburg: Smirdin, 1848), III, 597. I am indebted to A. G. Cross's useful article, "N. M. Karamzin's 'Messenger of Europe' *(Vestnik Evropy)*, 1802–3," *Forum for Modern Language Studies*, 5 (January 1969), 15, for calling this essay to my attention. For a similarly composite image of the Russian gentleman, see D. V. Davydov, "Nekotorye cherty iz zhizni Denisa Vasil'evicha Davydova," *Sochineniia* (Moscow: GIKhL, 1962), 37.

32. Vinogradov, *Ocherki po istorii russkogo literaturnogo iazyka XVII–XIX vv.*, 148–188; Lotman and Uspensky, "Spory o iazyke," 247–254; V. D. Levin, *Ocherk stilistiki russkogo literaturnogo iazyka kontsa XVIII-nachala XIX (Leksika)* (Moscow: Nauka, 1964), 116–153. For studies of the embodiment of this style in Western literature, see Erich Auerbach, *Mimesis: The Representation of Reality in Western Literature*, trans. Willard R. Trask (Princeton: Princeton University Press, 1953), chap. 15; Peter Brooks, *The Novel of Worldliness: Crébillon, Mar-*

ivaux, Laclos, Stendhal (Princeton University Press, 1969); Roland Barthes, "La Bruyère," in his *Essais critiques* (Paris: Éditions du Seuil, 1964), 221–237; Bakhtin, "Slovo v romane," 192–193.

33. Karamzin, "Otchego v Rossii malo avtorskikh talantov," *Izbrannye sochineniia*, II, 185.

34. Karamzin, "O liubvi k otechestvu i narodnoi gordosti," *Izbrannye sochineniia*, II, 286.

35. See Lotman and Uspensky, "Spory o iazyke," 242–254.

36. P. P. Pekarsky, *Istoriia Imperatorskoi Akademii Nauk v Peterburge*, 2 vols. (St. Petersburg: Tip. I. Akademii Nauk, 1870–1873), II, 270, 273.

37. For information on literacy in early nineteenth-century Russia, see below, Chap. 2.

38. A. S. Pushkin, *Eugene Onegin*, 2nd ed., rev. trans. Walter Arndt (New York: Dutton, 1981), 74. Unless otherwise noted, I shall use Arndt's verse translation, indicating chapter and stanza in parentheses.

39. Levin, *Ocherki*, 124. On contempt for "seminarists" among the gentry, see Gregory L. Freeze, *The Russian Levites: Parish Clergy in the Eighteenth Century* (Cambridge, Mass.: Harvard University Press, 1977), 97.

40. Hans Rothe, "Russ. *vkus*, 'Geschmack'," in *Romanica Europaea et Americana: Festschrift für Harri Meier, 8 Januar 1980*, ed. H. D. Bork et al. (Bonn: Bouvier Verlag Herbert Grundmann, 1980), 493–504, precisely charts the semantic broadening of the word "taste" in eighteenth-century Russia. For an analysis of the importance of "taste" in Enlightenment culture, see Peter Gay, "The Discovery of Taste," *The Enlightenment: An Interpretation* II (New York: Knopf, 1969), 290–318. For a defense of linguistic change, taste as a critical criterion, and the Europeanization of Russia, see Karamzin's speech to the Russian Academy, 5 December 1818, *Izbrannye sochineniia*, II, 233–242.

For illuminating reflections upon the nature of fashion, see Herbert S. Lindenberger, "On Fashion," in *Saul's Fall: A Critical Fiction* (Baltimore: Johns Hopkins University Press, 1979), 107–110; Fernand Braudel, "Costume and Fashion," in *Civilization and Capitalism, Fifteenth to Eighteenth Centuries*, vol. I, *The Structures of Everyday Life: The Limits of the Possible*, trans. Siân Reynolds (New York: Harper & Row, 1981), 311–333.

41. Quoted in Donald Fanger, *The Creation of Nikolai Gogol* (Cambridge, Mass.: Harvard University Press, 1981), 41.

42. On the importance of gestures in such a cultural situation, see Jonathan Swift, "A Compleat Collection of Genteel and Ingenious Conversation," in his *Satires and Personal Writings* (London: Oxford University Press, 1932), 199–201.

43. William Mills Todd III, *The Familiar Letter as a Literary Genre in the Age of Pushkin* (Princeton: Princeton University Press, 1976); P. M. Lazarchuk, *Druzheskoe pis'mo XVIII veka kak fakt literatury: Dissertatsiia na soiskanie uchenoi stepeni kandidata filologicheskikh nauk* (Leningrad: LGPI im Gertsena, 1972).

44. Mérimée's comment is cited in Lotman and Uspensky, "Spory o iazyke," 253; N. A. Polevoi, review of *Boris Godunov*, *Moskovskii telegraf*, 49 (1831), 433; J. Sękowski, letter to A. S. Pushkin of Jan.-Feb. 1834, in Pushkin, *Polnoe sobranie sochinenii*, XV, 109–110.

45. A. S. Shishkov, "Rech' pri otkrytii Besedy," *Chtenie v Besede liubitelei russkogo slova*, 1 (1811), 42–43.

46. For a list of his examples and a survey of the Gallicization of Russian, see Vinogradov, *Ocherki po istorii russkogo literaturnogo iazyka*, 160–173. Karamzin's 1818 speech to the Russian Academy, over which Shishkov presided, makes the essential point here: "We do not wish to imitate foreigners, but we write as they write because we live as they live, we read what they read, we have the same models of intelligence and taste." *Izbrannye sochineniia*, II, 238.

47. N. M. Karamzin, *Pis'ma N. M. Karamzina k I. I. Dmitrievu*, ed. Ia. Grot and P. Pekarsky (St. Petersburg: Imp. Akademiia Nauk, 1866), 97.

48. Levin, *Ocherki stilistiki*, 115; Lotman and Uspensky, "Spory o iazyke," 180. Vinogradov gives earlier examples of attacks on the chancellery language in literary usage, *Ocherki po istorii russkogo literaturnogo iazyka*, 137, but here it is a question of overcoming the chancellery language in its own territory.

49. Quoted by Marc Raeff, "The Russian Autocracy and its Officials," *Harvard Slavic Studies*, 4 (1957), 80–81. Raeff distinguishes between the poorly educated lower-level clerks and the members of "society" who took the requisite interest in literature and philosophy, 86.

It should be noted that Tolstoy's treatment of Speransky in *War and Peace* takes cognizance of these distinctions, capturing Speransky's variety of post-prandial interests, taste for light French verse, and contempt for lower members of the civil service; at the same time Tolstoy endows him with the social clumsiness, poor French, and pomposity that signified non-noble origins.

50. Emmons, *The Russian Landed Gentry*, 7–11; Brenda Meehan-Waters, *Autocracy and Aristocracy: The Russian Service Elite of 1730* (New Brunswick: Rutgers University Press, 1982). See also Raeff, *The Origins of the Russian Intelligentsia*, chap. 3; and Daniel T. Orlovsky, "Recent Studies on the Russian Bureaucracy," *Russian Review*, 35 (October 1976), 448–467. There had, of course, been a pre-Petrine nobility, and independent-minded Russians of the early nineteenth century, such as Pushkin, could reinforce their feelings of independence in tracing their origins from it.

51. On this obstruction, see James T. Flynn, "The Universities, the Gentry, and the Russian Imperial Services," *Canadian-American Slavic Studies*, 2 (Winter 1968), 486–503.

52. Walter M. Pintner, "The Social Characteristics of the Early Nineteenth-Century Russian Bureaucracy," *Slavic Review*, 29 (September 1970), 429–443; W. Bruce Lincoln, "The Ministers of Nicholas I: A Brief Inquiry into Their Backgrounds and Service Careers," *Russian Review*, 34 (July 1975), 308–323.

53. Sidney Monas, *The Third Section: Police and Society in Russia under Nicholas I* (Cambridge, Mass.; Harvard University Press, 1961), 95–96.

54. On Karamzin's intellectual and personal relationship with the autocracy, see Richard Pipes, "The Background and Growth of Karamzin's Political Ideas down to 1810," *Karamzin's Memoir on Ancient and Modern Russia: A Translation and Analysis* (Cambridge, Mass.: Harvard University Press, 1959); V. E. Vatsuro and M. I. Gillel'son, "Podvig chestnogo cheloveka," in their

Skvoz' "umstvennye plotiny": Iz istorii knigi i pressy pushkinskoi pory (Moscow: Kniga, 1972), 32–113.

55. Wacław Lednicki, *Russia, Poland and the West: Essays in Literary and Cultural History* (London: Hutchinson, 1954), 196. Duelling was subject to legal penalties, but these could be circumvented with proper precautions (a compliant priest or doctor, for example). See A. S. Pushkin, *Eugene Onegin*, trans. and commentary by Vladimir Nabokov, 4 vols., rev. ed. (Princeton: Princeton University Press, 1975), 44; Lotman, *Roman A. S. Pushkina "Evgenii Onegin": Kommentarii*, 105.

56. A. G. Rashin, *Naselenie Rossii za 100 let (1821–1913 gg): Statisticheskie ocherki* (Moscow: Gos. statisticheskoe izd-vo, 1956), 119. Rashin's figures do not permit direct comparison with later years.

57. Ibid., 128.

58. Lotman, *Roman A. S. Pushkina "Evgenii Onegin": Kommentarii*, 78–79.

59. W. Bruce Lincoln, "The Daily Life of St. Petersburg Officials in the Mid Nineteenth Century," *Oxford Slavonic Papers*, n.s. 8 (1975), 87–88.

60. Quoted in Vatsuro and Gillel'son, *Skvoz' "umstvennie plotiny,"* 89.

61. Freeze, *The Russian Levites*, 184. The term "caste-estate" is his. In a new study Gregory Freeze argues that this situation persisted into the twentieth century, despite the formal termination (1869) of the caste system, *The Parish Clergy in Nineteenth-Century Russia: Crisis, Reform, Counter-Reform* (Princeton: Princeton University Press, 1983), 312, 388, 454.

62. A. S. Pushkin, *Eugene Onegin*, trans. Nabokov, I, 281.

63. Robert L. Nichols, "Orthodoxy and Russia's Enlightenment, 1762–1825," in Robert L. Nichols and Theofanis George Stavrou, eds., *Russian Orthodoxy under the Old Regime* (Minneapolis: University of Minnesota Press, 1978), 69–72. See also Hugh McLean, "Eugene Rudin," in William Mills Todd III, ed., *Literature and Society in Imperial Russia* (Stanford University Press, 1978), 264–266.

64. Freeze, *The Russian Levites*, 101. The examples of these "manners," however, seem to fall far short of what it would have taken to pass as a member of society.

65. P. A. Viazemsky, *Staraia zapisnaia kniga*, ed. L. Ia. Ginzburg (Leningrad: Izd-vo. pisatelei v Leningrade, 1929), 76.

66. On this fad for Church Slavonic, see the standard history of the Russian Bible Society, A. N. Pypin, "Rossiiskoe Bibleiskoe Obshchestvo: 1812–1826," in his *Religioznye dvizheniia pri Aleksandre I*, intro. and notes by N. K. Piksanov (Petrograd: Ogni, 1916), 119–120.

67. Ibid., 55, 66, 76–77, 80.

68. Robert Pinkerton, *Russia: or, Miscellaneous Observations on the Past and Present State of that Country and its Inhabitants* (London: Seeley & Sons, 1833), 359–360.

69. Erving Goffman, *Frame Analysis: An Essay on the Organization of Experience* (New York: Harper & Row, 1974), 496–559. Goffman's subsequent essays on the subject, published in *Forms of Talk* (Philadelphia: University of Pennsylvania Press, 1981), elaborate upon linguistic aspects of this approach.

B. M. Gasparov, "Ustnaia rech' kak semioticheskii ob"ekt," *Semantika nominatsii i semiotika ustnoi rechi: Lingvisticheskaia semantika i semiotika*, I (Tartu, 1978), 63–112, makes a series of essential comparisons between oral and written speech.

70. See the *Slovar' iazyka Pushkina*. I. I. Sreznevsky, *Materialy dlia slovaria drevne-russkogo iazyka* (St. Petersburg: Imp. Akademiia Nauk, 1893–1909), does not list "remark" or "witty remark" among the many possible meanings of *slovo* in the pre-Petrine Russian language.

71. S. T. Atsakov, "Vospominanie ob Alexsandre Semenoviche Shishkove," *Sobranie sochinenii v piati tomakh* (Moscow: Pravda, 1966), II, 270–273, 287.

72. Iu. N. Tynianov, "Oda kak oratorskii zhanr," *Arkhaisty i novatory* (Leningrad: Priboi, 1929), 80–84.

73. Althusser, *Lenin and Philosophy*, 170–183.

74. Quoted in Nichols, "Orthodoxy and Russia's Enlightenment," 79.

75. V. S. Solov'ev, "Znachenie poezii v stikhotvoreniiakh Pushkina (1899)," *Sobranie sochinenii*, 9 vols. (St. Petersburg: Tovarishchestvo "Obshchestvennaia pol'za," 1902–1907), VIII, 339. Such analyses of Pushkin and his work occurred regularly during the nineteenth century, but were, however, often couched in more complimentary terms. The tribute to the poet's universal susceptibility in Dostoevsky's 1880 Pushkin speech is, no doubt, the salient example. F. M. Dostoevsky, *Polnoe sobranie sochinenii v tridtsati tomakh* (Leningrad: Nauka, 1972–), XXVI, 146–147.

76. Quoted in Louis Pedrotti, *Józef-Julian Sękowski: The Genesis of a Literary Alien* (Berkeley: University of California Press, 1965), 31.

77. See, for example, "Ob uchtivosti i khoroshem tone," *Vestnik Evropy*, 9 (May 1803), 25–26.

78. Zhukovsky, "Pisatel' v obshchestve," 37; Goffman, *Frame Analysis*, 508–510.

79. William James, *The Principles of Psychology* (New York: Holt, 1890), I, 294.

80. Karamzin, *Pis'ma N. M. Karamzina k I. I. Dmitrievu*, 138–139. Letter of 11 November 1820. On the *honnête homme* as a cultural phenomenon, see Domna C. Stanton, *The Aristocrat as Art: A Study of the Honnête Homme and the Dandy in Seventeenth- and Nineteenth-Century French Literature* (New York: Columbia University Press, 1980).

81. M. Lemke, *Nikolaevskie zhandarmy i literatura 1826–1855gg. po podlinnym delam tret'ego otdeleniia sobstv. E.I. velichestva kantseliarii*, 2nd ed. (St. Petersburg: S. V. Bunin, 1909), 286.

82. A. I. Koshelev, *Zapiski, 1806–1883* (1884; rpt. Newtonville, Mass.: Oriental Research Partners, 1976), 68–69.

83. V. K. Kiukhel'beker, *Puteshestvie, Dnevnik, Stat'i* (Leningrad: Nauka, 1979), 95–96.

84. M. H. Abrams, *The Mirror and the Lamp: Romantic Theory and the Critical Tradition* (1953: rpt. New York: Norton, 1958), 84–88; L. Ia. Ginzburg, *O lirike* (Moscow-Leningrad: Sovetskii pisatel', 1964), 171. Ginzburg's exemplary poet

here, Lermontov, begins to break down these generic boundaries to replace this system with another, the unified personality of the lyric poet.

85. Germaine Necker de Staël, *Madame de Staël on Politics, Literature, and National Character*, ed. and trans. Morroe Berger (New York: Doubleday Anchor, 1965), 206.

86. On representations of the "strange man" in early nineteenth-century Russian literature, see B. T. Udodov, *M. Iu. Lermontov: Khudozhestvennaia individual'nost' i tvorcheskie protsessy* (Voronezh: Izd. voronezhskogo universiteta, 1973), 510–543.

87. Aksakov, "Vospominanie ob Aleksandre Semenoviche Shishkove," II, 280–281.

88. Viazemsky, *Staraia zapisnaia kniga*, 178.

89. For a useful introduction to Russian epigrams, see V. E. Vasil'eva et al., eds., *Russkaia epigramma vtoroi poloviny XVII–nachala XX v.* (Leningrad: Sovetskii pisatel', 1975).

90. Todd, *The Familiar Letter as a Literary Genre*, chap. 4.

91. L. Ia. Ginzburg, "Viazemsky" in *Staraia zapisnaia kniga*, 45.

92. P. A. Viazemsky, "Ot perevodchika," *Polnoe sobranie sochinenii*, 12 vols. (St. Petersburg: S. D. Sheremetev, 1878–1896), X, vii-ix.

93. V. G. Belinsky, *Sobranie sochinenii v deviati tomakh* (Moscow: Khud. lit., 1976–1982), IX, 682. Letter to K. D. Kavelin of 22 November 1847. I am indebted to Robert Louis Jackson, *The Art of Dostoevsky: Deliriums and Nocturnes* (Princeton: Princeton University Press, 1981), 12, for calling this quotation to my attention.

94. "Ob uchtivosti i khoroshem tone," 24, 29.

95. N. M. Karamzin, "Pis'mo k izdateliu," *Izbrannye sochineniia*, II, 176.

96. V. A. Zhukovsky, "O kritike," *Polnoe sobranie sochinenii*, IX, 96.

97. One recalls that Petr Chaadaev addressed his provocative *Lettres philosophiques* (1829) "à une dame."

98. *Poliarnaia zvezda, izdannaia A. Bestuzhevym i K. Ryleevym*, ed. V. A. Arkhipov et al. (Moscow-Leningrad: ANSSSR, 1960), 199–205. For other of Kornilovich's works on the everyday life and entertainments of the eighteenth century, see A. G. Kornilovich, *Sochineniia i pis'ma*, ed. A. G. Grymm-Grzhimailo and V. V. Kafengaus (Moscow-Leningrad: ANSSSR, 1957). For an evaluation of Kornilovich as a historian, see I. Z. Serman, "Aleksandr Kornilovich kak istorik i pisatel'," *Literaturnoe nasledie Dekabristov*, 142–164.

99. The voluminous literature on the Decembrists is dominated by studies of their biographies and ideas. For bibliographical information, see N. M. Chentsov, *Vosstanie Dekabristov: Bibliografiia* (Moscow-Leningrad: Tsentrarkhiv, 1929); M. V. Nechkina, ed., *Dvizhenie Dekabristov: Ukazatel' literatury, 1928–1959* (Moscow: Izd-vo vsesoiuznoi knizhnoi palaty, 1960); and M. V. Nechkina, ed., *Dvizhenie Dekabristov: Ukazatel' literatury 1960–1976* (Moscow: Nauka, 1983). Readers without Russian will find a thorough study of the Decembrists in Anatole G. Mazour, *The First Russian Revolution, 1825*, 2nd printing (Stanford: Stanford University Press, 1961). A useful collection of primary sources is Marc Raeff, ed., *The Decembrist Movement* (Englewood Cliffs: Prentice-Hall, 1966).

100. For information on these groups, see Todd, *The Familiar Letter as a Literary Genre,* chap. 2, appendix 1; V. B. Tomashevsky, *Pushkin. Kniga I* (Moscow-Leningrad: ANSSSR, 1956), 193–222; V. G. Bazanov, *Vol'noe obshchestvo liubitelei rossiiskoi slovesnosti* (Petrozavodsk: GosIzd Karelo-Finskoi SSR, 1949).

101. Bazanov, *Vol'noe obshchestvo,* 5–6.

102. On the attitude of the Northern Society and of its predecessors toward the gentry, see Riasanovsky, *A Parting of Ways,* 82–100; Walicki, *A History of Russian Thought,* 57–70; Mazour, *The First Russian Revolution,* 72–98; Raeff, *The Decembrists,* 15, 29; and S. S. Landa, "O nekotorykh osobennostiakh formirovaniia revoliutsionnoi ideologii v Rossii, 1816–21," *Pushkin i ego vremia: issledovaniia i materialy* (Leningrad: Nauka, 1962), I: 67–71; Lotman, "Dekabrist v povsednevnoi zhizni," 28–29, 71; and Iu. M. Lotman, "P. A. Viazemsky i dvizhenie Dekabristov," *Uchenye zapiski Tartuskogo Gosudarstvennogo Universiteta,* 98 (1960), 24–142.

103. Lotman, "Dekabrist v povsednevnoi zhizni," 62. In an earlier study, Lotman persuasively used these refusals as a key to interpreting the narrator's rhetoric in *Eugene Onegin,* chap. 1, "K evoliutsii postroeniia kharakterov v romane 'Evgenii Onegin'," *Pushkin: issledovaniia i materialy,* III (Moscow-Leningrad: Nauka, 1960), 131–173.

104. On the importance of Roman models (the Senecan sage, the Ciceronian rhetor) in the development of the *honnête homme,* see Stanton, *The Aristocrat as Art,* 15–17. The Decembrists' version clearly foregrounded the elements of social commitment (to rectify injustice, to cure social ills) that the eighteenth century had added to the French seventeenth-century version (Stanton, 9). On the Decembrists' use of Roman and later heroic models (e.g., Schiller's *Don Carlos*), see Lotman, "Dekabrist v povsednevnoi zhizni," 39–47. Indeed, the Decembrists' understanding of the Roman Republic was itself colored by contemporary European liberalism, as Landa indicates, "O nekotorykh osobennostiakh formirovaniia revoliutsionnoi ideologii v Rossii, 1816–21," 102–105.

105. Raeff, *The Decembrist Movement,* 15.

106. M. Iu. Lermontov, *Sobranie sochinenii v chetyrekh tomakh,* 2nd ed., ed. V. A. Manuilov et al. (Leningrad: Nauka, 1979–1981), IV, 186. Subsequent references to this edition will appear in the text in parentheses.

107. The scene is described in the memoirs of the Decembrist A. P. Beliaev, which are quoted in M. Ia. Basina, "Pisateli-Dekabristy," in A. M. Dokusov, ed., *Literaturnye pamiatnye mesta Leningrada,* 2nd ed. (Leningrad: Lenizdat, 1968), 136–137.

108. Mazour, *The First Russian Revolution,* 204.

109. P. E. Shchegolev, *Dekabristy: Sbornik statei* (Moscow-Leningrad: GIZ, 1926), 200–201. Quoted in Mazour, *The First Russian Revolution,* 205.

110. Raeff, *The Decembrist Movement,* 29; Riasanovsky, *A Parting of Ways,* 100; Mazour, *The First Russian Revolution,* 199, 271.

111. Thomas W. Atkinson, *Travels in the Regions of the Upper and Lower Amoor and the Russian Acquisitions* (New York: Harper & Bros., 1860), 303. Quoted in Anatole G. Mazour, *Women in Exile: Wives of the Decembrists* (Tal-

lahassee: Diplomatic Press, 1975), 52. I have adapted Atkinson's haphazard transliteration to the system used throughout this book.

112. N. M. Karamzin, *Pis'ma N. M. Karamzina k kniaziu P. A. Viazemskomu: 1810–1826 (iz ostaf'evskogo arkhiva)*, ed. N. Barsukov (St. Petersburg, 1897), 171. Footnote to a letter of 11 January 1826.

113. The most thorough study of the Official Nationality appears in Nicholas Riasanovsky, *Nicholas I and Official Nationality in Russia, 1825–1855* (Berkeley: University of California Press, 1959). W. Bruce Lincoln's *Nicholas I: Emperor and Autocrat of All the Russias* (Bloomington: Indiana University Press, 1978), analyzes these intellectual developments against a background of social and political history and suggests that there was a systematic pattern to Nicholas I's rule. Both provide useful bibliographies.

2. Institutions of Literature

1. This definition is derived from Peter L. Berger and Thomas Luckmann, *The Social Construction of Reality: A Treatise in the Sociology of Knowledge* (Garden City: Doubleday Anchor, 1966).

2. Edward J. Brown, *Stankevich and his Moscow Circle: 1830–1840* (Stanford: Stanford University Press, 1966), 10–12; Donald Fanger, *The Creation of Nikolai Gogol* (Cambridge, Mass.: Harvard University Press, 1979), 25–28; and V. G. Belinsky, *Sobranie sochinenii v deviati tomakh* (Moscow: Khudozhestvennaia literatura, 1976–1982), I, 613, list the salient examples.

3. As Berger and Luckmann note, socialization, the individual's initiation into the institutional order, is a process that is never total and never completed, 137, 143–144, 148, 157.

4. Harry Levin, "Literature as an Institution," *Accent*, 6 (1945–46), 159–168.

5. Wilhelm Vosskamp, "Gattungen als literarisch-soziale Institutionen (Zu Problemen sozial- und funktsions-geschichtlich orientierter Gattungstheorie und -historie)," in Walter Hinck, ed., *Textsortenlehre-Gattungsgeschichte* (Heidelberg: Quelle und Meyer, 1977), 27–42.

6. Robert Escarpit, *Sociology of Literature*, 2nd ed., trans. Ernest Pick (London: Cass, 1971).

7. Hugh Dalziel Duncan, *Language and Literature in Society: A Sociological Essay on Theory and Method in the Interpretation of Linguistic Symbols with a Bibliographical Guide to the Sociology of Literature* (Chicago: University of Chicago Press, 1953), 58–74.

8. Peter Bürger, "Institution Kunst als literatursozialogische Kategorie: Skizze einer Theorie des historischen Wandels der gesellschaftlichen Funktion der Literatur," *Romanistische Zeitschrift für Literaturgeschichte*, 1 (1977), 50–74. An important application of Bürger's analysis appears in his book *Theory of the Avant-Garde*, trans. Michael Shaw (Minneapolis: University of Minnesota Press, 1984).

9. Raymond Williams, *The Sociology of Culture* (New York: Schocken Books, 1982), 33–56.

10. Boris Eikhenbaum, *Moi vremennik: Slovesnost', nauka, kritika, smes'* (Leningrad: Izd. pisatelei v Leningrade, 1929), 84. For more material on formalist conceptions of literature as an institution, see William Mills Todd III, "Literature as an Institution: Fragments of a Formalist Theory," in Robert Louis Jackson and Stephen Rudy, eds., *Russian Formalism: A Retrospective Glance* (New Haven: Yale Center for International and Area Studies, 1985), 15–26.

11. See, in particular, Frank Kermode, *The Genesis of Secrecy: On the Interpretation of Narrative* (Cambridge, Mass.: Harvard University Press, 1979); Jonathan Culler, *Structuralist Poetics: Structuralism, Linguistics, and the Study of Literature* (Ithaca: Cornell University Press, 1975); and Jonathan Culler, *The Pursuit of Signs: Semiotics, Literature, Deconstruction* (Ithaca: Cornell University Press, 1981).

12. Jürgen Habermas, *Zur Logik der Sozialwissenschaften* (Frankfurt: Suhrkamp, 1970), 287–288.

13. Paul Ricoeur, "The Model of the Text," *Social Research*, 38 (1971), 530–545.

14. Roman Jakobson, "Closing Statement: Linguistics and Poetics," in Thos. A. Sebeok, ed., *Style in Language* (New York: M.I.T. Press and John Wiley & Sons, 1960), 353.

15. Ibid., 371. Robert Scholes has argued that all six factors can become multiple or duplicitous in a text marked by literariness. "Towards a Semiotics of Literature," *Critical Inquiry*, 4 (Autumn 1977), 109. Tzvetan Todorov proposes a Bakhtinian model, opposed to this Jakobsonian one, with no "code" or "contact" preceding the act of communication, but rather produced uniquely in and by the situation of utterance, *Mikhail Bakhtine: Le principe dialogique* (Paris: Editions du Seuil, 1981), 86–88.

16. For a summary of these developments, see Seymour Chatman, *Story and Discourse: Narrative Structure in Fiction and Film* (Ithaca: Cornell University Press, 1978).

17. Gary Saul Morson, *Dostoevsky's "Diary of a Writer" and the Traditions of Literary Utopia* (Austin: University of Texas Press, 1981), 48–51.

18. Elizabeth Closs Traugott and Mary Louise Pratt, *Linguistics for Students of Literature* (New York: Harcourt Brace Jovanovich, 1980), 109.

19. Jakobson, "Linguistics and Poetics," 356; Northrop Frye, *Anatomy of Criticism* (Princeton: Princeton University Press,1957), 79; Roland Barthes, "From Work to Text," in Josué V. Harari, ed., *Textual Strategies: Perspectives in Post-Structuralist Criticism* (Ithaca: Cornell University Press, 1979), 73–81.

20. Alvin B. Kernan, *The Imaginary Library: An Essay on Literature and Society* (Princeton: Princeton University Press, 1982), proposes such an awareness of institutional "paradigm shifts," 29.

21. On the vitality of useful institutional forms and their expansion into different areas of life, see Elizabeth Burns, *Theatricality: A Study of Convention in the Theater and in Social Life* (New York: Harper & Row, 1972), 35.

22. M. N. Kufaev, *Istoriia russkoi knigi v XIX veka* (Leningrad: Nachatki znanii, 1927), 20. For a detailed empirical study of eighteenth-century Russian

publishing (public and private, provincial and metropolitan), see Gary Jon Marker, "Publishing and the Formation of a Reading Public in Eighteenth-century Russia," Ph.D. diss., University of Californa, Berkeley, 1977.

23. On the possibilities for liberty within this mode of institutionalization, see Paul Zumthor, "From History to Poem, or the Paths of Pun: The Grands Rhétoriquers of Fifteenth-Century France," *New Literary History*, 10 (Winter 1979), 245–246.

24. G. A. Gukovsky, *Russkaia literatura XVIII veka: Uchebnik dlia vysshikh uchebnykh zavedenii* (Moscow: Uchpedgiz, 1939), 419.

25. Samuel Johnson, *Johnson's Dictionary: A Modern Selection*, ed. E. L. McAdam, Jr. and George Milne (New York: Random House, Modern Library, 1965), 167.

26. T. Grits, V. Trenin, M. Nikitin, *Slovesnost' i kommertsiia (knizhnaia lavka A. F. Smirdina)*, ed. V. B. Shklovskii and B. M. Eikhenbaum (Moscow: Fede-ratsiia, 1929), see drunkenness as institutionalized among eighteenth-century Russian writers, 137. Pushkin wrote of Sumarokov that he was a "buffoon for all of the magnates of that time," XI, 253. For sensational examples of such subservience, see Vladimir C. Nahirny, *The Russian Intelligentsia: From Torment to Silence* (New Brunswick: Transaction, 1983), 36–41. For information on how important writers supported themselves during this period, see S. Shashkov, "Literaturnyi trud v Rossii (istoricheskii ocherk)," *Delo*, 8 (1876), 5–21.

27. P. A. Viazemsky, "O Sumarokove," *Literaturnaia gazeta*, 28 (16 May 1830), 222.

28. A. Kh. Benkendorff, letter to Pushkin of 14 December 1826, in Push-kin, *Polnoe sobranie sochinenii*, XIII, 313. It has subsequently been established that this comment was developed by Nicholas I from a report on Pushkin's play by the critic-informer Bulgarin. See G. O. Vinokur, "Kto byl tsenzorom 'Borisa Godunova'?" in *Pushkin: Vremennik pushkinskoi kommissii*, I (Moscow-Leningrad: ANSSSR, 1936), 203–214.

29. Sumarokov stated in the memorandum quoted above, "I am a gentle-man . . . descended from noble ancestors," Viazemsky, "O Sumarokove," 224. On Pushkin and the nobility, see Gerald Eugene Mikkelson, "Pushkin and the History of the Russian Nobility," Ph.D. diss., University of Wiscon-sin, 1971.

30. Grits, Trenin, and Nikitin, *Slovesnost' i kommertsiia*, 94–101. Some of the need for such patronage had disappeared when printers ceased to demand full payment from authors before publishing their works, Marker, "Publishing and the Formation of a Reading Public," 461.

31. For a taxonomy of modes of patronage and an account of their survival in a market economy, see Williams, *The Sociology of Culture*, 38–44.

32. For a taxonomic description of these forms of familiar association, see the formalist study by M. I. Aronson and S. A. Reiser, eds., *Literaturnye kruzhki i salony* (Leningrad: Priboi, 1929). Here, and in N. L. Brodsky, ed., *Literaturnye salony i kruzhki: Pervaia polovina XIX veka* (Moscow-Leningrad: Academia, 1930), may be found a wealth of contemporary accounts.

33. On this equality, see Mickiewicz's notes on Russian literary life of the 1820s and 1830s, quoted in Aronson and Reiser, *Literaturnye kruzhki i salony*, 70; and Jean-Paul Sartre, *Qu'est-ce que la littérature?* (Paris: Gallimard, 1948), 111–113.

34. C. B. Tinker, *The Salon and English Letters: Chapters on the Interrelations of Literature and Society in the Age of Johnson* (New York: Macmillan, 1915), 170, notes that this game was highly popular in England, too, and that a four-volume collection of them was published in Bath in 1776. For a Russian example, see S. P. Zhikharev, *Zapiski sovremennika* (Moscow-Leningrad: ANSSSR, 1955), 33.

35. Viktor Shklovsky, discussing the eighteenth century, attempted a taxonomy of dedications that we may now expand: a pulp-fiction writer addressed "the reader," and a "serious" work addressed its patron; now the literature of familiar groups addressed immediate friends, a salon hostess, or fellow poets: *Matvei Komarov: Zhitel' goroda Moskvy* (Leningrad: Priboi, 1929), 31.

36. Unpublished preface to the 1805 section. L. N. Tolstoy, *Polnoe sobranie sochinenii*, 90 vols. (Moscow: Knudozhestvennaia literatura, 1928–1958), XIII, 55.

37. For examples of how some contemporaries perceived Gogol within this tradition, see D. V. Dashkov, letter no. 27 to P. A. Viazemsky, Tsentralnyi gosudarstvennyi arkhiv literatury i iskusstva, Ostaf'evskii arkhiv, 195/1/1820, sheet 50; A. O. Smirnova, *Zapiski i dnevniki, vospominaniia, pis'ma* (Moscow, Federatsiia, 1929), 316. For treatment of Gogol as an outsider or Ukrainian in polite society, see Aronson and Reiser, *Literaturnye kruzhki i salony*, 200; S. T. Aksakov, *Istoriia moego znakomstva s Gogolem* (Moscow: ANSSSR, 1960), 60.

38. Aronson and Reiser, *Literaturnye kruzhki i salony*, 300–301.

39. Brodsky, *Literaturnye salony i kruzhki*, 109–110. For further information on these student circles of the early nineteenth century, see Iu. M. Lotman, "Andrei Sergeevich Kaisarov i literaturno-obshchestvennaia bor'ba ego vremeni," *Uchenye zapiski Tartuskogo Gosudarstvennogo Universiteta*, 63 (1958), 18–76; and V. M. Istrin, "Druzheskoe literaturnoe obshchestvo," *Zhurnal ministerstva narodnogo prosveshcheniia*, 7 (1910), 80–144.

40. See Aronson and Reiser, *Literaturnye kruzhki i salony*, 35–38. It is, however, impossible to accept Aronson's thesis that the circles lacked traditions.

41. Lotman, "Andrei Sergeevich Kaisarov," 22, 40–42, 63–66. The opposition between philosophical seriousness and fashionable frivolity has, as W. Bruce Lincoln notes, correlations with distinctions between Moscow and Petersburg, *Nicholas I: Emperor and Autocrat of all the Russias* (Bloomington: Indiana University Press, 1978), 255–257.

42. Brown, *Stankevich and his Moscow Circle*, records the legends that grew up around Stankevich and seeks the "reality" that these legends transformed.

43. Aronson and Reiser, *Literaturnye kruzhki i salony*, 167.

44. A. I. Koshelev, "Moi vospominaniia ob A. S. Khomiakove," *Russkii arkhiv*, 11 (1879), 266.

45. A. I. Koshelev, *Zapiski, 1806–1883* (1884; rpt. Newtonville, Mass.: Oriental Research Partners, 1976), 30.

46. For a discussion of this passage in the novel, see Chap. 3 below. The lyrics in question are Pushkin's "Akafest Ekaterine Nikolaevne Karamzinoi" (1827) and Lermontov's "Iz al'boma S. N. Karamzinoi" (1841). On the obligatory worship of the hostess, see Tinker, *The Salon and English Letters*, 27.

47. The sour comment belongs to I. I. Panaev, *Literaturnye vospominaniia* (Leningrad: Academia, 1928), 44; the rest of the material appears in A. F. Tiutcheva, *Pri dvore dvukh imperatorov: Dnevnik, 1853–1855* (Moscow: M. and S. Sabashnikov, 1928), 68–74.

48. For accounts of education in early nineteenth-century Russia, see N. A. Hans, *History of Russian Educational Policy, 1701–1917* (New York: Russell and Russell, 1964); B. V. Tomashevsky, *Pushkin*, vol. I (Moscow-Leningrad: Nauka, 1956), 11–15; Marcelle Ehrhard, *V. A. Joukovski et le préromantisme russe* (Paris: Champion, 1938), 15–41; Istrin, "Druzheskoe literaturnoe obshchestvo," 80–144; and Cynthia H. Whittaker, *The Origins of Modern Russian Education: An Intellectual Biography of Count Sergei Uvarov, 1786–1885* (DeKalb: Northern Illinois University Press, 1984).

49. Tinker, *The Salon and English Letters*, 25.

50. Carolyn C. Lougee, *Le Paradis des Femmes: Women, Salons, and Social Stratification in Seventeenth-Century France* (Princeton: Princeton University Press, 1977), 52.

51. P. A. Viazemsky, "Neskol'ko slov o polemike," *Literaturnaia gazeta*, 18 (27 March 1830), 143–144.

52. Lougee, *Le Paradis des Femmes*, 212–213.

53. Quoted in Zhikharev, *Zapiski sovremennika*, 427.

54. A. P. Kern, "Vospominaniia o Pushkine," in *Vospominaniia, dnevniki, perepiska*, ed. A. M. Gordin (Moscow: Khudozhestvennaia literatura, 1974), 30. In connection with this salon Mme Kern quotes the salon description from the eighth chapter of *Eugene Onegin*. A less idyllic vision of Olenin emerges from the biography of Baron Del'vig, who was fired from his post by Olenin for having visited the exiled Pushkin.

55. Viazemsky's biographer reminds us that Viazemsky constantly denied having class prejudices during the 1820s and 1830s. M. I. Gillel'son, *P. A. Viazemsky: Zhizn' i tvorchestvo* (Leningrad: Nauka, 1969), 328.

56. On Stankevich's egalitarian tendencies, see Brown, *Stankevich and his Moscow Circle*, 6, 7, 9, 42, 47, 53, 87, 89.

57. V. E. Evgen'ev-Maksimov et al., eds., *Ocherki po istorii russkoi zhurnalistiki i kritiki*, vol. I (Leningrad: Izd. Leningradskogo universiteta, 1950), 256–257.

58. Aronson and Reiser, *Literaturnye kruzhki i salony*, 286–287.

59. Rufus W. Mathewson, Jr., *The Positive Hero in Russian Literature*, 2nd ed. (Stanford: Stanford University Press, 1975), 21–23.

60. Letter of Pushkin to Nashchokin, in A. S. Pushkin, *Polnoe sobranie sochinenii*, XVI, 121; letter of Nashchokin to Pushkin, ibid., XVI, 181.

61. P. A. Viazemsky, *Polnoe sobranie sochinenii*, 12 vols. (St. Petersburg:

S. D. Sheremetev, 1878–1896), I, 268. Viazemsky is addressing here Zhukovsky's essay on "The Writer in Society."

62. *Istoriia russkoi zhurnalistiki,* 155–156, 199, 211, 300.

63. Viazemsky, quoted in M. S. Borovkova-Maikova, ed., *"Arzamas" i "arzamasskie" protokoly* (Leningrad: Izd. pisatelei v Leningrade, 1933), 239–242.

64. Iu. M. Lotman, "P. A. Viazemsky i dvizhenie Dekabristov," *Uchenye zapiski Tartuskogo Gosudarstvennogo Universiteta,* 98 (1960), 42, 112–114.

65. For an account of this enterprise, see Aronson and Reiser, *Literaturnye kruzhki i salony,* 290.

66. Gillel'son, *P. A. Viazemsky,* 258.

67. M. I. Gillel'son and V. A. Manuilov, eds., *Lermontov v vospominaniiakh sovremennikov* (Moscow: Khudozhestvennaia literatura, 1972), 239.

68. Quoted in Lotman, "P. A. Viazemsky i dvizhenie Dekabristov," 50.

69. On Zhukovsky's role in interceding for writers at court, see Ehrhard, *V. A. Joukovski,* 118–121. Bludov did intercede with Nicholas I to advance Koshelev's career. Koshelev, *Zapiski,* 23–26.

70. On M. F. Orlov, see S. Ia. Borovoi, "M. F. Orlov i ego literaturnoe nasledie," in M. F. Orlov, *Kapituliatsiia Parizha, Politicheskie souchineniia, Pis'ma* (Moscow: ANSSSR, 1963), 269–313, and part 2 of Alexander Herzen's *Byloe i dumy (My Past and Thoughts).* On the government's attitude toward the Slavophiles, see N. V. Riasanovsky, *A Parting of Ways: Government and the Educated Public, 1802–1855* (Oxford: Oxford University Press, 1976), 252–253.

71. From Uvarov's report to Nicholas I of February 1847, quoted in James T. Flynn, "Tuition and Social Class," *Slavic Review,* 35 (June 1976), 245. See also Cynthia H. Whittaker, "The Ideology of Sergei Uvarov: An Interpretive Essay," *Russian Review,* 37 (April 1978), 170–171, for a view of how a salon figure adapted his notion of Enlightenment to the policies of Nicholas' regime.

72. A. Kh. Benckendorff to Pushkin, 23 December 1826, in Pushkin, *Polnoe sobranie sochinenii,* XIII, 315.

73. Mikhail K. Lemke, *Nikolaevskie zhandarmy i literatura 1826–1855gg. po podlinnym delam tret'ego otdeleniia sobst. E. I. Velichestva kantseliarii,* 2nd ed. (St. Petersburg: S. V. Bunin, 1909), 19–27; W. Bruce Lincoln, "The Ministers of Nicholas I," *Russian Review,* 34 (July 1975), 112–119. See also Sidney Monas, *The Third Section: Police and Society under Nicholas I* (Cambridge, Mass.: Harvard University Press, 1961), 92–99. Nevertheless, the appeal of circles was such that even Benckendorff had once belonged to a circle, a Masonic lodge to which Chaadaev, the Decembrist Pestel', and Griboedov also belonged. Lemke, *Nikolaevskie zhandarmy,* 24.

74. Quoted by W. Bruce Lincoln, "The Daily Life of St. Petersburg Officials in the Mid Nineteenth Century," *Oxford Slavonic Papers,* n.s. 8 (1975), 90. The writers included the lexicographer Dal' and, briefly, Ivan Turgenev.

75. M. N. Longinov, cited in Gillel'son and Manuilov, *Lermontov v vospominaniiakh sovremennikov,* 156–157.

76. P. A. Viazemsky, *Zapisnye knizhki, 1813–1848,* ed. V. S. Nechaeva (Moscow: ANSSSR, 1963), 298–299. For a longer selection from this passage

and more information on Viazemsky's career, see Riasanovsky, *A Parting of Ways*, 267–268. A standard economic history of the time passes over Viazemsky's service in merciful silence, as it does the service of two other writers who found themselves in that ministry, N. V. Kukol'nik and V. G. Benediktov; Walter M. Pintner, *Russian Economic Policy under Nicholas I* (Ithaca: Cornell University Press, 1967).

77. Quoted in Aronson and Reiser, *Literaturnye kruzhki i salony*, 177–178. Other memoirists, such as Grigorovich (quoted ibid., 283), blame the intellectuals for the split, and one does sense a chip on their shoulder. The point remains that the split occurred, that the writers became constituted as a marginal group (an intelligentsia), and that the salons (and with them, polite society) lost their harmonizing function.

78. Quoted in Aronson and Reiser, *Literaturnye kruzhki i salony*, 171.

79. Panaev, *Literaturnye vospominaniia*, 143–144.

80. R. V. Ivanov-Razumnik, introduction to Panaev, *Literaturnye vospominaniia*, xiii–xiv.

81. I. I. Panaev, "Spal'nia svetskoi zhenshchiny (epizod iz zhizni poeta v obshchestve)," *Pervoe polnoe sobranie sochinenii*, 6 vols. (St. Petersburg: N. G. Martynov, 1888–1889), I, 1–43.

82. M. I. Gillel'son, *Molodoi Pushkin i Arzamasskoe bratstvo* (Leningrad: Nauka, 1974), 207–208.

83. *"Arzamas" i "arzamasskie" protokoly*, 242.

84. *Ocherki po istorii russkoi zhurnalistiki i kritiki*, 230–232.

85. Ibid., 307.

86. Ibid., 270.

87. E. M. Blinova, *"Literaturnaia gazeta" A. A. Del'viga i A. S. Pushkina, 1830–1831: Ukazatel' soderzhaniia* (Moscow: Kniga, 1966); Fanger, *The Creation of Nikolai Gogol*, 39.

88. S. P. Shevyrev, "Vzgliad na sovremennoe napravlenie russkoi literatury," *Moskvitianin* (1842), No. 1, xxxii.

89. P. A. Viazemsky, *Ostaf'evskii arkhiv kniazei Viazemskikh*, ed. V. I. Saitov, 5 vols. (St. Petersburg: S. P. Sheremetev, 1899), III, 149. Letter of 26 January 1842 to A. I. Turgenev.

90. On these developments, see A. Meynieux, *La Littérature et le métier d'écrivain en Russie avant Pouchkine* (Paris: Librairie des cinq continents, 1966); Grits, Trenin, and Nikitin, *Slovesnost' i kommertsiia;* and K. A. Papmehl, *Freedom of Expression in Eighteenth Century Russia* (The Hague: M. Nijhoff, 1971).

91. Grits, Trenin, and Nikitin, *Slovesnost' i kommertsiia*, 175.

92. Ibid., 80, 86; Kufaev, *Istoriia russkoi knigi*, 32; recent research by G. J. Marker challenges the common notion of Novikov's mass appeal, however; by analyzing the surviving subscription lists for Novikov's books and journals, Marker has determined that the greatest part (77 percent) of Novikov's readers belonged to the gentry; "Novikov's Readers," *Modern Language Review*, 77 (October 1982), 900. For statistics on the gentry's overwhelming presence on other subscription lists of the eighteenth century, see Marker, "Publishing and the Formation of a Reading Public," 393.

93. G. P. Makogonenko, *Nikolai Novikov i russkoe prosveshchenie XVIII veka* (Moscow: Gos. izd. khudozhestvennoi literatury, 1951), 507. See also L. B. Svetlov, *Izdatel'skaia deiatel'nost' N. I. Novikova* (Moscow: Gizlegprom, 1946).

94. Gukovsky, *Russkaia literatura XVIII veka*, 297–303.

95. Grits, Trenin, and Nikitin, *Slovesnost' i kommertsiia*, 83.

96. On the journalistic confrontation between Catherine and Novikov, see Makogonenko, *Nikolai Novikov i russkoe prosveshchenie*, chaps. 4–6.

97. Riasanovsky, *A Parting of Ways*, 22–23. Marker's statistics eloquently support these points on the absence of a "third estate" from the literary process, "Publishing and the Formation of a Reading Public," 397.

98. *Severnaia pchela*, 1833. Quoted in Grits, Trenin, and Nikitin, *Slovesnost' i kommertsiia*, 278.

99. Lemke, *Nikolaevskie zhandarmy i literatura*, 246–252, 260–261, 286.

100. On these problems, see ibid.; A. V. Nikitenko, *Dnevnik*, 3 vols. (Moscow: Goslitizdat, 1955–1956); Monas, *The Third Section;* Charles A. Rudd, *Fighting Words: Imperial Censorship and the Russian Press, 1804–1906* (Toronto: University of Toronto Press, 1982), chaps. 4–6.

101. Donald Fanger, "Gogol and his Reader," in William Mills Todd III, ed., *Literature and Society in Imperial Russia, 1800–1914* (Stanford: Stanford University Press, 1978), 74–75. See also Mariana Tax Choldin, "A Fence around the Empire: The Censorship of Foreign Books in Nineteenth-Century Russia," Ph.D. diss., University of Chicago, 1979; she reports that a number of writers served in the Foreign Censorship Committee, 35–37, but that their influence became noticeable only in the late 1850s, 56.

102. Nikitenko, *Dnevnik*, I, 89. It tells something about the morality of literary life at the time, that Bulgarin excused himself by saying that he had not actually read the novel. Lemke, *Nikolaevskie zhandarmy*, 269.

103. Monas, *The Third Section*, 196.

104. The edition of N. Polevoi's *Moscow Telegraph* that I consulted in Pushkinsky Dom once belonged to M. N. Longinov, a nineteenth-century Russian literary scholar. His marginal note to Part 55 (1834), in which an unfavorable review of a patriotic drama resulted in the banning of the journal, merits quotation: "Only a crude, shameless cavil of the censorship terror could have made a bill of indictment from this review, ruining the future and poisoning the days of an honest man."

105. Jeffrey Brooks, "Readers and Reading at the End of the Tsarist Era," in Todd, *Literature and Society in Imperial Russia*, 120–123; Shklovsky reports that the industry was still going strong in 1917, *Matvei Komarov*, 16.

106. V. V. Vinogradov, comp., *Slovar' iazyka Pushkina* (Moscow: Gos. izd. slovarei, 1956–1961).

107. K. N. Batiushkov, *Sochineniia*, 3 vols., ed. L. N. Maikov and V. I. Saitov (St. Petersburg: Kotomin, 1885–1887), II, 24. The producers of this material, like modern Soviet writers, were, in fact, paid by the signature.

108. On the historically variable importance of an author's name, see Michel Foucault, "What Is an Author?" in Harari, *Textual Strategies*, 145–148; Belinsky, *Sobranie sochinenii v deviati tomakh*, I, 229. For a scholarly analysis

of contemporary provincial reading which confirms the typicality of Tatiana's list, see A. V. Blium, "Massovoe chtenie v russkoi provintsii kontsa XVIII-pervoi chetverti XIXv.," *Trudy leningradskogo gos. instituta kul'tury N.K. Krupskoi,* vol. 25, *Istoriia russkogo chitatelia,* part I (Leningrad, 1973), 37–57.

109. *Eugene Onegin,* trans. Vladimir Nabokov, 4 vols., rev. ed. (Princeton: Princeton University Press, 1975), II, 514. On the shady practices of the popular press, see Shklovsky, *Matvei Komarov,* 44.

110. *Literaturnye listki,* 4 (3 March 1824), 148–149.

111. "Zhurnalnye zametki, *Severnaia pchela,*" (1834), 43.

112. On the history of the almanacs, see John Mersereau, Jr., *Baron Delvig's "Northern Flowers," 1825–1832; Literary Almanach of the Pushkin Pleiad* (Carbondale: Southern Illinois University Press, 1967), 7–25; Grits, Trenin, and Nikitin, *Slovesnost' i kommertsiia,* 188–208; V. E. Vatsuro, *"Severnye tsvety": Istoriia al'manakha Del'viga-Pushkina* (Moscow: Kniga, 1978).

113. See Ju. Ovsiannikov, *Lubok: Russkie narodnye kartinki XVII–XVIIIvv* (Moscow: Sovetsky khudozhnik, 1968), for examples of the former; *Poliarnaia zvezda, izdannaia A. Bestuzhevym i K. Ryleevym,* ed. V. A. Arkhipov et al. (Moscow-Leningrad: ANSSSR, 1960), for reproductions of the latter.

114. *Aonidy,* 2 (Moscow, 1797), ix–x.

115. Mersereau, *Baron Delvig's "Northern Flowers,"* 9–15.

116. "Ob al'manakhe 'Severnaia lira' " (1827). The almanac under review was edited by S. E. Raich, whose scruples prevented him from selling his own verse, but permitted him to publish almanacs, S. Gessen, *Knigoizdatel' A. S. Pushkin* (Leningrad: Academia, 1930), 127–130.

117. A. S. Pushkin, "O proze" (1822), *Polnoe sobranie sochinenii,* XI, 18–19. Joan Nabseth Stevenson convincingly argues, however, that Gogol was able to use organizational aspects of the almanac, particularly its fragmentariness, in assembling his collection *Arabeski,* "Literary and Cultural Patterns in Gogol's *Arabeski,*" Ph.D. diss., Stanford University, 1984, chap. 2.

118. Gessen, *Knigoizdatel' A. S. Pushkin,* 82; P. A. Chireisky, *Pushkin i ego okruzhenie* (Leningrad: Nauka, 1975), 36.

119. Grits, Trenin, and Nikitin, *Slovesnost' i kommertsiia,* 119; Gessen, *Knigoizdatel' A. S. Pushkin,* 19, estimates that the average government office worker earned 60–80 rubles per month; one of low rank, such as Gogol's Akaky Akakievich, had to support himself on 33 rubles. See also W. Bruce Lincoln, *In the Vanguard of Reform: Russia's Enlightened Bureaucrats, 1825–1861* (DeKalb: Northern Illinois University Press, 1982), 20–21.

120. Gnedich kept 13,000 rubles and turned a mere 2,000 over to Batiushkov; Gessen, *Knigoizdatel' A. S. Pushkin,* 32. Gnedich did similarly well with Pushkin's "Prisoner of the Caucasus": he made 5,000 rubles; the poet, 500 rubles and a free copy, ibid., 40. Each poet, of course, graciously thanked Gnedich for his efforts in polite epistolary form.

121. On publishing expenses, see Kufaev, *Istoriia russkoi knigi,* 135; and Gessen, *Knigoizdatel' A. S. Pushkin,* 21–22.

122. For an account of the British publishing industry during this period, see J. A. Sutherland, *Victorian Novelists and Publishers* (Chicago: University of Chicago Press, 1976), chaps. 1–3.

123. (1832) Quoted in Grits, Trenin, and Nikitin, *Slovesnost' i kommertsiia*, 171.

124. (1830) Quoted in ibid., 171.

125. Ibid., 343–346. On the vicious quarrels among Sękowski, Bulgarin, Grech, and N. Polevoi, see V. A. Kaverin, *Baron Brambeus: Istoriia Osipa Senkovskogo, zhurnalista, redaktora "Biblioteki dlia chteniia"* (Moscow: Nauka, 1966), 81–120.

126. Kufaev, *Istoriia russkoi knigi*, 140.

127. Grits, Trenin, and Nikitin, *Slovesnost' i kommertsiia*, 28, 224, 239.

128. Pushkin, for example, occasionally mentioned pulp literature in his writing—to compromise his opponents or to characterize fictional characters of low cultural attainments, but his 4,000-volume library contained virtually none of it. B. L. Modzalevsky, *Biblioteka A. S. Pushkina: Bibliograficheskoe opisanie* (St. Petersburg: Akademiia nauk, 1910), lists but one epistolary manual (1829), one of Orlov's Vyzhigin imitations, two old songbooks, and a collection of *skazki* (folktales). Some of Pushkin's own works were snapped up by the chapbook publishers—lyrics, narrative poems—but he ignored it, as he did not ignore it when his copyright was infringed upon by a publisher for the more exclusive public. Kufaev, *Istoriia russkoi knigi*, 144.

129. Statistical research, as I shall discuss in connection with the reading public below, is difficult to conduct for this period. Nahirny's survey of various biographical dictionaries finds that 71.3 percent of the 92 writers born between 1750 and 1799 belonged to the nobility; of the 120 writers born between 1800 and 1825—70.9 percent; *The Russian Intelligentsia*, 27–28.

130. A number have been written: Gillel'son, *P. A. Viazemsky*, 167–169, 186–201; M. P. Eremin, *Pushkin-publicist*, 2nd ed. (Moscow: Khudozhestvennaia literatura, 1976), chap. 3; *Ocherki po istorii russkoi zhurnalistiki i kritiki*, vol. 1, part III; V. V. Gippius, "Pushkin v bor'be a Bulgarinym v 1830–31gg," *Vremennik pushkinskoi kommissii*, 6 (1941), 235–255; Fanger, *The Creation of Nikolai Gogol*, 30–44; V. E. Vatsuro and M. I. Gillel'son, "Podvig chestnogo cheloveka," in their *Skvoz' "umstvennye plotiny": Iz istorii knigi i pressy pushkinskoi pory* (Moscow: Kniga, 1972), 32–113; Hans Rothe, "Karamzin and his Heritage: History of a Legend," in J. L. Black, *Essays on Karamzin: Russian Man-of-Letters, Political Thinker, Historian, 1766–1826* (The Hague: Mouton, 1975), 148–190; Abbott Gleason, *European and Muscovite: Ivan Kireevsky and the Origins of Slavophilism* (Cambridge, Mass." Harvard University Press: 1972), 45–74.

131. Pushkin, XI, 120; Belinsky, quoted in *Poliarnaia zvezda, izdannaia A. Bestuzhevym i K. Ryleevym*, 821. Ivan Kireevsky presented this in more dialectical fashion: "he was brought up for his audience, and his audience for him," quoted in Rothe, "Karamzin and his Heritage," 158.

132. Gogol, *Polnoe sobranie sochinenii*, XIII, 61, 266–267.

133. Shevyrev, 1842, quoted in Rothe, "Karamzin and his Heritage," 161.

134. "Otryvki iz pisem, mysli i zamechaniia," XI, 57. This was first published in the almanac *Severnye tsvety* in 1828. I have translated *chestnogo cheloveka* with the French term *honnête homme* because Pushkin's phrase echoes one from a review of Karamzin's history in *Le Moniteur universel* ("l'honnête

homme avant le savant"), quoted in Vatsuro and Gillel'son, "Podvig chest-nogo cheloveka," 95–96. This fine essay explores political aspects of the struggle for Karamzin's relics, but it neglects the institutional concerns that Pushkin's fragments so thoroughly address.

135. *Severnaia pchela*, 64 (29 May 1826). Quoted by Vatsuro and Gillel'son, "Podvig chestnogo cheloveka," 83–84.

136. Mikkelson, "Pushkin and the History of the Russian Nobility," 117 and passim.

137. Lemke, *Nikolaevskie zhandarmy*, 239–240. Bulgarin's denunciation of his chief competitors to the Third Section would invariably seek to link them with polite society, which he saw as a spawning ground for "unpatriotic" activities, such as the Decembrist movement.

138. Review of Bulgarin's *Dmitrii Samozvanets*, quoted in Eremin, *Pushkin-publicist*, 149.

139. Originally published in the almanac *Al'bom severnykh muz na 1828*, this brief memoir was reprinted in subsequent editions of Bulgarin's collected works.

140. Pushkin, letter to Del'vig, 31 July 1827, XIII, 334–335. Dmitriev is quoted in Vatsuro and Gillel'son, "Podvig chestnogo cheloveka," 86–87. Dmitriev's own mastery of the polite style had been hailed by Karamzin.

141. See, on this point, the skirmish between Raich and Viazemsky (1830), Gillel'son, *P. A. Viazemsky*, 195. Here "aristocratism" suggests a literary situation governed by the self-chosen few. Karamzin himself had criticized this sort of aristocracy, promising his readers, "we are not aristocrats in literature; we value works, not names." Karamzin, *Izbrannye sochineniia v dvukh tomakh*, ed. P. Berkov (Moscow-Leningrad: Khudozhestvennaia literatura, 1964), II, 228.

142. See Fanger, *The Creation of Nikolai Gogol*, 31. On the Russian pica-resque and "moral-satirical" novels, see Jurij Striedter, *Der Schelmenroman in Russland: Ein Beitrag zur Geschichte des russischen Romans vor Gogol'* (Berlin: Otto Harrassowitz, 1961); V. F. Pereverzev, *U istokov russkogo realisticheskogo romana* (Moscow: Khudozhestvennaia literatura, 1965), 7–113. Excerpts from Bulga-rin's novel are available in Christine Rydel, ed., *The Ardis Anthology of Russian Romanticism* (Ann Arbor: Ardis, 1984), 242–251.

143. *Ocherki po istorii russkoi zhurnalistiki i kritiki*, 310–311.

144. A subscription to *Severnaia pchela* cost the considerable sum of 50 rubles a year; Gessen, *Knigoizdatel' A. S. Pushkin*, 19.

145. Indicative of Bulgarin's successful synthesis is the presence of the tsar's name on the subscription list for *Petr Vyzhigin* and the diamond ring that he was awarded; Lemke, *Nikolaevskie zhandarmy*, 274–275. At the same time he did not neglect to thank the public for supporting him. In this com-bination, patron and reading public, Bulgarin had momentarily brought to-gether the writer-reader relationships that had once been characteristic of the patronage system and the chapbook trade, respectively.

In a private communication Donald Fanger has called my attention to a similar spirit of synthesis hovering over A. A. Bestuzhev, *Poezdka v Revel'* (St.

Petersburg: Pliushar, 1821). On the title page of this commercial venture Bestuzhev is not only careful to indicate his membership in two familiar associations, but also to note that the associations had been "imperially approved." "The lambs are safe and the wolves satisfied," as the Russian proverb has it.

146. Belinsky, *Sobranie sochinenii v devjati tomakh,* I, 264.

147. Comparisons are difficult because of incomplete statistics. The first printing of *Ivan Vyzhigin* sold out in seven days; 7,000 copies were sold in two years according to Grech; Grits, Trenin, and Nikitin, *Slovesnost' i kommertsiia,* 227. According to Gessen, Pushkin earned 25,000 rubles for the separate chapters of *Eugene Onegin* and 12,000 rubles for the first complete edition; *Knigoizdatel' A. S. Pushkin,* 100. Kufaev reports that the second (1837) edition was published in 5,000 copies, which sold out very quickly and earned Pushkin 3,000 rubles; *Istoriia russkoi knigi,* 135. These triumphs pale, however, by comparison with the successes that the English novel was beginning to enjoy as an institutionalized literary enterprise, supported by lending libraries, publishing firms, and stable market relationships. On this see Sutherland, *Victorian Novelists and Publishers.*

148. Karamzin, *Izbrannye sochineniia,* II, 228–229. Karamzin was, however anxious to discuss earlier Russian literature, as part of his efforts to make Russian readers aware of their past.

149. On this point Pushkin was forced to acknowledge an element of "aristocratic" pride (XI, 166). "The writers known among us under the title of 'aristocrats,' have introduced a custom that is harmful to literature," he confessed, "not to reply to criticism." Typically, Pushkin proposed to replace this socioliterary convention with one transferred from the social life of another European culture: "Look at an English lord: he is ready to respond to the polite challenge of a gentleman and shoot it out with Kuchenreiter pistols or to take off his frockcoat and box with a cabman in the street" (XI, 91).

150. Grits, Trenin, and Nikitin, *Slovesnost' i kommertsiia,* 179, mention the former problem, not the latter.

151. "O dvizhenii zhurnalnoi literatury v 1834 i 1835 g.," VIII, 175.

152. Grits, Trenin, and Nikitin, *Slovesnost' i kommertsiia,* chaps. 7–10; N. P. Smirnov-Sokol'sky, *Knizhnaia lavka A. F. Smirdina* (Moscow: Izd.-vo Vses. knizhnoi palaty, 1957).

153. Belinsky, "Literaturnye mechtaniia," *Sobranie sochinenii v deviati tomakh,* I, 121.

154. Gessen, *Knigoizdatel' A. S. Pushkin,* 111; Grits, Trenin, and Nikitin, *Slovesnost' i kommertsiia,* 247–250.

155. E. E. Naidich, " 'Geroi nashego vremeni' v russkoi kritike," in M. Iu. Lermontov, *Geroi nashego vremeni,* ed. B. M. Eikhenbaum and E. E. Naidich (Moscow: ANSSSR, 1962), 168–169. Another version has the bribe delivered by Lermontov's doting grandmother; ibid.

156. Belinsky, "Neskol'ko slov o 'Sovremennike,' " *Sobranie sochinenii v deviati tomakh,* I, 489.

157. *Severnaia pchela,* 300 (1833), 1186; S. P. Shevyrev, "Slovesnost' i tor-

govlia," *Moskovskii nabliudatel'*, 1, pt. 1 (1835), 24; Gogol and Belinsky also noted that Smirdin played no intellectual role in the *Biblioteka dlia chteniia.*

158. Kufaev, *Istoriia russkoi knigi*, 131. As an emblem of Pushkin's distance from Smirdin, see his scornful remark on Smirdin's language, quoted in Chap. 1 above. On the close association between printers and writers in the developing European republic of letters, see Elizabeth L. Eisenstein, *The Printing Press as an Agent of Change: Communications and Cultural Transformations in Early-Modern Europe* (Cambridge: Cambridge University Press, 1979), 139–140, 154–155.

159. Grits, Trenin, and Nikitin, *Slovesnost' i kommertsiia*, 241, exaggerate the "mass" nature of the public that Smirdin's editions could have reached.

160. Ibid., 238.

161. Kufaev, *Istoriia russkoi knigi*, 130; *Ocherki po istorii russkoi zhurnalistiki i kritiki*, 326.

162. Belinsky reports that Batiushkov's works cost 15 rubles; *Sobranie sochinenii v deviati tomakh*, I, 381. By the end of the century, a volume could cost as little as 30 kopecks. On the later nineteenth-century book trade, see Jeffrey Brooks, "Readers and Reading at the End of the Tsarist Era," in Todd, *Literature and Society in Imperial Russia*, 97–150. Smirdin did publish distinguished works of Russian literature at reduced rates, it is true, but this was only in the late 1840s, beyond the scope of this study.

163. On these shady practices, see Fanger, "Gogol and his Reader," 83; Belinsky, *Sobranie sochinenii v deviati tomakh*, I, 227.

164. Belinsky, *Sobranie sochinenii v deviati tomakh*, I, 263. Belinsky's point is supported by Shashkov, "Literaturnyi trud," 26–28.

165. Gogol, VIII, 157; Belinsky, *Sobranie sochinenii v deviati tomakh*, I, 226, 263; Pushkin, XII, 96.

166. Gogol, VIII, 165; Belinsky, *Sobranie sochinenii v deviati tomakh*, I, 227; letter of Pushkin to M. P. Pogodin, 11 July 1832, in Pushkin, *Polnoe sobranie sochinenii*, XV, 27.

167. Grits, Trenin, and Nikitin, *Slovesnost' i kommertsiia*, 300. Such syncretism helps distinguish this journal from the "thick journals" *(tolstye zhurnaly)* of the 1840s–1880s, journals which were marked by a stronger ideological identity, by the predominance of prose over verse, and by vigorous literary criticism. Robert Maguire offers this useful distinction between the types of journals in his *Red Virgin Soil: Soviet Literature of the 1920's* (Princeton: Princeton University Press, 1968), 44.

168. Gogol (VIII, 166–167), for one, immediately noted the Moscow journal's critical intentionality.

169. Shevyrev, "Slovesnost' i torgovlia," 3, 18–19, 25–27.

170. Belinsky, *Sobranie sochinenii v deviati tomakh*, I, 263–264.

171. *Ocherki po istorii russkoi zhurnalistiki i kritiki*, 381.

172. Belinsky, *Sobranie sochinenii v deviati tomakh*, I, 162.

173. Ibid., I, 241. It must be noted, however, that some of Sękowski's alterations merely reflected sound editorial policy (theretofore unknown in Russia, except in the coauthorship patterns of the familiar groups) and that

he had his contemporary defenders as well as critics. For balanced modern views, see Louis Pedrotti, *Józef-Julian Sękowski: The Genesis of a Literary Alien* (Berkeley: University of California Press, 1965); and Kaverin, *Baron Brambeus.*

174. Belinsky, *Sobranie sochinenii v deviati tomakh,* I, 245–246.

175. *Ocherki po istorii russkoi zhurnalistiki i kritiki,* 332.

176. *Biblioteka dlia chteniia,* vol. I, 1934, "Kritika," 36–36.

177. Compare, for example, Belinsky's point that criticism should put theory to practice, *Sobranie sochinenii v deviati tomakh,* I, 259.

178. *Biblioteka dlia chteniia,* vol. I, 1934, "Kritika," 1.

179. Kaverin, *Baron Brambeus,* 141.

180. See Fanger, *The Creation of Nikolai Gogol,* 76, for a similar suggestion which refers, in turn, to V. V. Gippius, "Tvorcheskii put' Gogolia," in his *Ot Pushkina do Bloka* (Moscow-Leningrad: Nauka, 1966), 113.

181. I. M. Bogdanov, *Grammotnost'i obrazovanie v dorevoliutsionnoi Rossii i v SSSR* (Moscow, 1964), 20. Maguire estimates this well over 90 percent of the population was illiterate at this time, *Red Virgin Soil,* 36.

182. Quoted in A. G. Rashin, "Gramotnost' i narodnoe obrazovanie v Rossii v XIX i nachale XIXv," *Istoricheskie zapiski,* 37 (1951), 50–52.

183. B. B. Veselovsky, *Istoriia zemstva za 40 let,* vol. I (St. Petersburg: O. N. Popovoi, 1909), 448–449. Quoted in Rashin, "Gramotnost' i narodnoe obrazovanie," 55.

184. Rashin, "Gramotnost' i narodnoe obrazovanie," 53. This figure excludes the university in Finland. By 1848 university enrollment would reach 4,566 and would serve as a "seedbed of opposition to the government." Patrick L. Alston, *Educaton and the State in Tsarist Russia* (Stanford: Stanford University Press, 1969), 36–37. For further information on the expansion of the educated public during the 1840s and 1850s, see V. P. Leikina-Svirskaia, "Formirovanie raznochinskoi intelligentsii v Rossii v 40-kh godakh XIX v.," *Istoriia SSSR,* 1 (January-February 1958), 83–104.

185. Rashin, "Gramotnost' i narodnoe obrazovanie," 72.

186. Walter J. Ong, S.J., "The Writer's Audience Is Always a Fiction," *PMLA,* 90, (January 1975), 9–21.

187. For an analysis of such "metapoetical" poems, see Victor Erlich, *The Double Image: Concepts of the Poet in Slavic Literatures* (Baltimore: Johns Hopkins University Press, 1964), 16–37.

188. Fanger, *The Creation of Nikolai Gogol,* 71. Fanger also mentions Kireevsky's description of the Russian public as a half-educated crowd, more interested in relevance than beauty. Pushkin, as we shall see in the next chapter, looked for a reader who could allow a work of art several functions.

189. N. Nadezhdin, "Zdravyi smysl i Baron Brambeus," *Teleskop,* 21 (1834), 329–330.

190. Belinsky, "Nechto o nichem," *Sobranie sochinenii v deviati tomakh,* I, 228.

191. Ibid., I, 229. for a similar experiment in critical judgment, see I. A. Richards, *Practical Criticism: A Study of Literary Judgment* (1929; rpt: New York: Harcourt, Brace & World, 1956). Richards' comments on the Cambridge un-

dergraduates are scarcely more charitable than Belinsky's on the fashionable readers of Moscow and St. Petersburg.

192. Belinsky, "Russkaia literatura v 1840 godu," *Sobranie sochinenii v deviati tomakh*, III, 195–98.

193. Bulgarin's denunciations—astute, pioneering works of literary sociology—characterized the readership of Belinsky's journal, *Otechestvennye zapiski*, as the "bankrupt and perverted gentry, senseless youths, and the huge class (increasing daily) of those who have nothing to lose . . . cantonists, seminarists, the children of poor clerks and so forth," Lemke, *Nikolaevskie zhandarmy*, 303. Kufaev reports that the provincial booksellers would fill out their orders according to Belinsky's reviews, *Istoriia russkoi knigi*, 122. On this new intelligentsia, see Abbott Gleason, *Young Russia: The Genesis of Russian Radicalism in the 1860's* (New York: Viking, 1980); Nahirny, *The Russian Intelligentsia*, chaps. 5–6.

194. Roland Barthes, *S/Z: An Essay*, trans. Richard Miller (New York: Hill and Wang, 1974), 4.

195. The genre of a letter to the editor of one's own journal was a relatively common one in early nineteenth-century Russian journalism. It created different voices (or the illusion of them) within the journal, and it served as a device for presenting the journal's program without seeming to preach to the readers.

196. N. L. Stepanov, in *Ocherki po istorii russkoi zhurnalistiki i kritiki*, 408.

3. Eugene Onegin

1. V. G. Belinsky, *Sobranie sochinenii v deviati tomakh* (Moscow: Khudozhestvennaia literatura, 1976–1982), VI, 425.

2. The dedicatory piece replaces a poem which prefaced the first edition of chap. 1, "Razgovor knigoprodavtsa s poetom" ("Conversation of a bookseller with a poet," 1824). This poem also celebrated a synthesizing process: the bookseller persuades the poet that commerce and inspiration are not incompatible.

3. In developing an approach to Pushkin's use of conventions I have found many useful insights in E. H. Gombrich, *Art and Illusion: A Study in the Psychology of Pictorial Representation* (Princeton: Princeton University Press, 1960); D. K. Lewis, *Convention: A Philosophical Study* (Cambridge, Mass.: Harvard University Press, 1969); L. Ia. Ginzburg, *O psikhologicheskoi proze* (Leningrad: Sovetskii pisatel', 1971); and Elizabeth Burns, *Theatricality: A Study of Convention in the Theater and in Social Life* (New York: Harper & Row, 1972). Two recent issues of *New Literary History*, 13 (Autumn 1981) and 14 (Winter 1983), have offered valuable elaboration upon these theories, but no major departures from them.

4. Leon Stilman, "Problemy literaturnykh zhanrov i traditsii v 'Evgenii Onegine' Pushkina," *American Contributions to the Fourth International Congress of Slavists: Moscow, September, 1958* (The Hague: Mouton, 1958), p. 329. This chapter will depart from Stilman's seminal essay primarily by viewing the

"creative process" in more insistently institutional and ideological terms.

5. Gombrich, *Art and Illusion*, 236. As far as literary texts are concerned, Wolfgang Iser has argued that, because literary reception involves processes of ideation, not visual perception, it is possible for the readers of a literary text to "watch" themselves having an illusion; *The Act of Reading: A Theory of Aesthetic Response* (Baltimore: Johns Hopkins University Press, 1978), 189.

6. Of these, the most forthright remains D. D. Blagoi, *Sotsiologiia tvorchestva Pushkina: Etiudy*, 2nd ed. (Moscow: Mir, 1931), chap. 4. Blagoi uses drafts when the final version will not substantiate his contentions and uses the Pushkin of the 1830s when the one who wrote *Eugene Onegin* lacks sufficient historical and class consciousness, as he admits. Blagoi does, however, avoid what he calls sociological "Calvinism" (39) in discovering cases in which Pushkin's consciousness and social being ran in opposite directions (42, 121, 155).

G. A. Gukovsky's reading of the novel, *Pushkin i problemy realisticheskogo stilia* (Moscow: GIKhL, 1957), chap. 3, excludes the author-narrator from the plot (167) although Gukovsky finds him the most attractive character in the novel (241). Gukovsky makes Pushkin a precursor of Chernyshevsky (172) in societal determinism. Reading the novel as a bitter commentary on "society's" perversion of Russian culture and crippling of Eugene, Gukovsky combs *Eugene Onegin* for evidence of Pushkin's national consciousness and use of national culture as a positive social norm.

7. Among essays which deal with the entire novel and do not limit themselves to specific formal problems (such as meter or style), the purest formalist reading belongs to Viktor Shklovsky, " 'Evgenii Onegin' (Pushkin i Stern)," *Ocherki po poetike Pushkina* (Berlin: Epokha, 1923), 199–220. It treats the plot of Pushkin's novel as a mere pretext for the deconstruction, à la Sterne, of novelistic conventions. Providing a useful illustration of Gombrich's point that we cannot simultaneously perceive illusionist art as representation and organized form, D. D. Blagoi followed his sociological reading with an equally unadulterated architectonic one, *Masterstvo Pushkina* (Moscow: Sovetskii pisatel', 1955), 178–198. Important points about genre, prose, and verse appear in a manuscript (1921–22) by Iu. N. Tynianov that has only recently been publised, "O kompozitsii 'Evgeniia Onegina,' " *Poetika: Istoriia literatury: Kino* (Moscow: Nauka, 1977), 52–77.

8. Iu. M. Lotman has faced the problem of the novel's complexity by calling attention to its narrator's many points of view and standards for evaluating the characters, the multiplicity of which will allow many readings of the novel; *Eugene Onegin* takes on its illusory "lack of structure" by creating a wealth of structural relationships: *Uchenye zapiski Tartuskogo gosudarstvennogo universiteta, 184, Trudy po russkoi i slavianskoi filologii*, 9 (1966), 5–32. Hugh McLean finds the novel's complexity in its modulation of ironic and lyrical tones, "The Tone(s) of Evgenii Onegin," *California Slavic Studies*, 6 (1971), 3–15. John Fennell concentrates on the novel's contrast of "poetic" and "prosaic" styles, "Evgeny Onegin," in *Nineteenth-century Russian Literature*, ed. J. L. I. Fennell (Berkeley: University of California Press, 1973), 36–55. In dif-

ferent ways all three call attention to structural features of the text which a social reading would be unwise to ignore.

9. This does not exclude the importance to the novel's structure of other cultural patterns, such as the dance. On this, see William Mills Todd III, " 'The Russian Terpsichore's Soul-Filled Flight': Dance Themes in *Eugene Onegin"* (forthcoming).

10. Georg Lukács, "Pushkin's Place in World Literature," *Writer and Critic and Other Essays* (New York: Universal Library, 1971), 233.

11. For example, Stilman, "Problemy literaturnykh zhanrov," 357, and Stanley Mitchell, "Tatiana's Reading," *Forum for Modern Language Studies,* 4 (January 1968), 20.

12. That Pushkin's characters relate their thoughts and actions to their reading has been discussed by a number of scholars and, of course, by the narrator of *Eugene Onegin* himself (3:10). What to make of this remains a critical problem, however, as can be seen from the differing emphasis put on it by Mitchell, "Tatiana's Reading"; Stilman, "Problemy literaturnykh zhanrov"; George Gibian, "Love by the Book: Pushkin, Stendhal, Flaubert," *Comparative Literature,* 3 (Spring 1956), 97–109; and V. V. Sipovsky, *Pushkin: zhizn' i tvorchestvo* (St. Petersburg: Trud, 1907), 555–618. Two more recent studies have called important attention to the role of literary references in structuring the reader's understanding of the novel: Riccardo Picchio accounts for the function of the novel's epigraphs, "Dante and J. Malfilâtre as Literary Sources of Tat'jana's Erotic Dream (Notes on the Third Chapter of Pushkin's *Evgenij Onegin),"* in *Alexander Pushkin: A Symposium on the 175th Anniversary of his Birth,* ed. Andrej Kodjak and Kiril Taranovsky (New York: New York University Press, 1976), 42–55. Iu. M. Lotman finds that literary references arouse expectations in the reader that are systematically frustrated by Pushkin, *Roman v stikhakh Pushkina "Evgenii Onegin"* (Tartu: Izd. T. G. U., 1975), 79.

My own procedure is to take the author-narrator seriously when he mentions what his characters are reading, as if he were putting quotation marks around his characters' thoughts and actions. In the process of rewriting the novel, Pushkin tended to cut down the length of his characters' reading lists and to focus the reader's attention on the entries that remained.

13. In the original Russian, the "you" here is more specific, namely *chitatel'* ("reader"). Pushkin may be having some fun, however, at the expense of his friend Viazemsky, who uses the frosts/roses association in his well-known poem "First Snow" ("Pervyi sneg," 1819), but Pushkin would himself turn to the rhyme in his greatest narrative poem, "The Bronze Horseman" ("Mednyi vsadnik," 1833) in order to conjure up the delight of a winter day. Iu. M. Lotman argues that Pushkin's rhyme is not so banal after all, because it encompasses the last syllable of the word preceding "roses"—*morozy/ -my rozy; Roman A. S. Pushkina "Evgenii Onegin": Kommentarii* (Leningrad: Prosveshchenie, 1980), 251.

14. See, for example, Baratynsky's comments, quoted in McLean, "The Tone(s) of *Evgenij Onegin,"* 3.

15. I am surprised that Pushkin's sociological commentators have not

glossed the nurse's account of her marriage (at age thirteen to an even younger boy) with a passage ("Edrovo") from Radishchev's *Journey from Petersburg to Moscow* in which a young peasant girl refuses to marry a ten-year-old boy because his father sleeps with his young daughters-in-law until his sons grow up. Pushkin's vague hint at this less than charming custom (*snokhachestvo*) of the folk suggests that he is hardly the unalloyed venerator of the national, folk culture that his more chauvinistic critics have made him. This passage, by the way, is excised from the standard school edition (Moscow: Detskaia literatura, 1966) of Radishchev's famous tract.

16. Cf. "Mistress into Maid" ("Baryshnia-Krest'ianka," 1830). Here the heroine with excellent connections and the wealthy hero are doomed to marry each other for economic reasons; however, her games and disguises and his Byronic posing make the marriage ultimately desirable in personal terms as well.

17. This was a common polemical gambit against cultural nationalism at the time. Essayists of the early 1800s used similar reminders of the foreign element (Greek, Mongolian) in medieval and folk culture to undermine the position of the linguistic purists, led by Admiral Shishkov, whom Pushkin laughingly evokes in *Eugene Onegin* (8:14). For examples, see N. I. Mordovchenko, *Russkaia kritika pervoi chetverti XIX veka* (Moscow: Nauka, 1959), 77–97.

18. Gukovsky, *Pushkin i problemy*, 215, holds that the dream is mostly folkloric; A. L. Slonimsky, *Masterstvo Pushkina*, 2nd ed. (Moscow: GIKhL, 1963), 356, and Lotman, *Roman A. S. Pushkina "Evgenii Onegin": Kommentarii*, 365–366, both of whom give excellent examples, hold that the dream is entirely folkloric. Blagoi states the folkloric thesis most emphatically, "The Inner, unconscious world of Pushkin's heroine is entirely woven from the motifs and images of Russian folk tales," *Sotsiologiia tvorchestva Pushkina*, 145.

19. A. S. Pushkin, *Eugene Onegin*, trans. and commentary Vladimir Nabokov, 4 vols., rev. ed. (Princeton: Princeton University. Press, 1975), II, 506–511; N. L. Brodsky, *"Evgenii Onegin": Roman A. S. Pushkina*, 5th ed. (Moscow: Prosveshchenie, 1964), 235–236; M. R. Katz, "Dreams in Pushkin," *California Slavic Studies*, II (1980), 91.

20. Slonimsky, *Masterstvo Pushkina*, 356–357, offers many examples of prophetic dreams (replete with rapid streams, dark forests, deserted houses, and wild beasts) in the ritual laments of the Russian folk wedding.

21. In *Eugene Onegin* Pushkin uses *son* both for "sleep" (15 times) and for "dream" (29 times). V. V. Vinogradov, ed., *Slovar' iazyka Pushkina* (Moscow: Gos. Izd. slovarei, 1956–1961). However, the ambiguity of the world leaves this distribution open to question. For a comprehensive treatment of such semantic problems, and related structural ones, see Katz, "Dreams in Pushkin," 71–103.

22. Samuel Richardson, *Clarissa*, 4 vols. (London: Everyman's Library, 1962), I, 433.

23. Ibid., I, 79. Combing the pages of Richardson's novel, one discovers an entire bestiary for Tatiana's imagination; for example, Miss Howe tells

Clarissa that men have horns for butting (I, 88) and Clarissa later imagines Lovelace as a lion cub, bear, or tiger (III, 206). Clarissa's description of Lovelace focuses on the repulsive: "His face is a fiery red, somewhat bloated and pimply . . . He has a great scar in his forehead with a dent, as if his skull had been beat in there . . . The turn of his fiery eye . . ." (II, 226–227). Apropos of fiery eyes, readers who sometimes find that Nabokov's invaluable commentaries roast Pushkin over a pale fire will be amused to learn that in this instance Pushkin's country miss is a more attentive reader than her distinguished commentator. Ignoring the epistolary novel as a source, Nabokov unjustly faults Pushkin for lending Tatiana a convention of the "Gothic novel or Byronic romance" before he let her read them in Chap. 7 (Nabokov, II, 410–411). In fact, here, as elsewhere, Tatiana's perceptions are guided by her reading of books that *Eugene Onegin* names.

24. J. W. von Goethe, *Gesammelte Werke in sieben Bänden* (Bielefeld: Sigbert Mohn Verlag, n.d.), IV, 52.

25. There is, of course, a rich tradition of treating *Eugene Onegin* as a historical work, beginning with Belinsky who called it the first historical narrative poem in Russia, not because it depicted historical characters, but because it was set in one of the most interesting moments in the development of Russian society, *Sobranie sochinenii v deviati tomakh*, VI, 363. Pushkin, in fact, toyed with the idea of making *Eugene Onegin* a historical novel in the usual sense by inserting his hero into the Decembrist uprising, but he never realized it, except in the fantasies of certain Soviet critics. The speculation about how Pushkin might have "finished" the novel has reached such extremes among *Pushkinisty* that one of them, B. S. Meilakh, has objected to contrived reconstructions of the text, "Evgenii Onegin," *Pushkin: itogi i problemy izucheniia,* ed. B. P. Gorodetsky et al. (Moscow-Leningrad: Nauka, 1966), 436. A more plausible approach to the historicity of the novel has been suggested by two scholars who develop the idea that while the characters of the novel are seen only until 1825, the author-narrator continued writing after the Decembrist uprising: G. P. Makogonenko, *"Evgenii Onegin" A. S. Pushkina,* 2nd ed. (Moscow: Khudozhestvennaia literatura, 1971), 131; I. M. Semenko, "O roli obraza 'avtora' v 'Evgenii Onegine,' " *Trudy leningradskogo bibliotechnogo instituta imeni N. K. Krupskoi,* 2 (1957), 139. Semenko finds that the chapters written after the uprising project a less ironic, more tragic authorial image.

26. For Weber's views on this, see Max Weber, *Max Weber on Law in Economy and Society,* ed. Max Rheinstein, 2nd ed. (Cambridge, Mass.: Harvard University Press, 1954), 20–21. Weber notes that the borderline between usage and convention is a fluid one.

27. Stanley Mitchell calls our attention to the line of demarcation that the French Revolution drew between the ages of sensibility and romanticism in Western Europe, "Tatiana's Reading," 2–3. But Pushkin himself, in recording this change in literary styles (3:11–12) presents it as a matter of changing taste and attaches no profound historical significance to it. By the end of the novel Eugene will be reading Rousseau (8:35), and Tatiana will have

come to grips with Eugene's novels about "contemporary man" (7:22). It is interesting in this regard to note that Pushkin at times uses Richardson's Lovelace as a recurring type, not a mere museum piece of literary history which has lost its relevance (XIII, 71; XIV, 33, 49).

28. This special relationship between a writer and his or her historical sources has been suggested to me by Herbert Lindenberger, *Historical Drama: The Relation of Literature and Reality* (Chicago: University of Chicago Press, 1975), chap. 1.

29. Lukács, "Pushkin's Place in World Literature," 250.

30. For a study of these inscribed readers, see Sona Stephan Hoisington, "The Hierarchy of Narrates in *Eugene Onegin*," *Canadian-American Slavic Studies*, 10 (Summer 1976), 242–249; and Lotman, *Roman A. S. Pushkina "Evgenii Onegin": Kommentarii*, 63, 66, 296.

31. I have borrowed this description of the functions of language from Roman Jakobson, whose communications model helped me describe the literary institutions in Chapter 2 above; "Closing Statement: Linguistics and Poetics," in Thos. A. Sebeok, ed., *Style in Language* (New York: M.I.T. Press and John Wiley & Sons, 1960), 353–358. Jakobson observes that the language of literature not only calls attention to its aesthetic function but, in diverse genres, evokes other functions as well (357). In an illuminating critique of Jakobson's description, Mary Louise Pratt, *Toward a Speech Act Theory of Literary Discourse* (Bloomington: Indiana University Press, 1977), indicates, among other problems, the narrowness of his conception of "conative" utterances, 31. I have taken her critique into account in using his description.

32. For useful surveys of these contemporary reactions, see Sona Stephan Hoisington, "Early Critical Responses to *Evgenij Onegin*: 1825–1845," Ph.D. diss., Yale University, 1971, chaps. 1–3. V. A. Zelinksy, comp., *Russkaia kriticheskaia lilteratura o proizvedeniiakh A. S. Pushkina*, vols. 3–4. (Moscow: Lissner and Roman, 1887–1888). Bulgarin's increasingly negative comments on the novel have been collected in P. N. Stolpiansky, comp., "Pushkin i 'Severnaia pchela' (1825–1837), I," *Pushkin i ego sovremenniki: Materialy i issledovaniia*, 23–24 (1916), 127–194. For a study of the novel's subsequent reception, see I. E. Usok, "Roman A. S. Pushkina 'Evgenii Onegin' i ego vospriiatie v Rossii XIX–XX v.," in N. V. Os'makov et al., eds., *Russkaia literatura v istoriko-funktsional'nom osveshchenii* (Moscow: Nauka, 1979), 239–302.

33. In the original Russian the "thrillers" are even more condescendingly titled—"toy" [*igrushka*]. Nadezhdin later borrowed the metaphor for a review of *Eugene Onegin, Teleskop*, 9 (1832), 110.

34. Nabokov calls to our attention that these lines are located at the very center of the text, I, 17.

35. The only one of the "two or three novels" that Pushkin identified was Constant's *Adolphe*. He did this in an anonymous announcement of Viazemsky's translation of the novel, for which he cited the last eight lines of *Eugene Onegin*, 7:22 (XI, 87). Shortly after this announcement was published, the first separate edition of *Eugene Onegin*, chapter 7 appeared; between its appearance and the publication of chapter 8 (January 1832), Russian

readers were presented with two translations of *Adolple* (by Viazemsky and N. A. Polevoi) and numerous reviews of them. Given this situation, it was hardly necessary for Pushkin to name the title of Constant's novel, as he had done in his drafts. Pushkin regarded Adolphe as one of the ancestors of Byron's Childe Harold, who replaced Adolphe in Pushkin's drafts, but not as a model for Eugene's speech and behavior toward Tatiana, as I shall discuss below. Readers would have been all the more tempted to catch Pushkin's use of *Adolphe* in *Eugene Onegin* because Viazemsky dedicated his translation, which Pushkin had helped edit, to Pushkin and called it "our favorite novel." On Pushkin and Constant, see Anna Akhmatova, " 'Adol'f' Benzhamena Konstana v tvorchestve Pushkina," *Pushkin: Vremennik pushkinskoi kommissii*, I (Moscow-Leningrad: ANSSSR, 1936); L. I. Vol'pert, *Pushkin i psikhologiches-kaia traditsiia vo frantsuzskoi literature* (Tallin: Eesti raamat, 1980), chap. 4.

36. Cf. A. F. Tiutcheva's memoir on Karamzin's daughter, co-hostess with the historiographer's widow of the salon discussed above in Chapter 2: "She raised the ability to treat people in society to an art and almost to a virtue," *Pri dvore dvukh imperatorov: Dnevnik, 1853–1855* (Moscow: M. and S. Sabashnikov, 1928), 71.

37. Iu. N. Tynianov, "Arkhaisty i Pushkin," *Arkhaisty i novatory* (Len-ingrad: Priboi, 1929), 150, and Lotman, *Roman A. S. Pushkina "Evgenii Onegin": Kommentarii*, 356, note that fashion had by now replaced the wit's old-fash-ioned eloquence with the English dandy's more clipped manner.

38. For a meticulous textological examination of these drafts, see N. Ia. Solovei, "Evoliutsiia temy bol'shogo sveta v VIII glave 'Evgeniia Onegina' (k voprosu o printsipakh publikatsii rukopisnykh materialov)," *Pushkinskii sbor-nik* (Pskov, 1968), 29–39.

39. V. K. Kiukhel'beker, reading chapter 8 in 1832, noted the similarity between Tatiana and the poet in terms of their ability to conceal their deepest feelings from "society"; *Puteshestvie, Dnevnik, Stat'i* (Leningrad: Nauka, 1979), 99–100.

40. Slonimsky, *Masterstvo Pushkina*, 344, has called my attention to this confluence of sources for Tatiana's famous refusal. Upon reexamining them, I find that she is closer to V. L. Pushkin's French version than to the Russian, which has no profession of love and is darkened by the shadow of death. The passage in *Eugene Onegin* reads "Ia vas liubliu (k chemu lukavit'?) / No ia drugomu otdana / I budu vek emu verna" (8:47). The folksong as published in Chulkov's collection reads "Ia dostanus' inomu drug / I verna budu po smert' moiu." V. L. Pushkin's translation is "Je t'aimerai toujours, ô mon ami, mais je serai fidelle à mon époux." This translation of Chulkov's version can be found in N. Trubitsyn, "Iz poezdki Vasiliia L'vovicha Pushkina za-granitsu (1803–1804gg.)," *Pushkin i ego sovremenniki: Materialy i issledovaniia*, 19–20 (1914), 168–169.

41. This suggests that the strength of Pushkin's heroine does not flow merely from her roots in the folk culture, as Lukács, "Pushkin's Place in World Literature," 251, and others have suggested, but from her understand-ing of her culture's various aspects: the intersection of its literary and social patterns, its popular and European heritage.

42. The most detailed analysis of Eugene as a dandy remains L. Grossman, "Pushkin i dendizm," *Etiudy o Pushkine* (Moscow-Petrograd: L. D. Frenkel', 1923), 3–36. However, Lotman draws some useful distinctions between the *petit maître* of the eighteenth-century and the English-style dandy of the 1820s, *Roman A. S. Pushkina "Evgenii Onegin": Kommentarii,* 141–142, 356.

A. A. Bestuzhev's letter of 9 March 1925 to Pushkin demonstrates the conventionality of Eugene's pose: "I see a fop who is soul and body devoted to fashion, I see a man of whom I meet thousands in real life; for coldness, misanthropy, and strangeness have now become toilet accessories," in Pushkin, *Polnoe sobranie sochinenii,* XIII, 149.

43. Among the tools of Eugene's artistry: hypocrisy, concealment of hope, jealousy, the gloomy appearance, dejection, pride, obedience, attentiveness, indifference, silence, fiery eloquence, casualness, self-obliviousness, the quick and tender gaze, shyness, daring tearfulness, novelty, flattery, intimidation, joking, the mind, the heart, imploring, demanding, lessons in discretion, the pursuit of love, disturbing, maligning. Underscoring the range of Eugene's talents is the far more modest list of the poet's resources in the dedicatory piece.

44. Because of these clear parallels between Eugene's imagined behavior here and similar scenes from *Adolphe,* and because of the parallels between incidents in that novel and Eugene's sermon and letter to Tatiana, it is difficult to accept Lotman's contention that Onegin's sermon and letter to Tatiana are free of literary reminiscences, *Roman A. S. Pushkina "Evgenii Onegin": Kommentarii,* 236, 362.

45. Nabokov, III, 16–17.

46. Writing in 1822, Pushkin could offer no better example of his period's periphrastic prose style than "friendship, that sacred feeling, whose noble flame . . ." (XI, 18).

47. Charles Baudelaire, "Le Dandy," *Oeuvres complètes,* ed. Claude Pichois, 2 vols. (Paris: Gallimard, 1975–1976), II, 710. Jürgen Habermas makes a similar point: "Without the normative background of routines, roles, and forms of life—in short, conventions—the individual action would remain indeterminate"; "What is Universal Pragmatics?" *Communication and the Evolution of Society,* trans. Thomas McCarthy (Boston: Beacon Press, 1979), 36.

48. There remains the possibility that Eugene might have shot to kill in self-defense. Eugene might safely assume that Lensky, the aggrieved party, would be firing in earnest. This is a mitigating circumstance, but it does not entirely excuse Eugene's choice of the more deadly alternative; had Eugene fired first and into the air, it is not at all certain that Lensky (by then reconciled with Olga) would have shot to kill. Anyway, Eugene, as a gentleman, would have faced his opponent's fire bravely. Pushkin presents Eugene's actions during the duel as coldly, automatically correct, which implies that Eugene was following a convention, not worrying about saving his skin. Eugene certainly does not use the excuse of self-preservation in his subsequent thoughts, letters, or dreams about the duel. Lotman, in an otherwise excellent account of duelling, refers to a 1908 codex which rules that the first shooter could not fire into the air. But textual examples closer to Pushkin's time suggest that

this was not necessarily so in the customs of the early nineteenth century, when duelling was so widespread that a gentleman hardly needed reference manuals. One recalls that Tolstoy's Vronsky resolved to fire into the air, had the aggrieved Karenin called him out, and that Lermontov's Pechorin, who challenged Grushnitsky, saw that Grushnitsky had the choice.

49. Mitchell, "Tatiana's Reading," 15; Gukovsky, *Pushkin i problemy*, 266–267. The source of this understanding of Onegin's resurrection, Gukovsky reports, is Belinsky, who adduces as evidence of Eugene's sincerity precisely the part of his letter to Tatiana which is plagiarized, consciously or unconsciously, from *Adolphe*, chap. 3. Tatiana, better read in this case than Belinsky and better attuned to the ways in which literature shapes life, cannot share the pioneering social critic's idealization of Eugene to such an unqualified degree. For structural analyses of Tatiana's decision and of her function in the novel, see Geraldine Kelley, "The Characterization of Tat'jana in Pushkin's *Evgenij Onegin*," Ph.D. diss., University of Wisconsin, 1976, and M. R. Katz, "Love and Marriage in Pushkin's *Eugene Onegin*" (unpublished manuscript).

50. "No chtob prodlilas' zhizn' moia," ("But so that my life could be prolonged"): "sans cette amitié je ne puis vivre," B. Constant, *Adolphe* (Paris: Garnier, 1966), 47.

51. Since presenting an early version of this chapter as a paper in 1975, I have found that two excellent works also comment upon the metaphor "life's novel." From different angles of approach, both S. G. Bocharov and Iu. M. Lotman see *Eugene Onegin* as a process of overcoming novelistic tradition. In Bocharov's subtle stylistic analysis this is, roughly speaking, a matter of translating literature into life and making *Eugene Onegin* reproduce the open-endedness of life: *Poetika Pushkina: Ocherki* (Moscow: Nauka, 1974), 103. Iu. M. Lotman, *Roman v stikhakh*, boldly speculates that Pushkin's motive force in writing *Eugene Onegin* was to create a work that would be perceived as a nonliterary reality (80), as life itself (65). Lotman's argument works splendidly for what I have been calling the ficton-making (narrator's and reader's) level of the novel, where he shows that Pushkin created the illusion of lack of literary structure by multiplying structural connections. Instead of carrying this awareness into his description of the interaction between Pushkin's characters, Lotman draws what seems to be an un-Pushkinian distinction between literature and life in finding that by the end of the novel Tatiana and Eugene are "completely" freed from "the fetters of literary associations" and have entered a "genuine, that is, simple and tragic world of real life" (79). "Real life" in *Eugene Onegin* is tragic to be sure, but it is tragic precisely because it is not simple, because it offers many conventional behavioral models and hence possibilities for tragically wrong decisions.

52. I am grateful to Irina Paperno for suggesting that *Eugene Onegin*, while breaking the novelistic convention here (young lovers, with whom the reader is well acquainted, marry), nevertheless observes Russian social conventions (girl marries older man) and follows some literary precedents as well (girl marries older warrior—*Othello*, Pushkin's own "Poltava").

4. A Hero of Our Time

1. Archival records show that these two editions of the novel, 2,400 copies in all, sold for a modest 5.60 rubles each. V. A. Manuilov, "Lermontov i Kraevsky," *Literaturnoe nasledstvo*, vol. 45–46 (Moscow: ANSSSR, 1948), 384.

2. Such as Belinsky, who, among others, thought that Lermontov might have surpassed Pushkin "in content" had he lived. V. G. Belinsky, *Sobranie sochinenii v deviati tomakh* (Moscow: Khudozhestvennaia literatura, 1976–1982), IX, 494; letter to V. P. Botkin of 17 March 1842.

3. From N. P. Ogarev, quoted in L. Ia. Ginzburg, *Tvorcheskii put' Lermontova* (Leningrad: Khudozhestvennaia literatura, 1940), 28.

4. M. I. Gillel'son and V. A. Manuilov, eds., *M. Iu. Lermontov v vospominaniikh sovremennikov* (Moscow: Khudozhestvennaia literatura, 1972), 133, 141, 201.

5. B. M. Eikhenbaum, "Literaturnaia pozitsiia Lermontova," *Literaturnoe nasledstvo*, vol. 43–44 (Moscow: ANSSSR, 1941), 3–82.

6. E. Diushen [M. E. Duchesne], *Poeziia M. Iu. Lermontova v ee otnoshenii k russkoi i zapadnoevropeiskim literaturam* (Kazan': M. A. Golubev, 1914); B. M. Eikhenbaum, *Lermontov: Opyt istoriko-literaturnoi otsenki* (Leningrad: Gos. Izd., 1924); B. V. Tomashevsky, "Proza Lermontova i zapadno-evropeiskaia literaturnaia traditsiia," *Literaturnoe nasledstvo*, vol. 43–44 (Moscow: ANSSSR, 1941), 469–516; A. V. Fedorov, *Lermontov i literatura ego vremeni* (Leningrad: Khudozhestvennaia literatura, 1967)—to name only the most important ones.

7. Tomashevsky mentions Alfred De Vigny's *Servitude et grandeur militaires* (1835) in this regard, "Proza Lermontova i zapadno-evropeiskaia traditsiia," 500–501.

8. For bibliographies and surveys of this academic *perpetuum mobile*, see B. T. Udodov, *M. Iu. Lermontov: Khudozhestvennaia individual'nost' i tvorcheskie protsessy* (Voronezh: Izd. Voronezhskogo Universiteta, 1973), 459–481; and V. A. Manuilov, *Roman M. Iu. Lermontova "Geroi nashego vremeni": Kommentarii*, 2nd ed. (Leningrad: Prosveshchenie, 1975), 20–28.

9. T. Levit, "Literaturnaia sreda Lermontova v Moskovskom Blagorodnom Pansione," *Literaturnoe nasledstvo*, vol. 45–46 (Moscow: ANSSSR, 1948), 225–254; B. V. Neiman, "Lermontov i dekabristy," in N. A. Glagolev, ed., *M. Iu. Lermontov: Sbornik statei* (Moscow: Uchpedgiz, 1941), 36–61; E. G. Gershtein, "Lermontov i 'kruzhok shestnadtsati,' " in N. L. Brodsky, ed., *Zhizn' i tvorchestvo M. Iu. Lermontova: Sbornik I: Issledovaniia i materialy* (Moscow: Goslitizdat, 1941), 7–124. For information and bibliography on all of these topics, see V. A. Manuilov, ed., *Lermontovskaia entsiklopediia* (Moscow: Sovetskaia entsiklopediia, 1981).

10. E.g., B. M. Eikhenbaum, "Geroi nashego vremeni," in his *O proze: Sbornik statei* (Leningrad: Khudozhestvennaia literatura, 1969), 234, 240, 243, 251, 253, 266, 268, 269 ff., 275, 281, 301, 303.

11. *M. Iu. Lermontov v vospominaniikh sovremennikov*, 133, 239, 244, 269, 443.

12. Belinsky, *Sobranie sochinenii v deviati tomakh*, IX, 365, letter to V. P.

Botkin, 16–21 April 1840. See also the accounts by I. I. Panaev and V. A. Sollogub, in *M. Iu. Lermontov v vospominaniikh sovremennikov*, 232, 236, 268.

13. On the quarrel and duel with Barante, see E. G. Gershtein, "Duel' Lermontova s Barantom," *Literaturnoe nasledstvo*, vol. 45–46 (Moscow: ANSSSR, 1948), 389–432.

14. On Lermontov's relationship with the Karamzins, see V. A. Manuilov, "Lermontov i Karamziny," in M. P. Alekseev et al., eds., *M. Iu. Lermontov: Issledovaniia i materialy* (Leningrad: Nauka, 1979), 323–342.

15. "Iz al'boma S. N. Karamzinoi," I, 469.

16. Letter 26 June 1839, original in French, quoted in E. V. Danilova et al., eds., "Pis'ma S. N. Karamzinoi k E. N. Meshcherskoi o Lermontove," in M. P. Alekseev et al., eds., *M. Iu. Lermontov: Issledovaniia i materialy* (Leningrad: Nauka, 1979), 356.

17. For another reading of the final poem, which, ignoring the salon thematics, sees it as a manifesto of literary "Realism," see Manuilov, *Roman M. Iu. Lermontova "Geroi nashego vremeni": Kommentarii*, 23.

18. V. A. Manuilov, comp., *Letopis' zhizni i tvorchestva M. Iu. Lermontova* (Moscow-Leningrad: Nauka, 1964), 107. For an account of the writing of *A Hero of Our Time*, for which there is little evidence, see Udodov, *M. Iu. Lermontov*, 482–509.

The difficulties of influence tracing may be seen from the motif of the partial laughter: one encounters it not just in the "Maksim Maksimych" section of Lermontov's novel (IV, 220), but also in such other contemporary texts as Stendhal's diary entry on Napolean (14 July 1804), Marie Henri Beyle, *Oeuvres intimes de Stendhal*, ed. H. Martineau (Paris: Gallimard, 1955), 516. It would be most appropriate to view such migratory motifs as elements of a discourse which attempted to "read" the inner life from outward gestures.

19. For a useful genre study of Lermontov's prose, see Helen Goscilo, "From Dissolution to Synthesis: The Use of Genre in Lermontov's Prose," Ph.D. diss., Indiana University, 1976. On "Princess Mary" and an important prose genre, the "society tale," see V. A. Ezerikhina, " 'Kniazhna Meri' M. Iu. Lermontova i 'svetskaia povest' ' 1830-kh godov,' *Uchenye zapiski Leningradskogo Ped. Instituta im. A. I. Gertzena* (1961), vol. 219, *Voprosy istorii russkoi literatury*, 51–72. On the generic variety of the gentlemen-littérateurs, see Chapter 1 above.

20. On *A Hero of Our Time* as a psychological novel, see Belinsky's essays on Lermontov; Ginzburg, *Tvorcheskii put' Lermontova*, 184; A. G. Tseitlin, *Masterstvo Turgeneva-romanista* (Moscow: Sovetskii pisatel', 1958), 57; John Mersereau, Jr., *Mikhail Lermontov* (Carbondale: Southern Illinois University Press, 1962), 158; John Garrard, *Mikhail Lermontov* (Boston: Twayne, 1982), 123; and C. J. G. Turner, *Pechorin: An Essay on Lermontov's "A Hero of Our Time,"* Birmingham Slavonic Monographs, no. 5 (Birmingham: Department of Russian Language and Literature, 1978), 79–80. Udodov sees the problem of "personality" as central to the novel, *M. Iu. Lermontov*, 545; E. M. Mikhailova's very detailed and intelligent reading sees "personality" as the criterion by which author and hero evaluate society, without, however, adequately

considering "personality" as an ideological construct, *Proza Lermontova* (Moscow: Khudozhestvennaia literatura, 1957), 310; Eikhenbaum convincingly relates the novel to the psychological insights of the Utopian Socialists, "Geroi nashego vremeni," 246–247, 275–282; and Mikhailova finds *A Hero of Our Time* more socially aware than the European novel of psychological analysis (e.g., Constant's *Adolphe*), *Proza Lermontova*, 372–381.

21. Of the many such studies, I have found particularly useful the studies mentioned in note 11 to the Introduction and D. D. Blagoi, "Ot 'Evgeniia Onegina' k 'Geroiu nashego vremeni' (k voprosu o khudozhestvennom metode Lermontova)," in U. R. Fokht, ed., *Problemy romantizma: Sbornik statei* (Moscow: Iskusstvo, 1967), 293–319; and V. Glukhov, " 'Geroi nashego vremeni' i 'Evgenii Onegin,' " in U. R. Fokht, ed., *Tvorchestvo M. Iu. Lermontova: 150 let so dnia rozhdeniia, 1814–1964* (Moscow: Nauka, 1964), 285–310.

22. A recent comparison between Pushkin's lexicon and Lermontov's suggests that here, too, the latter's range was significantly restrained, V. V. Borodin and A. Ia. Shaikevich, eds., "Chastotnyi slovar' iazyka M Iu. Lermontova," in Manuilov, *Lermontovskaia entsiklopediia*, 717–718.

23. On Lermontov's Byronism, see Ginzburg, *Tvorcheskii put' Lermontova*, 30–35 and 107–114.

24. For a reading which unconvincingly tries to connect Pechorin with young Morton's political ideals, see Eikhenbaum, "Geroi nashego vremeni," 271–273; on Lermontov's use of Scott in general, see D. P. Iakubovich, "Lermontov i Val'ter Skott," *Izvestiia ANSSSR: Seriia 7, Otdelenie obshchestvennykh nauk*, 3 (1935), 243–272.

25. Although I use my own translations of the novel, I consulted the best English version and refer to the titles of the sections as they are rendered in it: Mihail Lermotov, *A Hero of Our Time*, trans. Vladimir Nabokov in collaboration with Dmitri Nabokov (Garden City: Doubleday, 1958).

26. M. Iu. Lermontov, *Sochineniia v shesti tomakh* (Moscow-Leningrad: ANSSSR, 1954–1957), VI, 158.

27. Ibid., VI, 570.

28. On the vicissitudes of the "Caucasus" in Russian literature, see B. M. Eikhenbaum, *Lev Tolstoi: Kniga pervaia, 50-e gody* (Leningrad: Priboi, 1928), 127–142. On Lermontov's relations with his prominent Romantic predecessor, see V. E. Vatsuro, "Lermontov i Marlinskii," in U. R. Fokht, ed., *Tvorchestvo M. Iu. Lermontova: 150 let so dnia rozhdeniia, 1814–1964* (Moscow: Nauka, 1964), 341–363.

29. S. P. Shevyrev, " 'Geroi nashego vremeni,' " *Moskvitianin*, 1 (1841), 529.

30. Shevyrev, whose defense of polilte society's literary institutions was noted in Chapter 2, reveals the horizon of expectations against which Lermontov's novel is set, when, in a review of the novel, he sees the Caucasus as an arena for the "duel between two forces, educated and wild" and contrasts the "civil order" of Russia with the life of the mountain peoples, who lack any knowledge of a "social contract": " 'Geroi nashego vremeni,' " 518. Rousseau's "Second Discourse," which argues that tyranny and violence have

attended most social forms, would have had more bearing on the structure of Lermontov's novel than *The Social Contract*, to which Shevyrev may be referring.

31. Belinsky, " 'Geroi nashego vremeni': Sochinenie M. Lermontova," *Sobranie sochinenii v deviati tomakh*, III, 84.

32. Among modern treatments, Eikhenbaum expresses this double chronology most neatly as the "chronology of events" and "the chronology of the narration itself . . . the history of the author's (and, together with his, the reader's) growing familiarity with the hero," "Geroi nashego vremeni," 263–264.

33. See, for example, Eikhenbaum, "Geroi nashego vremeni," 264; Udodov, *M. Iu. Lermontov*, 581.

34. Eikhenbaum, "Geroi nashego vremeni," 302.

35. Vladimir Nabokov has noted Maksim Maksimych's opening and closing comments on fate, "Notes," Lermontov, *A Hero of Our Time*, 210; Udodov sees the recurrence of the fortress setting as an example of the novel's ringlike construction, *M. Iu. Lermontov*, 584.

36. Using a sort of analysis more appropriate to *Eugene Onegin*, which unlike *A Hero of Our Time* marks its place in history by referring to the past works and ongoing development its author, Vladimir Nabokov worked back from the publication date of "The Author's Introduction" to place the novel's action between 1830 and 1839, Vladimir Nabokov, "Translator's Foreword," *A Hero of Our Time*, viii–ix. According to this scheme the usually careful Nabokov would have Pechorin refer to *The Library for Reading* a year before it began publication. In an even more desperate attempt to date *A Hero of Our Time*, S. N. Durylin draws upon dates established in a different work by Lermontov, the unfinished "Princess Ligovskaia," *Kak rabotal Lermontov* (Moscow: Mir, 1934), 8–9.

37. Alfred de Musset, *La Confession d'un enfant du siècle*, in his *Oeuvres complètes*, 3 vols., ed. Maurice Allem (Paris: Gallimard, 1933–1952), III, 94.

38. On the novel's ironic sense of history, see Victor Ripp, "A Hero of Our Time and the Historicism of the 1830's: The Problem of the Whole and the Parts," *Modern Language Notes*, 92 (1977), 969–986.

39. Belinsky, " 'Geroi nashego vremeni': Sochinenie M. Lermontova: Izdanie vtoroe," *Sobranie sochinenii v deviati tomakh*, IV, 452.

40. In the course of writing the novel Lermontov eliminated such specific events as "the terrible story" of Pechorin's duel, *Sochineniia v shesti tomakh*, VI, 577.

41. On Pechorin's possible development as a character, see Garrard, *Mikhail Lermontov*, 136; Goscilo "From Dissolution to Synthesis," 266–267; Turner, *Pechorin*, 24; and Mikhailova, *Proza Lermontova*, 273–274. Belinsky contributed to such biographical interpretation by speculating that a sequel to the novel would have shown a new, reformed Pechorin, " 'Geroi nashego vremeni': Sochinenie M. Lermontova," III, 149–150. On the tradition of the "free character" in Russian fiction, see Donald Fanger, "On the Russianness of the Russian Nineteenth-Century Novel," in Theofanis G. Stavrou, ed., *Art*

and Culture in Nineteenth-Century Russia (Bloomington: Indiana University Press, 1983), 49–50.

42. On the *portrait moral* of the French salons and its rendering of "static, summary fixity," see Peter Brooks, *The Novel of Worldliness: Crébillon, Marivaux, Laclos, Stendhal* (Princeton: Princeton University Press, 1969), 15–17, 48–62, 77–80, 106–110, 148–149, 152–153, 178–179, 229; and Roland Barthes, "La Bruyère," in his *Essais critiques* (Paris: Editions du Seuil, 1964), 221–237.

43. Given this preponderance of references to the theater, it is to be expected that other critics have noted them: Gary Cox, "Dramatic Genre as a Tool of Characterization in Lermontov's *A Hero of Our Time*," *Russian Literature*, 11 (1982), 163–172; Turner, *Pechorin*, 45–54; G. M. Fridlender, "Lermontov i russkaia povestvovatel'naia proza," *Russkaia literatura*, 1 (1965), 44; N. Ia. D'iakonova, "Iz nabliudenii nad zhurnalom Pechorina," *Russkaia literatura*, 4 (1969), 123. My approach will differ from these by paying more attention to theatricality, especially to the cultural context, to the problem of "script," and to onstage/backstage regions. Lisa A. Schneider relates this novel's theatricalized conflicts to a different cultural context, the theatricalization of warfare during the Napoleonic era: *"Red Cavalry:* Babel's Theater of War," Ph.D. diss., Stanford University, 1985, chap. 3.

44. Nabokov, "Translator's Foreword," x.

45. For examples, see V. V. Vinogradov, ed., *Slovar' iazyka Pushkina* (Moscow: Gos. Izd. slovarei, 1956–1960). In analyzing the novel's use of this theatricality, I have found valuable insight in a number of sociological and aesthetic studies, such as Elizabeth Burns, *Theatricality: A Study of Convention in the Theater and in Social Life* (New York: Harper & Row, 1972); Michael Fried, *Absorption and Theatricality: Painting and Beholder in the Age of Diderot* (Berkeley: University of California Press, 1980); Erving Goffman, *The Presentation of Self in Everyday Life* (Garden City: Anchor Books, 1959); David Marshall, "Adam Smith and the Theatricality of Moral Sentiments," *Critical Inquiry*, 10 (June 1984), 592–613; and a special issue devoted to "Drama, Theater, Performance: A Semiotic Perspective," *Poetics Today*, 2 (Spring 1981).

46. For much useful data on this situation, see Iu. M. Lotman, "Theater and Theatricality in the Order of Early Nineteenth Century Culture," *Soviet Studies in Literature*, 11 (Spring-Summer 1975), 155–185; Iu. M. Lotman, "Poetika bytovogo povedeniia v russkoi kul'ture XVIII veka," *Uchenye zapiski Tartuskogo Gosudarstvennogo Universiteta, Vyp. 411: Trudy po znakovym sistemam*, 7 (1977), 65–89.

47. Iu. M. Lotman, *roman A. S. Pushkina "Evgenii Onegin": Kommentarii* (Leningrad: Prosveshchenie, 1980), 53; J. S. Curtiss, *The Russian Army under Nicholas I, 1825–1855* (Durham: Duke University Press, 1965), 184.

48. I borrow this distinction between impressions "given" and "given off" from Goffman, *The Presentation of Self*, 2–3.

49. See Goffman on "dramaturgical discipline," "dramaturgical circumspection," and other "defensive attributes and practices," ibid., 216, 218, 228.

50. By turning self-presentation into a contest, *A Hero of Our Time* anticipates Clifford Geertz's critique of Goffman's *Presentation of Self in Everyday*

Life, namely that Goffman's "theater" is the arena for "information games"; "Blurred Genres: The Refiguration of Social Thought," *The American Scholar,* 49 (Spring 1980), 170.

51. Goffman, *The Presentation of Self,* 13.

52. For a detailed reading of Pechorin's comic failures in this section, see R. A. Peace, "The Role of *Taman'* in Lermontov's *Geroi nashego vremeni,*" *Slavonic and East European Review,* 45 (January 1967), 12–29.

53. For an elaboration of this antithesis between "ritual" and "game," see Claude Lévi-Strauss, *The Savage Mind* (Chicago: University of Chicago Press, 1966), 30–33.

54. Lotman, "Theater and Theatricality," 179.

55. Ibid., 167; Goffman, *The Presentation of Self,* 106–140. Lotman's "intermission"—"a break during which the semioticity of behavior is reduced to a minimum"—is more rigorously covered by Goffman's distinction between "backstage" (a place where performances are prepared and where the performers can relax from, even contradict, the impression their performance is to foster) and "outside" (which is neither front nor back with respect to a given performance).

56. See, for example, Seymour Chatman, *Story and Discourse: Narrative Structure in Fiction and Film* (Ithaca: Cornell University Press, 1978), 170–172, who uses the category of "audience" to distinguish diary narrative from interior monologue.

57. B. Constant, *Adolphe* (Paris: Garnier, 1966), 38.

58. For good examples, see Marshall, "Adam Smith and the Theatricality of Moral Sentiments," 593, 611–612.

59. Useful surveys of the nineteenth-century criticism may be found in E. E. Naidich, " 'Geroi nashego vremeni' v russkoi kritike," in M. Iu. Lermontov, *Geroi nashego vremeni,* ed. B. M. Eikhenbaum and E. E. Naidich (Moscow: ANSSSR, 1962), 163–197; Ginzburg, *Tvorcheskii put' Lermontova,* chap. 7; and Mikhailova, *Proza Lermontova,* chap. 1.

60. Belinsky, " 'Geroi nashego vremeni': Sochinenie M. Lermontova," III, 125.

61. For an attempt to equate Lermontov's position with Belinsky's, see N. I. Mordovchenko, *Belinskii i russkaia literatura ego vremeni* (Moscow-Leningrad: Gosizdat, 1950), 120–125.

62. Letter of 14 June 1840 to the empress, quoted in *M. Iu. Lermontov v vospominaniikh sovremennikov,* 394.

63. "Tragic escapade," "to dramatize feelings and actions," "pompous phrases and declamations," Lermontov, *Sochineniia v shesti tomakh,* VI, 604–605.

64. Among the many critics who have for various reasons stressed the novel's lyricisim are Belinsky, " 'Geroi nashego vremeni': Sochinenie M. Lermontova," III, 141; Mikhailova, *Proza Lermontova,* 262, 333–334, 350; Udodov, *M. Iu. Lermontov,* 528, 570, 601; Manuilov, *Kommentarii,* 50; Eikhenbaum, *Lermontov: Opyt istoriko-literaturnoi otsenki,* 82, 129; and Paul Debreczeny, "Elements of the Lyrical Verse Tale in Lermontov's *A Hero of Our Time,*" in Victor

Terras, ed., *American Contributions to the Seventh International Congress of Slavists: Warsaw, August 21–27, 1973*, vol. II, *Literature and Folklore* (The Hague: Mouton, 1973), 93–117.

65. On "strangeness" and "eccentricity" in the ideology of polite society, see Chapter 1 above. Their literary heritage is discussed in Udodov, *M. Iu. Lermontov*, 510–543.

66. Georg Lukács, *The Theory of the Novel: A Historico-Philosophical Essay on the Forms of Great Epic Literature*, trans. Anna Bostock (Cambridge, Mass.: M.I.T. Press, 1971), 97.

5. Dead Souls

1. S. G. Bocharov, "O stile Gogolia," in *Teoriia literaturnykh stilei: Tipologiia stilevogo razvitiia novogo vremeni*, ed. N. K. Gei et al. (Moscow: Nauka, 1976), 409–445; on the problem of dating of the novel's action, see E. C. Smirnova-Chikina, *Poema N. V. Gogolia "Mertvye dushi": Kommentarii*, 2nd ed. (Leningrad: Prosveshchenie, 1974), 190–192. Assuming that Gogol intended to provide an accurate image of Russia's legal and governmental institutions, she places the action in the early 1830s, but cites less literal-minded readers who have placed it as early as the 1810s and 1820s. The novel's sense of deathly stasis virtually requires that the action take place in a historical vacuum.

2. For a useful collection of contemporary comments on the title, see Smirnova-Chikina, *Poema N. V. Gogolia "Mertvye dushi": Kommentarii*, 27–29. From all accounts "dead souls" was a theretofore unknown combination of noun and epithet in the Russian language.

3. Quoted in S. T. Aksakov, *Istoriia moego znakomstva s Gogolem so vkliucheniem vsei perepiski s 1832 po 1852 g.* (Moscow: ANSSSR, 1960), 90.

4. Ibid., 71.

5. K. P. Masal'sky, quoted in Paul Debreczeny, *Nikolai Gogol and his Contemporary Critics*, Transactions of the American Philosophical Society, new series, vol. 56, part 3 (1966), 35.

6. P. A. Pletnev, "Chichikov ili Mertvye dushi Gogolia," *Sovremennik*, 26 (1842), 55. Pletnev, it must be added, placed the blame for the novel's focus on triviality squarely on society, adding that "Gogol was returning to society what it itself could give him," 56.

7. Anon. [K. S. Aksakov], *Neskol'ko slov o poeme Gogolia "Mertvye dushi"* (Moscow, 1842), 14–15. Useful surveys of the novel's reception are provided by V. I. Shenrok, "Literaturnye otzyvy sovremennikov o pervom tome 'Mertvykh dush,' " *Russkaia starina*, 82 (October 1894), 143–178; Debreczeny, *Nikolai Gogol and his Contemporary Critics*, 29–50; and Donald Fanger, *The Creation of Nikolai Gogol* (Cambridge, Mass.: Harvard University Press, 1979), 201–205. D. N. Ovsianiko-Kulikovskii, " 'Liudi 40-kh godov' i Gogol'," *Istoriia russkoi intelligentsii*, part I (Moscow: V. M. Sablin, 1908), 205–233, sensitively analyzes the affinities and dissimilarities between Gogol and his socially conscious readers; a very useful account of subsequent Gogol criticism appears in

R. A. Maguire, "The Legacy of Criticism," *Gogol from the Twentieth Century: Eleven Essays* (Princeton: Princeton University Press, 1974), 4–51.

8.   V. G. Belinsky, *Sobranie sochinenii v deviati tomakh* (Moscow: Khudozhestvennaia literatura, 1976–1982), V, 53–55, and VIII, 511.

9.   Ovsianiko-Kulikovsky, " 'Liudi 40-kh godov' i Gogol'," 211.

10.   Smirnova-Chikina's useful commentaries to the novel, intended for an audience of teachers and students, represent a concerted effort to "place" the novel in this particular way. The émigré criticism that strenuously denies the novel's relationship to the old regime is, no doubt, itself engaged in a process of legitimation.

11.   Although few, if any, of the novel's first readers failed to relate the world of the novel to their own, it was Belinsky's criticism that started this trend. The socially oriented critics of the 1850s and 1860s, such as Chernyshevsky, amplified it and passed it on to the academic scholarship of the Soviet period, where it has become obligatory to find all of nineteenth-century Russian literature "realistic," especially the oeuvre of Nikolai Gogol. The genealogy of Russian social criticism is thoroughly studied by Rufus W. Mathewson, Jr., *The Positive Hero in Russian Literature*, 2nd ed. (Stanford: Stanford University Press, 1975); the Gogolian stages in this genealogy are crisply outlined by Simon Karlinsky, *The Sexual Labyrinth of Nikolai Gogol* (Cambridge, Mass.: Harvard University Press, 1976), 281–290.

12.   Pletnev, "Chichikov ili Mertvye dushi Gogolia," 56; Belinsky, *Sobranie sochinenii v deviati tomakh*, IX, 682, letter to K. D. Kavelin, 22 November 1847.

13.   A. V. Nikitenko, *Dnevnik v trekh tomakh*, ed. I. Ia. Aizenshtok (Leningrad: Goslitizdat, 1955), I, 346, entry of 24 February 1852; N. G. Chernyshevsky, *Polnoe sobranie sochinenii v piatnadtsati tomakh* (Moscow: GIKhL, 1934–1953), III, 20; F. M. Dostoevsky, *Dnevnik pisatelia* (April, 1876), *Polnoe sobranie sochinenii* (Leningrad: Nauka, 1972–), XXII, 106.

14.   For a perceptive analysis of Rozanov's challenge to the Belinsky tradition, an analysis which calls due attention to Rozanov's own political animus, see Robert Louis Jackson, "Two Views of Gogol and the Critical Synthesis: Belinskij, Rozanov, and Dostoevskij; An Essay in Literary-Historical Criticism," *Russian Literature*, 15 (1984), 223–242. Rozanov's insistence on the static quality of Gogol's characters and on the waxen monotony of his language appears most forcefully in two essays on Gogol appended to the third edition of his study of Dostoevsky's "Legend of the Grand Inquisitor": *Legenda o velikom inkvizitore F. M. Dostoevskogo: Opyt kriticheskogo kommentariia: S prilozheniem dvukh etiudov o Gogole*, 3rd ed. (St. Petersburg: M. V. Pirozhkov, 1906), 253–282.

15.   For useful anthologies of such modern readings, see Maguire, *Gogol from the Twentieth Century*; and Victor Erlich, ed., *Twentieth-Century Russian Literary Criticism* (New Haven: Yale University Press, 1975).

16.   The most important among such exceptions are undoubtedly the studies by Iu. M. Lotman, "Problema khudozhestvennogo prostranstva v proze Gogolia," *Uchenye zapiski Tartuskogo Gosudarstvennogo Universiteta, No.*

209: *Trudy po russkoi i slavianskoi filologii, IX, Literaturovedenie* (Tartu, 1968), 5–50; Bocharov, "O stile Gogolia," 409–445; an Iu. V. Mann, *Poetika Gogolia* (Moscow: Khudozhestvennaia literatura, 1978). For a cogent literary historical challenge to the "realism" of Gogol's work, see V. V. Kozhinov, "K metodologii istorii russkoi literatury (o realizme 30-kh godov XIX veka), *Voprosy literatury*, 5 (1968), 60–82.

17. V. F. Pereverzev, *Tvorchestvo Gogolia* (Moscow: Sovremennye problemy, 1914); G. A. Gukovsky, *Realizm Gogolia* (Moscow-Leningrad: GIKhL, 1959); A. A. Elistratova, *Gogol i problemy zapadno-evropeiskogo romana* (Moscow: Nauka, 1972). Gukovsky's brilliant monograph, it should be noted, was published posthumously from an incomplete manuscript, which came to an abrupt halt in the chapter on *Dead Souls*.

18. B. M. Eikhenbaum, "How Gogol's 'Overcoat' Is Made," in Maguire, *Gogol from The Twentieth Century*, 269–291. The article first appeared in 1918, constituting, after the symbolists' assaults, one of the most important challenges to the established reading habits of the Russian intelligentsia.

19. Vladimir Nabokov, *Nikolai Gogol* (Norfolk, Conn.: New Directions, 1944), 63–70. Nabokov explains the stability of *poshlost'* as follows: "so beautifully timeless and so cleverly painted over with protective tints that its presence (in a book, in a soul, in an institution, in a thousand other places) often escapes detection." The ties to ideological analysis become particularly suggestive when Nabokov compares his project to Flaubert's dictionary of "idées reçues." Victor Erlich's discussion of the novel, which rejects the realist classification as well as the extremes of Nabokov's ahistoricism, follows Nabokov's important insight into a discussion of Gogol's "wacky" style as a cognitive instrument: *Gogol* (New Haven: Yale University Press, 1969), 115–141. Donald Fanger, also questioning the realist interpretation, located the novel's historical function in its representation of a provocative nothingness, in its offering of the "raw material of an unborn national self-consciousness": *The Creation of Nikolai Gogol*, 190.

20. A. de Jonge, "Gogol," in John Fennell, ed., *Nineteenth-Century Russian Literature: Studies of Ten Russian Writers* (Berkeley: University of California Press, 1973), 125. Compare Erlich, on Gogol's language as the "only active protagonist, the only dynamic force," *Gogol*, 221. James B. Woodward has discussed the characters' distorting and falsifying use of language in *Gogol's Dead Souls* (Princeton: Princeton University Press, 1978), chap. 8.

21. The idiosyncrasy of Gogol's oeuvre has been so often noted in literary scholarship, by representatives of all the hostile parties, that the source-hunting scholarship which has pursued Pushkin and Lermontov has generally avoided Gogol. The best comparative studies of Gogol have, for the most part, been typological, and, therefore, not so concerned with sources. Gogol himself predetermined this tendency by being remarkably reticent about his own reading. On this problem, see S. T. Aksakov, *Istoriia moego znakomstva*, 13; and Fanger, *The Creation of Nikolai Gogol*, 12–13. A substantial attempt to discover the literary sources, G. I. Chudakov, *Otnoshenie tvorchestva*

N. V. Gogolia k zapadno-evropeiskim literaturam (Kiev: Univ. St. Vladimira, 1908), cannot solve the mysteries, but it does offer valuable bibliograpical information on works that Gogol *might* have known.

22. S. A. Vengerov, "Gogol sovershenno ne znal real'noi russkoi zhizni," *Sobranie sochinenii*, vol. II (St. Petersburg: Prometei, 1913), 125, 130.

23. A. N. Karamzin, "Rimskie pis'ma A. N. Karamzina k svoei materi Ekaterine Andreevne," *Starina i novizna*, 20 (1916), 164.

24. Analyses of Gogol's position during the early 1830s appear in Donald Fanger, *The Creation of Nikolai Gogol*, part 2; and Boris Eikhenbaum, *Moi vremennik: Slovesnost', Nauka, Kritika, smes'* (Leningrad: Izd. pisatelei v Leningrade, 1929), 89–92.

25. On the collection's nonconversational tone, see Joan Nabseth Stevenson, "Literary and Cultural Patterns in Gogol's *Arabeski*," Ph.D. diss., Stanford University, 1984, chap. 1.

26. On the importance of Pushkin as an "imaginary interlocutor" for Gogol, see V. Sh. Krivonos, *Problema chitatelia v tvorchestve Gogolia* (Voronezh: Izd. Voronezhskogo universiteta, 1981), 45–47; of the many studies of the relationship the most detailed and insightful remains V. V. Gippius, "Literaturnoe obshchenie Gogolia s Pushkinym," *Uchenye zapiski Permskogo gos. universiteta*, no. 2 (1931), 61–126; a useful bibliography on the subject appears in E. A. Voitolovskaia and A. N. Stepanov, comps., *N. V. Gogol': Seminarii* (Leningrad: Gos. Uchebno-ped. izd., 1962), 205–209. See also Fanger, *The Creation of Nikolai Gongol*, 69–72 and 150–53; and Donald Fanger, "Influence and Tradition in the Russian Novel," in John Garrard, ed., *The Russian Novel from Pushkin to Pasternak* (New Haven: Yale University Press, 1983), 36–41.

27. Gogol's chosen mode of publication provides institutional corraboration for Bocharov's thesis that no genuine dialogue is possible in Gogol's fictive world, but that "penetration" by a word or transfiguration are real possibilities, "O stile Gogolia," 431.

28. Aksakov, *Istoriia moego znakomstva*, 24–36, 56, 60, captures this rivalry and its more ridiculous aspects.

29. See, for example, Aksakov, *Istoriia moego znakomstva*; I. S. Turgenev, *Polnoe sobranie sochinenii i pisem v dvadtsati vos'mi tomakh* (Moscow-Leningrad: ANSSSR, 1960–1968), XIV, 66; Chernyshevsky went so far as to equate Gogol's behavior in society with that of the insinuating *picaro* of *Dead Souls*, Chichikov, *Polnoe sobranie sochinenii v piatnadtsati tomakh*, IV, 639–640. Among recent scholars only Karlinsky pays much attention to Gogol's associations during these years abroad, *The Sexual Labyrinth of Nikolai Gogol*, 185–202.

30. A. N. Karamzin, "Rimskie pis'ma," 119.

31. Charles Augustin Sainte-Beuve, *Revue des deux mondes*, 12 (1845), 883–889; A. S. Sturdza, quoted in V. Veresaev, *Gogol' v zhizni: Sistematicheskii svod podlinnykh svidetel'stv sovremennikov* (Moscow: Academia, 1933), 171.

32. See, for example, the memoirs of Count Sollogub, I. I. Panaev, D. M. Pogodin, and L. I. Arnol'di, quoted in S. O. Mashinsky, ed., *Gogol' v vospominaniikh sovremennikov* (Moscow: GIKhL, 1951), 77, 213, 412, 478; S. T. Aksakov, *Istoriia moego znakomstva*, 11–13, 60–61, 65.

33. Aksakov, *Istoriia moego znakomstva*, 60.

34. Turgenev, *Polnoe sobranie sochinenii*, XIV, 66, 69–71.

35. P. V. Annenkov, who remembered the humor in all of Gogol's conversation, was, nevertheless, hard pressed to give specific examples, "N. V. Gogol' v Rime letom 1841 goda," *Literaturnye vospominaniia*, ed. V. P. Dorofeev (Moscow: GIKhL, 1960), 101.

36. Turgenev, *Polnoe sobranie sochinenii*, XIV, 70. It should be noted that Dickens and Gogol performed under very different institutional circumstances: Dickens for large, paying audiences, Gogol for small groups of friends, fellow students, and salon habitué(e)s.

37. Panaev is quoted in *Gogol v vospominaniaikh sovremennikov*, 44, 215; Aksakov, *Istoriia moego znakomstva*, 37.

38. Annenkov, *Literaturnye vospominaniia*, 87.

39. Quoted in M. I. Gillel'son, "N. V. Gogol' v dnevnikakh A. I. Turgeneva," *Russkaia literatura*, no. 2 (1963), 138. Repeating earlier reactions of Pushkin and Belinsky, no doubt independently, Aleksandr Turgenev found it both "funny and sad."

40. Aksakov, *Istoriia moego znakomstva*, 56.

41. Pletnev, "Chichikov ili Mertvye dushi Gogolia," 23.

42. Pletnev, letter to V. A. Zhukovsky of 5 June 1842, "Iz pisem P. A. Pletneva k V. A. Zhukovskomu," *Russkii arkhiv* (1870), 1277.

43. Letter to Gogol, 1842, quoted in Aksakov, *Istoriia moego znakomstva*, 91.

44. On cooperation and implicature in oral speech situations, see H. P. Grice, "Logic and Conversation," in Peter Cole and Jerry L. Morgan, eds., *Syntax and Semantics*, vol. III, *Speech Acts* (New York: Academy Press, 1975). For a seminal literary appropriation of his discussion, see Mary Louise Pratt, *Toward a Speech Act Theory of Literary Discourse* (Bloomington: Indiana University Press, 1977), chaps. 4–5. On politeness and cooperation, see Robin Lakoff, "The Logic of Politeness; or Minding Your p's and q's," *Papers from the Ninth Regional Meeting, Chicago Linguistic Society*, April 1973 (Chicago: Chicago Linguistic Society, 1973), 292–305.

45. Smirnova-Chikina, in fact, labels this a "careless syntactic construction," *Poema N. V. Gogolia "Mertvye dushi": Kommentarii*, 145. Grammatically speaking, she is, of course, correct. But more so is Andrei Bely, who noted that Gogol was fluent in Russian, if not in its formal grammar, *Masterstvo Gogolia* (Moscow-Leningrad: GIKhL, 1934), 279. Perhaps Alexander Pope's "Essay on Criticism" might have the last word here:

> Those oft are *Strategems* which *Errors* seem
> Nor is it *Homer Nods*, but *We* that *Dream*.

46. Compare Pletnev on the narrator: "You not infrequently cease to suspect his presence, where he, as a narrator, ought to be. He is entirely immersed in the sphere of the society which is moving about him, he shares its way of thinking, speaks its language, and takes its every false idea for The Truth. In this way the charm of the reality he has created is not disturbed"; "Chichikov ili Mertvye dushi Gogolia," 25.

47. The Academy edition of Gogol's works prints the successive surviving drafts of the novel. For the second draft, dated 1840–41, Gogol added a passage on the education of women (chap. 2), a passage inviting the reader to compare Korobochka and the ladies of St. Petersburg (chap. 3), a paean to the Russian word (chap. 5), Chichikov's meditation on the immutability of the "kulak" (chap. 5). For the final drafts of 1841–42 Gogol reworked the digressions considerably. He made the digression on the fate of the comic writer more lyric and less essayistic in style (chap. 7), polished considerably the passages on the language of society ladies (chaps. 8 and 9), cut references to Chichikov's reading and his own (chap. 11), and devoted considerable efforts to the cadences and rhetorical organization of the digressions on Russia (chap. 11). Sergei Aksakov reports that Gogol continued to make substantive changes even on the final proofs, *Istoriia moego znakomstva*, 64. An adequate account of this process remains to be written. The abandoning of the essayistic manner in favor of the lyrical or sermonical is particularly significant in institutional terms.

48. On the multiplicity of languages, sociolects, and generic fragments as a determining marker of the "novel," see M. M. Bakhtin, "Slovo v romane," in his *Voprosy literatury i estetiki* (Moscow: Khudozhestvennaia literatura, 1975), 72–233. His brief essay on Gogol and Rabelais appears in the same volume, 484–495; although it is not very specific in defining the "official" language that is subverted by Gogol's laughter, although it may overplay the role of folk humor in Gogol's later work, and although it ignores the darker aspects of Gogol's comedy, it is methodologically useful for its attention to clashing styles and transgressed boundaries. Less methodologically productive, but more specific linguistically on the plurality of "voices," styles, and genres in Gogol's oeuvre are V. V. Vinogradov's studies on Gogol, written in the 1920s and republished in his *Izbrannye trudy: Poetika russkoi literatury* (Moscow: Nauka, 1976). See, especially, pp. 194 ("multiplicity of voices" in the Gogolian narrator), 211 (Gogol as a generic "ragpicker"), 284 (Gogol's style as a "verbal mosaic"), and 295–344 (on K. P. Masal'sky's parody of *Dead Souls*). Andrei Bely also captures, with greater attention to innovations, syntax, and figures of speech, the multiple perspectives of Gogol's prose, *Masterstvo Gogolia*, chap. 4.

49. Gogol first wrote of the future *Dead Souls* in an 1835 letter to Pushkin, whom he would later credit, perhaps accurately, with having given him the subject of *Dead Souls*, VIII, 439–440. In a draft of the novel, Gogol's chatty author-narrator lists Fielding (together with Shakespeare, Ariosto, Cervantes, and Pushkin) as writers who truly "reflected nature," VI, 553; Gogol cut the comment, which was too cultivated for the narrator at this point. For commentary on *Dead Souls* as a "poema," see Fanger, *The Creation of Nikolai Gogol*, 165–168; Mann, *Poetika Gogolia*, 328–352.

50. This characterization of the genre is derived from a very substantial essay on the subject by Claudio Guillén, "Toward a Definition of the Picaresque," in his *Literature As System* (Princeton: Princeton University Press, 1971), 71–106; and from Walter L. Reed, *An Exemplary History of the Novel:*

The Quixotic versus the Picaresque (Chicago: University of Chicago Press, 1981). For Guillén *Dead Souls* departs from the picaresque tradition with its use of a "dazzling" third-person narrator, who overwhelms Chichikov, 95. It could be argued, however, that the narrator's position, stylistically and ethically, often approaches Chichikov's. For Karl Ludwig Selig, *Dead Souls* is clearly a picaresque novel: "Concerning Gogol's *Dead Souls* and *Lazarillo de Tormes*," *Symposium*, 8 (Summer 1954), 138. Elistratova concurs, but qualifies this by suggesting that such novelists as Fielding mediated between *Dead Souls* and the picaresque tradition, *Gogol i problemy zapadno-evropeiskogo romana*, 29–34, 93, 153, 160, 167, 192. She notes, 33, that the picaresque title of the novel's first edition, "The Adventures of Chichikov" *(Pokhozhdeniia Chichikova)* was added to deflect the censor's attention from Gogol's potentially blasphemous title, *Dead Souls*. On the picaresque and everyday life, see M. Defourneaux, *Daily Life in Spain in the Golden Age* (Stanford: Stanford Universty Press, 1979); a similar service is provided for early nineteenth-century Russia by Iu. M. Lotman, "O Khlestakove," *Uchenye zapiski Tartuskogo Gosudarstvennogo Universiteta, Trudy po russkoi i slavianskoi filologii, XXVI: Literaturovedenie* (1977), 19–53. On earlier Russian picaresques, see Jurij Striedter, *Der Schelmenroman in Russland: Ein Beitrag zur Geschichte des russischen Romans vor Gogol'* (Berlin: Otto Harrassowitz, 1961); and V. F. Pereverzev, *U istokov russkogo realisticheskogo romana*, 2nd ed. (Moscow: Khudozhestvennaia literatura, 1965), 7–113.

51. On Chichikov and Kopeikin as contrasting rogues, see Iu. M. Lotman, "Povest' o kapitane Kopeikine (rekonstruktsiia zamysla i ideino-kompozitsionnaia funktsiia)," *Uchenye zapiski Tartuskogo Gosudarstvennogo Universiteta, 467: Semiotika teksta: Trudy po znakovym sistemam*, 11 (1979), 39–42. For Smirnova-Chikina the tale's contrast to the main plot line resides in its folkloric origins ("Kopeikin" is a brigand who figures in a series of songs), *Poema N. V. Gogolia "Mertvye Dushi": Kommentarii*, 168–70.

52. Although *Dead Souls* merits further discussion as a picaresque novel, a number of important studies have meditated upon the thematic and structural functions of "the road" in it: Bely, *Masterstvo Gogolia*, 191; Lotman, "Problema khukozhestvennogo prostranstva v proze Gogolia," 47–50 (an important distinction between "road," *doroga*, and "path," *put'*); and Fanger, *The Creation of Nikolai Gogol*, 169, 242–247.

53. In its repeated emphasis on seeing the everyday world before one's eyes, *Dead Souls* echoes a central preoccupation of the picaresque: "How many people must there be in the world who run away from others in flight because they can't see themselves?" muses Lazarillo de Tormes, *Two Spanish Picaresque Novels: Lazarillo de Tormes, The Swindler*, trans. Michael Alpert (Baltimore: Penguin Books, 1969), 26.

54. Guillén, "Toward a Definition of the Picaresque," 85.

55. The parody of Karamzin was identified by V. V. Vinogradov, *Ocherki po istorii russkogo literaturnogo iazyka XVII–XIXvv.*, 2nd ed. (Moscow: Uchpedgiz, 1938), 362.

56. Compare "The most important vehicle of reality maintenance is con-

versation," Peter J. Berger and Thomas Luckmann, *The Social Construction of Reality: A Treatise in the Sociology of Knowledge* (Garden City: Doubleday Anchor, 1966), 153.

57. Such theatricality, too, falls within the picaresque tradition, but Gogol crafts the performances to stress the verbal, stylistic aspects of the impersonation, as Chichikov changes his manner of speaking to match the peculiarities of each landowner. By contrast, Quevedo's "swindler" is more dependent upon costumes and other physical properties: *Two Spanish Picaresque Novels*, 115, 116, 118.

58. In particular, the indefiniteness of the positive terms has frequently been noted by Gogol scholars of all sorts. See, for example, Mann, who traces this awareness of Gogol's indefiniteness back to Belinsky, *Poetika Gogolia*, 308; and Lotman, who notes Gogol's inconsistent use of Enlightenment and romantic vocabularies, "Problema khudozhestvennogo prostranstva v proze Gogolia," 49.

59. Gogol was rereading Molière as he began serious work on his novel, XI, 73 (letter of 12 November 1836 to Zhukovsky); XI, 82 (letter of 25 January 1837 to Prokopovich). Pushkin had connected Gogol's name with Molière as early as 1831, XI, 216. Gogol himself praised Molière for his completely developed and nuanced characters, but expressed a wish for "Russian characters . . . our own rogues, our own eccentrics," VIII, 186.

60. I borrow the rendering "fervor" from Robert A. Maguire's superb translation of V. V. Gippius, *Gogol* (Ann Arbor: Ardis, 1981), 130. Because of its accurate citations of Gogol's texts and its up-to-date references, the translation is generally more useful than the 1924 Russian original.

61. Gregory Freidin, in a personal communication, suggests that this loose pattern of parallel motifs is imitative of verbal, associative performance rather than systematic or logical. At the same time, confirming the institutional ambiguity of the novel, these chapters have struck James B. Woodward as the vehicle of an intricately wrought allegory on the "mortification of the soul," *Gogol's "Dead Souls,"* chaps. 1–5.

62. This passage was called to my attention by Fanger, *The Creation of Nikolai Gogol*, 189. I have preserved the roughness of Gogol's manuscript in my translation. Horst-Jürgen Gerigk pursues Gogol's treatment of character toward similar conclusions with help from Heidegger's concept of "Das Man" (that is, a being dominated by the Other, lacking memory and an awareness of consequences): "Gogol: 'Die Toten Seelen,' " in Bodo Zelinsky, ed., *Der Russische Roman* (Düsseldorf: August Bagel Verlag, 1979), 100–110.

63. The author-narrator's incoherence has occasioned disagreement in the critical literature between those who see it as one person and those who see it as multiple persons, positions, or voices. The majority accept the former view; versions of the latter view appear in Fanger, *The Creation of Nikolai Gogol*, 171–172; Gukovsky, *Realizm Gogolia*, 505–516 (although the voices, he claims, are joined in "dialectical unity"); Gary Duane Cox, "A Study of Gogol's Narrators," Ph.D. diss., Columbia University, 1978, 231. Vinogradov's thesis that the narrator lacks psychological coherence is a powerful one,

although "cultural" or "biographical" coherence might be as much, or more, to the point, *Izbrannye trudy*, 220, 313, 326.

64. Certainly "plot" has been one of the most controversial aspects of *Dead Souls*, and many readers, starting with Sergei Aksakov, have counseled other readers to seek the novel's genius elsewhere, dismissing Gogol's plots as trivial, rudimentary, or anecdotal. Aksakov, *Istoriia moego znakomstva*, 75; Eikhenbaum, "How Gogol's 'Overcoat' Is Made," 270; Iu. N. Tynianov, "Dostoevsky i Gogol (k teorii parodii)," *Arkhaisty i novatory* (Leningrad: Priboi, 1929), 420–421; Nabokov, *Nikolai Gogol*, 39; Bely, *Masterstvo Gogolia*, 46; A. L. Slonimsky notes Gogol's frequent ellipsis of plot motivation and finds that objects in Gogol's oeuvre, encountering no resistence from significant events, can themselves mushroom into plots, *Tekhnika komicheskogo u Gogolia* (Petrograd: Academia, 1923), 56–57; in a lengthy and interesting chapter, M. S. Gus has taken issue with this dominant view, basing his "algorithm" of plot movement on a Hegelian dialectic of movement (the lyric hero) and stasis (the characters), *Zhivaia Rossiia i "Mertvye dushi"* (Moscow: Sovetskii pisatel', 1981), chap. 3. Gogol was himself well aware that the construction of plots was not the strongest aspect of his talent, and he later admitted this to Zhukovsky, claiming in one of his juicier mystifications to have taken lessons from "our dear Homer," XIV, 35 (Jan. 1848).

65. Iu. M. Lotman, *Struktura khudozhestvennogo teksta* (Moscow: Iskusstvo, 1970), 282.

66. Ibid., 282–283.

67. As Seymour Chatman notes, this latter possibility becomes increasingly prominent in modern narratives, *Story and Discourse: Narrative Structure in Fiction and Film* (Ithaca: Cornell University Press, 1978), 48.

68. Gogol's most successful translator, Bernard Guilbert Guerney, goes out of his way to avoid the autoerotic suggestiveness of the last sentence: "And for a long while yet did he keep on lifting now this foot and now the other and inspecting the deftly and wondrously turned heel of each boot." Nicholai V. Gogol, *Dead Souls* (New York: Random House, Modern Library, 1965), 181. I believe it important to preserve this emblem of isolation and self-gratification.

69. The functional identity of absence and fullness in Gogol is suggested by the similarly disruptive effects of two women: the governor's daughter (a nonentity), and the "wench, as fresh and powerful as a juicy turnip" (VI, 237), whose presence occasioned the failure of Chichikov's smuggling caper.

70. For a substantial discussion of the author-narrator's attack on the readers he addresses (narratees), see Richard Peace, *The Enigma of Gogol: An Examination of the Writings of N. V. Gogol and their Place in the Russian Literary Tradition* (Cambridge: Cambridge University Press, 1981), 273–281. Picaresque fiction, too, could feature a sardonic relationship to its readers, as one sees in the preface to *The Swindler*, *Two Spanish Picaresque Novels*, 83.

71. The reader who complained to Sergei Aksakov (*Istoriia moego znakomstva s Gogolem*, 75) that Gogol's police chief plays a larger role in the novel than he would in a normal town missed the point of the passage: as polite

society breaks down, its members fall back upon the protection and logic of the police state. Compare Gogol's story "The Nose," in which only the policeman can explain how the nose could be both a civil servant of the fifth rank *and* something found in a loaf of bread.

Conclusion

1. The term *honnête homme*, once replete with significance, appears in a similarly impoverished form in Turgenev's novel *Rudin* (1856) and in Tolstoy's *Childhood* (1852). In the former it is applied to Volyntsev, who lacks social grace and cultural attainment, in the latter it is used for the father, who lacks all but the most superficially conventional ethics.

2. Compare Abram Tertz's insightful comments on Gogol's peculiar blend of economics and eschatology, *V Teni Gogolia* (London: Collins and Overseas Publications Interchange, 1975), 47.

3. On the datedness of Gogol's argument, see G. V. Florovsky, *Puti russkogo bogosloviia*, 2nd ed. (Paris: YMCA Press, 1981), 260–269, where it is linked to the "ideology of the times of Alexander I"; and Victor Erlich, *Gogol* (New Haven: Yale University Press, 1969), 197–199. A more detailed analysis is now available in Ruth Sobel, *Gogol's Forgotten Book: Selected Passages and its Contemporary Readers* (Washington, D.C.: University Press of America, 1981).

4. Belinsky, *Sobranie sochinenii v deviati tomakh* (Moscow: Khudozhestvennaia literatura, 1976–1982), VI, 377.

5. Ibid., IX, 682.

6. As A. G. Tseitlin has noted, *Masterstvo Turgeneva-romanista* (Moscow: Sovetskii pisatel', 1958), 58.

7. Quoted in F. M. Dostoevsky, *Polnoe sobranie sochinenii v tridtsati tomakh* (Leningrad: Nauka, 1972–), XXII, 105.

8. Ibid., 106.

9. Ibid., XIII, 453.

Index